The Future of Criminology

The Future
of Criminology

Edited by

Rolf Loeber and
Brandon C. Welsh

OXFORD
UNIVERSITY PRESS

OXFORD
UNIVERSITY PRESS

Oxford University Press, Inc., publishes works that further
Oxford University's objective of excellence
in research, scholarship, and education.

Oxford   New York
Auckland   Cape Town   Dar es Salaam   Hong Kong   Karachi
Kuala Lumpur   Madrid   Melbourne   Mexico City   Nairobi
New Delhi   Shanghai   Taipei   Toronto

With offices in
Argentina   Austria   Brazil   Chile   Czech Republic   France   Greece
Guatemala   Hungary   Italy   Japan   Poland   Portugal   Singapore
South Korea   Switzerland   Thailand   Turkey   Ukraine   Vietnam

Published by Oxford University Press, Inc.
198 Madison Avenue, New York, New York 10016

www.oup.com

Oxford is a registered trademark of Oxford University Press

Library of Congress Cataloging-in-Publication Data
The future of criminology / edited by Rolf Loeber and Brandon C. Welsh.
p.   cm.
Includes bibliographical references and index.
ISBN 978-0-19-991793-8; ISBN 978-0-19-991795-2 (pbk.)
1. Criminology. 2. Crime prevention.
I. Loeber, Rolf. II. Welsh, Brandon, 1969–
HV6025.F88   2012
364—dc23   2011042957

1 3 5 7 9 8 6 4 2

Printed in the United States of America
on acid-free paper

{ CONTENTS }

PART II Criminal Careers and Justice

PART III Prevention

{ CONTRIBUTORS }

Gaylene Styve Armstrong is an Associate Professor in the College of Criminal Justice at Sam Houston State University. She has published extensively on correctional practices and treatment programs.

Leena K. Augimeri, Director, Centre for Children Committing Offences and Program Development, Child Development Institute and Adjunct Professor, University of Toronto, Canada. For the past 26 years this scientist-practitioner's work has focused on the development of a comprehensive crime prevention model for young children engaged in antisocial behavior with a focus on police-community referral protocols, evidence-based interventions (cofounder of the gender-sensitive SNAP(r) models), and risk/need assessment tools (EARL-20B and EARL-21G). She is a noted author, trainer, consultant, and a Fellow of the Academy of Experimental Criminology.

Alfred Blumstein is a University Professor and the J. Erik Jonsson Professor of Urban Systems and Operations Research and former Dean (from 1986 to 1993) at the H. John Heinz III College of Public Policy and Management of Carnegie Mellon University. He is a Fellow of the American Society of Criminology, was the 1987 recipient of the Society's Sutherland Award for "contributions to research," and was the president of the Society in 1991–92. He was awarded the 2007 Stockholm Prize in Criminology.

Richard F. Catalano is the Bartley Dobb Professor for the Study and Prevention of Violence and Director of the Social Development Research Group at the University of Washington's School of Social Work. His work focuses on discovering risk and protective factors for positive and problem behavior, designing and testing programs to address these factors, and using this research to understand and improve the prevention service systems in states and communities. He has published over 250 articles and book chapters and has been recognized by practitioners, criminologists, and prevention scientists.

Raymond R. Corrado is a Professor in the School of Criminology at Simon Fraser University and Co-director of the Centre for Social Responsibility. His research and publications have focused on youth violence, youth justice, mental health and law, Aboriginal young offenders, risk-management instruments for serious and violent children and youth, and political terrorism. He also is a Visiting Fellow, Clare Hall College and the Institute of Criminology, Cambridge University, and Adjunct Professor, Faculty of Law, University of Bergen.

John E. Eck is Professor of Criminal Justice at the University of Cincinnati. He has written extensively on crime places, crime prevention, and police effectiveness. He received his doctorate from the University of Maryland.

Manuel Eisner is Professor of Comparative and Developmental Criminology at the Institute of Criminology, Cambridge University. His research interests include the history of violence, individual development and aggression, cross-cultural comparative analysis of violence, and violence prevention. He is the Principal Investigator of the Zürich Project on the Social Development of Children, a longitudinal study of 1,200 children age 7 to age 15.

David P. Farrington, O.B.E., is Professor of Psychological Criminology at the Institute of Criminology, Cambridge University, and Adjunct Professor of Psychiatry at Western Psychiatric Institute and Clinic, University of Pittsburgh. His major research interest is in developmental criminology, and he is Director of the Cambridge Study in Delinquent Development, which is a prospective longitudinal survey of over 400 London males from age 8 to age 48. In addition to over 500 published journal articles and book chapters on criminological and psychological topics, he has published over 75 books, monographs, and government publications.

Rob T. Guerette is an Associate Professor of Criminal Justice in the School of International and Public Affairs at Florida International University. He holds a doctorate from Rutgers University–Newark and was a Fellow at the Eagleton Institute of Politics, Rutgers University–New Brunswick. His research interests include situational crime prevention, community and problem-oriented policing, transnational crime, and program and policy evaluation.

J. David Hawkins is Endowed Professor of Prevention and Founding Director of the Social Development Research Group, School of Social Work, University of Washington. His research focuses on the prevention of adolescent behavioral and health problems.

Karl G. Hill is a Research Associate Professor at the University of Washington's School of Social Work. He has worked with the Social Development Research Group since 1994, seeking to understand the factors that influence the development of substance use disorder and crime, and the mechanisms of continuity and discontinuity in these behaviors across generations. His current work examines gene-environment interplay in the development of addiction and related problems.

Ross Homel is Foundation Professor of Criminology and Criminal Justice at Griffith University in Brisbane, Australia. Formerly he has been Head of the School of Criminology and Criminal Justice and Director of both the Griffith Institute for Social and Behavioural Research and the Key Centre for Ethics, Law, Justice and Governance.

Darrick Jolliffe is a Senior Lecturer in Criminology at the University of Leicester and a Chartered Scientist. His research interests and publications focus on empathy, developmental life course criminology, reconviction, and quantitative evaluations.

Lila Kazemian is an Associate Professor in the Department of Sociology at John Jay College of Criminal Justice in New York. Her research interests include life-course and criminal career research, desistance from crime, offender reentry, and comparative criminology. Her work has been published in the *Journal of Research in Crime and Delinquency*, the *Journal of Quantitative Criminology*, the *European Journal of Criminology*, *Crime and Delinquency*, and the *Journal of Contemporary Criminal Justice*.

Christopher J. Koegl is the Director of Research at the Ontario Correctional Institute and Senior Research Associate with the Centre of Children Committing Offences at the Child Development Institute. His research interests include evidence-based risk assessment and treatment approaches for children in conflict with the law, medical and mental health outcomes associated with antisocial behavior, co-occurring substance use and mental disorders, and the monetary costs associated with antisocial behavior over the life course.

Rick Kosterman is a research scientist with the Social Development Research Group at the University of Washington. He is currently Principal Investigator of a NIDA-funded study investigating depression and anxiety disorders and their co-occurrence with drug abuse and sexual risk behavior in young adulthood.

Brian Lawton is an assistant professor in the Department of Criminology, Law and Society at George Mason University. He received his B.A. from Rhode Island College and his M.A. and Ph.D. from Temple University. His research interests include patterns of crime over both time and place, and the discretionary use of force by police. His work has been published in the *Journal of Research in Crime and Delinquency*, *Journal of Quantitative Criminology*, and the *Journal of Criminal Justice*, among others.

Rolf Loeber is Distinguished University Professor of Psychiatry and Professor of Psychology and Epidemiology at the University of Pittsburgh, and Professor of Juvenile Delinquency and Social Development, Free University, Amsterdam. He is Co-director of the Life History Program and is Principal Investigator of a number of longitudinal studies, including the Pittsburgh Youth Study and the Pittsburgh Girls Study. He has published widely in the fields of juvenile antisocial behavior and delinquency, substance use, and mental health problems.

Friedrich Lösel is Director of the Institute of Criminology at Cambridge University and Professor of Psychology at the University of Erlangen–Nuremberg. Previously, he was Professor of Psychology at Bielefeld, Director of the Social Science Research Centre at Nuremberg, Senior Lecturer at Bamberg, Assistant Professor at Erlangen, and Principal Investigator in two Advanced Research Centres of the German Research Council.

Doris Layton MacKenzie is Director, Justice Center for Research, and Professor of Sociology and Crime, Law and Justice at The Pennsylvania State University. Author of *What Works in Corrections: Examining the Criminal Activities of Offenders and Delinquents* (2006), Dr. MacKenzie has an extensive record of publication and research in the areas of corrections and offender behavior.

Tara Renae McGee is a Senior Lecturer in the School of Criminology and Criminal Justice and Deputy Director of the Key Centre for Ethics, Law, Justice and Governance at Griffith University. She is a developmental criminologist with a particular interest in examining the key postulates of developmental and life-course theories of crime.

Steven F. Messner is Distinguished Teaching Professor of Sociology at the University at Albany, State University of New York. His research focuses on social institutions and crime, understanding spatial and temporal patterns of crime, and crime and social control in China. In addition to his publications in professional journals, he is coauthor of *Crime and the American Dream, Perspectives on Crime and Deviance, Criminology: An Introduction Using ExplorIt*, and coeditor of *Theoretical Integration in the Study of Deviance and Crime* and *Crime and Social Control in a Changing China*. He served as the 2010–2011 President of the American Society of Criminology.

Terrie E. Moffitt studies how genetic and environmental risks work together to shape the developmental course of abnormal human behaviors, crime, and psychiatric disorders. She is associate director of the Dunedin Longitudinal Study, and director of the Environmental-Risk Longitudinal Twin Study. She works at Duke University in the United States, at the Institute of Psychiatry, King's College London, and at the Dunedin School of Medicine in New Zealand.

Joseph Murray is a Wellcome Trust Research Fellow and Senior Research Associate at the Department of Psychiatry, Cambridge University. Until 2010, he studied and worked at the Institute of Criminology, Cambridge University, where he completed his M.Phil. and Ph.D., supervised by David Farrington. He graduated from the University of Oxford with a B.A. in Philosophy, Politics and Economics.

Amy Nivette is a Ph.D. student in the Institute of Criminology at Cambridge University. Her research interests are in cross-societal patterns of violence, particularly in relation to the structure and legitimacy of the state.

D. Wayne Osgood is Professor of Crime, Law and Justice and Sociology at Pennsylvania State University, lead editor of the journal *Criminology*, and a Fellow of the American Society of Criminology. He has published research on peer relations and delinquency, time use and problem behavior, the transition to adulthood, criminal careers, and the effectiveness of prevention programs.

Alex R. Piquero is Ashbel Smith Professor of Criminology in the School of Economic, Political and Policy Sciences at the University of Texas at Dallas, Adjunct

Professor at the Key Centre for Ethics, Law, Justice, and Governance, Griffith University, and Co-editor of the *Journal of Quantitative Criminology*. His research interests include criminal careers, criminological theory, and quantitative research methods. He has received numerous research, teaching, and service awards and is a Fellow of both the American Society of Criminology and the Academy of Criminal Justice Sciences.

Jill Portnoy is a graduate student in criminology at the University of Pennsylvania. She is interested in the role of biological and social forces in explaining criminal behavior. Her current research focuses on the psychophysiological and hormonal bases of antisocial behavior.

Adrian Raine is University Professor and the Richard Perry Professor of Criminology, Psychiatry, and Psychology at the University of Pennsylvania. For the past 34 years his interdisciplinary research has focused on the biosocial bases of child and adult antisocial behavior, together with prevention implications.

Justin Ready is an Assistant Professor in the School of Criminology and Criminal Justice at Arizona State University. He has conducted research on crime hot spots, displacement, and policing technology such as conducted electrical devices and surveillance cameras. His articles have appeared in journals such as *Justice Quarterly*, *Crime and Delinquency*, *Criminology*, and *Police Quarterly*.

Frederick P. Rivara is the holder of the Seattle Children's Guild Endowed Chair in Pediatrics, Professor of Pediatrics and adjunct Professor of Epidemiology at the University of Washington. He is chief of the Division of General Pediatrics and vice chair of the Department of Pediatrics in the School of Medicine. He is editor-in-chief of *Archives of Pediatrics and Adolescent Medicine*.

Jonathan P. Shepherd is Professor of Oral and Maxillofacial Surgery and Vice Dean at Cardiff University, where he directs the Violence Research Group. He won the 2008 Stockholm Criminology Prize. He is an elected member of Council and a trustee of the Royal College of Surgeons and was elected a Fellow of the Academy of Medical Sciences in 2002. Awards include the Sellin Glueck Award (2003) of the American Society of Criminology for outstanding international contributions to criminology and honorary fellowship of the Royal College of Psychiatrists (2008). He was appointed CBE in the 2008 New Year Honours for services to the criminal justice system and health care.

Lawrence W. Sherman is Wolfson Professor of Criminology at Cambridge University, where he is the Director of the Jerry Lee Centre of Experimental Criminology and Director of the Police Executive Programme, both at the Institute of Criminology, and a Fellow of Darwin College. He is also Distinguished Professor of Criminology at the University of Maryland. His work has received awards from learned societies in the United States, Germany, and Great Britain, including the Benjamin Franklin Medal of the Royal Society for the Arts. He is President of the

Division of Experimental Criminology of the American Society of Criminology, and Honorary President of the Society of Evidence-Based Policing.

Peter K. Smith is Emeritus Professor of Psychology at the Unit for School and Family Studies at Goldsmiths, University of London. He is editor of *Violence in Schools: The Response in Europe* (New York, 2002), and coeditor of *Bullying in Schools: How Successful Can Interventions Be?* (Cambridge, 2004) and *Bullying in the Global Village: Research on Cyberbullying from an International Perspective* (Oxford, 2012). He has recently carried out research on the effectiveness of antibullying strategies in schools, for the Department for Education, London. He is Chair of COST Action IS0801 on Cyberbullying (www.gold.ac.uk/iso801/), which has representatives from 28 countries.

Howard N. Snyder is Deputy Director of the Bureau of Justice Statistics within the US Department of Justice. He oversees BJS activities in law enforcement, prosecution, courts, and recidivism and BJS's special projects. He was honored in 2010 by the American Society of Criminology for his contributions to the field of criminal justice with its August Vollmer Award.

Magda Stouthamer-Loeber is an Associate Professor of Psychiatry and Psychology (retired). Dr. Stouthamer-Loeber's career has involved the management of data collection and data management of large longitudinal studies on antisocial and delinquent behavior as well as depression in male and female youth. She has also written on protective factors, early fatherhood, and the effects of child abuse on the development of males.

Terence P. Thornberry is a Professor in the Department of Criminology and Criminal Justice at the University of Maryland. He is also the Principal Investigator of the Rochester Youth Development Study, a multigenerational longitudinal study that began in 1986.

Michael Tonry is Professor of Law and Public Policy and director of the Robina Institute of Criminal Law and Criminal Justice at the University of Minnesota Law School and Senior Fellow at the Netherlands Institute for the Study of Crime and Law Enforcement, Free University, Amsterdam.

Richard E. Tremblay is Emeritus Professor of Pediatrics, Psychiatry and Psychology at the University of Montreal, Professor of Early Childhood Development at University College Dublin, and coordinator of the Marie Curie International Network on Early Childhood Development. He is a fellow of the Royal Society of Canada, a fellow of the Academy of Experimental Criminology, and a Grand Officer of Chile's Mistral Order. He received the American Society of Criminology's Sellin-Glueck Award, the Academy of Experimental Criminology Joan McCord Award, the International Society for Research on Aggression JP Scott career award, the French Academy of Moral and Political Sciences Laufer Award, and the Italian Societa Libera International Research Award.

Maria M. Ttofi is Leverhulme-Newton Trust Early Career Fellow at the Institute of Criminology at Cambridge University. Her interests include systematic/meta-analytic reviews in social science topics and experimental and developmental criminology.

Irvin Waller is a Professor of Criminology at the University of Ottawa and author of popular books for legislators and taxpayers. He is internationally consulted on implementing policies that stop crime and advance victim rights, for which he has received international awards. He served as a senior Canadian public servant and was founding CEO of the UN-affiliated International Centre for Prevention of Crime.

David Weisburd is the Walter E. Meyer Professor of Law and Criminal Justice and Director of the Institute of Criminology of the Hebrew University Faculty of Law in Jerusalem, and a Distinguished Professor of Criminology, Law and Society at George Mason University and Director of its Center for Evidence Based Crime Policy.

Brandon C. Welsh is a Professor in the School of Criminology and Criminal Justice at Northeastern University and a Senior Research Fellow at the Netherlands Institute for the Study of Crime and Law Enforcement. His research interests include the prevention of delinquency and crime, with an emphasis on developmental and situational approaches, and evidence-based crime policy. He has written nine books, including *The Oxford Handbook of Crime Prevention*.

Per-Olof H. Wikström is Professor of Ecological and Developmental Criminology at the Institute of Criminology, Cambridge University, and Professorial Fellow of Girton College. He is the director of the Peterborough Adolescent and Young Adult Development Study (PADS+). His main research interests are developing unified theory of the causes of crime (Situational Action Theory), its empirical testing, and its application to devising knowledge-based prevention policies.

James Q. Wilson was Professor of Government at Harvard University for 26 years and then Professor of Public Policy at the University of California, Los Angeles for 12 years. He now teaches at Pepperdine University. He is the author of *Thinking About Crime*, the coauthor (with Richard J. Herrnstein) of *Crime and Human Nature*, and the coeditor (with Joan Petersilia) of *Crime and Public Policy*. For six years he was chairman of the Committee on Law and Justice at the National Research Council / National Academy of Sciences.

Georgia Zara is an Associate Professor of Criminal Psychology, University of Turin, and is a Visiting Scholar of the Institute of Criminology, Cambridge University. She is a psychologist and a criminologist. Her major research interests are criminal careers, criminal persistence and recidivism, psychopathy, and sexual offending.

Gregory M. Zimmerman is an Assistant Professor in the School of Criminology and Criminal Justice at Northeastern University. His research focuses on the interrelationships among individual and contextual causes of criminal offending. He has recently been published in *Criminology* and *American Sociological Review*.

David P. Farrington

In a letter to Robert Hooke in 1676, Isaac Newton said, "If I have seen a little further it is by standing on the shoulders of giants." This is how I feel. I am not sure that I have seen a little further than anyone else (probably not!) but I have certainly "stood on the shoulders of giants," metaphorically of course.

In this foreword, I will first pay tribute to the older generation of scholars who inspired me and from whom I learned a great deal (most of whom, sadly, are now deceased). This is the "looking backward" part. I could spend just as much time paying tribute to my contemporaries and to the younger generations of scholars, but I do not have space to do this, and many excellent examples of their work are included in this book. I am extremely gratified by the number of prominent scholars who have found time in their busy schedules to contribute a chapter to this book, and of course I am particularly grateful to Rolf Loeber and Brandon Welsh for their great efforts to bring this project to fruition. Lee Robins used to joke that I could write faster than she could think, but this statement would apply more accurately to Rolf and Brandon!

In the second part of this foreword, I will look forward, identifying some key issues in criminology and making recommendations about what research is needed to advance knowledge. This part could equally be entitled "Toward a Scientific Criminology."

Looking Back

It is always invidious to single out particularly influential scholars, but I decided to limit myself to only 10. I could, of course, have paid tribute to many more people. First, Alan Watson, my Ph.D. supervisor, taught me to think and write clearly. He would go through my drafts with a fine-tooth comb, constantly asking, "How does this follow from that?" Second, Donald West, the first director of the Cambridge study, set very high standards of meticulous data collection and analysis, and would never allow any problems to be swept under the table. In a longitudinal study, any problems have to be fully resolved now or they will come back to haunt you in days to come! Donald had another life as a psychical researcher, and his experience in this field (where no one believed any results and looked for every possible alternative explanation) meant that he never accepted any finding uncritically and rigorously challenged every result. Third, Nigel Walker, director of the Institute of Criminology in the 1970s, was very important in my career, because (contrary to the dominant sociological approach in British criminology at the time) he believed that psychology could make an important contribution to criminology and he appointed me in Cambridge as a university teaching officer!

I was very much influenced by the giants of longitudinal research in criminology. Fourth, Lee Robins made outstanding contributions and constantly came up with brilliant, thoughtful, insightful comments. Fifth, Joan McCord always bubbled over with enthusiasm about everything. She was a wonderful role model who energized younger scholars with her intellectual excitement. Sixth, Marvin Wolfgang was incredibly influential in the United States, and his book *Delinquency in a Birth Cohort* (Wolfgang, Figlio, and Sellin 1972) really put longitudinal and criminal career research on the map there. He even embarked on a birth cohort study in China, at a time when few Westerners went there. I visited all three of these scholars in their homes, and Joan's home, in particular, contained a treasure trove of books, journals, and the Cambridge-Somerville data.

The greatest pioneer of criminal career research was my seventh giant, Alfred Blumstein. I was very privileged to be a member of the National Academy of Sciences panel on criminal career research that he chaired in the 1980s. This was incredibly exciting, and we really felt that we were pushing back (or is it forward?) the frontiers of knowledge and establishing a new paradigm in criminology. I was especially excited to collaborate with Al in formulating and testing simple theories that made quantitative predictions about a wide range of criminal career features. Al and his wife Dolores were amazingly hospitable in allowing me to stay in their house on my many visits to Pittsburgh, and Al and I often discussed exciting developments until late in the night!

Eighth, Albert Reiss was a brilliant scholar who came up with incredibly stimulating ideas. He really put co-offending on the map in criminology, and I was delighted to collaborate with him on this topic and learned a lot. However, Al Reiss was a divergent thinker who was always moving up to the next level of complexity, and it was a bit difficult to bring projects with him to closure. In contrast, Al Blumstein is a convergent thinker who is very concerned to keep to the point and reach a solution. Having Al Blumstein as (a very focused) chair of the criminal career panel and Al Reiss as a member was a good combination!

Ninth, Lloyd Ohlin was a wonderful man who was universally liked. I was very impressed as we sat together in my house and he laid out the skeleton of our book *Understanding and Controlling Crime* (Farrington, Ohlin, and Wilson 1986). While I always planned my papers in advance, Lloyd's planning and foresight were brilliant. Last but not least, James Q. Wilson is a wonderfully clear and persuasive lecturer and writer. Jim would say: What do we know? What do we need to know? How can we find out? His writing was always very clear, gripping, and entertaining—very different from the rather turgid and pedantic style sometimes seen in criminological journal articles. I am very pleased that both Al Blumstein and Jim Wilson have contributed to this book.

I learned a lot from all of these scholars, and from many other clever and stimulating people. To my mind, the 1980s was a golden age of criminological research in the United States, and I was very privileged to participate in the exciting developments there. In the 1980s, there was a great deal of funding of experimental, longitudinal, and criminal career research. Unlike previous and later decades, many randomized field experiments were carried out and several major longitudinal studies were initiated. I am not sure whether I will ever see such a golden age of funding again. It is very sad that, despite crime being a major social problem with enormous costs to society, the funding of criminological research (e.g., compared with medical research) is so tiny.

Looking Forward

Looking forward, my main suggestion is that criminology should aim to become more scientific. Sciences are based on systematic observation and experimentation, on testing quantitative predictions from theories, and on replication of key results. There are many key issues and questions that could and should be addressed in criminology, and many new studies that could and should be funded, but I will outline a few of my priorities, in no particular order.

First, there should be more systematic observation of offending as it happens. For example, we (Buckle and Farrington 1984; 1994) systematically observed shoplifting and found that shoplifters tended to spend more time in the store, tended to look around a lot, and tended to buy goods as well as stealing them. We estimated the number of items stolen per 10 customer-hours in the store. I think that there should be more attempts to observe offending and to try to estimate how often (per unit time) different types of crimes are committed.

Second, there should be more efforts to carry out field experiments to investigate causes or immediate influences on offending. For example, we (Farrington and Knight 1979, 1980) used the "lost letter" technique to investigate stealing. We left stamped, addressed, unsealed letters containing money (except in control conditions) and messages on the streets of London and observed members of the public pick them up. We experimentally manipulated the amount and form of the money and the nature of the apparent victim (e.g., male or female, young or old, rich or poor). We found that hardly anyone stole the money (compared with the control "no money" condition) when the apparent victim was a poor older female, whereas about 80 percent stole the money when the apparent victim was a rich young male. Surely we could develop an experimental criminology (perhaps inspired by experimental social psychology; see Farrington 1979) of the causes of offending as well as an experimental criminology of the prevention and treatment of offending.

Third, there should be more prospective longitudinal studies of the development of offending, especially documenting relative continuity and absolute changes in behavior. In order to speed up results, accelerated longitudinal designs could be used (Tonry, Ohlin, and Farrington 1991). A key priority in criminology is to measure self-reported and official offending from childhood to adulthood. This would require regular, repeated interviews at different ages, seen to best advantage in the pioneering Pittsburgh Youth Study (Loeber et al. 2008). It is very important to estimate the "scaling-up" factor from official to self-reported offending for different types of crimes and people at different ages, not only to assess the effectiveness of the police and courts but also to assess the true effectiveness of intervention programs that generally have only official measures of recidivism. It is also very important to maximize response rates, because the most elusive and uncooperative people (who are the hardest to include in surveys) are the most interesting to criminologists (Farrington et al. 1990).

In new longitudinal studies, there should be more efforts to study not only the development of offending but also situational factors that influence why offenses are committed. Research on developmental and situational influences on offending needs to be brought together. Similarly, there should be more efforts in future longitudinal studies to measure biological and neighborhood/community influences on offending. Past research has tended to focus on individual, family, peer, school, and socioeconomic factors. There are many key issues that need to be addressed. For example, what mechanisms link hyperactivity / impulsiveness / attention deficit / low self-control / poor ability to delay gratification (etc.) to offending? How and why are anxiety and depression related to offending? To what extent do family factors predict offending after controlling for genetic influences? Why does offending vary with age, gender, and race? Are all these demographic relationships mediated by differences in risk factors? Are there demographic differences in the levels of risk factors or in the strength of relationships between risk factors and offending?

Fourth, while a great deal is known about risk factors for offending, there is a particular need to study protective factors in new longitudinal studies. These can be factors that predict a low rate of offending, factors that predict a low rate of offending in a risk category (e.g., low income), or factors that interact with a risk factor to nullify its influence (Farrington, Loeber, and Ttofi 2012 ; Farrington and Ttofi in press). Protective factors also need to be included in risk assessment devices and targeted in intervention programs.

Fifth, there is a special need to carry out quasi-experimental within-individual analyses in new longitudinal studies to investigate the effect on offending of life events such as getting married or becoming unemployed (Farrington 1988; Theobald and Farrington 2009). The real strength of longitudinal studies lies in their ability to study within-individual change over time, but relatively few longitudinal researchers have used their data to do this. In the Pittsburgh Youth Study, Farrington et al. (2002) found that poor parental supervision predicted delinquency within individuals, but peer delinquency did not. This suggests that poor supervision might be a cause but peer delinquency is merely a marker for delinquency (measuring the same underlying construct).

Sixth, more research is needed on co-offending. Many crimes, especially in the teenage years, are carried out with others, but there has been relatively little research on this topic (see e.g., Reiss and Farrington 1991; van Mastrigt and Farrington 2009). Estimates of co-offending are needed to link up offenders and crimes. For example, the familiar age-crime curve does not show aggregate changes in the number of crimes with age but instead shows aggregate changes in the number of offender-offense combinations. For example, if three offenders are jointly convicted for four different offenses at age 16, 12 offender-offense combinations will be added to the curve, not four offenses. As another example, if 1,000 burglaries are committed in an area and 100 people are convicted for burglary, the probability of an offender being convicted is not necessarily 0.10 (100/1000). If, for example, two offenders on average commit each burglary, there are 2,000 offender-offense combinations, but only 100 convictions (and one conviction is usually one offender-offense combination). In this case, then, the true probability of an offender being convicted is 0.05. More research is especially needed on recruiters, defined as offenders who constantly commit crimes with younger, less experienced or first offenders (van Mastrigt and Farrington 2011). These recruiters are prime targets for intervention because, if their behavior could be changed, this would have a disproportionate effect on the number of crimes.

Seventh, it is important to propose and test falsifiable theories that make quantitative predictions. For example, Barnett, Blumstein, and Farrington (1987; 1989) proposed that there were two categories of offenders: "frequents" had a high rate of offending per year and a low probability of terminating their criminal careers after each offense, while "occasionals" had a lower rate of offending per year and a higher termination probability. Barnett and his colleagues showed that this simple model fitted and predicted a range of criminal career features. It would be desirable to extend this type of a simple theory to specify the influence of risk factors on offending at different ages and to self-reported offending as well as convictions. If criminological theories are to be scientific, they should make exact quantitative predictions.

Eighth, there should be more randomized experiments, especially in Europe, to test the effectiveness of methods of preventing and treating offending. It would be desirable to carry out experiments not just on special types of offender treatment such as cognitive-behavioral therapy but also on mainstream sentences such as imprisonment, fines, probation, and community service (see e.g., Killias et al. 2010). Experiments are especially needed on area-based situational interventions such as CCTV (closed-circuit television) and improved street lighting (Welsh and Farrington 2009). It should be possible to design intervention experiments to advance knowledge about criminological theories (Robins 1992).

Ninth, it would be highly desirable to evaluate the impact of interventions within prospective longitudinal surveys, as advocated by Farrington et al. (1986). There should be a number of measures, covering several years, then an intervention, then more measures, covering several years afterward. It seems that no large-scale study of this kind has ever been carried out on offending using interview data. Such studies could simultaneously advance knowledge about the development and causes of offending and about the effects of interventions. Also, the impact of interventions can be better understood in the context of preexisting trends or developmental sequences, and the prior information about participants could make it possible to investigate interactions between types of persons (and their risk/protective factors and prior histories) and types of interventions (Farrington, Loeber, and Welsh 2010). Long-term follow-up information after an experiment is highly desirable to show effects of an intervention that are not immediately apparent and to compare short-term and long-term effects and investigate developmental sequences that link them.

Tenth, and finally, more attempts to replicate results in cross-national and cross-cultural comparisons are needed (Farrington and Loeber 1999). More systematic reviews and meta-analyses are needed to determine the generalizability of findings (Welsh and Farrington 2006). It is crucial to include cost-benefit analyses in evaluating interventions and in systematic reviews, in order to establish which interventions have the highest benefit-to-cost ratios (Welsh, Farrington, and Sherman 2001). And it is especially important to communicate findings to policymakers and practitioners so that the research has an impact. For example, I think that there should be a national agency to coordinate early prevention initiatives (Farrington and Welsh 2007), and that there should be special court and correctional treatments for young adult offenders (Loeber and Farrington in press).

In conclusion, many criminologists seem to choose easy topics and easy methods that are guaranteed to produce results within a short time frame. I believe that it is more important to choose the more risky, challenging scientific methods that I have recommended in order to advance knowledge significantly, such as systematic observation, field experiments, longitudinal studies, randomized experiments on interventions, and the holy grail of the longitudinal-experimental study. And it is a lot more fun when you are convinced that you are really pushing back (or forward!) the frontiers of knowledge!

References

Barnett, Arnold, Alfred Blumstein, and David P. Farrington. 1987. "Probabilistic Models of Youthful Criminal Careers." *Criminology* 25: 83–107.

Barnett, Arnold, Alfred Blumstein, and David P. Farrington. 1989. "A Prospective Test of a Criminal Career Model." *Criminology* 27: 373–388.

Buckle, Abigail, and David P. Farrington. 1984. "An Observational Study of Shoplifting." *British Journal of Criminology* 24: 63–73.

Buckle, Abigail, and David P. Farrington. 1994. "Measuring Shoplifting by Systematic Observation: A Replication Study." *Psychology, Crime and Law* 1: 133–141.

Farrington, David P. 1979. "Experiments on Deviance with Special Reference to Dishonesty." In *Advances in Experimental Social Psychology*, vol. 12, edited by Leonard Berkowitz, 207–252. New York: Academic Press.

Farrington, David P. 1988. "Studying Changes within Individuals: The Causes of Offending." In *Studies of Psychosocial Risk: The Power of Longitudinal Data*, edited by Michael Rutter, 158–183. New York: Cambridge University Press.

Farrington, David P., Bernard Gallagher, Lynda Morley, Raymond St. Ledger, and Donald J. West. 1990. "Minimizing Attrition in Longitudinal Research: Methods of Tracing and Securing Cooperation in a 24-year Follow-up." In *Data Quality in Longitudinal Research*, edited by David Magnusson and Lars Bergman, 122–147. Cambridge: Cambridge University Press.

Farrington, David P., and Barry J. Knight. 1979. "Two Non-reactive Field Experiments on Stealing from a 'Lost' Letter." *British Journal of Social and Clinical Psychology* 18: 277–284.

Farrington, David P., and Barry J. Knight. 1980. "Stealing from a 'Lost' Letter: Effects of Victim Characteristics." *Criminal Justice and Behavior* 7: 423–436.

Farrington, David P., and Rolf Loeber. 1999. "Transatlantic Replicability of Risk Factors in the Development of Delinquency." In *Historical and Geographical Influences on Psychopathology*, edited by Patricia Cohen, Cheryl Slomkowski, and Lee N. Robins, 299–330. Mahwah, NJ: Lawrence Erlbaum.

Farrington, David P., Rolf Loeber, and Maria M. Ttofi. 2012. "Risk and Protective Factors for Offending." In *The Oxford Handbook of Crime Prevention*, edited by Brandon C. Welsh and David P. Farrington, 46–69. Oxford: Oxford University Press.

Farrington, David P., Rolf Loeber, and Brandon C. Welsh. 2010. "Longitudinal-Experimental Studies." In *Handbook of Quantitative Criminology*, edited by Alex R. Piquero and David Weisburd, 503–518. New York: Springer.

Farrington, David P., Rolf Loeber, Yanming Yin, and Stewart Anderson. 2002. "Are Within-Individual Causes of Delinquency the Same as Between-Individual Causes?" *Criminal Behaviour and Mental Health* 12: 53–68.

Farrington, David P., Lloyd E. Ohlin, and James Q. Wilson. 1986. *Understanding and Controlling Crime: Toward a New Research Strategy*. New York: Springer.

Farrington, David P., and Maria M. Ttofi. In press. "Protective and Promotive Factors in the Development of Offending." In *Antisocial Behaviour and Crime: Contributions of Theory and Evaluation Research to Prevention and Intervention*, edited by Thomas Bliesener, Andreas Beelman, and Mark Stemmler. Göttingen: Hogrefe.

Farrington, David P., and Brandon C. Welsh. 2007. *Saving Children from a Life of Crime: Early Risk Factors and Effective Interventions*. New York: Oxford University Press.

Killias, Martin, Gwladys Gillieron, Francoise Villard, and Clara Poglia. 2010. "How Damaging is Imprisonment in the Long Term? A Controlled Experiment Comparing Long-Term Effects of Community Service and Short Custodial Sentences on Reoffending and Social Integration." *Journal of Experimental Criminology* 6: 115–130.

Loeber, Rolf, and David P. Farrington. In press. *From Juvenile Delinquency to Adult Crime: Criminal Careers, Justice Policy and Prevention*. Oxford: Oxford University Press.

Loeber, Rolf, David P. Farrington, Magda Stouthamer-Loeber, and Helene R. White. 2008. *Violence and Serious Theft: Development and Prediction from Childhood to Adulthood*. New York: Routledge.

Reiss, Albert J., and David P. Farrington. 1991. "Advancing Knowledge about Co-offending: Results from a Prospective Longitudinal Survey of London Males." *Journal of Criminal Law and Criminology* 82: 360–395.

Robins, Lee N. 1992. "The Role of Prevention Experiments in Discovering Causes of Children's Antisocial Behavior." In *Preventing Antisocial Behavior: Interventions from Birth through Adolescence*, edited by Joan McCord and Richard E. Tremblay, 3–20. New York: Guilford.

Theobald, Delphine, and David P. Farrington. 2009. "Effects of Getting Married on Offending: Results from a Prospective Longitudinal Survey of Males." *European Journal of Criminology* 6: 496–516.

Tonry, Michael, Lloyd E. Ohlin, and David P. Farrington. 1991. *Human Development and Criminal Behavior: New Ways of Advancing Knowledge*. New York: Springer.

Van Mastrigt, Sarah B., and David P. Farrington. 2009. "Co-offending versus Age, Gender and Crime Type: Implications for Criminal Justice Policy." *British Journal of Criminology* 49: 552–573.

Van Mastrigt, Sarah B., and David P. Farrington. 2011. "Prevalence and Characteristics of Co-offending Recruiters." *Justice Quarterly* 28: 325–359.

Welsh, Brandon C., and David P. Farrington, eds. 2006. *Preventing Crime: What Works for Children, Offenders, Victims and Places*. Dordrecht: Springer.

Welsh, Brandon C., and David P. Farrington. 2009. "Public Area CCTV and Crime Prevention: An Updated Systematic Review and Meta-analysis." *Justice Quarterly* 26: 716–745.

Welsh, Brandon C., David P. Farrington, and Lawrence W. Sherman, eds. 2001. *Costs and Benefit of Preventing Crime*. Boulder, CO: Westview Press.

Wolfgang, Marvin E., Robert M. Figlio, and Thorsten Sellin. 1972. *Delinquency in a Birth Cohort*. Chicago: University of Chicago Press.

{ A FUTURE OF CRIMINOLOGY AND A CRIMINOLOGIST FOR THE AGES }

Rolf Loeber and Brandon C. Welsh

Criminology is a dynamic and evolving field of study. The last few decades have witnessed major advances in scientific knowledge, legendary scholarly debates, and pivotal contributions to research, policy, and practice. The volume of studies has increased dramatically, the number of authors has skyrocketed, and the number of areas covered by publications has been augmented in many different ways. This enormous output calls out for taking stock of the field, an effort to address two key questions: Where are we now? What does the future hold?

It is these two questions that are at the heart of this book. Providing insights to these questions is a group of leading scholars, representing a wide range of disciplines in the social and behavioral sciences as well as medicine and public health. Five important topical areas are covered: development and causation; criminal careers and justice; prevention; intervention and treatment; and public policy strategies. Also at the heart of this book is one of the most influential criminologists of the last four decades: David Farrington. Through David's lifework, these topical areas have come to form major areas of study in the field of criminology, and they were the inspiration for the substantive framework of this book. This introduction sketches some of the milestone contributions made by David Farrington, introduces the five topical areas, and offers a view of the 33 chapters to come.

David P. Farrington

It is not easy to describe David Farrington as a person. He is a vigorous worker with an amazing curiosity about disparate topics. He has a prodigious memory, including the best memory for numbers that we have ever met in anyone. His outlook on solving problems of all kinds is unwaveringly positive, and he rarely admits that something cannot be solved. He believes in empirical verification and looks down on boundless speculation without the possibility of falsification and without the impetus for empirical proof. He is uniformly encouraging to young scholars and students. Although at home in England, his mental work extends well into Europe and North America, to which he traveled in some years almost every month. When discussing criminology and data sets, his appetite for solving problems often leads him to volunteer to undertake writing papers. For us, he is an ideal cochair for a meeting, which is one of the ways that he, as a former football player, excels as a team player.

Born in Lancashire, David excelled at school and received a scholarship to study at Cambridge. In rapid tempo he obtained his Ph.D., after which, in 1969, he became a research assistant to Donald West, a pioneering psychiatrist, who had set up the first longitudinal study on crime in England, the now famous Cambridge Study in Delinquent Development. David succeeded Donald West as director of the study in 1982. Under David's guidance, the study has become the longest-running longitudinal study ever conducted on the development of antisocial behavior and delinquency from childhood into adulthood (over 40 years, from ages 8 to 48–50). The prodigious output of four books and 186 articles (and counting) are every bit the result of David's profound inquiries and energy.

David Farrington also has been a key mover behind the setup, execution, and analyses of another major longitudinal study, the Pittsburgh Youth Study (PYS). So far, he has coauthored three books and 37 articles with investigators of the PYS, covering a great variety of topics on the study of antisocial behavior and juvenile delinquency.

David Farrington has also pioneered international comparisons of crime from adolescence into adulthood (using longitudinal studies) and cross-national comparisons of crime and punishment. Another major breakthrough engineered by David Farrington is establishing the links between research on antisocial behavior and delinquency and preventive and remedial interventions. This is no small achievement because sociology, including much of criminology, had been predominantly oriented toward theories while neglecting to link theory and research findings to preventive and remedial approaches to reduce crime. David Farrington focused on the reduction of children's and adolescents' behavioral precursors to serious delinquency, and improving family conditions and school circumstances that facilitate prosocial behavior and reduce bullying. There is no doubt that David Farrington has made substantive contributions to the establishment of more rational and effective public policies in several Western countries.

Another key breakthrough concerns the ways that David Farrington has advanced the study of causality of factors associated with antisocial and delinquent behavior. A multitude of past empirical studies has attempted to ascertain the causal status of these factors by means of between-group comparisons. However, this method is quite limited because it does not address to what extent causes apply to individuals and to what extent individual-level change in behavior happens because of these factors. David Farrington has been one of the first to recognize this and undertake within-individual change analyses to identify causes of crime. In this context he executed pioneering papers on the role of marriage in reducing crime, and the role of unemployment in increasing crime.

David Farrington's scholarly achievements are no doubt tremendous (for a listing of his publications, see http://www.crim.cam.ac.uk/people/academic_research/david_farrington/). He ranks number *one* in citations in the English scientific literature concerning antisocial behavior and crime (Cohen 2011). He holds this ranking not only in the most recent five-year period, but has ranked as the most cited author over the past 15 years (Cohen 2011). We are unaware of another talented colleague who has achieved such an incredible record. But more important to David are his collaborations with any number of his students and a wide range of colleagues from different disciplines.

David Farrington is highly esteemed by his peers. This is evident from his election to president of several international and national scientific societies. He is the only scholar who has been president of four major criminological societies: the American Society of Criminology (which is quite extraordinary for a Brit), the British Society of Criminology, the European Association of Psychology and Law, and the Academy of Experimental Criminology.

David Farrington's achievements are truly international in other ways as well. He has served as a consultant to many governments and their agencies. Interestingly, he is the only British scholar who has been a member of several US National Academy of Sciences (NAS) panels on different topics, and even served as vice chair of the NAS panel on violence in the early 1990s. David Farrington is also the founding chair of the Campbell Collaboration Crime and Justice Group. Rightly, these and his many contributions to science have been recognized throughout the Western world.

In summary, David Farrington is an exceptional scientist, whose publications and scholarly achievements place him at the top of the criminology profession. His contributions to the welfare of children and adolescents have been profound and extend from the study of the causes of antisocial behavior and delinquency to preventive and remedial interventions to reduce crime. His work on both sides of the Atlantic has been facilitated by his enormous energy, wisdom, and ability to collaborate with a wide range of scholars in a number of disciplines.

Development and Causation

Part I of this volume deals with the future of studies on the development of offending and its causes. This topic continues to be a central focus of the steady stream of publications generated by David Farrington and his colleagues over decades using the wonderful data from the Cambridge Study in Delinquent Development. Whereas initially the focus was on group differences in development and causation, David's emphasis increasingly has focused on within-individual differences. This is due in part to the belief that causes that apply to individuals are more important than causes that apply to categories of offenders, as well as because within-individual causes are more relevant than between-group causes for preventive and remedial interventions.

Chapter 1 by Wayne Osgood focuses on life course criminology, and particularly the relationship between crime and age as expressed in the age-crime curve. He considers within-individual differences such as persistence and desistance, and the impact of life transitions, such as marriage and entering the workforce, on offending. He advocates future studies on the explanation of the age-crime curve, and particularly changes in within-individual explanations rather than permanent individual differences.

In chapter 2, Rolf Loeber considers the properties of the age-crime curve. He revisits factors—such as neighborhoods, cohorts, and impulsivity—that influence the height and the breadth of the curve, and he shows by means of simulation studies that interventions are likely to reduce the curve and, thereby, decrease the prevalence of offenders in populations of young people.

In chapter 3, Richard Tremblay explains that in the course of executing the Montreal Longitudinal-Experimental Study, he became convinced that some of the developmental origins of antisocial behavior were situated in the period prior to kindergarten. He especially focuses on toddler's aggression, anger, oppositional behavior, defiance, and overt disregard for rules. He is much aware of environmental factors that impinge on the development of antisocial behaviors, including intergenerational transmission of the behaviors. He stresses the importance of gene expression studies (epigenetic) that indicate that environmental risk factors related to the mother "may start to have their impact on the child's developing brain and eventual self-control problems during fetal life, and soon after, through their impact on gene expression."

Adrian Raine and Jill Portnoy, in chapter 4, focus on biomarkers for conduct disorder, antisocial behavior, and delinquency, with a special emphasis on low resting heart rate. This factor has been extensively replicated in different populations and different negative outcomes even when possible confounds were taken into account. Heart rate is related to other concepts such as unpleasant physiological state and fearlessness, and may be a marker for noradrenergic and reduced right brain functioning. The authors advocate future studies to demonstrate the extent to which heart rate is a good biological and predictive marker for conduct problems, antisocial behavior, and delinquency.

Terrie Moffitt, in chapter 5, advances the need to improve the physical and financial health of populations and reduce crime. She focuses on the role of poor self-control in predicting delinquency, health outcomes, substance use dependence, and financial wealth, providing supporting data from the Dunedin longitudinal study and the Environmental-Risk Longitudinal Twin Study. The role of sibling comparisons is stressed to examine differences in self-control among siblings reared in the same family environment. The findings are highly relevant for future intervention programs aimed at enhancing self-control at all levels in the population.

In chapter 6, Terence Thornberry reviews the state of past monothematic, and current multithematic and multidisciplinary, integrated theories of crime, particularly developmental and life course theories explaining why some individuals and not others become serious offenders. He argues that major advances have been made by the measurement of official and self-reported delinquency, and the understanding of the heterogeneity of criminal careers. He recognizes the role of individuals' decision-making and human agency in offending, and desistance from offending and nonoffending. He notes that future theories will become more encompassing, incorporating biological and economic factors. At the same time, he finds that it is desirable to counteract the proliferation of different theories by the creation of an unified theory, which should link the development and explanation of offending with interventions.

Per-Olof Wikström, in chapter 7, focuses on one neglected aspect of theories, namely, the integration of the person, including human agency, with environmental approaches in the study of crime causation. He calls "analytical criminology" the study of why people engage in acts of crime, and advances this type of criminology through a combination of action theory-driven and empirically testable research. He advocates better distinctions between markers of causation and causal processes and mechanisms. He describes Situational Action Theory, which he illustrates by way of new findings from the Peterborough Adolescent and Young Adult Development Study.

Among all causes of offending, Darrick Jolliffe and Joe Murray, in chapter 8, focus on the role of empathy to explain offending and the absence of offending in the context of risk and intervention studies. They show that there is considerable, replicated evidence that poor empathy predicts offending, but that several issues— such as the measurement of empathy and its causal status—remain perplexing. Using the Cambridge Quality Checklist to establish the causal status of empathy, they conclude that past studies on empathy score low on the checklist. Rather than taking this as a defeat, they suggest several ways to advance studies on empathy and its relationship to offending.

Gregory Zimmerman and Steven Messner, in chapter 9, argue that research on neighborhood influences on crime should involve both conceptual and methodological multilevel analyses of the characteristics of individuals and their environments. After describing the current state of the macrosociological approach to the study of crime, they review the integration of this perspective with individual-level explanations of crime, and present several future challenges for research.

Increasingly studies have assessed protective factors in addition to risk factors to explain deviant behaviors. Also, a multitude of studies have shown the relevance of bullying—both as instigator and victim—to later delinquency. Maria Ttofi and Peter Smith, in chapter 10, review a range of risk and protective factors relevant to school bullies and victims. Building on the work by David Farrington and others, they stress the replicated efficacy of bullying prevention studies. They show that whereas earlier studies have focused on the impact of bullying on externalizing behaviors, studies also document the impact on internalizing problems. They make a case that longitudinal studies should better examine risk and protective factors related to individuals' careers in school bullying. In addition, they argue that future intervention studies focusing on bullying should not just see the removal of risk factors as a central management strategy, but that prevention and intervention programs should include the enhancement of protective factors.

In chapter 11, Georgia Zara focuses on the much neglected criminal career aspect of adult-onset offenders. She stresses that risk factors do not always need to have an immediate and direct effect, that some early risk factors have a long-term impact, that many factors play a protective role in childhood and adulthood, but that this protective effect may cease in adulthood, that psychological insulation or resilience toward antisocial and criminogenic factors may not last long, and that delinquency abstention is not necessarily a sign of good adjustment in adolescence. Using data from the Cambridge Study in Delinquent Development, she presents important findings, and formulates an agenda for future work on adult-onset offending.

Advances in the study of crime and its causes are much dependent on the quality and quantity of longitudinal studies. Magda Stouthamer-Loeber, in chapter 12, examines the important role that David Farrington has played in the start-up and design of the Pittsburgh Youth Study and how he always stressed hands-on data collection and management. Stouthamer-Loeber contrasts past with future data collection techniques and improved issues of confidentiality in the current world of data sharing. She also discusses optimal management conditions for the execution of longitudinal studies, stressing the need for ongoing quality controls for data collection, and advances in methods of data storage, multidisciplinary collaboration within and across studies, and the need to optimize the yields of longitudinal studies through secondary data analyses.

Criminal Careers and Justice

Part II of this volume concentrates on the future of criminal careers and justice studies and builds on many of the studies published by David Farrington. There is no doubt that David and Alfred Blumstein are among the top pioneers of criminal career research. Al Blumstein, in chapter 13, summarizes key quantitative aspects of criminal career studies, including such parameters as initiation, duration, and termination, and in between, frequency, seriousness of the offenses, and crime mix including specialization. Blumstein stresses that despite advances, there is a great need to build a more complete and comprehensive knowledge base of delinquency career characteristics using official and self-reported delinquency records based on longitudinal data from multiple sites and from multiple countries. He stresses the importance of trajectory research and research on co-offending, that future studies should include measures of genetics and brain functioning, and that the study of gene-environment interactions will become more important than it is now. He makes the case that more research is needed to examine the impact of different justice policies and practices on criminal career parameters.

Alex Piquero, in chapter 14, uses David Farrington's Cambridge Study in Delinquent Development as an example of a study that has generated hundreds of papers and several books relevant to criminal career research. He contrasts these findings with a discussion of contentious and unresolved substantive, theoretical, and methodological issues in criminal career research and provides pointers to areas in which future research is likely to pay off.

Much of the criminal career research has relied on official data of delinquency, derived from police and court records. Howard Snyder, in chapter 15, chronicles the attempts by US agencies to collect uniform crime data from thousands of precincts and courts. In addition, federal surveys such as the National Criminal Victimization Survey (NCVS) provide essential periodic information on crime levels at different geographic units, but also are the basis for criminal career research. He states that currently many national statistical systems are facing serious challenges with increasing costs and not meeting the demands of policymakers, researchers, and the public at large. For example, the NCVS is dogged by decreasing response rates and poor documentation of different forms of crime. Snyder makes the case that improvements are needed before administrative data are analyzed, including "(1) establishing data transfer agreements with the administrative agencies, (2) developing a detailed understanding of the structure, logic and content of the administrative database, and (3) creating programs able to extract the needed statistical information from the administrative databases." Once such objectives are achieved, the gains for crime reporting and criminal career research are expected to be enormous.

In chapter 16, Marc Le Blanc takes a fresh look at developmental criminology and examines the extent to which deviant behavior in general conforms to findings from developmental criminology. Drawing on his lifelong research on a population of young people and a sample of known delinquents, he argues that the age-crime curve applies to many other deviant behaviors as well and that qualitative and quantitative changes known from developmental criminology also apply to various forms of deviant behavior. The same is true for the classification of individuals according to their developmental trajectories. Further, he argues that problems in self-regulation are germane to both crime and deviant behaviors, and that qualitative and quantitative changes in self-regulation underlie the manifestations of all deviant behaviors. Finally, he makes a case that most explanatory models are more complex than ones that are currently in use and that the next generation of statistical tests will need to advance to more complex levels.

Most of the research on developmental criminology has been concerned with the beginning and persistence of the criminal careers rather than with desistance from offending. Lila Kazemian, in chapter 17, summarizes current knowledge about desistance, the study of which has moved from event to process analyses based on a combination of social and cognitive factors. She argues that future research needs to better integrate several criminal career parameters, including desistance in frequency, seriousness, and versatility, and involve multiple outcomes such as improvements in mental and physical health and substance use. She also favors a better integration of desistance research with prisoner reentry programs and resiliency research.

In chapter 18, Ray Corrado examines psychopathy as a key correlate of serious delinquency and violence. He summarizes the considerable and varied debate on how to best measure psychopathy and compares different measurements of the construct, and which aspects of psychopathy have the best predictive utility. He considers the evidence on whether problems in anxiety and disinhibition are central to psychopathy and the degree to which psychopathy can be related to the Five Factor Model of Personality. He rightly faces the issue to what extent the features of psychopathy developed in adults can be applied to younger people and which developmental model of psychopathy is best for adolescents. He also explores whether development of brain anatomy and chemistry can explain the etiology of psychopathy. He concludes his chapter with recommendations on improvements in the measurement of psychopathy.

Prevention

Part III of this volume focuses on the future of prevention studies to reduce delinquency. The study of the prevention of delinquency and crime seems to have been a natural path for David Farrington. From early on in his career he began to think and write about how early risk factors for delinquency and criminal offending—among the major discoveries of his longitudinal research—could be counteracted through effective prevention programs. His work was soon contributing to the emerging area of risk-based prevention in criminology. The basic idea of this approach is rather straightforward: identify the key risk factors for offending and implement prevention methods designed to counteract them. One article, entitled "Early Developmental Prevention of Delinquency" (Farrington 1994), proved tremendously influential; many others soon followed. While his early research had a special focus on developmental crime prevention, his interest in the prevention of crime more generally led him to also explore the effectiveness of the two other major crime prevention strategies: community prevention and situational prevention.

This part brings together five chapters that examine the current state and future of crime prevention research, covering the full range of prevention strategies. Developmental prevention with a special focus on the family domain is the subject of chapter 19 by Brandon Welsh. Here it is argued that families matter and by putting families first we can go a long way toward improving the effectiveness of delinquency prevention in the years to come. The importance of family-based prevention is evident not just in the early childhood years but also for system-involved youth.

In chapter 20, Frederick Rivara looks at the future of preventive public health as applied to interpersonal violence. Drawing on the latest advances in brain violence research, he argues that we need to address from an early age the toxic stress (i.e., repetitive and/or prolonged stress that overwhelms the body's coping mechanisms) that puts children and youth at greatest risk for involvement in delinquency and violence and can impair long-term social and emotional functioning. This will not come easy, and opportunities for criminology and public health are explored.

Situational crime prevention is the focus of chapter 21 by John Eck and Rob Guerette. They take stock of the research evidence on the effectiveness of a wide range of situational measures implemented in a number of public and private places (e.g., retail, transportation). They find that many situational measures are effective in preventing different crimes in the settings. Drawing on these findings and key theoretical and policy issues on places and ownership for crime in those places, the authors explore the future possibilities for tailor-made interventions and what they call "own the place, own the crime" prevention.

The next two chapters have a shared focus on community crime prevention. In chapter 22, Ross Homel and Tara McGee report on key emerging issues facing this approach, with a special emphasis on the needs and challenges of building community capacity to deliver effective and sustainable prevention programs. In chapter 23, David Hawkins, Richard Catalano, Karl Hill, and Rick Kosterman profile the effective school-based Seattle Social Development Project and Communities That Care, a community prevention operating system, and discuss some of the future benefits of rolling out effective prevention programs for wider public use.

Intervention and Treatment

Some criminologists argue that more attention needs to be paid to crime prevention, especially before a crime takes place. There are others who argue that more attention needs to be paid to intervening with and treating criminally involved populations. These are by no means mutually exclusive camps (see Cullen 2011). But there are sizable bodies of literature that favor one approach over the other. Perhaps not surprisingly, David Farrington's interest in crime prevention in no way precluded an interest in intervention and treatment. This is because his research and the work of others convinced him of the benefits of subscribing to a more comprehensive approach, which is best captured by the phrase "never too early, never too late." What this means is that it is never too early to help improve the life chances of an at-risk child and it is never too late to provide treatment to an offender who one day will return to the community. While David's research on intervention and treatment began when he was a young scholar, it is his more recent research and writing as part of two national study groups on serious and violent juvenile offenders and child delinquents (Loeber and Farrington 1998, 2001) that really identified him with both camps.

Part IV includes five chapters that examine the current state and future of intervention and treatment research in criminology. Two chapters, one by Doris MacKenzie and Gaylene Armstrong and the other by Friedrich Lösel, focus on the current era of correctional treatment, one that places increasing emphasis on evidence-based programs. MacKenzie and Armstrong, in chapter 24, highlight the role that high-quality evaluations, especially randomized experiments, and rigorous techniques of research synthesis (which include high-quality evaluations) have played in recent years in drawing attention to the importance and effectiveness of correctional treatment for offenders as well as the ineffectiveness of many popular "get tough" programs. Lösel, in chapter 25, also discusses the next stage of this development, which involves the translation of effective programs into policy and practice. In some countries this is done through accreditation. While the future looks bright for this new approach in corrections, the authors draw attention to a number of future perspectives, including the challenges of identification and management of special populations of offenders and the need for more attention to treatment fidelity.

Chapter 26, by Leena Augimeri and Christopher Koegl, focuses on interventions for young children with conduct problems who come in conflict with the law. The authors note that there is a dearth of evidence-based and developmentally appropriate programs and services for this population, often resulting in punitive measures or no treatment at all. The authors highlight one program that they developed and outline a number of priorities for future intervention research and practice to better serve this vulnerable population.

In chapter 27, Jonathan Shepherd considers the future of public health as it relates to violence, with a focus on two key roles: the prevention of violence and the organization and commissioning of research in and for health services. He argues that this dual focus (rather than just a focus on violence prevention) is particularly important because it "allows comparisons between, on the one hand, the development of research and, on the other, research infrastructure in health and in crime and justice and points to reforms that could usefully be made." One of these reforms is the integration of victim services with mental health services.

Manuel Eisner and Amy Nivette, in chapter 28, examine the intriguing prospect of how to lower the global homicide rate to 2 per 100,000 in the next 50 years. The authors show that this would require a 75 percent reduction in homicides worldwide, an ambitious goal but one that is plausible based on historical patterns. The authors argue that to achieve this global violence reduction plan will require advances in knowledge on three main topics. There is a need for a greater cross-cultural understanding of causal risk factors for violence; a need to expand the evidence base on effective prevention and intervention programs beyond its current focus on developed countries; and a need to understand the pacification of societies.

Public Policy Strategies

The focus of part V on public policy strategies is not just a logical end-point for a book about the future of criminology. It is also in recognition of the important contributions that David Farrington has made to crime policy in England, the

United States, Canada, and other parts of the world. Any reluctance to broach the research-policy divide—something that plagues many scholars—is not evident in David's lifework. One can always count on sound, research-based policy prescriptions following from his scholarly works, not to mention David taking the time to meet with political leaders, policymakers, and others to discuss the policy implications of his research.

This part includes five chapters that discuss public policy strategies that concern crime and justice. In chapter 29, James Wilson takes on the challenges facing macrocriminology, a field of study, he argues, that has "made very little progress" in understanding changes in the national crime rate. He contrasts this with the advances that have been made in understanding individual differences in offending, what he refers to as microcriminology. A discussion ensues on some of the key factors that have been put forth to explain changes in the crime rate.

In chapter 30, David Weisburd, Brian Lawton, and Justin Ready offer a mix of research and policy. Here the authors outline their proposal for the next generation of studies of the "criminology of place" and discuss how this can contribute to basic knowledge and more informed public policy. Building on the work of David Farrington to advance prospective longitudinal studies to investigate within- and between-individual differences in offending, a similar research strategy is called for (and sketched out) to investigate important questions concerning the criminology of place.

Experimental criminology is the subject of chapter 31 by Lawrence Sherman. It begins by describing two different models that have greatly advanced field experiments on crime and justice in the last few decades (center to periphery and periphery to center), but owing to political realities have lost some of their influence. Sherman reminds us that experimental criminology remains a vibrant and robust field of study and outlines a number of promising directions to guide the field in the coming years.

In chapter 32, Irvin Waller addresses government crime policy and the need for more and improved implementation in an effort to translate what works in crime prevention into effective practice. This begins with funding. Waller describes how modest reallocations of government spending on traditional criminal justice to effective crime prevention can lead to impressive reductions in crime. The next step begins with promoting improved governance and what amounts to a science of implementation, and he outlines what is needed to bring this about.

In chapter 33, the final chapter of the book, Michael Tonry takes on the future of sentencing and its control in the United States and in England and Wales. He sketches out how sentencing and punishment policies in these two countries need to change and his views on how they will change by the year 2025. Tonry argues for repealing a range of punitive sentencing options (e.g., three-strikes laws, mandatory minimums) for which there is no "credible evidence" of their effectiveness and have been applied inconsistently and disproportionately to minority offenders. Presumptive sentencing guidelines, sentencing reviews, and proportionate maximum sentences are among the needed reforms to bring about more effective, just, and humane sentences for offenders.

Acknowledgments

The editors are much indebted to Jennifer Wilson for her careful and dedicated assistance with this volume. Work on this volume was supported by grant 2005-JK-FX-0001 from the Office of Juvenile Justice and Delinquency Prevention (OJJDP), grants MH 50778 and 73941 from the National Institute of Mental Health, grant No. 11018 from the National Institute on Drug Abuse, and a grant from the Department of Health of the Commonwealth of Pennsylvania.

References

Cohen, Ellen G. 2011. "Changes in Scholarly Influence in Major International Criminology Journals, 1986–2005." *Canadian Journal of Criminology and Criminal Justice* 53: 157–188.

Cullen, Francis T. 2005. "The Twelve People Who Saved Rehabilitation: How the Science of Criminology Made a Difference." *Criminology* 43: 1–42.

Farrington, David P. 1994. "Early Developmental Prevention of Delinquency." *Criminal Behaviour and Mental Health* 4: 209–227.

Loeber, Rolf, and David P. Farrington, eds. 1998. *Serious and Violent Juvenile Offenders: Risk Factors and Successful Interventions.* Thousand Oaks, CA: Sage.

Loeber, Rolf, and David P. Farrington, eds. 2001. *Child Delinquents: Development, Intervention, and Service Needs.* Thousand Oaks, CA: Sage.

PART I

Development and Causation

1

Some Future Trajectories for Life Course Criminology

D. Wayne Osgood

I am grateful for the opportunity of adding my thoughts on the future of life course criminology to this volume in honor of David Farrington. David was a key member of the small group whose work created this field, and he consistently has been a major contributor shaping its short history. I could easily spend all my allotted space reviewing his influence on life course criminology as a whole and my own work in particular, but the editors have asked us to be brief in that regard. I will follow their direction and offer my views about the current state of life course criminology and where it should be heading, mentioning some aspects of David's contributions as I go.

The Launching of Life Course Criminology

When I entered criminology in the late 1970s, developmental or life course criminology did not exist. The strong relationship between age and crime was widely acknowledged, as indeed it is one of the oldest findings in all of social science (Quetelet 1984 [1833]). Criminologists' primary response to that fact was to focus their attention on the teen years, when crime rates peak. Indeed, the leading investigations were devoted to teenaged, inner-city males because they represent the intersection of the best-known demographic correlates of crime (e.g., Glueck and Glueck 1950; Wolfgang, Figlio, and Sellin 1972). I learned that criminology had a rich body of theory and evidence about ways that the experiences, circumstances, and personalities of these adolescents related to whether they were involved in delinquency.

After I had worked in the field for a few years, I began to think that criminologists' treatment of age was not working out so well. Though focusing on teenagers appeared to take age seriously, doing so also precluded meaningful analysis of age by making it a constant. The study of juvenile delinquency was a vital tradition with a rich history. Yet my new field seemed to present teenagers as oddly frozen in time, as though 16-year-olds would always be 16 (Sampson and Laub 1992). The exclusive focus on the teen years meant losing sight of its essential nature as a brief period of rapid change, with childhood close behind and adulthood looming on the horizon. Criminological research was largely limited to comparisons between different people, asking how delinquents differ from nondelinquents. As David has reminded us, however, the meaning of age is to be found in within-person comparisons (Farrington 2003). The age-crime curve can arise only because people change, that is, because most of the many 16-year-olds who break the law did not do so at age twelve and will not at age thirty. Something happens over that time, and we can only find out what if we study at other ages in addition to when they are teenagers.

It turned out that enough criminologists were already concerned about these issues that the field of life course criminology was being born. The movement came from several directions. On the methodological front was a growing appreciation of the value of the longitudinal studies required for developmental and life course research. With his already sustained involvement in the long-term Cambridge Study in Delinquent Development (West and Farrington 1973, 1977), David was a leader in advancing this work, for instance heading the influential MacArthur Foundation–sponsored volume on directions for longitudinal research on crime (Farrington, Ohlin, and Wilson 1986). From criminal justice research came the prominent criminal careers model (Blumstein et al. 1986), stressing the value of examining involvement in crime as a pattern over the entire life course, and David was a key contributor to this work as well (Blumstein, Farrington, and Moitra 1985; Blumstein, Cohen, and Farrington 1988). A third stream was input from the psychological study of human development, with its tradition of attention to contributions of genetics, early temperament, and family socialization to continuities in development, exemplified by influential theoretical positions of Moffitt (1993) and Patterson (Patterson and Yoerger 1993). Consistent with David's background in psychology, he contributed to the emergence and progress of life course criminology from this direction as well, such as his work as a member of the MacArthur research group addressing human development and crime (Tonry, Ohlin, and Farrington 1991), involvement in the trajectory typology research that combined developmental and criminal career approaches (Nagin, Farrington, and Moffitt 1995), and collaboration with David Rowe on behavioral genetic underpinnings of crime (Rowe and Farrington 1997). A final major source for developmental and life course criminology was the emergence of the life course model in sociology, as exemplified by the work of Elder (1974), and most notably presented to criminologists by Sampson and Laub (1992, 1993). This tradition has become an important part of David's work as well (Farrington 2003).

Where Are We Now? Life Course Criminology Comes of Age

Life course criminology has come a long way fast, to the point that it is clearly a prominent part of the discipline. Articles on life course topics appear in almost every issue of our leading journals, and key publications have been cited hundreds and even thousands of times. The most prestigious awards in criminology have gone to leading figures in life course criminology, including not only David Farrington but also Al Blumstein, John Laub, Terrie Moffitt, Dan Nagin, and Rob Sampson.

There can be no doubt that life course criminology has accomplished a great deal, for we now know much that we did not before. In my view, progress is most evident in two areas that have been major concentrations. The first of these is the nature of patterns of offending over time. Long before the advent of life span criminology, abundant evidence demonstrated substantial continuity in offending over considerable age spans (Olweus 1979; Robins 1966), but more recent research refined and clarified our understanding in many ways. Key studies have traced offending over much longer age spans than ever before (Blokland and Nieuwbeerta 2005; Laub and Sampson 2003). The criminal careers model brought a host of parameters for calibrating offending over the life span, which researchers have used to describe offending patterns in considerable detail (e.g., Piquero, Farrington, and Blumstein 2003, 2007). Nagin and Land's (1993) method of identifying groups based on trajectories of offending over time has been widely adopted, providing a valuable heuristic for holistically portraying typical patterns of offending across ages. New statistical models have helped to parse the source of continuity between stable individual differences (persistent heterogeneity) and the tendency for committing crime to generate more crime (state dependence, Nagin and Paternoster 1991).

A second focal area for life course criminology has been the effects on crime of the major role transitions of early adulthood, such as marriage, entering the work-force, and becoming a parent. Criminologists had long studied the movement from childhood to adolescence in seeking to understand the onset of crime. A key insight underlying life course criminology is that it is also important to understand the desistance that comes later. Why do some people keep on committing crime as they enter adulthood, perhaps spending many years in prison, when most other offenders stop? Sampson and Laub (1993) saw the relevance of examining the key events in people's lives in the postteen years, and they led the way with their analyses of marriage and employment in the Gluecks' data. In league with Julie Horney and Ineke Marshall, I was not too far behind (Horney, Osgood, and Marshall 1995), and as usual, so were David Farrington and Donald West (1995). The volume and sophistication of research on this topic has grown continuously since that time (for a recent review see Siennick and Osgood 2008).

Where Should We Be Going? One Future for Life Course Criminology

Though many important topics in life course criminology merit further study, I want to encourage attention to one that is largely neglected but in my view is most central of all: I believe that we should do more research aimed at determining why crime rates differ with age. Though the age-crime curve is one of the strongest, most consistent, and longest-standing findings in criminology, we have not put much effort into determining its source.

This is not to say that life course criminologists have failed to delve into the relationship between age and crime. Far from it! For instance, in 1986 David Farrington initiated a topic that remains of major interest (e.g., Petras, Nieuwbeerta, and Piquero 2010) when he reported that the shape of the age/crime curve was primarily due to change in how many people engage in crime, rather than change in how much crime offenders commit.

Hirschi and Gottfredson's 1983 article on age and crime stimulated a great deal of the research in life course criminology with their argument that the age/crime curve is so consistent that it should be regarded as a constant that is beyond explanation. Life course criminologists responded to this as a challenge and produced an impressive array of studies seeking to demonstrate variation in patterns of age-related change in offending and to predict that variation. For instance, we have a great deal of research concerning predictors of who will have longer versus shorter criminal careers, which is a major focus of the typological theories that focus on age of onset (Moffitt 1993; Patterson and Yoerger 1993). It is now widely accepted that people vary in their trajectories of offending, though controversy remains about some key aspects, such as the degree to which the variation in timing of offending (as distinct from mean level) is meaningful and predictable by early precursors (e.g., Sampson and Laub 2005).

In my view both Hirschi and Gottfredson's (1983) original argument and most of the work addressing the issues they raised has shared a notable feature that keeps the focus away from the most interesting question. Hirschi and Gottfredson sought to demonstrate the constancy of the relationship between age and crime by showing that it held for different groups of people, and subsequent research correspondingly attended to differences in relation to various personal attributes. Further, the growth curve and trajectory grouping statistical models we now rely on for such research can bias us toward a focus on such between-person explanations through their convenient summary of the entire offending pattern over time (Osgood, Anderson, and Shaffer 2005). As a result, the study of age and crime has been largely the study of between-person differences in effects of age, which is a bit odd considering that age is the quintessential within-person variable (Farrington 2003).

It is logically possible for between-person variables, such as gender, ethnicity, genetic factors, early child rearing, and stable personality traits, to predict patterns of change, but I see two shortcomings of the approach. First, prediction about any fine-grained differences in change from measures taken at a great distance in time strikes me as implausible. Given the stability of offending across ages, early prediction of average levels (or rank order) of offending is understandable. I am doubtful, however, that we will ever be very successful at using early information to predict that certain high-level offenders and low-level offenders (or nonoffenders) will change places at particular ages, many years later. Though offense trajectory models give us tidy pictures of seemingly orderly change, groups differ far more in average rates of offending than timing. Differences in timing prove very hard to predict in the long run (Laub and Sampson 2003; Sampson and Laub 2005), and change over time in actual individual patterns of offending is not so orderly at all (Osgood, Anderson, and Shaffer 2005).

The second shortcoming of focusing on between-individual variables in relation to age and crime is that such variables necessarily leave unanswered the fundamental question about the relationship between age and crime. Why do crime rates rapidly rise in early adolescence and then more gradually decline through the rest of life? Hirschi and Gottfredson's (1985) response to a critic nicely summarizes what is required for a satisfactory answer to this question: Find a variable with a similar pattern of change over the age span that also is strongly associated with crime. Permanent differences between people cannot account for the aggregate, overall age/crime curve. We can only explain it with variables on which people change over time (Farrington 2003).

In my view, life course criminology would be enormously enriched by greater attention to relevant ways that people and their lives change with age. I concur with Sampson and Laub that criminologists have tended to adopt the tacit ontological view that the development of criminal careers is a gradual unfolding of a future that was predetermined early in life (Laub and Sampson 2003; Osgood, Anderson, and Shaffer 2005; Sampson and Laub 2005). The result is research that treats life after childhood as one long outcome, paying little attention to the complex interplay when people whose capacities are evolving grapple with the shifting circumstances of their lives.

The one area of strength for criminological research on effects of time-varying variables is the study of role transitions associated with the transition to adulthood (Siennick and Osgood 2008). I am a devotee of this work, and from it we now have a rich menu of theoretical approaches (Giordano, Cernkovic, and Rudolph 2002; Laub and Sampson 2003; Massoglia and Uggen 2010) and methodological strategies (Horney, Osgood, and Marshall 1995 ; King, Massoglia, and MacMillan 2007; Sampson, Laub, and Wimer 2006) for studying time-varying explanatory variables. Yet success in investigating these role transitions must not mislead us to believe that it is remotely close to a sufficient range of research on relationships between crime and time-varying explanatory variables. Important as these transitions are, they obviously represent a limited age span and a slice of life's content.

Furthermore, focusing on the role transitions of early adulthood does not take us very far toward explaining the overall trend in offending over the life course. Despite the mass of evidence that marriage brings reductions in offending, a direct test indicates that it accounts for only a small portion of age-related variation in crime (Blokland and Nieuwbeerta 2005). The reasons are straightforward: Much of the reduction in crime happens well before marriage is common, and the effect of marriage on offending is considerably less than the age-related decline.

We also have good evidence that exploring other life domains can be fruitful. Among the few direct attempts to explain the relationship of age and crime, considerably greater success has come in studies of peer processes, specifically Warr's (1993, 1998) investigations of association with deviant peers and my own research on time spent in unstructured socializing (Osgood, Anderson, and Shaffer 2005). Even so, these factors leave most variation in the age-crime relationship unexplained. A great deal of exciting research awaits us as we take up the challenge of exploring the many domains in which life changes with age and seek to determine which account for the dramatic shifts in crime rates over the life course.

References

Blokland, Arjan A. J., and Paul Nieuwbeerta. 2005. "The Effects of Life Circumstances on Longitudinal Trajectories of Offending." *Criminology* 43: 1203–1240.

Blumstein, Alfred, Jacqueline Cohen, and David P. Farrington. 1988. "Criminal Career Research: Its Value for Criminology." *Criminology* 26: 1–36.

Blumstein, Alfred, Jacqueline Cohen, Jeffrey A. Roth, and Christy Visher. 1986. *Criminal Careers and "Career Criminals"*. Vol. 1. Washington, DC: National Academy Press.

Blumstein, Alfred, David P. Farrington, and Soumyo Moitra. 1985. "Delinquency Careers: Innocents, Desisters, and Persisters." *Crime and Justice: An Annual Review of Research*, vol. 6, edited by Michael Tonry and Norval Morris, 187–219. Chicago: University of Chicago Press.

Elder, Glen H., Jr. 1974. *Children of the Great Depression*. Chicago: University of Chicago Press.

Farrington, David P. 1986. "Age and Crime." In *Crime and Justice: An Annual Review of Research*, vol. 7, edited by Michael Tonry and Norval Morris, 189–250. Chicago: University of Chicago Press.

Farrington, David P. 2003. "Developmental and Life-Course Criminology: Key Theoretical and Empirical Issues—The 2002 Sutherland Award Address." *Criminology* 41: 221–255.

Farrington, David P., Lloyd E. Ohlin, and James Q. Wilson. 1986. *Understanding and Controlling Crime: Toward a New Research Strategy*. New York: Springer.

Farrington, David P., and Donald J. West. 1995. "Effects of Marriage, Separation and Children on Offending by Adult Males." In *Current Perspectives on Aging and the Life Cycle*, vol. 4: *Delinquency and Disrepute in the Life Course*, edited by John Hagan, 249–281. Greenwich, CT: JAI Press.

Giordano, Peggy C., Stephen A. Cernkovich, and Jennifer L. Rudolph. 2002. "Gender, Crime, and Desistance: Toward a Theory of Transformation." *American Journal of Sociology* 107: 990–1064.

Glueck, Sheldon, and Eleanor Glueck. 1950. *Unraveling Delinquency*. New York: Commonwealth Fund.

Hirschi, Travis, and Michael Gottfredson. 1983. "Age and the Explanation of Crime." *American Journal of Sociology* 89: 552–584.

Hirschi, Travis, and Michael Gottfredson. 1985. "All Wise after the Fact Learning Theory, Again: Reply to Baldwin." *American Journal of Sociology* 90: 1330–1333.

Horney, Julie, D. Wayne Osgood, and Ineke Haen Marshall. 1995. "Criminal Careers in the Short-Term: Intra-Individual Variability in Crime and Its Relation to Local Life Circumstances." *American Sociological Review* 60: 655–673.

King, Ryan D., Michael Massoglia, and Ross MacMillan. 2007. "The Context of Marriage and Crime: Gender, the Propensity to Marry, and Offending in Early Adulthood." *Criminology* 45: 33–65.

Laub, John H., and Robert J. Sampson. 2003. *Shared Beginnings, Divergent Lives: Delinquent Boys to Age 70.* Cambridge: Harvard University Press.

Massoglia, Michael, and Christopher Uggen. 2010. "Settling Down and Aging Out: Toward an Interactionist Theory of Desistance and the Transition to Adulthood." *American Journal of Sociology* 116: 543–582.

Moffitt, Terrie E. 1993. "Adolescence-Limited and Life-Course-Persistent Antisocial Behavior: A Developmental Taxonomy." *Psychological Review* 100: 674–701.

Nagin, Daniel S., David P. Farrington, and Terrie E. Moffitt. 1995. "Life-Course Trajectories of Different Types of Offenders." *Criminology* 33: 111–139.

Nagin, Daniel S., and Kenneth C. Land. 1993. "Age, Criminal Careers, and Population Heterogeneity: Specification and Estimation of a Nonparametric, Mixed Poisson Model." *Criminology* 31: 327–362.

Nagin, Daniel S., and Raymond Paternoster. 1991. "On the Relationship of Past to Future Delinquency." *Criminology* 29: 163–189.

Olweus, Dan. 1979. "Stability of Aggressive Reaction Patterns in Males: A Review." *Psychological Bulletin* 86: 852–875.

Osgood, D. Wayne, Amy L. Anderson, and Jennifer N. Shaffer. 2005. "Unstructured Leisure in the After-School Hours." In *Organized Activities as Contexts of Development: Extracurricular Activities, After-School and Community Programs*, edited by Joseph L. Mahoney, Reed W. Larson, and Jacquelynne S. Eccles, 45–64. Mahwah, NJ: Lawrence Erlbaum.

Patterson, Gerald R., and Karen Yoerger. 1993. "Developmental Models for Delinquent Behavior." In *Crime and Mental Disorder*, edited by Sheilagh Hodgins, 140–172. Newbury Park, CA: Sage.

Petras, Hanno, Paul Nieuwbeerta, and Alex R. Piquero. 2010. "Participation and Frequency during Criminal Careers across the Life Span." *Criminology* 48: 607–637.

Piquero, Alex R., David P. Farrington, and Alfred Blumstein. 2003. "The Criminal Career Paradigm." In *Crime and Justice: A Review of Research*, vol. 30, edited by Michael Tonry, 359–506. Chicago: University of Chicago Press.

Piquero, Alex R., David P. Farrington, and Alfred Blumstein. 2007. *Key Issues in Criminal Career Research: New Analyses of the Cambridge Study in Delinquent Development.* New York: Cambridge University Press.

Quetelet, Adolphe. 1984. [1833.] *Adolphe Quetelet's Research on the Propensity for Crime at Different Ages.* Cincinnati: Anderson.

Robins, Lee N. 1966. *Deviant Children Grown Up: A Sociological and Psychiatric Study of Sociopathic Personality.* Baltimore: Williams and Wilkins.

Rowe, David C., and David P. Farrington. 1997. "The Familial Transmission of Criminal Convictions." *Criminology* 35: 177–201.

Sampson, Robert J., and John H. Laub. 1992. "Crime and Deviance in the Life Course." *Annual Review of Sociology* 18: 63–84.

Sampson, Robert J., and John H. Laub. 1993. *Crime in the Making: Pathways and Turning Points through Life.* Cambridge: Harvard University Press.

Sampson, Robert J., and John H. Laub. 2005. "A Life-Course View of the Development of Crime." *Annals of the American Academy of Political and Social Science* 602: 12–45.

Sampson, Robert J., John H. Laub, and Christopher Wimer. 2006. "Does Marriage Reduce Crime? A Counterfactual Approach to Within-Individual Causal Effects." *Criminology* 44: 465–508.

Siennick, Sonja E., and D. Wayne Osgood. 2008. "A Review of Research on the Impact on Crime of Transitions to Adult Roles." In *The Long View of Crime: A Synthesis of Longitudinal Research*, edited by Akiva M. Liberman, 161–187. New York: Springer.

Tonry, Michael, Lloyd E. Ohlin, and David P. Farrington. 1991. *Human Development and Criminal Behavior: New Ways of Advancing Knowledge*. New York: Springer.

Warr, Mark. 1993. "Age, Peers, and Delinquency." *Criminology* 31: 17–40.

Warr, Mark. 1998. "Life Course Transitions and Desistance from Crime." *Criminology* 36: 183–216.

West, Donald J., and David P. Farrington. 1973. *Who Becomes Delinquent?* London: Heinemann.

West, Donald J., and David P. Farrington. 1977. *The Delinquent Way of Life*. London: Heinemann.

Wolfgang, Marvin E., Robert M. Figlio, and Thorsten Sellin. 1972. *Delinquency in a Birth Cohort*. Chicago: University of Chicago Press.

2

Does the Study of the Age-Crime Curve Have a Future?

Rolf Loeber

About 150 years after the first identification of the relationship between age and crime by Quetelet (1833), David Farrington was the first to comprehensively review empirical knowledge about the *age-crime curve* (Farrington 1986). The term refers to the fact that the prevalence of offending in populations increases from late childhood, peaks during mid to late adolescence, and then decreases in adulthood (see also Tremblay and Nagin 2005; Laub and Sampson 2003). This bell-shaped age curve is universal in all Western populations and possibly beyond. For example, the age-crime curve applies to males and females, and to individuals of different ethnic backgrounds (but see details below). In contrast to a vast body of research on juvenile delinquency, the age-crime curve highlights the onset of delinquency in some individuals prior to adolescence and a gradual decrease in the prevalence of offenders during adulthood.

In this chapter, I celebrate David's insights into the age-crime curve, and I review the ways that the age-crime curve systematically varies for populations of youth exposed to different levels of risk factors. I also show novel research on prediction of the age-crime curve, after which I point to future openings for research on the age-crime curve.

Whereas David recognized the importance of the age-crime curve and its universality in different populations of young offenders, he also noted that the curve can vary for different populations. Some age cohorts may start delinquency earlier and stop later, or may have a higher frequency (height of curve) of offending. He also noted that there was an absence of explanations of the curve. The variables that influence the width and height of the curve and its decrease over time have not been studied extensively. Information about which factors influence the age-crime curve is of great importance for public policy and for reducing future crime waves.

Why Is the Age-Crime Curve Important?

In the conventional use of the term, the age-crime curve indicates when a population of youth starts to engage in offending, at what age the largest proportion of youth engages in offenses, and in which period much desistance takes place.[1] There are several reasons why the population age-crime curve is important:

a. In longitudinal data sets, the shape of the age-crime curve represents the number of individuals who engage in crime in at least the first three decades of life.
b. The sum of different age-crime curves of successive cohorts represents community level of crime as it changes over time. Thus, the age-crime curve of a given cohort is a building block toward understanding the community level of crime.
c. One of the litmus tests for interventions is whether interventions eventually reduce community levels of crime or, on a narrower level, reduce the age-crime curve. There are two major ways that the age-crime curve can be reduced: first, by lowering the peak of the curve and, second, by reducing the base of the curve.
d. Both lowering of the peak and reducing of the base of the curve reduce the number of active offenders. Important is which methods promote desistance among active offenders.
e. Most of the serious offenders—including violent offenders—are situated in the down-slope of the age-crime curve. Thus, the lowering of the tail end of the age-crime curve is likely to affect the volume of serious crime in populations.
f. The higher and longer the down-slope of the age-crime curve, the larger the population of people who may not have outgrown offending or who may have started offending during adulthood.

Measurement Issues

Although many reports on the age-crime curve use cross-sectional information (Farrington 1986), such information confuses age, period, and cohort effects. Therefore, the best quantification of the age-crime curve is accomplished in cohort studies in which a defined population of the *same* participants may contribute to the age-crime curve from childhood to subsequent ages.

Most published age-crime curves are based on official records, fewer on self-reports, and fewest on combinations of self-report and official records (Loeber et al. 2008). Age-crime curves based on self-reported delinquency tend to show an earlier peak than official records (Blokland and Palmen in press; Piquero et al. in press). This earlier peaking may reflect the fact that more self-reported juvenile offenders at a young age may be undetected in official records until a later age (Piquero et al. in press). In addition, since official records miss self-reported delinquency often over several years, age-crime curves based on official records tend to be lower than those based on self-reports.

Variations in the Age-Crime Curve for Different Populations

Even though the age-crime curve is universal, the shape of the curve varies for different populations. First, studies show that the age-crime curve for females peaks earlier than males (e.g., Blokland and Palmen in press; Farrington 1986). The curve is higher and wider for young males (especially those of a minority status) growing up in the most disadvantaged neighborhoods (Fabio et al. 2011; Elliott, Pampel, and Huizinga 2004). Third, the age-crime curve for violence tends to peak later than that of property crime (Blokland and Palmen in press; Piquero et al. in press). Since most of the violence is directed at same-age victims, it is not surprising that the down-slope of the age crime curve overlaps with the age period 16 to 24 years, when violent victimization is common (e.g., Kershaw, Nicholas, and Walker 2008). However, we are not aware of age-crime victimization curves and their relationship to the age-crime curve. Fourth, the age-crime curve is higher for some cohorts than for others, indicating the presence of period effects (i.e., some age cohorts are more delinquent than other age cohorts; Farrington 1986).

It should be understood that the typical published age-crime curve is a cross-sectional prevalence curve and not an indicator of individuals' persistence or desistance in offending. Information about persistence and desistance derives from longitudinal follow-up data and is the key for understanding age-normative versus delayed outgrowing of delinquency (see below). In summary, the down-slope of the age-crime curve varies between different populations of young people and often extends from adolescence into adulthood (Loeber and Farrington in press).

Explanations

Traditionally, explanations in criminology have focused on either group or individual differences in offending. A key question is the following: What are the best predictors of serious offenses, and which individual differences distinguish between, for example, those individuals who will commit serious offenses and those who will not? Examples of individual differences are whether an individual's offense frequency changes as a result of marriage or employment. Usually, linear statistical models are used to answer either type of question because the emphasis is on explaining group or individual differences.

Linear tests are useful for these outcomes, but are not for predictors of the age-crime curve, because the key issue is what explains the up-slope *and* the down-slope of the age-crime curve, which is a quadratic or cubic function. The key issue is what factor(s) can explain relatively few individual differences in offending at the end of childhood, a ballooning of individual differences in offending during adolescence, and a narrowing down of individual differences in offending between late adolescence and early adulthood. Thus, the crucial question is this: Which factors explain why individuals become increasingly involved in offending *and* why a high proportion of the same individuals decrease their offending? We propose that many predictors of delinquency also predict the age-crime curve in that individual differences in factors such as neighborhood quality or parenting style differentiate between different levels of the age-crime curve (e.g., Fabio et al. 2011). Individual differences on predictors of delinquency, however, are not necessarily illustrative of processes that explain the waxing and waning of delinquency in individuals' lives.

I propose that what is needed is the study of predictors of the age-crime curve that are either situated in the brain, directly measure brain maturation, or are markers of maturational processes. The following example may serve this purpose. In the Pittsburgh Youth Study, we extended earlier research on the middle sample (first studied at age 10; White et al. 1994) and focused on a version of cognitive impulsivity, which we thought would best measure frontal brain functioning and individuals' ability to control their behavior. We focused on three psychometric tasks that measured aspects of cognitive impulsivity (i.e., the Trail Making Test, the Stroop Color, Word Association Test, and Time Perception). We also took into account intelligence, which had been measured at about age 12 (Loeber et al. n.d.). Follow-up was in the form of arrest for moderate to serious forms of offenses from ages 11 to 28. The results of the prospective analyses showed that cognitive impulsivity and intelligence and their interaction positively predicted the probability of being arrested for any offense (i.e., total arrests) and arrest for violence, but not arrest for theft. Cognitive impulsivity (and intelligence) predicted the *increase*, *decrease*, and *stabilization* of arrest from adolescence into early adulthood (see figure 2.1).

As far as I am aware, this is the only research to date showing that psychometric test results predicted the age-crime curve for arrest, especially violence. Although the study did not demonstrate a link with brain maturation, cognitive impulsivity is likely to be a marker of brain maturation, and the results are in line with notions that brain maturation influences the age-crime curve. Since brain maturation is probably malleable, it is less clear, however, to what extent *improved self-control* through specific training or through appropriate parenting is associated with accelerated brain maturation, a faster outgrowing of impulsive and sensation-seeking behaviors during adolescence, a lowering of the age-crime curve for these individuals, and a curtailing of the age-crime curve into early adulthood.

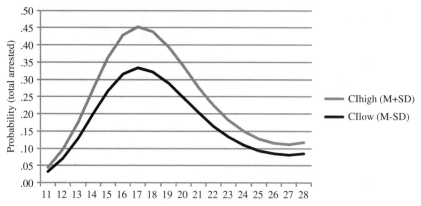

FIGURE 2.1 *Estimated male age-crime curve (probability of total arrest between age 11 and 28) for high and low cognitive impulsivity (CI; M + SD vs. M – SD) (Loeber et al. 2011).*

Lowering the Age-Crime Curve

It is rare that intervention studies have yearly follow-ups to measure self-reported delinquency over time. It is more feasible to obtain official records of offending. Yet very few published evaluation studies have demonstrated the degree to which interventions lowered the age-crime curve for experimental participants compared to controls, and to what extent the experimental lowering and shrinking of the age-crime curve affected related outcomes such as incarceration time.

We used the longitudinal data from the PYS to simulate the impact of an intervention, such as improved self-control training, on offending by at-risk youths in the youngest, middle, and oldest samples (Loeber and Stallings 2011). The effectiveness of the intervention took into account a conservative difference between experimental and control groups, which was based on prior intervention studies. The modeled intervention showed a lowering of the age-crime curve during adolescence and early adulthood by reducing the prevalence of convicted homicide offenders and homicide victims, thus benefiting the justice system by greatly reducing arrests and weeks of incarceration (figure 2.2).

In conclusion, there are many intervention programs available outside of the justice system that reduce recidivism and prevent persistence of offending from adolescence into early adulthood. Preliminary results indicate that such interventions may lower the age-crime curve.

The Future of Age-Crime Curve Research

The preceding makes it clear that several key aspects of the age-crime curve are missing in current research. Some examples of important unresolved issues are discussed in the following.

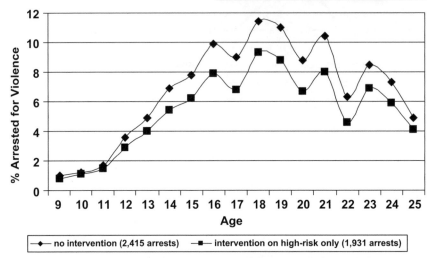

FIGURE 2.2 *Age-crime curves of percentage arrested for violence before and after intervention on high-risk participants only (youngest, middle, and oldest cohorts in the PYS) (Loeber and Stallings 2011).*

PREVALENCE AND FREQUENCY

- The age-crime curve essentially is a prevalence curve. A key unanswered question is whether the frequency of offending with age follows the age-crime curve or not, and whether changes in frequency represent increases in some types of offenses and decreases in other types of offenses.
- The age-crime curve may represent different developmental trajectories of categories of offenders (Piquero in press). However, a key issue is how best to combine trajectory analyses with analyses of the overall age-crime curve.

EXPLANATIONS

- As David Farrington (1986) has pointed out, we need to know why offending prevalence reaches a peak in adolescence, and why it declines afterward. I would add that we also need to know why offending prevalence increases between late childhood and adolescence.

- Among the putative explanation of the age-crime curve is brain maturation. However, the relationship between brain maturation and the age-crime curve, although often hypothesized, remains without firm foundation. Necessary are longitudinal research studies in which the same participants are studied from late childhood until early adulthood by means of brain imaging or other brain investigative techniques.
- It is also necessary to establish whether the degree to which there are individual differences in the up-slope, peak, and down-slope of the age-crime curve can be linked to individual differences in the development of brain functioning.
- Alongside this research it is necessary to establish which psychometric tests of cognitive impulsivity best link to individual differences in brain maturation and behavioral impulsivity.
- This basic research should take into account known risk factors for offending such as parents' child-rearing practices, peer influences, school factors, and neighborhood factors.
- There are many brain locations and mechanisms that need to be researched to address the above points. To narrow down these options, investigators may want to establish the extent to which systematic training in improved self-control changes in which areas of brain functioning.
- Because studying the age-crime curve by definition takes decades, it is advisable for researchers to explore techniques to statistically model individual differences in the age-crime curve. For instance, to what extent is it possible to determine at a young age what the likelihood will be that the age-crime curve for that individual will have a certain range of values?

EVALUATION OF INTERVENTIONS

- Interventions should be evaluated by showing how the interventions affect the age-crime curve. For example, is the intervention effect concentrated in lowering the peak of the curve, or does it primarily affect the down-slope of the curve, indicating an earlier outgrowing of delinquency?
- Which interventions and at what ages are superior in lowering the age-crime curve?
- Is an intervention at an early age combined with interventions at later ages superior to interventions at an early age only to reduce the age-crime curve?

In many ways the above research agenda is much inspired by working with David Farrington for almost three decades, for which I am tremendously grateful.

Acknowledgments

Work on this chapter was supported by grant 2005-JK-FX-0001 from the Office of Juvenile Justice and Delinquency Prevention (OJJDP), grants MH 50778 and 73941 from the National Institute of Mental Health, grant No. 11018 from the National Institute on Drug Abuse, and a grant from the Department of Health of the Commonwealth of Pennsylvania.

Note

1. Desistance from offending tends to occur throughout the age-crime curve, but is concentrated in the down-slope of the curve (Loeber and Farrington, in press).

References

Blokland, Arjan A. J., and Hanneke Palmen. In press. "Criminal Career Patterns." In *Persisters and Desisters in Crime from Adolescence into Adulthood: Explanation, Prevention and Punishment*, edited by Rolf Loeber, Machteld Hoeve, N. Wim Slot, and Peter van der Laan. Aldershot, UK: Ashgate.

Elliott, D. S., Fred Pampel, and David Huizinga. 2004. *Youth Violence: Continuity and Desistance. A Supplemental Report to Youth Violence: A Report of the Surgeon General*. Boulder: Center for the Study and Prevention of Violence, Institute of Behavior Science, University of Colorado.

Fabio, Antony, Li-Chan Tu, Rolf Loeber, and Jacqueline Cohen. In press. "Neighborhood Socioeconomic Disadvantage and the Shape of the Age-Crime Curve." *American Journal of Public Health* 101: S325–S332.

Farrington, David P. 1986. "Age and Crime." In *Crime and Justice: An Annual Review of Research*, vol. 7, edited by Michael Tonry and Norval Morris, 189–250. Chicago: University of Chicago Press.

Kershaw, Chris, Sian Nicholas, and Alison Walker. 2008. *Crime in England and Wales 2007/08*. London: Home Office. www.homeoffice.gov.uk/rds/pdfs08/hosb0708.pdf.

Laub, John H., and Robert J. Sampson. 2003. *Shared Beginnings, Divergent Lives: Delinquent Boys to Age 70*. Cambridge: Harvard University Press.

Loeber, Rolf, and David P. Farrington, eds. In press. *Transitions from Juvenile Delinquency to Adult Crime: Criminal Careers, Justice Policy and Prevention*. New York: Oxford University Press.

Loeber, Rolf, David P. Farrington, Magda Stouthamer-Loeber, and Helene R. White. 2008. *Violence and Serious Theft: Development and Prediction from Childhood to Adulthood*. New York: Routledge.

Loeber, Rolf, Barbara Menting, Don Lynam, Terri Moffitt, Magda Stouthamer-Loeber, Rebecca Stallings, David Farrington, and Dustin Pardini. N.d. "Findings from the Pittsburgh Youth Study: Cognitive Impulsivity and Intelligence as Predictors of the Age-Crime Curve." Manuscript in preparation.

Loeber, Rolf, and Rebecca Stallings. 2011. "Modeling the Impact of Interventions on Local Indicators of Offending, Victimization, and Incarceration." In *Young Homicide Offenders and Victims: Development, Risk Factors and Prediction from Childhood*, edited by Rolf Loeber and David P. Farrington, 137–152. New York: Springer.

Piquero, Alex R., J. David Hawkins, and Lisa Kazemian. In press. "Criminal Career Patterns." In *Transitions from Juvenile Delinquency to Adult Crime: Criminal Careers, Justice Policy and Prevention*, edited by Rolf Loeber and David P. Farrington. New York: Oxford University Press.

Quetelet, Adolphe. 1984. [1833.] *Adolphe Quetelet's Research on the Propensity for Crime at Different Ages*. Cincinnati: Anderson.

Tremblay, Richard E., and Daniel S. Nagin. 2005. "The Developmental Origins of Physical Aggression in Humans." In *Developmental Origins of Aggression*, edited by Richard E. Tremblay, William H. Hartup, and John Archer, 83–106. New York: Guilford Press.

White, Jennifer L., Terri E. Moffitt, Avshalom Caspi, Dawn J. Bartusch, Douglas J. Needles, and Magda Stouthamer-Loeber. 1994. "Measuring Impulsivity and Examining Its Relationship To delinquency." *Journal of Abnormal Psychology* 103: 192–205.

3

Developmental Origins of Aggression

FROM SOCIAL LEARNING TO EPIGENETICS

Richard E. Tremblay

A few months after having started my Ph.D. at the University of London, my upstairs neighbor, a postdoctoral student in cancer genetics, gave me a newspaper clipping of a book review on juvenile delinquency. He knew that my thesis was on the treatment of juvenile delinquents and wondered if I had heard of the study described in the book. At that time I was far from realizing that the study I discovered in *Who Becomes Delinquent* (West and Farrington 1973) would have such a profound effect on my career. Indeed, my Ph.D. research on the effects of residential treatment for delinquent boys (Tremblay 1984) made me realize the importance of understanding the early development of antisocial behavior, and the Cambridge Study in Delinquent Development (Farrington 2003) was a model. The other model was a prevention randomized control trial, the Cambridge-Somerville Study initiated in 1935 by the Harvard physician Richard C. Cabot and made famous by Joan McCord's long-term follow-up of its impact (McCord 1978; 1992).

Both Richard C. Cabot and David West had realized that understanding and preventing the development of chronic antisocial behavior meant starting studies long before the police and the courts started arresting and processing adolescents in the juvenile justice system. The youngest subjects enrolled in the Cambridge-Somerville study were seven years old at its initiation in 1935, and the subjects in the Cambridge study were eight to nine years old at its initiation in 1961–1962. Twenty years after the start of the Cambridge study I initiated the Montreal Longitudinal-Experimental Study with a sample of kindergarten boys from low socioeconomic areas. The study was a cross between the US and UK Cambridge studies. The first aim was to understand the development of delinquent behavior with a longitudinal design, and the second aim was to experiment a preventive intervention with a randomized control trial embedded in the longitudinal study (Tremblay et al. 2003; Lacourse et al. 2003; Boisjoli et al. 2007). There were two other important differences: the sample was much larger, and the assessments were yearly until the end of adolescence, providing detailed information on the boys' developmental trajectories from kindergarten to the end of high school (Nagin and Tremblay 1999).

However, the first five years of results from the Montreal Longitudinal-Experimental Study convinced me that kindergarten was too late to understand the developmental origins of antisocial behavior. It took another six years to get the funding to initiate a birth cohort and start assessing antisocial behavior in the crib. There were two related major obstacles to doing this: first, my colleagues resisted including aggression items before the children reached two years of age, arguing that it would be seen as ridiculous by the parents; second, early childhood experts had decided that any form of aggression before children were "conscious" of their behavior could not be considered "aggression" (Kagan 1974). Consciousness is still part of many experts' definition of "aggression," although assessments of violence in adolescents and adults very rarely attempt to measure to what extent the aggressor was conscious. Fortunately, animal behavior specialists have managed to study fish, rat, and baboon aggression without requiring a proof of consciousness and their work has been extremely useful to understand human aggression (Tremblay 2000).

Development of Antisocial Behavior before the Age of Reason

A number of studies published in the past decade and a half on the development of antisocial behaviors during the preschool years clearly show that they are universal (Tremblay 2010).

Physical aggression: From the available data on the development of physical aggression we can conclude that: (1) the vast majority of preschool children use physical aggression; (2) the vast majority also learn with age to use other means of solving problems; (3) some need more time than others to learn; (4) girls learn more quickly than boys; (5) most of the cases of chronic physical aggression during adolescence were chronic cases since early childhood; (6) attempting to use retrospective information to determined "age of onset" of physical aggression is futile because recall of specific age is unreliable and in all cases it will have been in early childhood.

Anger, opposition, defiance, and overt disregard for rules: From the available data on the preschool development of overt anger, opposition, defiance, and overt disregard for rules, which is admittedly thin, we can conclude that: (1) all children frequently manifest anger from the first month after birth; (2) the vast majority of preschool children frequently manifest opposition, defiance, and overt disregard for rules; (3) the vast majority also learn during the preschool years to use other means of solving problems; (4) some need more time than others to learn; (5) there does not appear to be substantial differences between females and males; (6) approximately 7 percent of children could be considered chronic cases from childhood to adolescence.

Covert rule-breaking: Very few studies have focused on covert rule-breaking during early childhood; apparently because of its covert nature it is more difficult to observe than overt behaviors such as physical aggression and overt rule-breaking. For the same reasons it is also difficult to obtain reliable parent reports. Thus better data is needed to understand the development of covert rule-breaking during early childhood. Laboratory observations are probably the best approach to collect appropriate data. It will be important to rethink where rule breaking fits in the antisocial behavior spectrum because the traditional focus on truanting from school, staying out late, and running away from home are by definition creating a late onset group because they do not apply to young children. Appropriate rule-breaking criteria for each developmental period are needed.

Theft: The comparison between developmental trajectories of theft and physical aggression is striking. Frequency of physical aggression apparently decreases substantially from the preschool years to the end of adolescence, except for a very small group, while frequency of theft apparently increases for all from 10 years onward at the latest (Tremblay 2010). This developmental difference makes it hard to understand why diagnostic categories, developmental theories, etiological studies, and studies meant to test preventive and corrective interventions aggregate physical violence and theft assessments. Physical aggression and theft have different destructive consequences (person vs. property), are at opposite ends of the overt-covert continuum, and require different skills (brawn vs. brain). There are good reasons why infants start by physically aggressing to obtain property rather than commit simple theft: they do not have the cognitive control needed for the covert behavior, but they have the strong desire and enough impulsive brute force for the overt behavior. It seems obvious that physical violence and theft require different bio-psycho-social skills and different interventions are needed to prevent or correct these problems. Yet they have been systematically aggregated to create antisocial behavior (ASB), conduct disorder (CD) scores, and developmental taxonomies. Unfortunately, there is a paucity of theft studies during the early years. We need to study more attentively theft before the age when self-reporting becomes reliable. It is clear that taking things from others (with and without force) starts during early childhood, and it is most likely that the individual differences in the frequency of this behavior are as stable as physical aggression. What changes with time is the type of property that is stolen. The chronic stealer will steal the stylish red Tonka car at 3 years and the stylish red BMW at 17 years. However, it appears clear that theft, like indirect aggression, substantially increases among humans with increase in cognitive ability and opportunity. Interestingly, although extremely disruptive for victims and society, the more skilled at these covert behaviors generally managed not to get caught.

General Conclusions on the Development of Antisocial Behavior from Early Childhood to Adulthood

Developmental taxonomies: Developmental trajectories of the two overt behavioral categories (physical aggression and opposition-defiance) and the two covert behavioral categories (rule breaking and theft-vandalism) indicate that the frequency of overt behavior generally decreases with age, while the frequency of covert behavior generally increases with age. If indirect aggression was also considered part of the antisocial domain, we would also see that indirect aggression increases with age. These developmental differences are not surprising when we consider the behavioral impact of brain maturation, which increases the ability to inhibit impulses with age. Because aggregated scales of conduct problems or antisocial behavior have been the norm, very few studies have addressed these issues. The available studies suggest very strongly that the a priori developmental taxonomy "early and late onset" of conduct disorder or antisocial behavior confounds early development of overt DB and later development of covert disruptive behaviour. The aggregation of overt and covert DB also masks the timing of the appearance and disappearance of important sex differences.

Sex differences: Most studies indicate that males are largely overrepresented in the chronic trajectories of each antisocial category. The best available data is for aggression. From infancy sex differences increase with age; however these tendencies are inversed for overt (physical) and covert (indirect) aggression. Girls appear to learn the covert aggression strategy earlier and increase their frequency up to late adolescence. These sex differences can best be observed among the chronic cases. Physical violence of females during adolescence is generally so rare that modeling their developmental trajectories fails. Thus the differences in type of aggression between males and females are at their peak when they start mating.

Comorbidity. Comorbidity is ubiquitous among antisocial behaviors, and this is true at all ages, including for preschoolers. However, high comorbidity should not lead to an aggregation of dimensions that are meaningful for the advancement of research, prevention, and treatment. First, there is good psychometric evidence of significant differences between these types of antisocial behavior at a given point in time. Second, the developmental trajectories reviewed above evince important developmental differences. Finally, our taxonomies are meant to guide treatment. If the same diagnosis is given to individuals who, for example, have theft problems only, those who simply break age-appropriate rules, and those who have a serious physical aggression problem, it is unlikely that we will find the adequate intervention for each category. This is obviously also true for the emotional and cognitive dimensions of these problems, which, for example, lead to more or less proactive and reactive aggressions (Barker et al. 2006; Frick and Viding 2009; Vitaro et al. 2006).

Risk Factors and Bio-Psycho-Social Mechanisms

Research on the development of antisocial behavior during early childhood has helped us understand the early environmental risk factors for chronic trajectories of antisocial behavior (Tremblay 2010). Most of these risk factors can be identified prior to or at the start of pregnancy: mother's behavior problems during adolescence, mother's poor education, mother's first pregnancy at a young age, mother's depression, mother's smoking during pregnancy, dysfunctional relations between mother and father, and low family income.

Sex of the child, a genetic characteristic, is by far the most robust predictor. There is also good evidence from quantitative genetic studies (mainly twin studies) and molecular genetic studies that genetic factors are strongly implicated in effects that can be observed soon after birth. New evidence from gene expression studies (epigenetic) suggest that the numerous environmental risk factors related to the mother may start to have their impact on the child's developing brain and eventual self-control problems during fetal life and, soon after, through their impact on gene expression. There is a strong possibility that this mechanism, a well-kept secret until very recently, is possibly the main nature-nurture mechanism through which antisocial behavior is transmitted, amplified, or muted from generation to generation. Because we did not study antisocial behavior problems during early childhood, our interventions targeted the toxic environment very far downstream after the original damage was done. From an epigenetic perspective, that damage is carried throughout development by genetic programming. It will be important to unravel the intricacies of that mechanism during the perinatal period, but all the evidence suggests that preventing the development of chronic antisocial behavior problems should start at conception, at the latest, and needs to target females who have a history of social adjustment problems. In essence we need to turn on its head our thinking about prevention of chronic antisocial behavior: males are much more affected, but females should be our prime target to prevent a new generation of males and females with chronic antisocial behavior. It is clear that the perinatal bio-psycho-social environment that impacts gene expression is very largely related to pregnant women's health status and lifestyle. This epigenetic perspective suggests that successful prevention of antisocial behavior may be easier to achieve by ameliorating the early environment than by chasing bad genes. In case these conclusions are read as blaming mothers for their children's behavior problems, I will emphasize that mothers, fathers, and children should not be blamed for the genes and the environment they receive at conception. The main argument here is that we probably need to give intensive support to parents from conception, at the latest, to help children become more responsible and prevent other generations of victims.

The Future of Crib Criminology: Experiment, Experiment, Experiment

Preventive and corrective experiments for antisocial behavior have targeted school-age children much more frequently than preschoolers. A meta-analysis published a few years ago found 249 experimental studies with antisocial behavior symptoms as outcome, and only 8 percent of these included children younger than six years of age at the start of the intervention (Wilson and Lipsey 2007). Interestingly, the authors set out to assess impact of the interventions on aggression but found so few studies specifically assessing impact on aggression that they widened their scope to general concepts of antisocial-disruptive behavior. So, in line with developmental studies, prevention and treatment research to date provides very little information on impact for specific types of antisocial behavior. The majority of experimental intervention studies target preadolescents and adolescents (59 percent). The logic behind developmentally late interventions appears to be based on the social learning and "adolescent onset" paradigms. The media and the general public support such interventions because adolescents create more apparent social disruption than elementary school children and the latter more than toddlers. Public reactions put pressure on politicians at all levels of government, and resources follow, even if the intended effects are far from attained (Gatti, Tremblay, and Vitaro 2009). For example, although the Canadian public was bombarded for close to a decade with information on the importance of prevention of violent behavior during early childhood, a national survey showed that the public believed the problem was mainly during adolescence and that resources should mainly target adolescents (Tremblay 2003a). Complex explanations can be given for these beliefs, but the most parsimonious is that physically aggressive males are feared more at the peak of their physical growth and strength (adolescence) than during their early childhood.

To my knowledge only three preschool randomized controlled preventive trials evinced encouraging effects on DB at least up to adolescence. First, between 1962 and 1965 the High/Scope Preschool preventive intervention program was implemented with low-IQ three- to four-year-olds ($N = 123$) living in poverty with parents who had low education. Impressive reductions of antisocial behavior during adolescence and adulthood were observed (Schweinhart et al. 2005). Second, in 1973 the Mauritius Child Health Project randomly distributed to enriched and control nursery schools three-year-olds ($N = 200$) with varying risk for schizotypal behavior. Follow-up assessments at 17 and 23 years showed impressive reductions of antisocial behavior and schizotypal personality (Raine et al. 2001; 2003; Venables et al. 2006). Finally, between 1978 and 1980 the Elmira Nurse Home Visitation program randomly distributed over four treatment conditions 400 young pregnant women who had no previous live birth and were unmarried or poor. Results showed reduction of DB symptoms for boys when they were 15 years of age (Olds et al. 1998) and for girls when they were 19 years of age (Eckenrode et al. 2010). Interestingly, the original aim of these three studies was not to reduce antisocial behavior; consequently, the development of antisocial behavior was not monitored from early childhood to adolescence. Thus, we do not know when and how these preschool interventions managed to impact antisocial behavior. One recent randomized control trial suggests that an effective early preventive intervention may not be effective if used as an early corrective intervention. In this case the effective home visitation with at-risk pregnant women was applied to parents who were found to abuse their child (MacMillan et al. 2005) and did not show any positive short-term effects. There is some evidence that preschool interventions specifically targeting DB can have significant positive effects, but the follow-up evaluations are too short to know if the effects will last into late childhood, adolescence, and early adulthood (e.g., Webster-Stratton, Reid, and Stoolmiller 2008). However, we can expect that intensive targeted preschool corrective interventions will have long-term impacts, because at least one intensive early elementary school intervention with disruptive kindergarten males from low socioeconomic environments showed significant positive impacts on high-school completion and early adulthood criminality (e.g., Boisjoli et al. 2007; Lacourse et al. 2002).

Based on the logic of developmental trajectories, the presently known risk factors and developmental mechanisms, it appears clear that interventions starting more than 12–17 months after birth are corrective interventions with reference to the child's antisocial behavior. All the early risk factor studies for antisocial behavior suggest that early interventions should start as close as possible to conception and continue supporting the family and the child as long as needed. Such interventions are in fact corrective interventions for women who have a long history of social and mental adjustment problems. Interestingly, this was one of the main conclusions of the Swiss child psychiatrist Lucien Bovet in the first report the World Health Organization commissioned after its creation (Bovet 1951). These interventions will not modify genes, but they will likely change gene expression. Epigenetic studies are giving tools to assess the epigenetic effects of the preventive intervention during pregnancy and infancy. Because these short-term effects on gene expression are possibly good markers of long-term effects, we can use them to compare the effectiveness of different forms of interventions. These experimental preventive interventions can also be used to test environmental effects on the cascade of biological effects that follow gene expression and lead to behavior problems. For example, smoking cessation experimental interventions during pregnancy can test their effects on gene expression and eventually on antisocial behavior (Caporaso et al. 2009).

Finally, one of the major conclusions I can draw from five decades of longitudinal studies on antisocial behavior is that the time is ripe for investments in large collaborative early experimental preventive interventions. Randomized controlled trials are the best tools to test causal hypotheses while testing effective interventions (Schwartz, Flamant, and Lelouch 1981; Tremblay 2003b). It is amazing that there have been so few bio-psycho-social experimental interventions with pregnant women at risk of intergenerational transmission of social and mental health problems that start during early childhood. Good models were implemented two decades ago (Donelan-McCall, Eckenrode, and Olds 2009). We need to use these interventions that are well tested and study carefully the development of their potential bio-psycho-social effects from the prenatal period to at least the third generation's prenatal period. Without experiments and long-term follow-ups we cannot claim to know how to socialize children to prevent chronic criminal behavior.

Note

This chapter was adapted from Tremblay 2010.

References

Barker, Edward D., Richard E. Tremblay, Daniel S. Nagin, Frank Vitaro, and Eric Lacourse. 2006. "Development of Male Proactive and Reactive Physical Aggression During Adolescence." *Journal of Child Psychology & Psychiatry* 47: 783–790.

Boisjoli, Rachel, Frank Vitaro, Eric Lacourse, Edward Barker, and Richard E. Tremblay. 2007. "Impact and Clinical Significance of a Preventive Intervention for Disruptive Boys: 15-year Follow-Up. *British Journal of Psychiatry* 191: 415–419.

Bovet, Lucien. 1951. *Psychiatric Aspects of Juvenile Delinquency*. Geneva: World Health Organization / Organisation Mondiale de la Santé.

Caporaso, Neil, Fangyi Gu, Nilanjan Chatterjee, Jin Sheng-Chih, Kai Yu, Meredith Yeager, Constance Chen, Kevin Jacobs, William Wheeler, Maria T. Landi, Regina G. Ziegler, David J. Hunter, Stephen Chanock, Susan Hankinson, Peter Kraft, and Andrew W. Bergen. 2009. "Genome-Wide and Candidate Gene Association Study of Cigarette Smoking Behaviors." *PloS One* 4: e4653.

Donelan-McCall, Nancy, John Eckenrode, and David L. Olds. 2009. "Home Visiting for the Prevention of Child Maltreatment: Lessons Learned during the Past 20 Years." *Pediatric Clinics of North America* 56: 389–403.

Eckenrode, John, Mary Campa, Dennis Luckey, Charles R. Henderson, Robert Cole, Harriet Kitzman, Elizabeth Anson, Kimberly Sidora-Arcoleo, Jane Powers, and David Olds. 2010. "Long-Term Effects of Prenatal and Infancy Nurse Home Visitation on the Life Course of Youths: 19-Year Follow-up of a Randomized Trial." *Archives of Pediatrics & Adolescent Medicine* 164: 9–15.

Farrington, David P. 2003. "Key Results from the First Forty Years of the Cambridge Study in Delinquent Development." In *Taking Stock of Delinquency: An Overview of Findings from Contemporary Longitudinal Studies*, edited by Terence P. Thornberry and Marvin D. Krohn, 137–183. New York: Kluwer Academic / Plenum.

Frick, Paul J., and Essi Viding. 2009. "Antisocial Behavior from a Developmental Psychopathology Perspective." *Development and Psychopathology* 21: 1111–1131.

Gatti, Uberto, Richard E. Tremblay, and Frank Vitaro. 2009. "Iatrogenic Effect of Juvenile Justice." *Journal of Child Psychology and Psychiatry* 50: 991–998.

Kagan, Jerome. 1974. "Development and Methodological Considerations in the Study of Aggression." In *Determinants and Origins of Aggressive Behavior*, edited by Jan de Wit and William W. Hartup, 107–114. The Hague: Mouton.

Lacourse, Eric, Sylvana Côté, Daniel S. Nagin, Frank Vitaro, Mara Brendgen, and Richard E. Tremblay. 2002. "A Longitudinal-Experimental Approach to Testing Theories of Antisocial Behavior Development." *Development and Psychopathology* 14: 909–924.

Lacourse, Eric, Daniel S. Nagin, Richard E. Tremblay, Frank Vitaro, and Michel Claes. 2003. "Developmental Trajectories of Boys' Delinquent Group Membership and Facilitation of Violent Behaviors during Adolescence." *Development and Psychopathology* 15: 183–197.

MacMillan, Harriet L., B. Helen Thomas, Ellen Jamieson, Christine A. Walsh, Michael H. Boyle, Harry S. Shannon, and Amiram Gafni. 2005. "Effectiveness of Home Visitation by Public-Health Nurses in Prevention of the Recurrence of Child Physical Abuse and Neglect: A Randomized Controlled Trial. *Lancet* 365: 1786–1793.

McCord, Joan. 1978. "A Thirty-Year Follow-Up of Treatment Effects." *American Psychologist* 33: 284–289.

McCord, Joan. 1992. "The Cambridge-Somerville Study: A Pioneering Longitudinal Experimental Study of Delinquency Prevention." In *Preventing Antisocial Behavior: Interventions from Birth through Adolescence*, edited by Joan McCord and Richard E. Tremblay, 196–206. New York: Guilford Press.

Nagin, Daniel, and Richard E. Tremblay. 1999. "Trajectories of Boys' Physical Aggression, Opposition, and Hyperactivity on the Path to Physically Violent and Nonviolent Juvenile Delinquency." *Child Development* 70: 1181–1196.

Olds, David, Charles R. Henderson, Robert Cole, John Eckenrode, Harriet Kitzman, Dennis Luckey, Lisa Pettit, Kimberly Sidora, Pamela Morris, and Jane Powers. 1998. "Long-Term Effects of Nurse Home Visitation on Children's Criminal and Antisocial Behavior: 15-year Follow-Up of a Randomized Controlled Trial." *Journal of the American Medical Association* 280: 1238–1244.

Raine, Adrian, Kjetil Mellingen, Jianghong Liu, Peter H. Venables, and Sarnoff A. Mednick. 2003. "Effects of Environmental Enrichment at Ages 3–5 Years on Schizotypal Personality and Antisocial Behavior at Ages 17 and 23 Years. *American Journal of Psychiatry* 160: 1627–1635.

Raine, Adrian, Peter H. Venables, Cyril Dalais, Kjetil Mellingen, Chandra Reynolds, and Sarnoff A. Mednick. 2001. "Early Educational and Health Enrichment at Age 3–5 Years Is Associated with Increased Autonomic and Central Nervous System Arousal and Orienting at Age 11 Years: Evidence from the Mauritius Child Health Project." *Psychophysiology* 38: 254–266.

Schwartz, Daniel, Robert Flamant, and Joseph Lelouch. 1981. *Clinical Trials*. London: Academic Press.

Schweinhart, Lawrence J., Jeanne Montie, Zongping Xiang, William S. Barnett, Clive R. Belfield, and Milagros Nores. 2005. *Lifetime Effects: The High/Scope Perry Preschool Study through Age 40*. Vol. 14. Ypsilanti, MI: High/Scope Press.

Tremblay, Richard E. 1984. "Treatment of Hard-Core Delinquents in Residential Establishments." *British Journal of Criminology* 24: 384–393.

Tremblay, Richard E. 2000. "The Development of Aggressive Behaviour during Childhood: What Have We Learned in the Past Century?" *International Journal of Behavioral Development* 24: 129–141.

Tremblay, Richard E. 2003a. "Public Opinion and Violence Prevention." http://www.excellence-jeunesenfants.ca/documents/BulletinVol2No1Avril03ANG.pdf.

Tremblay, Richard E. 2003b. "Why Socialization Fails: The Case of Chronic Physical Aggression." In *Causes of Conduct Disorder and Juvenile Delinquency*, edited by Benjamin B. Lahey, Terrie E. Moffitt, and Avshalom Caspi, 182–224. New York: Guilford Publications.

Tremblay, Richard E. 2010. "Developmental Origins of Disruptive Behaviour Problems: The 'Original Sin' Hypothesis, Epigenetics and Their Consequences for Prevention. *Journal of Child Psychology and Psychiatry* 51: 341–367.

Tremblay, Richard E., Frank Vitaro, Daniel Nagin, Linda Pagani, and Jean R. Séguin. 2003. "The Montreal Longitudinal and Experimental Study: Rediscovering the Power of Descriptions." In *Taking Stock of Delinquency: An Overview of Findings from Contemporary Longitudinal Studies*, edited by Terence Thornberry, 205–254. New York: Kluwer Academic / Plenum.

Venables, Peter H., Adrian Raine, Sarnoff A. Mednick, Fini Schulsinger, and Cyril Dalais. 2006. "The Mauritius Child Health Project: Its Origins, Procedures, Ethical Issues, and Outcome." In *Crime and Schizophrenia: Causes and Cure*, edited by Adrian Raine, 315–334. New York: Hauppauge, Nova Science Publishers.

Vitaro, Frank, Edward Barker, Michel Boivin, Mara Brendgen, and Richard E. Tremblay. 2006. "Do Early Difficult Temperament and Harsh Parenting Differentially Predict Reactive and Proactive Aggression?" *Journal of Abnormal Child Psychology* 34: 685–695.

Webster-Stratton, Carolyn, M. Jamila Reid, and Mike Stoolmiller. 2008. "Preventing Conduct Problems and Improving School Readiness: Evaluation of the Incredible Years Teacher and Child Training Programs in High-Risk Schools." *Journal of Child Psychology and Psychiatry* 49: 471–488.

West, Donald James, and David P. Farrington. 1973. *Who Becomes Delinquent*. London: Heinemann.

Wilson, Sandra Jo, and Mark W. Lipsey. 2007. "School-Based Interventions for Aggressive and Disruptive Behavior: Update of a Meta-analysis." *American Journal of Preventative Medicine* 33: S130–S143.

4

Biology of Crime

PAST, PRESENT, AND FUTURE PERSPECTIVES

Adrian Raine and Jill Portnoy

Thirty-three years ago the first author sat as a graduate student at 5:00 p.m. in the audience of a psychology departmental colloquium at York University, listening in rapt attention as a mesmerizing David Farrington gave a beguiling talk on his Cambridge Study in Delinquent Development. He was invited to have dinner with Farrington that evening and wanted to go, but how could he possibly sit in the company of such a giant in the field of criminology. His anxiety overcame him and he did not attend.

Thirty-three years later the second author sits less anxiously as a graduate student in the Cambridge University library making her contributions to this chapter. She has after all had the privilege to work with David Farrington on her master's dissertation, a meta-analysis focusing on resting heart rate and antisocial behavior. While the man who was a giant in the field three decades ago has now become a criminology legend in his own lifetime, he is a gentle giant whose enthusiasm, kindheartedness, thoughtfulness, sincerity, optimism, and excitement over the future of criminology places young mentees at ease and continues to inspire them to push the boundaries of criminology to new territories.

Together, inspired by the early work that David himself created (Farrington 1987; 1997), we suggest here that one of the future directions of criminology will be research on "biomarkers" to both understand and predict future offending. As one example, we will highlight low resting heart rate as a candidate for a bio-marker. We first outline what biomarkers are, then turn to the empirical evidence that provides initial support for this view, and then provide some theoretical interpretation of why heart rate is a marker for antisocial behavior. Finally, we provide pointers for future research on the relationship between heart rate and antisocial /criminal behavior.

Evidence of Low Resting Heart Rate as a Biomarker

Biomarkers are biological correlates of specific behavioral states or conditions that can be used to objectively index the presence of the behavior in question. Currently there are no biomarkers for most psychiatric conditions, including conduct disorder and antisocial personality disorder. Potential biomarkers for conduct disorder and antisocial behavior include low resting heart rate (Ortiz and Raine 2004), prefrontal deficits (Raine 2002), low serotonin (Moore, Scarpa, and Raine 2002), and reduced P300 event-related-potential amplitudes (Iacono et al. 2002). Among these, resting heart rate is likely the best replicated biological correlate of antisocial behavior in children and adolescents (Ortiz and Raine 2004; Moffitt et al. 2008). In one meta-analysis of 40 independent studies, 45 independent effect sizes, and a total sample of 5,868 children, an overall effect size of $d = -0.44$ was calculated, indicating lower resting heart rates in antisocial children as compared to both normal and psychiatric controls (Ortiz and Raine 2004).

The relationship between resting heart rate and antisocial behavior is characterized by a range of features that both lend support to its importance as a biomarker and increase its relevance to criminological research. First, the relationship is generalizable across multiple populations. Resting heart rate is related to antisocial behavior in studies of children (e.g., Maliphant et al. 1990b; Moffitt et al. 2001), adolescents (e.g., Mezzacappa et al. 1997; Raine and Venables 1984a), and adults (e.g., Armstrong et al. 2009; Scarpa et al. 2000). The relationship is not confined to males and has also been observed in populations of females (Rogeness et al. 1990a; Maliphant et al. 1990a; Raine et al. 1997; Moffitt and Caspi 2001). Though most studies of resting heart rate have been conducted within noninstitutionalized populations (Raine 1993), the resting heart rate–antisocial behavior relationship has also been observed within clinical samples (Kruesi et al. 1992; Raine and Jones 1987; Zahn-Waxler et al. 1995). Additionally, low resting heart rate is a robust marker of antisocial behavior independent of cultural context. The low resting heart rate–antisocial behavior relationship has been replicated in countries in both hemispheres, including England (e.g., Farrington 1987), Germany (Schmeck and Poustka 1995), New Zealand (Moffitt and Caspi 2001), the United States (e.g., Rogeness et al. 1990a), Mauritius (Raine et al. 1997), Siberia (Slobodskaya et al. 1999), and Canada (Mezzacappa et al. 1997).

Low resting heart has also been found to characterize a range of antisocial behaviors, including aggression (e.g., Kindlon et al. 1995; Raine and Jones 1987), externalizing behavior problems (e.g., Scarpa et al. 2000; El-Sheikh et al. 1994), and conduct disorder (e.g., Herpertz et al. 2001). Resting heart rate is also predictive of later violence independent of all other psychosocial and family risk factors. In a series of six regression analyses aimed at establishing the best independent predictors of convictions for violence in the Cambridge Study in Delinquent Development (Farrington 1997), out of 48 family, socioeconomic, attainment, and personality predictors, low resting heart rate was one of only two risk factors that was *independently* related to violence (i.e., independent of all other risk factors). Perhaps surprisingly, studies of adults psychopaths have often failed to find resting heart rate differences (Raine 1993). However, these studies have almost exclusively compared psychopaths to criminals who are not psychopaths, leaving open the possibility that both these groups may have lower heart rates than noncriminal controls.

Importantly, it is unlikely that the relationship between resting heart and antisocial behavior is artifactual. Studies have repeatedly ruled out a range of potential confounds including height, weight, body bulk, physical development, and muscle tone (Raine et al. 1997; Farrington 1997; Wadsworth 1976), poor scholastic ability and low IQ (Farrington 1997; Raine et al. 1990); excess motor activity and inattention (Farrington 1997; Raine et al. 1997), drug and alcohol use (Raine et al. 1997); engagement in physical exercise and sports (Farrington 1997; Wadsworth 1976), and low social class, divorce, family size, teenage pregnancy, and other psychosocial adversity (Farrington 1997; Raine et al. 1990; Wadsworth 1976). Confounds, such as smoking, that both artificially increase resting heart and are also associated with higher levels of antisocial behavior have rarely been taken into account (for an exception see Farrington 1997). Therefore, it is possible that controlling for additional confounds may actually *increase* the strength of the relationship between resting heart rate and antisocial behavior.

Importantly, several prospective studies have ruled out the possibility that living a delinquent way of life could in some way cause low heart rate (Wadsworth 1976; Farrington 1987; Moffitt and Caspi 2001; Raine et al. 1997). One of these studies found that resting heart rate measured as early as age 3 was related to aggressive behavior at age 11 (Raine et al. 1997).

Resting heart rate has particular relevance to socially oriented criminological researchers that are interested in incorporating biomarkers into their research. Heart rate measurements made using relatively cheap and easy-to-use equipment (e.g., heart rate and blood pressure cuff) have been found to produce equally strong effect sizes as those made with more technically sophisticated equipment (Ortiz and Raine 2004). Therefore, resting heart rate can be easily and cheaply integrated into criminological research protocols. Because it is likely that biosocial interactions are part of the explanation of antisocial behavior (Raine 2002), resting heart rate provides the criminological research community with the potential to contribute to a more integrated, multidisciplinary approach to understanding antisocial behavior. Indeed, initial findings already reveal that resting heart rate and social factors likely interact to predict antisocial behavior (Farrington 1997; Scarpa et al. 2008).

Theoretical Considerations and Conclusions

While the evidence supporting resting heart rate as a biomarker for antisocial behavior is robust, the mechanisms whereby low resting heart rate predisposes to antisocial behavior are less well understood. Several theoretical possibilities have been proposed. These include stimulation seeking, fearlessness, reduced noradrenergic functioning, reduced right hemisphere functioning, and increased vagal tone.

Stimulation-seeking theory argues that low arousal represents an unpleasant physiological state. Antisocial individuals seek stimulation in order to increase their arousal levels to an optimal or normal level (Eysenck 1997; Quay 1965; Raine et al. 1997), and antisocial, aggressive behavior may be viewed as a form of stimulation-seeking for some children. In support of this theory, resting heart rate at age 3 years has been found to characterize both stimulation-seeking behavior at 3 years as well as aggressive behavior at 11 years (Raine et al. 1997, 1998). A meta-analysis of 43 independent effect sizes found that stimulation-seeking and aggression were positively related (Wilson and Scarpa 2011), lending further support to stimulation-seeking theory.

A related interpretation, fearlessness theory recognizes that the measurement of resting heart rate frequently co-occurs with a series of other more stressful procedures (e.g., interview/medical examination, exposure to aversive stimuli). It argues that low levels of arousal during these mildly stressful psychophysiological test sessions are markers of low levels of fear (Raine 1993). At a situational level, the commission of antisocial and violent acts requires a degree of fearlessness. Meanwhile, children who lack fear are less likely to be responsive to socializing punishments, which may in turn contribute to poor fear conditioning and lack of conscience development (Raine 1993). Fearlessness theory is bolstered by the finding that particularly fearless individuals, such as decorated bomb disposal experts and decorated paratroopers have particularly low heart rate levels (Cox et al. 1983; McMillan and Rachman 1987; O'Connor et al. 1985). It should be noted, however, that Farrington (1997) found no relationship between resting heart rate and measures of nervousness, casting some doubt on the fearlessness interpretation.

Rather than being an immediate cause of antisocial behavior, low resting heart may be a marker for other biological processes that are more directly implicated in antisocial behavior. One biological process that may underlie this relationship is reduced noradrenergic functioning. The monoamine norepinephrine, which is found in autonomic nervous system neurons and produced in the locus coeruleus, is centrally involved in attention and vigilance and forms one of the four arousal systems in the brain stem. Like low resting heart rate, reduced noradrenergic functioning is associated with strong underarousal of the sympathetic nervous system. Reduced levels of norepinephrine are also associated with antisocial behavior. A meta-analytic review found a significant negative effect size of 0.41 between reduced central (cerebrospinal fluid) measures of norepinephrine and increased antisocial behavior (Raine 1993). In addition, Rogeness et al. (1990a, 1990b) found both reduced heart rate and reduced noradrenaline in conduct-disordered children.

Reduced right hemisphere functioning may also underlie the relationship between resting heart rate and antisocial behavior. The right hemisphere is dominant for the control of autonomic functions, including heart rate (Lane and

Jennings 1995) and both lesion and intracarotid amobarbital studies confirm that reduced heart rate is associated with decreased right hemisphere functioning (Zamrini et al. 1990; Yokoyama et al. 1987). Poor right hemisphere functioning has also been found in antisocial and violent populations as measured by functional magnetic resonance imaging (fMRI; Raine et al. 2001), computerized tomography (CT; Hucker et al. 1988), neuropsychological tests (Day and Wong 1996), EEG deficits (Evans and Park 1997), and event-related potentials (ERPs; Drake et al. 1988). Poor right hemisphere functioning (particularly the anterior regions) has been associated with deficits in the withdrawal system, a system that promotes retreat from aversive and dangerous situations (Davidson et al. 1990; Davidson 1998). Furthermore, patients with right hemisphere lesions, compared to those with left hemisphere lesions, have been shown to have reduced heart rate and skin conductance responses to films depicting negative emotions (e.g., anger) (Zoccolotti et al. 1986). Reduced right hemisphere functioning and a consequent weaker withdrawal system could make children less averse to dangerous, risky situations that increase the probability of antisocial behavior.

A further biological process that could account for this relationship is increased vagal tone. Raine and Venables (1984b) suggested that the low heart rate recorded in antisocial individuals may be a function of increased vagal tone and reflect a passive coping response to mildly stressful situations, a response that attenuates painful experiences and may make such children less responsive to socializing punishments. However, data since then have not supported this hypothesis. Mezzacappa et al. (1997) found that antisocial 15-year-old boys were characterized by low resting heart rates, but also found evidence for *reduced*, not increased, vagal functioning. Furthermore, Pine et al. (1996) found that reduced—and not increased vagal tone—was associated with aggressive behavior in children. El-Sheikh et al. (2001) found increased vagal tone actually *protected* against externalizing problems in 8- to 12-year-olds exposed to parental conflict. If reduced vagal tone does prove a systematic correlate of antisocial behavior, it will indicate that the resting heart rate–antisocial relationship is driven by particularly strong sympathetic underarousal that is powerful enough to overcompensate for low vagal tone, which would otherwise be expected to increase heart rate in antisocial children. The counterhypothesis that needs to be tested is that the resting heart–antisocial relationship is driven by parasympathetic dominance and *increased* vagal tone (Raine and Venables 1984b).

In addition to the interpretations outlined above, several alternative explanations for the resting heart rate–antisocial behavior relationship exist. For example, as both antisocial behavior and heart rate are partly heritable (Ditto 1993; Eley et al. 1999), it may be the case that the same set of genes encodes for both low resting heart rate and other neurophysiological processes that give rise to antisocial behavior. Such an explanation, if correct, would have particular relevance to developmental criminologists and could contribute to our understanding of the intergenerational transmission of offending. In a twin study, Baker et al. (2009)

found that the relationship between low resting heart and antisocial behavior was explained almost entirely by their genetic covariation, lending initial support to this possibility.

While some interpretations of the resting heart rate–antisocial behavior relationship seem more promising than others (e.g., stimulation-seeking, reduced noradrenergic functioning), it is likely that no one process will fully account for the link between resting heart rate and antisocial behavior. Instead, it is likely that several explanations will be relevant in explaining this relationship. Nonetheless, future research should focus on identifying which of these processes plays a key role in shaping the resting heart rate–antisocial behavior relationship. Such research could have important implications for the treatment of antisocial behavior.

In conclusion, low resting heart rate is a potentially promising biomarker for antisocial behavior and conduct disorder. Strengths include the wide replication of this finding in multiple countries, prospective longitudinal research showing that low heart rate predicts later crime and violence, its quick and reliable assessment, and the fact that it is diagnostically specific—no other mental health condition has been associated with low resting heart rate (Raine 1993). Such diagnostic specificity is very rare in the field. At the same time, future research is needed to assess the predictive utility of low resting heart rate in order to bolster the case for treating it as a biomarker (Moffitt et al. 2008). Are antisocial and conduct disordered children with low heart rate more likely to have more negative future social and behavioral outcomes? What cut-point for defining "low" resting heart rate best predicts later outcome? Importantly, can low heart rate help delineate a subgroups who may be more amenable to treatment? With regard to this last question, Stadler et al. (2008) demonstrated heart rate to be a predictor of treatment success, with aggressive and delinquent children being less responsive to parent training intervention if they had low resting heart rates. Further research along these lines would enhance the case for low resting heart rate as a biomarker for antisocial behavior, and bring to fruition one of the many lines of longitudinal research that David Farrington has stimulated.

References

Armstrong, Todd A., Shawn Keller, Travis W. Franklin, and Scott N. Macmillan. 2009. "Low Resting Heart Rate and Antisocial Behavior: A Brief Review of Evidence and Preliminary Results from a New Test." *Criminal Justice and Behavior* 36: 1125–1140.

Baker, Laura A., Catherine Tuvblad, Chandra Reynolds, Mo Zheng, Dora Isabel Lozano, and Adrian Raine. 2009. "Resting Heart Rate and the Development of Antisocial Behavior from Age 9 to 14: Genetic and Environmental Influences." *Development and Psychopathology* 21: 939–960.

Cox, David., Richard Hallam, Kieron O'Connor, and Stanley Rachman. 1983. "An Experimental Study of Fearlessness and Courage." *British Journal of Psychology* 74: 107–117.

Davidson, Richard J. 1998. "Anterior Electrophysiological Asymmetries, Emotion, and Depression: Conceptual and Methodological Conundrums." *Psychophysiology* 35: 607–614.

Davidson, Richard J., Paul Eckman, Clifford D. Saron, Joseph A. Senulis, and Wallace V. Friesen. 1990. "Approach-Withdrawal and Cerebral Asymmetry: Emotional Expression and Brain Physiology I." *Journal of Personality and Social Psychology* 58: 330–341.

Day, Rodney, and Stephen Wong. 1996. "Anomalous Perceptual Asymmetries for Negative Emotional Stimuli in the Psychopath." *Journal of Abnormal Psychology* 105: 648–652.

Ditto, Blaine. 1993. "Familial Influences on Heart Rate, Blood Pressure, and Self-Report Anxiety Responses to Stress: Results from 100 Twin Pairs." *Psychophysiology* 30: 635–645.

Drake, Miles E., Ann Pakalnis, Modestine E. Brown, and Sharon A. Hietter. 1988. "Auditory Event Related Potentials in Violent and Nonviolent Prisoners." *European Archives of Psychiatry & Neurological Sciences* 238: 7–10.

Eley, Thalia C., Paul Lichtenstein, and Jim Stevenson. 1999. "Sex Differences in the Etiology of Aggressive and Nonaggressive Antisocial Behavior: Results from Two Twin Studies." *Child Development* 70: 155–168.

El-Sheikh, Mona, Mary Ballard, and E. Mark Cummings. 1994. "Individual Differences in Preschoolers' Physiological and Verbal Responses to Videotaped Angry Interactions." *Journal of Abnormal Child Psychology* 22: 303–320.

El-Sheikh, Mona, JoAnn Harger, and Stephanie M. Whitson. 2001. "Exposure to Interparental Conflict and Children's Adjustment and Physical Health: The Moderating Role of Vagal Tone." *Child Development* 72: 1617–1636.

Evans, James R., and Nan-Sook Park. 1997. "Quantitative EEG Findings among Men Convicted of Murder." *Journal of Neurotherapy* 2: 31–39.

Eysenck, Hans J. 1997. "Personality and the Biosocial Model of Antisocial and Criminal Behavior." In *Biosocial Bases of Violence*, edited by Adrian Raine, Patricia Brennan, David P. Farrington, and Sarnoff A. Mednick, 21–38. New York: Plenum.

Farrington, David P. 1987. "Implications of Biological Findings for Criminological Research." In *The Causes of Crime: New Biological Approaches*, edited by Sarnoff A. Mednick, Terrie E. Moffitt, and Susan A. Stack, 42–64. New York: Cambridge University Press.

Farrington, David P. 1997. "The Relationship between Low Resting Heart Rate and Violence." In *Biosocial Bases of Violence*, edited by Adrian Raine, Patricia Brennan, David P. Farrington, and Sarnoff A. Mednick, 89–106. New York: Plenum.

Garralda, M. Elena, John Connell, and David C. Taylor. 1989. "Peripheral Psychophysiological Changes in Children with Conduct and Emotional Disorders: A Study of Resting Levels and Reactivity to Sounds." *Behavioral Neurology* 2: 125–133.

Herpertz, Sabine C., Britta Wenning, Bodo Mueller, Mutaz Qunaibi, Henning Sass, and Beate Herpertz-Dahlmann. 2001. "Psychophysiological Responses in ADHD Boys with and without Conduct Disorder: Implications for Adult Antisocial Behavior." *Journal of the American Academy of Child and Adolescent Psychiatry* 40: 1222–1230.

Hucker, S., R. Langevin, G. Wortzman, R. Dickey, J. Bain, L. Handy, J. Chambers, and S. Wright. 1988. "Cerebral Damage and Dysfunction in Sexually Aggressive Men." *Annals of Sex Research* 1: 33–47.

Iacono, William G., Scott R. Carlson, Stephen M. Malone, and Matthew McGue. 2002. "P3 Event-Related Potential Amplitude and the Risk for Disinhibitory Disorders in Adolescent Boys." *Archives of General Psychiatry* 59: 750–757.

Kindlon, Daniel J., Richard E. Tremblay, Enrico Mezzacappa, Felton Earls, Denis Laurent, and Benoist Schaal. 1995. "Longitudinal Patterns of Heart Rate and Fighting Behavior in 9- through 12-Year-Old Boys." *Journal of the American Academy of Child and Adolescent Psychiatry* 34: 371–377.

Kruesi, Markus J. P., Euthymia D. Hibbs, Theodore P. Zahn, Cynthia S. Keysor, Susan D. Hamburger, John J. Bartko, and Judith L. Rappaport. 1992. "A 2-year Prospective Follow-up Study of Children and Adolescents with Disruptive Behavior Disorders: Prediction by Cerebrospinal Fluid 5-Hydroxyindolecetic Acid, Homovanillic Acid, and Autonomic Measures." *Archives of General Psychiatry* 49: 429–435.

Lane, Richard D., and J. Richard Jennings. 1995. "Hemispheric Asymmetry, Autonomic Asymmetry, and the Problem of Sudden Cardiac Death." In *Brain Assymetry*, edited by Richard J. Davidson and Kenneth Hugdahl, 271–304. Cambridge: MIT Press.

Maliphant, R., F. Hume, and A. Furnham. 1990a. "Autonomic Nervous System Activity, Personality Characteristics and Disruptive Behavior in Girls." *Journal of Child Psychology and Psychiatry* 31: 619–628.

Maliphant, Rodney, Sally-Ann Watson, and Denver Daniels. 1990b. "Disruptive Behavior in School, Personality Characteristics and Heart Rate Levels in 7–9 Year Old Boys." *Educational Psychology* 10: 199–205.

McMillan, Tom M., and Stanley J. Rachman. 1987. "Fearlessness and Courage: A Laboratory Study of Paratrooper Veterans of the Falklands War." *British Journal of Psychology* 78: 375–383.

Mezzacappa, Enrico, Richard E. Tremblay, Daniel Kindlon, J. Phillip Saul, Louise Arseneault, Jean Seguin, Robert O. Pihl, and Felton Earls. 1997. "Anxiety, Antisocial Behavior, and Heart Rate Regulation in Adolescent Males." *Journal of Child Psychology and Psychiatry* 38: 457–469.

Moffitt, Terrie, E., Louise Arseneault, Sara R. Jaffee, Julia Kim-Cohen, Karestan C. Koenen, Candice L. Odgers, Wendy S. Slutske, and Essi Viding. 2008. "Research Review: DSM-V Conduct Disorder: Research Needs for an Evidence Base." *Journal of Child Psychology and Psychiatry* 49: 3–33.

Moffitt, Terrie E., and Avshalom Caspi. 2001. "Childhood Predictors Differentiate Life-Course Persistent and Adolescent Limited Pathways among Males and Females." *Development and Psychopathology* 13: 355–375.

Moffit, Terrie E., Avshalom Caspi, Michael Rutter, and Phil A. Silva. 2001. *Sex Differences in Antisocial Behavior: Conduct Disorder, Delinquency, and Violence in the Dunedin Longitudinal Study*. Cambridge: Cambridge University Press.

Moore, Todd M., Angela Scarpa, and Adrian Raine. 2002. "A Meta-analysis of Serotonin Metabolite 5-HIAA and Antisocial Behavior." *Aggressive Behavior* 28: 299–316.

O'Connor, K., R. Hallam, and S. Rachman. 1985. "Fearlessness and Courage: A Replication Experiment." *British Journal of Psychology* 76: 187–197.

Ortiz, James, and Adrian Raine. 2004. "Heart Rate Level and Antisocial Behavior in Children and Adolescents: A Meta-analysis." *Journal of the American Academy of Child and Adolescent Psychiatry* 43: 154–161.

Pine, Daniel S., Gail Wasserman, Jeremy Coplan, Jane Fried, Richard Sloan, Michael Myers, Laurence Greenhill, David Shaffer, and Bruce Parsons. 1996. "Serotonergic and Cardiac Correlates of Aggression in Children." *Annals of the New York Academy of Sciences* 794: 391–393.

Quay, Herbert C. 1965. "Psychopathic Personality as Pathological Stimulation-Seeking." *American Journal of Psychiatry* 122: 180–183.

Raine, Adrian. 1993. *The Psychopathology of Crime: Criminal behavior as a Clinical Disorder*. San Diego: Academic Press.

Raine Adrian. 2002. "Annotation: The Role of Prefrontal Deficits, Low Autonomic Arousal, and Early Health Factors in the Development of Antisocial and Aggressive Behavior in Children." *Journal of Child Psychology and Psychiatry* 34: 417–434.

Raine, Adrian, and Fiona Jones. 1987. "Attention, Autonomic Arousal, and Personality in Behaviorally Disordered Children." *Journal of Abnormal Child Psychology* 15: 583–599.

Raine, Adrian, Sohee Park, Todd Lencz, Susan Bihrle, Lori LaCasse, Cathy Spatz Widom, Loual-Al-Dayeh, and Manbir Singh. 2001. "Reduced Right Hemisphere Activation in Severely Abused Violent Offenders during a Working Memory Task as Indicated by fMRI." *Aggressive Behavior* 27: 111–129.

Raine, Adrian, Chandra Reynolds, Peter A. Venables, Sarnoff A. Mednick, and David P. Farrington. 1998. "Fearlessness, Stimulation-Seeking, and Large Body Size at Age 3 Years as Early Predispositions to Childhood Aggression at Age 11 Years." *Archives of General Psychiatry* 55: 745–751.

Raine, Adrian, and Peter H. Venables. 1984a. "Tonic Heart Rate Level, Social Class and Antisocial Behavior in Adolescents." *Biological Psychology* 18: 123–132.

Raine, Adrian, and Peter H. Venables. 1984b. "Electrodermal Nonresponding, Schizoid Tendencies, and Antisocial Behavior in Adolescents." *Psychophysiology* 21: 424–433.

Raine, Adrian, Peter H. Venables, and Sarnoff A. Mednick. 1997. "Low Resting Heart Rate at Age 3 Years Predisposes to Aggression at Age 11 Years: Findings from the Mauritius Joint Child Health Project." *Journal of the American Academy of Child and Adolescent Psychiatry* 36: 1457–1464.

Raine Adrian, Peter H. Venables, and Mark Williams. 1990. "Relationships between Central and Autonomic Measures of Arousal at Age 15 Years and Criminality at Age 24 Years." *Archives of General Psychiatry* 47: 1003–1007.

Rogeness, Graham A., Claudio Cepeda, Carlos A. Macedo, Charles Fischer, and William R. Harris. 1990a. "Differences in Heart Rate and Blood Pressure in Children with Conduct Disorder, Major Depression, and Separation Anxiety." *Psychiatry Research* 33: 199–206.

Rogeness, Graham A., Martin A. Javors, James W. Mass, and Carlos A. Macedo. 1990b. "Catecholamines and Diagnoses in Children." *Journal of the American Academy of Child and Adolescent Psychiatry* 29: 234–241.

Scarpa, Angela, Deniz Fikretoglu, and Kristen Lucher. 2000. "Community Violence Exposure in a Young Adult Sample: II. Psychophysiology and Aggressive Behavior." *Journal of Community Psychology* 28: 417–425.

Scarpa, Angela, Akiho Tanaka, and Sara Chiara Haden. 2008. "Biosocial Bases of Reactive and Proactive Aggression: The Roles of Community Violence Exposure and Heart Rate." *Journal of Community Psychology* 36: 969–988.

Schmeck, K., and F. Poustka. 1995. "Psychophysiological Vulnerability of Children with Externalizing Symptoms." Poster session presented at the annual meeting of the American Academy of Child and Adolescent Psychiatry, New Orleans, October.

Slobodskaya, H. R., M. D. Roifman, and S. G. Krivoschekov. 1999. "Psychological Health, Physical Development and Autonomic Nervous System Activity in Siberian Adolescents." *International Journal of Circumpolar Health* 58: 176–187.

Stadler, Christina, Dorte Grasmann, Jorg M. Fegert, Martin Holtmann, Fritz Poustka, and Klaus Schmeck. 2008. Heart Rate and Treatment Effect in Children with Disruptive Behavior Disorders. *Child Psychiatry and Human Development* 39: 299–309.

Wadsworth, Michael E. J. 1976. "Delinquency, Pulse Rate and Early Emotional Deprivation." *British Journal of Criminology* 16: 245–256.

Wilson, Lauren C., and Angela Scarpa. 2011. "The Link between Sensation Seeking and Aggression: A Meta-analytic Review." *Aggressive Behavior* 37: 81–90.

Yokoyama, K., R. Jennings, P. Ackles, P. Hood, and F. Boller. 1987. "Lack of Heart Rate Changes during an Attention-Demanding Task after Right Hemisphere Lesions." *Neurology* 37: 624–630.

Zahn-Waxler, Carolyn, Pamela M. Cole, Jean Darby Welsh, and Nathan A. Fox. 1995. "Psychophysiological Correlates of Empathy and Prosocial Behaviors in Preschool Children with Behavior Problems." *Development and Psychopathology* 7: 27–48.

Zamrini, E. Y., K. J. Meador, D. W. Loring, F. T. Nichols, G. P. Lee, R. E. Figueroa, and W. O. Thompson. 1990. "Unilateral Cerebral Inactivation Produces Differential Left /Right Heart Rate Responses." *Neurology* 40: 1408–1411.

Zoccolotti, P., C. Caltagirone, N. Benedetti, and G. Gainotti. 1986. "Pertubations des réponses végétatives aux stimuli émotionnels au cours des lesions hémisphériques unilatérales." *Encephale* 12: 263–268.

5

Self-Control, Then and Now

Terrie E. Moffitt

Among David Farrington's most visionary contributions to the understanding of crime have been his elegant theoretical and empirical arguments that low impulse control plays a central role in the developmental origins of lawbreaking (Farrington 1988; Farrington, Coid, and West 2009; Jolliffe and Farrington 2009; Farrington, Loeber, and Van Kammen 1990). David Farrington's writings inspired my own research team's past work on impulse control and delinquency (Caspi et al. 1994; White et al. 1994), and thus we honor his career with a new study, reported here.

Self-control is an umbrella construct that bridges concepts and measurements from different disciplines (e.g., impulsivity, conscientiousness, self-regulation, delay of gratification, inattention-hyperactivity, executive function, willpower, intertemporal choice). Now policymakers are considering large-scale early-childhood education programs to promote children's self-control skills, with the aim of reducing the crime rate and improving citizens' health and wealth as well. Experiments and economic models suggest such programs could reap benefits. Yet evidence was needed that self-control is truly important for the health, wealth, and public safety of the whole population. By following a cohort of 1,000 children from birth to age 32, we showed that childhood self-control predicts physical health, substance dependence, personal finances, and criminal offending outcomes, following a gradient of self-control. In another cohort of 500 sibling-pairs, we found that the sibling with lowest self-control had poorest outcomes, despite both siblings sharing their family background.

Economists are drawing attention to individual differences in self-control as a key consideration for policymakers who seek to enhance the physical and financial health of the population and reduce the crime rate (Heckman 2007). Although Farrington made the case 25 years ago that self-control was important determinant of adult crime and other social outcomes, the current emphasis on self-control skills of conscientiousness, self-discipline, and perseverance arises from the empirical observation that preschool Headstart programs that targeted poor children 50 years ago, although failing to achieve their stated goal of lasting improvement in children's IQ scores, somehow produced by-product reductions in teen pregnancy, school dropout, delinquency, and work absenteeism (Carneiro and Heckman 2003; Doyle et al. 2009; Heckman 2006).

In the context of this timely, ubiquitous, and intense policy interest in self-control, we report findings from the Dunedin longitudinal study of a complete birth cohort of 1,037 children born in one city in one year, whom we have followed from birth to age 32 years with minimal attrition. Our study design is observational and correlational; this is in contrast to experimental behavioral-economics experiments that yield compelling information about the consequences of low self-control. However, some economists have cautioned that "behavior in the lab might be a poor guide to real-world behavior" (Levitt and List 2008, 909). The naturalistic Dunedin Study complements experimental research on self-control by providing badly needed information about how well children's self-control, as it is distributed in the population, predicts real-world outcomes after children reach adulthood. The Dunedin Study's birth-cohort members with low self-control and poor outcomes have not dropped out of the study (96 percent retention). This enabled us to study the full range of self-control and to estimate effect sizes of associations for the general population, information that is requisite for informed policymaking.

We assessed children's self-control during their first decade of life. Reports by parents, teachers, researcher-observers, and the children themselves gathered across ages 3, 5, 7, 9, and 11 years were combined into a single highly reliable composite measure. Mean levels of self-control were higher among girls than boys, but the health, wealth, and public-safety implications of childhood self-control were equally evident and similar among both males and females. Dunedin children with greater self-control were more likely to have been brought up in socioeconomically advantaged families and had higher IQs; we thus tested whether childhood self-control influenced adults' health, wealth, and crime independently of their social-class origins and IQ.

Predicting Crime

We obtained records of study members' court convictions at all courts in New Zealand and Australia by searching the central computer systems of the New Zealand police; 24 percent of the study members had been convicted of a crime by age 32. As anticipated by David Farrington's work, children with poor self-control were significantly more likely to be convicted of a criminal offense as adults, even after accounting for social-class origins and IQ. This prediction applies to property offending and violent offending, whether measured by official police records or self-report interviews.

Predicting Health

When the Dunedin children reached age 32 years, we assessed their cardiovascular, respiratory, dental, and sexual health, as well as their immune functioning by carrying out physical examinations to assess metabolic syndrome, airflow limitation, periodontal disease, sexually transmitted infection, and inflammation status, respectively. We summed these five clinical measures into a simple physical health index for each study member; 43 percent of study members had none of the bio-markers, 37 percent had one, and 20 percent had two or more. Childhood self-control predicted the number of adult health problems, even after accounting for social-class origins and IQ.

Predicting Substance Dependence

We also conducted clinical interviews with the study members at age 32 to assess sub-stance dependence (tobacco, alcohol, and cannabis dependence, as well as dependence on other street and prescription drugs), following DSM-IV criteria (American Psychiatric Association 1994). As adults, children with poor self-control had elevated risk of substance-dependence, even after accounting for social-class and IQ. This longitudinal link between self-control and substance-dependence was verified by people study members had nominated as informants who knew them well: As adults, children with poor self-control were rated by their informants as having alcohol and drug problems.

Predicting Wealth

Childhood self-control foreshadowed the study members' socioeconomic status and income in adulthood. At age 32, children with poor self-control were also less financially planful. Compared to other 32-year-olds they were less likely to save money and they had acquired fewer financial building blocks for the future (such as homeownership, investment funds, or retirement plans). Children with poor self-control reported more money-management difficulties and had accumulated more credit problems. This longitudinal link between self-control and adult financial problems was verified by informants who knew them well: As adults, children with poor self-control were rated by their informants as poor money managers. Furthermore, self-control predicted single-parent child-rearing. By age 32, 47 percent of study members had become parents. Childhood self-control predicted whether or not these study members' offspring were being reared in one-parent versus two-parent households (e.g., the study member was an absent father or single mother). Poor self-control in childhood was a stronger predictor of all of these financial difficulties than study members' social-class origins and IQ.

Sibling Comparisons

Policymaking requires evidence that isolates self-control as the active ingredient affecting health, wealth, and crime, as opposed to other influences on children's futures. In the Dunedin Study, statistical controls revealed that self-control had its own associations with outcomes, apart from childhood social-class and IQ. However, each Dunedin Study member grew up in a different family, and their families varied widely on many features that affect children's adult outcomes. A compelling quasi-experimental research design that can isolate the influence of self-control is to track and compare siblings. To apply this design, we turned to a second sample, the Environmental-Risk Longitudinal Twin Study (aka E-risk), where we have been tracking a birth cohort of British twins since their birth in 1994–1995 with 96 percent retention. When the E-risk twins were 5 years old, research staff rated each child on the same observational measure of self-control originally used with Dunedin children as preschoolers. Although the E-risk children have been followed only up to age 12 years, their self-control already forecast many of the adult outcomes we saw in the Dunedin Study. We applied sibling fixed-effects models to the 504 same-sex dizygotic pairs because they are no more alike than ordinary siblings (with the added advantages of being the same age and sex. Models showed that the 5-year-old sibling with poorer self-control, as compared to his/her sibling with better self-control, was significantly more likely as a 12-year-old to begin smoking (a precursor of adult poor health), perform poorly in school (a precursor of adult wealth accumulation), and engage in antisocial conduct problems (a precursor of adult crime).

Conclusions

For all of these associations, we observed a self-control gradient in which boys and girls with less self-control had less health, less wealth, and more crime as adults than those with more self-control, at every level of the distribution of self-control. Effects were marked at the extremes of the self-control gradient. For example, by adulthood, the highest and lowest fifths of the population on measured childhood self-control had respective rates of multiple health problems of 11 percent versus 27 percent; rates of poly-substance dependence of 3 percent versus 10 percent; rates of annual income under NZ$20,000 of 10 percent versus 32 percent; rates of offspring reared in single-parent households of 26 percent versus 58 percent; and crime-conviction rates of 13 percent versus 43 percent.

Two cohorts born in different countries and different eras support the inference that individuals' self-control is a key ingredient in health, wealth, and public safety, and a sensible policy target. That many Dunedin Study members with low self-control had unplanned babies now growing up in low-income single-parent households reveals that one generation's low self-control disadvantages the next generation. Modern history is seeing a marked increase in human life expectancy, requiring individuals to pay more strategic attention to their health and wealth to avoid disability and poverty in old age. Modern history has also seen marked increases in food availability, sedentary occupations, access to harmful addictive substances, ease of divorce, self-management of retirement savings, and imprisonment of lawbreakers. These historical shifts are enhancing the value of individual self-control in modern life, not just for well-being, but for survival.

Our findings were consistent with a universal approach to early intervention to enhance self-control at all levels in the population. The observed gradient implies room for better outcomes even among the segment of the population whose childhood self-control skills were somewhat above average. And our controls for SES and IQ imply that even bright children from well-to-do homes can benefit from improving their self-control skills. Programs to enhance children's self-control have been developed and positively evaluated by Farrington and others (Augimeri et al. 2007; Diamond et al. 2007; Greenberg 2006; Piquero, Jennings, and Farrington 2010). The challenge remains to improve these programs and scale them up for universal dissemination (Layard and Dunn 2009; National Scientific Council on the Developing Child 2007). Innovative policies addressing self-control might reduce a panoply of societal costs, improve public safety, enhance quality of life in old age, save taxpayers money, and promote prosperity.

Acknowledgments

This research received support from the US NIA (AG032282), NIMH (MH077874), NICHD (HD061298), NIDCR (DE015260), NIDA (DA023026), the UK MRC (G0100527, G0601483) and ESRC (RES-177-25-0013), and New Zealand Health Research Council.

References

American Psychiatric Association. 1994. *Diagnostic and Statistical Manual of Mental Disorders.* 4th ed. Washington, DC: American Psychiatric Association.

Augimeri, Leena K., David P. Farrington, Christopher J. Koegl, and David M. May. 2007. "The SNAP Under 12 Outreach Project: Effects of a Community Based Program for Children with Conduct Problems." *Journal of Child and Family Studies* 16: 799–807.

Caspi Avshalom, Terrie E. Moffitt, Phil A. Silva, Magda Stouthamer-Loeber, Robert F. Krueger, and Pamela S. Schmutte. 1994. "Are Some People Crime-Prone: Replications of the Personality-Crime Relationship across Countries, Genders, Races, and Methods." *Criminology* 32: 163–195.

Carneiro, Pedro, and James J. Heckman. 2003. "Human Capital Policy." In *Inequality in America: What Role for Human Capital Policy?* edited by James J. Heckman and Alan Krueger, 327–354. Cambridge: MIT Press.

Diamond, Adele, W. Steven Barnett, Jessica Thomas, and Sarah Munro. 2007. "Preschool Program Improves Cognitive Control." *Science* 318: 1387–1388.

Doyle, Orla, Colm P. Harmon, James J. Heckman, and Richard E. Tremblay. 2009. "Investing in Early Human Development: Timing and Economic Efficiency." *Economics & Human Biology* 7: 1–6.

Farrington, David P. 1988. "Studying Changes within Individuals: The Causes of Offending." In *Studies of Psychosocial Risk*, edited by Michael Rutter, 158–183. Cambridge: Cambridge University Press.

Farrington, David P., Jeremy W. Coid, and Donald J. West. 2009. "The Development of Offending from Age 8 to Age 50: Recent Results from the Cambridge Study in Delinquent Development." *Monatsschrift fur Kriminologie und Strafrechtsreform* 92: 160–173.

Farrington, David P., Rolf Loeber, and Welmoet B. Van Kammen. 1990. "Long-Term Criminal Outcomes of Hyperactivity-Impulsivity-Attention Deficit and Conduct Problems in Childhood." In *Straight and Devious Pathways from Childhood to Adulthood*, edited by Lee N. Robins and Michael Rutter, 62–81. Cambridge: Cambridge University Press.

Greenberg, Mark T. 2006. "Promoting Resilience in Children and Youth: Preventive Interventions and Their Interface with Neuroscience." *Annals of the New York Academy of Science* 1094: 139–150.

Heckman, James J. 2006. "Skill Formation and the Economics of Investing in Disadvantaged Children." *Science* 312: 1900–1902.

Heckman, James J. 2007. "The Economics, Technology, and Neuroscience of Human Capability Formation." *Proceedings of the National Academy of Sciences of the United States of America* 104: 13250–13255.

Jolliffe, Darrick, and David P. Farrington. 2009. "A Systematic Review of the Relationship between Childhood Impulsiveness and Later Violence." In *Personality, Personality Disorder, and Violence*, edited by Mary McMurran and Richard C. Howard, 41–61. New York: John Wiley and Sons.

Layard, Richard, and Judy Dunn. 2009. *A Good Childhood: Searching for Values in a Competitive Age*. London: Penguin.

Levitt, Steven D., and John A. List. 2008. "Homo Economicus Evolves." *Science* 319: 909–910.

National Scientific Council on the Developing Child. 2007. "The Science of Early Childhood Development." http://www.developingchild.net.

Piquero, Alex R., Wesley G. Jennings, and David P. Farrington. 2010. "On the Malleability of Self-Control: Theoretical and Policy Implications Regarding a General Theory of Crime." *Justice Quarterly* 27: 803–834.

White, Jennifer L., Terrie E. Moffitt, Avshalom Caspi, Dawn J. Bartusch, Douglas J. Needles, and Magda Stouthamer-Loeber. 1994. "Measuring Impulsivity and Examining its Relationship to Delinquency." *Journal of Abnormal Psychology* 103: 192–205.

6

Criminological Theory

PAST ACHIEVEMENTS AND FUTURE CHALLENGES

Terence P. Thornberry

I have long admired David Farrington's many contributions to criminological research and theory and it is fitting that his colleagues recognize those contributions. In particular, I have been asked to comment on the growth and development of criminological theory, as well as to comment on its future development. I will try to address it with the same gusto that David Farrington has shown in addressing so many criminological topics over the years.

The Development of Theoretical Criminology

I am often struck by the relative youth of criminology as a scholarly discipline, as well as the newness of theoretical criminology as a specific part of it. Few criminological theories were proposed prior to the twentieth century. There is, of course, the work of Beccaria (1764), Lombroso (1876), Tarde (1890), and a few others, but in that era there was really no such thing as an organized field of theoretical criminology. And while some of the themes that these early writers identified remain vibrant—free will versus determinism, biological versus environmental influences, and so on—the theories themselves have long since fallen by the wayside. Over the years, numerous problems with their structure and internal logic were identified and empirical studies failed to offer strong support for them (e.g., Goring 1913).

The first theories that still have currency—for example, the work of Sellin (1938), Shaw and McKay (1942), Sutherland (1939), and Merton (1938)—were all developed in the late 1930s. Thus, we are separated by less than 100 years from the very founding of our area of inquiry. Even other social sciences, like psychology, sociology, and economics, are older and were more developed by such notable scholars as Freud (1930), Durkheim (1897), and Weber (1905) well before criminology emerged. And, compared to physical and biological sciences, we are obviously much younger still. I think it is helpful to keep this young history in mind when we evaluate the development of criminological theory and its current status. We are in many ways a discipline in its childhood, moving toward adolescence, not yet a mature discipline. There are too many basic questions—both empirical and theoretical—that are as yet unanswered for criminology to be considered a mature area of inquiry. That is not to say that we have not made progress over the past 100 years. Indeed, I think we have made tremendous inroads in a rather short time into gaining a fuller understanding of criminal behavior, but that does not alter the fact that we differ in many ways from more mature disciplines.

Early Theories

The early theories mentioned above all emerged from the perspective of American sociology at the turn of the last century. In many ways those theories arose in reaction to the theoretical world they inherited. Rather than focus on the crime and on philosophical argumentation as Beccaria (1764) did, they focused on the individual from a scientific and positivist perspective. Rather than focus on criminal behavior as an individual pathology as Lombroso (1876) and several of Freud's followers (e.g., Alexander and Healey 1935) did, they focused on crime as a rational response to the social environment, often a pathological environment, in which individuals found themselves. These theories had many features in common. They were all sociological in orientation and emphasized social and environmental influences in their explanations for offending behavior. They also adopted a scientific orientation and their theories were grounded in empirical observations and designed to be tested by the scientific method.

These theories were also monothematic. That is, they adopted a certain explanatory theme and focused almost exclusively on that single theme in their explanation of offending. Sutherland (1939) focused on the learning process, Shaw and McKay (1942) on social disorganization, Sellin (1938) on culture conflict, and Merton (1938) on anomie. There was little effort to expand beyond the theme of choice and to incorporate multiple influences.[1] These theories remained dominant throughout the middle part of the twentieth century when they were eventually joined by additional theories such as social control theory (Hirschi 1969), labeling theory (Becker 1963), conflict theory (Quinney 1970), and others. But these theories were also predominately monothematic. Theories were viewed, to a considerable extent, as being in competition with one another (Hirschi 1989) even though they emerged from the same dominant paradigm—early American sociology—and shared a common intellectual history.

More Recent Theoretical Developments

The latter part of the twentieth century was a very fertile time for theoretical development. This is in part due to the increasingly interdisciplinary orientation of criminology with the advent of separate programs in criminology and criminal justice representing multiple disciplines. Breaking away from its largely sociological roots, criminology embraced psychological, biosocial, economic, family process, rational choice, and other orientations. As a result, there has been a proliferation of new theoretical models offered to explain criminal offending. Several of these developments are particularly noteworthy.

One of the first departures from traditional, monothematic theories came with the development of integrated theoretical models such as those proposed by Elliott and colleagues (1985), Johnson (1979), and Le Blanc et al. (1988). Recognizing both the common intellectual heritage and the complementary nature of monothematic theories—such as control, learning, strain, and labeling theories—integrated models attempted to incorporate the strongest features of each into broader explanatory statements. For example, they combined the strong familial influences of control theory with the strong peer influences of learning theories in an effort to provide a more comprehensive theoretical statement. Although not without controversy (Messner, Krohn, and Liska 1989), the integrated approach has made a valuable contribution to the long-term development of criminological theory. It broke down the somewhat narrow focus of traditional theories, demonstrated that these "rival" theories actually had many points of similarity and complementarity, and opened the way for more comprehensive theoretical statements.

A second important advance during this time period was to move beyond the overwhelmingly sociological orientation of the earlier theories. Given their sociological focus, individual and biological factors were often downplayed in the explanation of offending. This may, in part, have been a reaction to the particular biological theory offered by Lombroso and its focus on "born criminals." Nevertheless, whatever the reason, these influences were not incorporated systematically into most traditional theories. Work by such scholars as Mednick (1977), Raine (1993), and Moffitt and Silva (1988) has helped remedy the situation, and now the role of neuropsychological deficits, temperament, brain development, and genes and gene-environment interactions is increasingly built into our understanding of the origins and development of criminal behavior. Relatedly, new theories adopted a population heterogeneity approach (e.g., Wilson and Herrnstein 1985; Gottfredson and Hirschi 1990) and argued that traits established early in the life course, but heterogeneously distributed in the population, explain offending.

The final, and arguably most important, development in theoretical criminology stems from improvements in the measurement and description of criminal behavior. Traditional theories were overwhelmingly informed by official measures of crime and by cross-sectional data. The advent and refinement of the self-report method (Thornberry and Krohn 2011) changed our under-standing of the correlates of crime and led to new theoretical orientations, for example, labeling theory (Becker 1963). Insights from longitudinal studies, especially the pioneering work of Wolfgang colleagues (Wolfgang, Figlio, and Sellin 1972; Wolfgang, Thornberry, and Figlio 1987), fundamentally changed our understanding of criminal behavior. No longer was crime viewed as a static at-tribute, delinquent versus nondelinquent; instead, we came to understand that delinquent careers unfold over the life course (Blumstein et al. 1986) and that there is substantial heterogeneity in those careers (Nagin 1999). These and sub-sequent longitudinal studies (Elliott, Huizinga, and Menard 1989; Farrington 1995) led to new empirical insights and theoretical challenges. For example, an-tisocial behavior, but not official reactions to it, was shown to have a much ear-lier onset than adolescence. For some offenders there is notable consistency in offending from childhood to adulthood, while for other offenders there is no-table change, with some desisting from involvement in crime and others exhibiting an unusually late onset.

All of this new information has led to what is currently called developmental, life course criminology (Farrington 2005b). A variety of life course theories have been proposed, including the work of Catalano and colleagues (2005), Farrington (2005a), Moffitt (1993), Sampson and Laub (1993), and Thornberry and Krohn (2005). Life course theories have a number of appealing characteristics. First, rather than simply trying to explain why some individuals are delinquents and others are not, they at-tempt to account for multiple aspects of delinquent careers including onset, persis-tence, and change. Second, life course theories are not monothematic and are not simply sociological in orientation, although the social environment is an important ingredient. Recognizing the breadth of human development, these theories incorpo-rate a wider array of explanatory factors ranging from individual characteristics to community and contextual influences. Third, these theories are increasingly incor-porating decision-making and human agency (Giordano, Cernkovich, and Rudolph 2002; Laub and Sampson 2003) rather than relying entirely on deterministic models.

Current and Future Developments

Putting this all together, at the current time there seems to be a tremendous proliferation of theoretical models. Old theories do not leave the stage; they are simply joined by new ones. The original theories developed in the early part of the twentieth century—by Sellin, Sutherland, Merton, and Shaw and McKay—still have currency both in their own right and as restated and refor-mulated by more contemporary theorists. For example, Sampson and col-leagues (Sampson and Groves 1989) extended the work of Shaw and MacKay (1942), and Akers (1973) recast Sutherland's theory to focus on social learning processes, Wolfgang and Ferracuti (1967) developed Sellin's model to explain violent behavior, and Cloward and Ohlin (1960) as well as Messner and Rosenfeld (1994) extended Merton's anomie theory. Few if any theories have been falsified and discarded. Each seems to have at least a kernel of truth and a modicum of empirical support.

In addition to the maintenance of traditional theories, new models have been offered as indicated in the previous section. Some expand disciplinary boundaries, for example, by incorporating biological and economic approaches. Some integrate various aspects of monothematic theories to offer broader, more comprehensive explanations. Some adopt a developmental, life course perspective. Regardless of the orientation of these models, the result is a rather cluttered field. There are more and more theories, but not necessarily greater and greater explanatory power.

To be sure, I believe that we have made progress in theoretical criminology during the past century and have gained new and important insights into the origins and development of criminal behavior. Nevertheless, there is a slightly discomforting feeling from the sheer proliferation of theoretical statements. What is currently lacking is movement toward what might be called a unified theory—if not yet a grand unified theory. By this I do not mean an integrated model (Thornberry 1989), but a new theoretical statement, developed in its own right, that supersedes and incorporates existing theories. A theoretical statement of this nature, when it is developed, will offer parsimony to the field, focus attention on the more central and powerful causes of crime, and yield more directed suggestions for prevention, treatment, and policy.

There are clearly aspects of existing theories that are overlapping and redundant. The same concepts and similar propositions are found in many of them. Notice, for example, how individual characteristics, family dynamics, and peer relationships are incorporated into virtually all theories of delinquency and crime, with slight variations on exactly how they influence criminal behavior. Although there seems to be agreement on their importance, theoretical criminology is lacking a general, synthesizing statement that capitalizes on the theoretical insights from these different but overlapping theories to offer a more complete and parsimonious explanation for offending. I believe that movement in this direction is inevitable as the field of criminology matures and becomes a more complete science.

Part of this movement will come from improvements in measurement and empirical testing. Surely some aspects of existing theories—and by extension some theories—will be falsified. Also, as criminology makes greater use of experimental designs and advances in statistical modeling such as propensity score models (Rosenbaum and Rubin 1983) that more accurately identify causal relationships, there will be a gradual movement away from risk factor approaches to the identification of the smaller set of factors that are actually causally related to criminal offending. As the discipline of criminology matures, there will hopefully be more agreement on critical tests and more acceptance of the results, even by proponents of each theory, to reduce some of the theoretical clutter that we currently experience.

Part of this movement toward a unifying theory will come from new efforts at theory construction. Building on existing theories and empirical observations, some criminologist will eventually see things differently and will put the building blocks of a causal explanation—which we probably have before us today—together in a new and different way. That is certainly the history of more mature sciences with scholars such as Darwin, Einstein, Freud, and Durkheim reorienting their disciplines with critical insights and unifying statements. It is not clear to me when this will happen in criminology, but I am confident that it will as we continue to gradually build our understanding of the causes of criminal behavior.

I am equally confident that movement in this direction will be influenced by David Farrington's empirical and theoretical contributions. There are several characteristics of David's work that set it apart. One is the sheer volume of his research. He has informed our understanding of virtually all aspects of criminal careers— prevalence, onset, persistence, and desistance. He has examined family, school, labeling, and employment effects to name just a few. His work has influenced the development of both population heterogeneity and state dependence models. He has extensively examined how criminal behavior "runs" in families and how it is transmitted across generations.

Perhaps most importantly, David's work is always carefully grounded in data. His theoretical work is strongly and clearly informed by first-rate empirical analysis that paints a vivid picture of offending. His empirical results set the stage both for the development of the theoretical propositions and for the empirical testing of the theory. An excellent example of this approach is found in David's early and influential studies of labeling theory.

Another feature of David's contributions is the thoroughness of his approach, both empirically and theoretically. His analyses look at an issue from every possible angle. His theoretical work then follows suit. Not satisfied with addressing a few basic questions, David is concerned with identifying and answering as many aspects of the phenomenon as possible. No better example of this can be found than in his life course, developmental theory. In that theory David addresses many issues about onset, continuity, change, and desistance; he poses theoretical questions at the individual and aggregate level; and he challenges other life course theorists (Farrington 2005a) to account for the same stubborn facts that his model addresses. Clearly, the volume, detail, and quality of his many contributions will help shape the future of theoretical criminology and movement toward a synthesizing and unifying framework.

Note

1. The Gluecks' multifactor approach is a notable exception, but it was more empirically based than theoretically derived (Glueck and Glueck 1950).

References

Akers, Ronald L. 1973. *Deviant Behavior: A Social Learning Approach*. Belmont, CA: Wadsworth.

Alexander, Franz, and William Healey. 1935. *Roots of Crime*. New York: Alfred A. Knopf.

Beccaria, Cesare. [1764] 1963. *Essays on Crimes and Punishment*. Translated by Henry Paolucci. Indianapolis: Bobbs-Merrill.

Becker, Howard S. 1963. *Outsiders: Studies in the Sociology of Deviance*. New York: Free Press of Glencoe.

Blumstein, Alfred, Jacqueline Cohen, Jeffrey A. Roth, and Christy A. Visher. 1986. *Criminal Careers and "Career Criminals"*. Washington, DC: National Academy Press.

Catalano, Richard F., Jisuk Park, Tracy W. Harachi, Kevin P. Haggerty, Robert D. Abbott, and J. David Hawkins. 2005. "Mediating the Effects of Poverty, Gender, Individual Characteristics, and External Constraints on Antisocial Behavior: A Test of the Social Development Model and Implications for Developmental Life-Course Theory." In *Integrated Developmental and Life-Course Theories of Offending*, edited by David P. Farrington, 93–123. New Brunswick, NJ: Transaction Publishers.

Cloward, Richard A., and Lloyd E. Ohlin. 1960. *Delinquency and Opportunity*. Glencoe, IL: Free Press.

Durkheim, Emile. [1897] 1951. *Suicide: A Study in Sociology*. Translated by John A. Spaulding and George Simpson. New York: Free Press.

Elliott, Delbert S., David Huizinga, and Suzanne S. Ageton. 1985. *Explaining Delinquency and Drug Use*. Beverly Hills, CA: Sage.

Elliott, Delbert S., David Huizinga, and Scott Menard. 1989. *Multiple Problem Youth: Delinquency, Substance Use, and Mental Health Problems*. New York: Springer.

Farrington, David P. 1995. "The Development of Offending and Antisocial Behaviour from Childhood: Key Findings from the Cambridge Study in Delinquent Development." *Journal of Child Psychology and Psychiatry* 360: 929–964.

Farrington, David P. 2005a. "The Integrated Cognitive Antisocial Potential (ICAP) Theory." In *Integrated Developmental and Life-Course Theories of Offending*, edited by David P. Farrington, 73–92. New Brunswick, NJ: Transaction Publishers.

Farrington, David P., ed. 2005b. *Integrated Developmental and Life-Course Theories of Offending*. New Brunswick, NJ: Transaction Publishers.

Freud, Sigmund. 1930. *Civilization and Its Discontents*. Translated by James Strachey. New York: Cape and Smith.

Giordano, Peggy C., Stephen A. Cernkovich, and Jennifer L. Rudolph. 2002. "Gender, Crime, and Desistance: Toward a Theory of Cognitive Transformation." *American Journal of Sociology* 107: 990–1064.

Glueck, Sheldon, and Eleanor T. Glueck. 1950. *Unraveling Juvenile Delinquency*. New York: Commonwealth Fund.

Goring, Charles. 1913. *The English Convict: A Statistical Study*. London: His Majesty's Stationery Office.

Gottfredson, Michael R., and Travis Hirschi. 1990. *A General Theory of Crime*. Stanford: Stanford University Press.

Hirschi, Travis. 1969. *Causes of Delinquency*. Berkeley: University of California Press.

Hirschi, Travis. 1989. "Exploring Alternatives to Integrated Theory." In *Theoretical Integration in the Study of Deviance and Crime: Problems and Prospects*, edited by Steven F. Messner, Marvin D. Krohn, and Allen E. Liska, 37–49. Albany: State University of New York Press.

Johnson, Richard E. 1979. *Juvenile Delinquency and Its Origins: An Integrated Theoretical Approach*. New York: Cambridge University Press.

Laub, John H., and Robert J. Sampson. 2003. *Shared Beginnings, Divergent Lives: Delinquent Boys to Age 70*. Cambridge: Harvard University Press.

Le Blanc, Marc, Marc Ouimet, and Richard E. Tremblay. 1988. "An Integrative Control Theory of Delinquent Behavior: A Validation 1976–1985." *Psychiatry* 51: 164–176.

Lombroso, Cesare. 1876. *L'uomo delinquente*. Milan: Hoepli.

Mednick, Sarnoff A. 1977. "A Bio-Social Theory of the Learning of Law-Abiding Behavior." In *Biosocial Bases of Criminal Behavior*, edited by Sarnoff A. Mednick and Karl O. Christiansen, 1–8. New York: Gardner Press.

Merton, Robert K. 1938. "Social Structure and Anomie." *American Sociological Review* 3: 672–682.

Messner, Steven F., Marvin D. Krohn, and Allen E. Liska. 1989. *Theoretical Integration in the Study of Deviance and Crime: Problems and Prospects*. Albany: State University of New York Press.

Messner, Steven F., and Richard Rosenfeld. 1994. *Crime and the American Dream*. Belmont, CA: Wadsworth.

Moffitt, Terrie E. 1993. "Adolescence-Limited and Life-Course-Persistent Antisocial Behavior: A Developmental Taxonomy." *Psychological Review* 100: 674–701.

Moffitt, Terrie E., and Phil A. Silva. 1988. "Neuropsychogical Deficit and Self-Reported Delinquency in an Unselected Birth Cohort." *Journal of the American Academy of Child and Adolescent Psychiatry* 27: 233–240.

Nagin, Daniel S. 1999. "Analyzing Developmental Trajectories: A Semiparametric, Group-Based Approach." *Psychological Methods* 4: 139–157.

Quinney, Richard. 1970. *The Social Reality of Crime*. Boston: Little, Brown.

Raine, Adrian. 1993. "Neurochemistry." In *The Psychopathology of Crime: Criminal Behavior as a Clinical Disorder*, edited by Adrian Raine, 81–102. San Diego: Academic Press.

Rosenbaum, Paul R., and Donald B. Rubin. 1983. "The Central Role of the Propensity Score in Observational Studies for Causal Effects." *Biometrika* 70: 41–55.

Sampson, Robert J., and W. Byron Groves. 1989. "Community Structure and Crime: Testing Social-Disorganization Theory." *American Journal of Sociology* 94: 774–802.

Sampson, Robert J., and John H. Laub. 1993. *Crime in the Making: Pathways and Turning Points through Life*. Cambridge: Harvard University Press.

Sellin, Thorsten. 1938. *Culture Conflict and Crime*. New York: Social Science Research Council.

Shaw, Clifford R., and Henry D. McKay. 1942. *Juvenile Delinquency and Urban Areas*. Chicago: University of Chicago Press.

Sutherland, Edwin H. 1939. *Principles of Criminology*. 3rd ed. Philadelphia: J.P. Lippincott.

Tarde, Gabriel. 1890. *Les lois de l'imitation*. 5th ed. Paris: Alcan.

Thornberry, Terence P. 1989. "Reflections on the Advantages and Disadvantages of Theoretical Integration." In *Theoretical Integration in the Study of Deviance and Crime: Problems and Prospects*, edited by Steven F. Messner, Marvin D. Krohn, and Allen E. Liska, 51–60. Albany: State University of New York Press.

Thornberry, Terence P., and Marvin D. Krohn. 2005. "Applying Interactional Theory to the Explanation of Continuity and Change in Antisocial Behavior." In *Integrated Developmental and Life-Course Theories of Offending*, edited by David P. Farrington, 183–209. New Brunswick, NJ: Transaction Publishers.

Thornberry, Terence P., and Marvin D. Krohn. 2011. "The Self Report Method and the Development of Criminological Theory." In *Measuring Crime and Criminality*, edited by John MacDonald, 1–19. New Brunswick, NJ: Transaction Publishers.

Vold, George B. 1979. *Theoretical Criminology*. New York: Oxford University Press.

Weber, Max. [1905] 1958. *The Protestant Ethic and the Spirit of Capitalism*. Translated by Talcott Parsons. New York: Charles Scribner and Sons.

Wilson, James Q., and Richard J. Herrnstein. 1985. *Crime and Human Nature*. New York: Simon and Schuster.

Wolfgang, Marvin E., and Franco Ferracuti. 1967. *The Subculture of Violence: Towards an Integrated Theory in Criminology*. London: Tavistock.

Wolfgang, Marvin E., Robert M. Figlio, and Thorsten Sellin. 1972. *Delinquency in a Birth Cohort*. Chicago: University of Chicago Press.

Wolfgang, Marvin E., Terence P. Thornberry, and Robert M. Figlio. 1987. *From Boy to Man, from Delinquency to Crime*. Chicago: University of Chicago Press.

7

Individuals' Situational Criminal Actions

CURRENT KNOWLEDGE AND TOMORROW'S PROSPECTS

Per-Olof H. Wikström

David Farrington clearly has academic celebrity status within criminology. I remember having breakfast at the conference hotel of an American Society of Criminology meeting some years ago when I saw a young criminologist at the table next to mine pointing toward David, who had just entered the room, and overheard him saying to another young criminologist, "That is David Farrington," and he respectfully continued, "He is the most famous criminologist in the world."

David Farrington has without a doubt earned his academic celebrity status through his many seminal contributions to criminological research. He is one of a handful of people who have laid the foundation for our current understanding of criminal careers and our knowledge about what aspects of people's social and psychological conditions and development are related to their differential crime involvement and its changes.

Not only has David Farrington played a central role in the creation of modern criminal career and risk factor research but he has also helpfully highlighted many of the key theoretical and methodological issues facing this research that need to be addressed to further advance our knowledge about crime, its causes and prevention (e.g., Farrington 1992; 1993; 1999; 2000; 2002). These issues include the problems of distinguishing between correlation and causation ("a major problem of the risk factor prevention paradigm is to determine which risk factors are causes and which are merely markers or correlated with crime"; Farrington 2000, 7), understanding the situational factors that move people to engage in acts of crime ("existing research tells us more about the development of criminal potential than about how that potential becomes actuality of offending in any given situation"; Farrington 2000, 5), and the integration of person and environmental approaches in the study of crime causation ("researchers interested in neighborhood influences have generally not adequately measured individual and family influences, just as researchers interested in individual and family influences have generally not adequately measured neighbourhood influences"; Farrington 1993, 30).

The key argument I put forward in this short chapter is that we need to move to a more analytical criminology to better address these (and related) issues in order to advance our knowledge about crime, its causes and prevention. Specifically, I propose that we need to take more seriously issues of causation, human agency, and the person-environment interaction (for a more extensive treatment of this argument, see Wikström 2011).

Analytical Criminology

Analytical criminology is concerned with the understanding of *why* people engage in acts of crime. More specifically the focus is on identifying the key social, developmental, and situational processes (mechanisms) involved in crime causation. The aim is to move beyond mapping out correlations and making predictions to establishing causation and, crucially, providing explanation. "The hallmark of modern science is the search for mechanisms behind facts, rather than the mindless search for data and statistical correlation among them" (Bunge 2006, 119).

Analytical criminology advocates theory-driven empirical research, arguing that empirical study without guiding theory (at its worst) risks just being the charting of (mostly causally irrelevant) correlations, but also that theorizing without supporting empirical research (at its worst) risks just being (inadequate) guesswork. It stresses the importance of developing integrative theory with clear (empirically) testable implications. It maintains that without knowing why people engage in acts of crime (and how the factors and processes involved work) it is difficult (other than by chance) to devise effective crime prevention policies and measures.

Does Everything Matter? The Problem of Correlation and Causation

Criminological research has produced a wealth of findings of stable statistical associations between offending and personal characteristics and environmental features. In fact, as Farrington (1992, 256) has pointed out, "there is no shortage of factors that are significantly correlated with offending and antisocial behavior; indeed, literally thousands of variables differentiate significantly between official offenders and non-offenders or correlate significantly with self-reported offending" (for a recent overview of crime correlates, see Ellis, Beaver, and Wright 2009). In a situation like this it is difficult to get clear guidance from criminological research about what the key causal factors are in crime causation and, thus, what key factors should be targeted in efforts to develop effective crime prevention. The question whether "everything" (or 'anything') matters in crime causation is clearly justified.

The problem of correlation and causation is well illustrated by the commonly used but ambiguous concept of "risk factor." A risk factor is often defined as a correlate that is shown to precede the outcome and is generally discussed in causal terms (i.e., that the factor influences, affects, etc.). Although a causal relation implies covariation and the possibility of prediction, this is not enough to establish causation (e.g., barometers predict but do not cause weather conditions). Causation also, and crucially, involves the requirement that the proposed cause (causal factor) produces (or help produce) the outcome (the effect). In fact, a cause may be thought of as an event that initiates a causal process that brings about the effect (see further Wikström 2011).

It is a safe assumption that most statistical relationships (risk factors) demonstrated in criminological research are of a noncausal nature (and hence irrelevant for our understanding of crime causation and the development of effective crime prevention). People do not shoplift or kill other people because they are male, 16 years old, or African American (attributes cannot be causes). Neither do people vandalize streetlights or blow up buildings because they have many siblings, live in public housing, or have a mother who smoked during pregnancy. At best, correlates like these may be markers of true causally effective factors, although some (nonattributes) may potentially play a role as "causes of the causes," that is, may influence (or help influence) the emergence of personal and environmental factors (i.e., crime propensity and criminogenic exposure) whose interaction may move people to engage in acts of crime (see further Wikström 2011).

The main challenge to advancing knowledge about crime causation is to identify which few of all the many crime correlates (risk factors) have causal efficacy and, among those that do, what role they play in crime causation (e.g., as causes or causes of the causes). The safest way to establish causation is through manipulation (experimentation). If it can be demonstrated that by changing the proposed cause/s we can (repeatedly) alter the outcome (effect) in predicted ways, there is good reason to assume the two are causally related.

However, even if we can ascertain causation by experimentation, this does not provide explanation. We can establish that if we change a, then b will change in predicted ways without knowing how this happens. To explain, we need to provide a plausible mechanism by which a produces b, and that is primarily a theoretical question (since the hypothesized mechanism is rarely observable). As Bunge (1999, 63) contends, "in the natural sciences no event or process is regarded as having been satisfactorily understood unless its actual or possible mechanism has been unveiled." There is no reason it should be otherwise in the social sciences.

Experimentation is seldom a possibility in the study of crime causation, and, therefore, we generally have to depend on nonexperimental observational studies (such as causal modeling) based upon adequate theorizing to test our ideas about causation. I have previously argued (given the ethical and practical difficulties of experimentation in our field of research) that "advancing knowledge about crime causation will, in the first instance, be a question of more extensive analytical work which aims to sort causes from correlates by identifying plausible causal mechanisms" (Wikström 2006, 69).

Habit and Deliberation: The Role of Agency

People are not merely puppets at the sole mercy of psychological and social forces. It is, therefore, essential to aim to model how (the process by which) social and psychological forces impact people's actions. However, the role of human agency (i.e., people's powers to make things happen intentionally) is poorly, if at all, treated in criminological theory and research. Moreover, criminology lacks a satisfactory and generally accepted action theory.[1] An adequate action theory is arguably crucial to help identify which few of all the many personal and environmental correlates are causally relevant in the study of crime causation.

Situational Action Theory (SAT) was developed to fill this gap. SAT proposes that human action (including acts of crime) is an outcome of a moral perception-moral choice process initiated and guided by the interaction of people's crime propensity and criminogenic exposure (see further, e.g., Wikström 2006; 2010a; 2010b). This perception-choice process is the proposed situational mechanism that links a person and his or her environment to his and her actions. Only personal and environmental factors that directly (or indirectly as causes of the causes) influence the input to the perception-choice process are causally relevant factors. Consequently, only personal and environmental factors that directly (or indirectly) influence a person's moral perception of an act of crime as a viable action alternative, and his or her moral choice whether or not to carry out such an act are causally relevant in the study of the causes of crime. SAT proposes that a person's crime propensity depends on his or her morality (personal moral rules and emotions) and ability to exercise self-control, and that a setting's criminogenic features depend on its moral context (its moral norms and their level of enforcement).

People exercise agency within the constraint of rule-guided choice. SAT maintains that such choices are expressed through habit or rational deliberation, implying that they may be more or less determined depending on the circumstances.

When people commit acts of crime out of moral habit, they essentially react (in a stimulus-response fashion) to environmental cues. They see only one causally effective alternative, although they are likely to be aware, in the back of their mind, that there are other alternatives. Habitual action involves "automatically" applying experienced-based rules of conduct to a setting and its circumstances. People are most likely to act habitually when they are operating in familiar circumstances (but habitual reactions may also be triggered by high levels of stress or emotion).

When people deliberate, they see several potent action alternatives. If at least one alternative involves an act of crime, whether or not he or she will form an intention to engage in an act of crime depends on the outcome of his or her deliberation. When people deliberate (make moral judgments), they may be seen as exercising "free will" within the constraint of perceived action alternatives. The process of choice is one in which the person aims to choose the best alternative among those perceived. People are most likely to deliberate when they are in new or unfamiliar circumstances, or when the rule-guidance is unclear (see further Wikström 2006; 2010b).

Kinds of People in Kinds of Settings: The Importance of Causal Interactions

It is difficult to imagine human action as anything other than an outcome of a causal interaction between the person and his or her environment.[2] Crime propensity is activated by criminogenic features, and criminogenic features are made relevant by crime propensity. Yet criminology still tends to be divided, theoretically and empirically, into person-oriented and environment-oriented approaches. The study of person-environment interactions is rather rare in criminology. To advance our knowledge about crime causation it is, arguably, essential that these approaches are properly integrated.

A major hurdle to testing hypotheses about the role of the person-environment interaction in crime causation is the fact that few criminological studies have collected adequate measures of environments and, particularly, people's exposure to different kinds of environments. The Peterborough Adolescent and Young Adult Development Study (PADS+) was developed specifically to address this problem and includes, among more traditional measures of person, family, peer, and school characteristics, a small-area community survey coupled with a space-time budget that provides data about people's activity fields (see further Wikström, Treiber, and Hardie 2011). This methodology enables, for the first time, the proper study of the role of the person-environment interaction in crime causation. The major findings from the first phase of PADS+ (testing key propositions of SAT) are published in Wikström et al. (2011). The results strongly support the proposition that acts of crime depend on kinds of people in kinds of settings. For example, those with a low crime propensity (strong morality and ability to exercise self-control) were practically situationally immune to influences of criminogenic settings, while those with a high crime propensity (weak morality and poor ability to exercise self-control) were situationally vulnerable to such influences.

Coda

In this short chapter I have argued that we need to take causation, human agency, and the person-environment interaction more seriously to advance our knowledge about crime, its causes and prevention. This requires (1) more advanced theoretical work with a particular focus on better understanding relevant causal processes and the role human agency play in these processes, (2) the development of new methodologies, particularly as regards measuring people's exposure to different kinds of environments, and (3) improving statistical techniques for the analysis of person-environment interactions in crime causation, particularly longitudinally.

Notes

1. Rational Choice Theory is sometimes used or alluded to, but, in my opinion, it has serious limitations as an explanation of moral action and crime.

2. A causal interaction may be seen as a cause—two or more factors or processes coming together—that initiates a causal process that brings about the action.

References

Bunge, Mario. 1999. *The Sociology-Philosophy Connection*. New Brunswick, NJ: Transaction Publishers.

Bunge, Mario. 2006. *Chasing Reality: Strife over Realism*. Toronto: University of Toronto Press.

Ellis, Lee, Kevin Beaver, and John Wright. 2009. *Handbook of Crime Correlates*. San Diego: Academic Press.

Farrington, David. P. 1992. "Explaining the Beginning, Progress, and Ending of Antisocial Behavior from Birth to Adulthood." In *Advances in Criminological Theory*, vol. 3: *Facts, Frameworks, and Forecast*, edited by Joan McCord, 253–286. New Brunswick, NJ: Transaction Publishers.

Farrington, David P. 1993. "Have any Individual, Family or Neighbourhood Influences on Offending Been Demonstrated Conclusively?" In *Integrating Individual and Ecological Aspects of Crime* (BRÅ-report 1993), edited by David P. Farrington, Robert J. Sampson, and Per-Olof H. Wikström, 3–37. Stockholm: Fritzes.

Farrington David P. 1999. "A Criminological Research Agenda for the Next Millennium." *International Journal of Offender Therapy and Comparative Criminology* 43: 154–167.

Farrington, David P. 2000. "Explaining and Preventing Crime: The Globalization of Knowledge—The American Society of Criminology 1999 Presidential Address." *Criminology* 38: 1–24.

Farrington, David P. 2002. "Are Within-individual Causes of Delinquency the Same as Between-Individual Causes?" *Criminal Behaviour and Mental Health* 12: 53–68.

Farrington, David P., Robert J. Sampson, and Per-Olof H. Wikström 1993. *Integrating Individual and Ecological Aspects of Crime*. BRÅ-report vol. 1. Stockholm: Fritzes.

Wikström, Per-Olof H. 2006. "Individuals, Settings and Acts of Crime: Situational Mechanisms and the Explanation of Crime." In *The Explanation of Crime: Context, Mechanisms and Development*, edited by Per-Olof H. Wikström and Robert J. Sampson, 61–107. Cambridge: Cambridge University Press.

Wikström, Per-Olof H. 2010a. "Situational Action Theory." In *Encyclopedia of Criminological Theory*, edited by Francis T Cullen and Pamela Wilcox, 1000–1007. Beverly Hills, CA: Sage.

Wikström, Per-Olof H. 2010b. "Explaining Crime as Moral Actions." In *Handbook of the Sociology of Morality*, edited by Steven Hitlin and Stephen Vasey, 211–240. New York: Springer.

Wikström, Per-Olof H. 2011. "Does Everything Matter? Addressing Problems of Causation and Explanation in the Study of Crime." In *When Crime Appears: The Role of Emergence*, edited by Jean M. McGloin, Christoper J. Sullivan, and Leslie W. Kennedy, 53–72. London: Routledge.

Wikström, Per-Olof H., Kyle Treiber, and Beth Hardie. 2011. "Examining the Role of the Environment in Crime Causation: Small-Area Community Surveys and Space-Time Budgets." In *The SAGE Handbook of Criminological Research Methods*, edited by David Gadd, Susanna Karstedt, and Steven Messner, 111–127. Los Angeles: Sage.

Wikström, Per-Olof H., Dietrich Oberwittler, Kyle Treiber, and Beth Hardie. 2011. *Breaking Rules: The Social and Situational Dynamics of Young People's Urban Crime*. Oxford: Oxford University Press.

8

Lack of Empathy and Offending

IMPLICATIONS FOR TOMORROW'S RESEARCH
AND PRACTICE

Darrick Jolliffe and Joseph Murray

This chapter reviews some of the most important facts and controversies surrounding the proposed relationship between empathy and offending. Like many areas of criminology, this topic has been the beneficiary of some of David Farrington's research efforts. Also, as in many areas of criminology, the understanding of the relationship between empathy and offending would benefit considerably by adopting David's trademark systematic and methodologically rigorous approach.

Several observations suggest that criminologists view empathy (or more accurately a lack of empathy) as relatively important for understanding the causes of crime. Empathy is referred to in influential theories used to explain crime, such as Gottfredson and Hirschi's General Theory (1990, 89–90). A "lack of empathy" is included as a key and possibly the defining characteristic of the concept of psychopathy (e.g., Blair 2007; Hare 1999). And there is conceptual overlap between empathy and a host of factors that have been associated with explaining crime, such as poor social cognition (Bennett, Farrington, and Huesmann 2004), and lack of guilt (Loeber et al. 2008) among others. In addition, empathy enhancement (through role-play and various perspective-taking exercises) is viewed as standard practice in many offender rehabilitation programs (e.g., Mulloy, Smiley, and Mawson 1991).

Perhaps this evidence for the importance of empathy could be considered qualitative, suggesting that some criminologists view a lack of empathy as significant. However, any chapter to celebrate David's work must have quantitative evidence, and this exists as well. In a postal survey of 1,218 criminologists (on the register of the American Society of Criminology) the most highly rated explanation for the persistence of criminal behavior was "a lack of empathy and concern for others" (Ellis, Cooper, and Walsh 2008).

David Farrington himself has articulated a view about the importance of a lack of empathy for characterizing offenders and their behavior. Farrington (1998,

257) suggests that offenders are "callous with low empathy. They are relatively poor at role-taking and perspective-taking, and may misinterpret other people's intentions. This lack of awareness or sensitivity to other people's thoughts and feelings impairs their ability . . . to appreciate the effects of their behavior on other people." Empathy has also been promoted to one of the main individual differences that David discusses in his reviews of individual differences in offending, with the others being low intelligence and high impulsivity (e.g., Farrington 2004; Farrington and Welsh 2008).

What Is Empathy?

Although the concept of "sympathy" has a long history, the term "empathy" is relatively new, being in widespread use for less than 50 years (Hanson 2003). Currently there remain many definitions of the term empathy in the literature, and these tend to either emphasize the proposed emotional component of empathy (i.e., being able to experience the emotions of another person) or the cognitive component (i.e., being able to understand the emotions of another person). However, a broad consensus seems to be forming that empathy contains both affective and cognitive components (e.g., Cohen and Strayer 1996; Davis 1983; Jolliffe and Farrington 2006a).

The theoretical relationship between low empathy and offending is seductively simplistic. Individuals who have lower levels of empathy are more likely to offend because they are free from experiencing or understanding the emotional consequences of their actions on others. Whereas people with relatively high empathy may comprehend or experience another's fear, distress, sadness when committing antisocial acts, these are not factored in as a cost or consequence of the antisocial act among those with low empathy. Thus, people with relatively low levels of empathy do not have the same behavioral inhibitions imposed by these experiences and understandings. A number of more detailed models of the relationship between empathy and antisocial behavior exist (e.g., Hanson 2003; Hoffman 2000), but in essence these models all have the same overall formula: low empathy increases the likelihood of committing criminal offenses.

Is Low Empathy Related to Offending?

Addressing this question marks one of David Farrington's early footprints on the study of empathy. David was approached by a hapless Ph.D. student perplexed with how to summarize the evidence on the relationship between empathy and criminal offending. Some of the studies clearly showed that people who committed offenses scored lower on measures of empathy, while others found no discernible difference in scores on empathy measures. David immediately handed over a copy of Lipsey and Wilson's (2001) Practical Meta Analysis and directed the student to undertake a systematic review. With more than a little support from David this systematic review was completed (Jolliffe and Farrington 2004).

The review included 35 studies that compared offenders (defined as those who committed acts that if detected could result in a criminal conviction) to nonoffenders on questionnaire measures of empathy. The results suggested that offenders had significantly lower empathy than nonoffenders, but the relationship was stronger for cognitive than for affective empathy. More importantly, the relationship between low empathy and offending was greatly reduced after controlling for intelligence and socioeconomic status, suggesting that these might be more relevant factors, or that empathy might mediate the relationship between these factors and offending (Jolliffe and Farrington 2004).

Measurement of Empathy

While the systematic review suggested that low cognitive empathy was strongly related to offending, this could have been partly attributable to the poor measurement of empathy. That is, most of the studies in the review that measured cognitive empathy used a scale that lacked face validity, making it unclear whether empathy was the actual variable being compared between offenders and nonoffenders. The other questionnaire measures of empathy used, while having higher face validity, seemed to contain some items that might be assessing levels of sympathy as opposed to empathy. Sympathy and empathy are interlinked but separate constructs (Hanson 2003) with empathy defined as the understanding or sharing of another's emotion and sympathy usually defined as how one feels about the emotions of another. The typical overlap between empathy and sympathy in the questionnaire measurement of empathy meant it was unclear to what degree empathy was actually being assessed. Additionally, there is some evidence to suggest that items that assess sympathy are more open to social desirability bias than those that assess empathy (Jolliffe and Farrington 2006a).

Prisoners as Offenders

One of David's lasting contributions to criminology, through his tireless work on the Cambridge Study in Delinquent Development, was to move forward the debate about who "offenders" are. That is, many people who self-report committing offenses don't get convicted, and few convicted people serve time in prison (e.g., Farrington 2003a). Studying prisoners as "offenders"[1] actually provides very little information about the potential link between empathy and the likelihood of committing offenses because prisoners are a unique (and biased) sample of all those who commit offenses. Further complicating the issue is the problem that empathy levels might be reduced by periods of incarceration (e.g., Neal and Clements 2010). This might account for the lower empathy scores identified among "offenders" (identified as prisoners) in many of the studies included in the systematic review of empathy and offending.

Correlation or Cause: The Relationship between Empathy and Offending

David has written extensively about the methodological quality of evaluation studies and risk factor research (e.g., Farrington 2003b; Farrington and Petrosino 2001), and recently he was involved in the development of a series of checklists designed to assess the methodological quality of studies included in systematic reviews of risk factors (Murray et al. 2009). These Cambridge Quality Checklists (CQC) were developed to draw attention to key features of studies so that an assessment could be made whether the variable of interest (in this instance empathy) is a correlate (i.e., associated with offending), a risk factor (i.e., associated with and preceding offending), or a causal risk factor (associated with and preceding offending, and changes in levels of empathy change the likelihood of offending).

On the CQC, the correlate score ranges from 0 to 5 depending on the method of sampling, the response rate, the sample size, and the method and quality of measuring the correlate and the outcome. The risk factor score is ordinal (out of three) depending on whether the data used in the study were cross-sectional, retrospective, or prospective. The causal risk factor score ranges from 1 to 7 with the lowest level being "A study without a comparison group and no analysis of change" and the highest being "A randomized experiment targeting the risk factor" (Murray et al. 2009).

Applying the CQC to the studies in the systematic review of empathy and offending makes for grim reading. Of the 35 studies included, the highest score achieved by any study on the correlate checklist was 1. This means that based on the studies included in the review, we can have little confidence that empathy is a correlate of offending. In addition, all 35 studies used cross-sectional data. This means that, given the studies included in the review, low empathy could lead to offending or, equally, low empathy could be a consequence of offending. Also, the highest level achieved on the causal risk factor scale was 2. This means that there was no evidence to suggest that empathy was a causal risk factor for offending.

In summary, the current state of the evidence regarding the relationship between empathy and offending is poor because of weak measurement of empathy and weak measurement of offending and because studies have employed relatively low methodological quality standards. David has been involved in some research undertaken to address some of these issues, however. For example, David contributed to the creation of a new questionnaire to measure empathy (the Basic Empathy Scale: BES) that appears promising especially as it has shown some cross-cultural validity (Albiero et al. 2009; D'Ambrosio et al. 2009; Jolliffe and Farrington 2006a). Also, studies that related this measure of empathy to self-reported offending and bullying among a medium-sized group (n = 720) of secondary school students found an interesting pattern of results. Low affective empathy was related to high levels of self-reported offending and bullying among both males and females. Affective empathy was also independently related to serious male bullying, controlling for other important individual differences (e.g., high impulsivity, low intelligence) (Jolliffe and Farrington 2006b; 2007; 2011). This fits well with evidence emerging from other areas of psychology suggesting that it is deficits in affective empathy that characterize more serious offending (Blair 2007).

Following David Farrington's Example to Improve Research on Empathy and Offending

David Farrington's past research on other risk factors for offending could be used as a useful blueprint for improving our understanding of the relationship between empathy and offending. One of the first areas that need to be addressed is the measurement of empathy. The BES empathy scale might be a good start, but it is unclear how well questionnaire measures capture empathy, especially affective empathy (Eisenberg and Fabes 1990).

Ideally a multimethod study of empathy and potentially overlapping traits such as impulsiveness and intelligence would be undertaken, much like the multimethod, multisource study of impulsivity carried out by White et al. (1994) in the Pittsburgh Youth Study.

The assessment of empathy should involve the administration of a number of questionnaire measures of empathy (e.g., the Basic Empathy Scale); recording of verbal responses to movie vignettes, perhaps while monitoring galvanic skin response; and measurement of autonomic arousal (as another way to assess the experience of emotions), among a large number of both males and females. The intercorrelations of these measures would be very informative, but it would also be essential that the measures of empathy were compared to measures of potentially overlapping constructs such as sympathy, perspective taking, and emotional intelligence, as well as established risk factors such as intelligence and impulsivity. Future research could then select measures of empathy that minimize this overlap.

Once a device or set of devices have been established to adequately measure empathy, high-quality prospective longitudinal studies are required. These should assess levels of empathy of a large group of children from an early age, before the onset of antisocial behavior, and include repeated measurements of empathy and offending during development. Such studies would help address the lack of evidence surrounding the predictive validity of empathy. It could also be assessed whether changes in empathy predict changes in delinquency within individuals, thus allowing for stronger inferences about causal effects. By measuring additional established explanatory risk factors that are important in predicting offending (e.g., intelligence, impulsivity, parental supervision), the mechanisms linking low empathy and offending could be explored (e.g., Farrington 2003b). For example, empathy may be spuriously related to later offending (e.g., because both low empathy and offending are the result of low intelligence); empathy may measure an underlying cause of offending (e.g., low empathy is a proxy measure of high impulsivity), or empathy may mediate the effects of another risk factor (e.g., low intelligence leads to low empathy, which increases the likelihood of offending). Currently, each mechanism is equally plausible, but in only one mechanism (empathy mediating another risk factor) could interventions for offenders designed to increase empathy hope to result in a reduction in later offending. For the other mechanisms, even if interventions successfully increased empathy, offending would not be prevented because empathy is not causally related to offending.

In conclusion, the research surrounding empathy and its potential relationship to offending is in its infancy. More work on how best to measure empathy and higher-quality studies of its relationship to offending are needed to create an empirical basis with which to properly evaluate a potential relationship. David Farrington's adherence to careful measurement and high-quality research (especially prospective longitudinal studies) should serve as the blueprint for moving forward in this challenging but important area.

Note

1. All but one of the studies located for the systematic review of empathy and offending used prisoners as offenders.

References

Albeiro, Paolo, Giada Matricardi, Daniela Speltri, and Diana Toso. 2009. "The Assessment of Empathy in Adolescence: A Contribution to the Validation of the Italian Version of the Basic Empathy Scale." *Journal of Adolescence* 32: 393–408.

Bennett, Sarah, David P. Farrington, and L. Rowell Huesmann. 2004. "Explaining Gender Differences in Crime and Violence: The Importance of Social Cognitive Skills." *Aggression and Violent Behavior* 10: 263–288.

Blair, James R. 2007. "Empathy Dysfunction in Psychopathic Individuals." In *Empathy in Mental Illness*, edited by Tom Farrow, 3–16. New York: Cambridge University Press.

Cohen, Douglas, and Janet Strayer. 1996. "Empathy in Conduct-Disordered and Comparison Youth." *Developmental Psychology* 32: 988–998.

D'Ambrosio, Fanny, Marie Oliver, Davina Didon, and Chrystel Besche. 2009. "The Basic Empathy Scale: A French Validation of a Measure of Empathy in Youth." *Personality and Individual Differences* 46: 160–165.

Davis, Mark H. 1983. "Measuring Individual Differences in Empathy: Evidence for a Multidimensional Approach." *Journal of Personality and Social Psychology* 44: 113–126.

Eisenberg, Nancy, and Richard A. Fabes. 1990. "Empathy: Conceptualization, Measurement, and Relation to Prosocial Behavior." *Motivation and Emotion* 14: 131–149.

Ellis, Lee, Jonathon A. Cooper, and Anthony Walsh. 2008. "Criminologists' Opinions about Causes and Theories of Crime and Delinquency." *Criminologist* 33: 23–25.

Farrington, David P. 1998. "Individual Differences and Offending." In *The Handbook of Crime and Punishment*, edited by Michael Tonry, 241–268. New York: Oxford University Press.

Farrington, David P. 2003a. "Methodological Quality Standards for Evaluation Research." *Annals of Social and Political Science* 587: 49–68.

Farrington, David P. 2003b. "Key Results from the First 40 years of the Cambridge Study in Delinquent Development." In *Taking Stock of Delinquency: An Overview of Findings from Contemporary Longitudinal Studies*, edited by Terrence P. Thornberry and Marvin D. Krohn, 137–184. New York: Kluwer/Plenum.

Farrington, David P. 2004. "Criminological Psychology in the Twenty-first Century." *Criminal Behaviour and Mental Health* 14: 152–166.

Farrington, David P., and Anthony Petrosino. 2001. "The Campbell Collaboration Crime and Justice Group." *Annals of the American Academy of Political and Social Science* 578: 35–49.

Farrington, David P., and Brandon Welsh. 2008. *Saving Children from a Life of Crime*. Oxford: Oxford University Press.

Gottfredson, Michael R., and Travis Hirschi. 1990. *A General Theory of Crime*. Stanford, CA: Stanford University Press.

Hanson, Karl R. 2003. "Empathy Deficits of Sexual Offenders: A Conceptual Model." *Journal of Sexual Aggression* 9: 13–23.

Hare, Robert D. 1999. "Psychopathy as a Risk Factor for Violence." *Psychiatric Quarterly* 70: 181–197.

Hoffman, Martin L. 2000. *Empathy and Moral Development: Implications for Caring and Justice*. New York: Cambridge University Press.

Jolliffe, Darrick, and David P. Farrington. 2004. "Empathy and Offending: A Systematic Review and Meta-analysis." *Aggression and Violent Behavior* 9: 441–476.

Jolliffe, Darrick, and David P. Farrington. 2006a. "The Development and Validation of the Basic Empathy Scale." *Journal of Adolescence* 29: 589–611.

Jolliffe, Darrick, and David P. Farrington. 2006b. "Examining the Relationship between Low Empathy and Bullying." *Aggressive Behavior* 32: 540–550.

Jolliffe, Darrick, and David P. Farrington. 2007. "The Relationship between Low Empathy and Self-Reported Offending." *Legal and Criminological Psychology* 12: 265–286.

Jolliffe, Darrick, and David P. Farrington. 2011. "Is Low Empathy Related to Bullying Controlling for Other Factors?" *Journal of Adolescence* 34: 59–71.

Lipsey, Mark W., and David B. Wilson. 2001. *Practical Meta-analysis*. Thousand Oaks, CA: Sage.

Loeber, Rolf, David P. Farrington, Magda Stouthamer-Loeber, and Helene Raskin White. 2008. *Violence and Serious Theft: Development and Prediction from Childhood to Adulthood*. New York: Routledge.

Mulloy, Rachel, Carson W. Smiley, and Diana L. Mawson. 1999. "The Impact of Empathy Training on Offender Treatment." *Focus on Corrections Research* 11: 15–18.

Murray, Joseph, David P. Farrington, and Manuel P. Eisner. 2009. "Drawing Conclusions about Causes from Systematic Reviews of Risk Factors: The Cambridge Quality Checklists." *Journal of Experimental Criminology* 5: 1–23.

Neal, Tess M. S., and Carl B. Clements. 2010. "Prison Rape and Psychological Sequelae." *Psychology, Public Policy, and Law* 16: 284–299.

White, Jennifer. L., Terri E. Moffitt, Avshalom Caspi, Dawn J. Bartusch, Douglas J. Needles, and Magda Stouthamer-Loeber. 1994. "Measuring Impulsivity and Examining Its Relationship to Delinquency." *Journal of Abnormal Psychology* 103: 192–205.

9

Person-in-Context

INSIGHTS AND ISSUES IN RESEARCH ON NEIGHBORHOODS AND CRIME

Gregory M. Zimmerman and Steven F. Messner

If one wants to significantly advance the frontiers of criminological research, one should take on one of the core theoretical or methodological challenges that David Farrington has so aptly highlighted over the course of his distinguished career (e.g., Farrington 1992; 1993; 1999; 2000; 2002). One such challenge pertains to the complex interplay between persons and their environments. Over 20 years ago, David Farrington observed that "researchers interested in neighbourhood influences have generally not adequately measured individual and family influences, just as researchers interested in individual and family influences have generally not adequately measured neighbourhood influences" (1993, 30). This led him to argue that research accounting for *either* individual- *or* community-level processes would likely be inconclusive, at best.

Our main objective in this chapter is to highlight research on neighborhood influences on crime and stress the importance of multilevel research, at both the conceptual and methodological levels. We explain the current state of the macrosociological approach to the study of crime, discuss the integration of this perspective with individual-level explanations of crime, and present some of the challenges that must be confronted to advance this promising area of criminology.[1]

Intellectual Foundations: The Chicago School

During the early part of the twentieth century, Chicagoans Clifford Shaw and Henry McKay (1931; 1942) mapped the residential location of youths who had been referred to juvenile court over several decades. They found that delinquency rates were highest in lower-class neighborhoods concentrated toward the inner city (i.e., in the transitional zone) and decreased as the distance from the city center increased. They also found that the relative rankings of crime rates across the zones of the city remained quite stable over time. This observation of stability suggested to them that something about the area, and not about the characteristics of the individuals living there, was responsible for the crime rates, particularly since the "kinds of persons" living there were constantly changing. Shaw and McKay also identified distinctive structural correlates of crime and delinquency rates. High-crime areas were characterized by residential instability, high percentages of families on public assistance, low median income, low home ownership, high percentages of immigrants, and high percentages of racial and ethnic minorities. Shaw and McKay (1942) argued that these structural characteristics promoted a breakdown of social organization, or "social disorganization." In socially disorganized neighborhoods, social controls (both internal and external) were relatively weak, which led to crime and delinquency through criminogenic situational factors and antisocial cultural frames.

Early studies in the social disorganization tradition, however, did not empirically investigate Shaw and McKay's (1942) suggestions that social disorganization leads to crime through a breakdown of societal institutions and weakened social controls (Sampson 2006). Contemporary work following the tradition of social disorganization theory has an explicit theoretical and empirical focus on the underlying *mechanisms* that link features of neighborhoods with levels of crime.

Unpacking Mechanisms

In the "systemic model of crime," Bursik and Grasmick (1993) extended the classical variant of social disorganization by locating the social controls that can effectively limit criminal activity in the networks of social relations that exist among neighborhood residents. "Private control" relies on friendship and kinship ties in the neighborhood; "parochial control" involves the supervision and monitoring of the public space in the neighborhood, primarily by neighbors; and "public control" entails the application of resources external to the neighborhood, typically those associated with government and law enforcement agencies, for collective purposes. The systemic model of crime postulates that the effectiveness of these controls depends on the extensiveness and density of both primary networks (e.g., social ties among kin and close friends) and secondary networks (e.g., social ties among acquaintances). In doing so, the systemic model of crime "unpacks the mechanisms" of neighborhood effects by highlighting the ways in which relational networks and various forms of social control intervene between structural neighborhood conditions and levels of crime.

Subsequent research has indicated that the relationship between neighborhood social ties and levels of crime is more complicated than depicted in the systemic model. For example, there is evidence that certain social ties may actually inhibit rather than enhance social controls aimed at reducing crime, suggesting that it is important to pay attention to *whom* the ties connect (Browning, Feinberg, and Dietz 2004; Patillo-McCoy 1999; Wilson 1987). Research also indicates that it may be possible to achieve high levels of informal social control and to fight crime in the absence of strong ties (Bellair 1997; Hampton and Wellman 2003). Moreover, social ties might need to be activated and the resources associated with them mobilized in order to achieve social control (Kubrin and Weitzer 2003; Sampson 2006).

Largely in response to the issues raised about the adequacy of the systemic model of crime, Robert Sampson and colleagues introduced the concept of "collective efficacy" to the neighborhood effects literature (Sampson, Raudenbush, and Earls 1997). Collective efficacy refers to the linkage of social cohesion in a neighborhood, which depends on high levels of trust and mutual support, with shared expectations among neighbors to intervene for the common good. Collective efficacy, the neighborhood-level analogue of "self-efficacy," relies on a basic level of working trust among neighbors, rather than on close personal ties, and incorporates the key factor of purposeful action that is often assumed in other "social capital" interpretations. Research has demonstrated that collective efficacy provides a causal mechanism through which structural neighborhood conditions influence neighborhood crime levels (e.g., Morenoff, Sampson, and Raudenbush 2001; Sampson, Morenoff, and Earls 1999; Sampson et al. 1997).

Our review thus far has revealed that much of the contemporary research following in the tradition of social disorganization theory has focused primarily on the regulatory capacity of neighborhood social ties and the activation of these ties for collective purposes. Yet, as we noted, Shaw and McKay (1942) argued that high crime rates in socially disorganized areas reflect exposure to criminal cultures in addition to weakened social controls. As described in the contemporary literature, concentrated disadvantage isolates lower-class neighborhoods from middle- and upper-class resources and opportunities (e.g., Sampson and Wilson 1995), which weakens residents' conventional value systems and causes some residents to embrace an alternative set of norms that condone antisocial behavior. As a result, residents of these areas face divergent value systems that are "culturally transmitted" through successive generations.

The classical cultural transmission thesis has been recast in the "cultural attenuation" hypothesis, which maintains that most residents in high-crime areas do not condone crime per se; rather, informal social control is compromised in these areas because the strength of residents' attachment to conventional value systems is weakened or attenuated (e.g., Warner 2003; Warner and Rountree 1997). Persistently weak cultural commitments are thus assigned responsibility for continuity in high rates of crime.

Another example of cultural research that conforms more closely to the logic underlying the earlier studies of the Chicago School's theorists is the work by Anderson (1999) on conflicting cultural orientations in highly disadvantaged, primarily minority neighborhoods. Drawing upon his ethnographic research in Philadelphia, Anderson proposed that two distinct orientations can be detected in these neighborhoods: a "decent" orientation, which embraces mainstream goals and norms and emphasizes hard work and self-reliance; and a normative orientation directly opposed to that of mainstream society. The rules of this "oppositional culture" are manifested in a "code of the streets," which stresses respect and deference. Only a minority of residents in these neighborhoods embraces the values of the "street code," but all must master it to avoid being easy targets for victimization. As a result, the pervasive acceptance of the code of the streets in disadvantaged, largely minority areas increases the likelihood that routine social interactions and interpersonal conflicts escalate into violence.

Multilevel Analysis

Research focusing on individual influences on crime has developed largely in isolation of macrosociological research on deviant behavior (Farrington 1993; Wikström and Sampson 2003). Yet there is an emergent view that crime is not dependent on *either* individual *or* community characteristics but rather on *who is in what setting* (Wikström 2004). This has pushed researchers to integrate insights about individual- and neighborhood-level processes and formulate more comprehensive explanations of crime (Tonry, Ohlin, and Farrington 1991; Wikström and Loeber 2000). These approaches involve "multilevel analysis," which is a natural extension of hierarchical data structures that exist naturally in time and space. For example, individuals are nested within families and peer groups, which are in turn nested within social contexts such as communities.

By linking levels of analysis, multilevel modeling (Raudenbush and Bryk 2002) has bridged the gap between theory and empiricism and provided researchers the opportunity to model more accurately a realistic view of criminal offending. Multilevel analysis allows researchers (1) to assess the percentage of variation in crime explained by individual- and community-level variables (i.e., partition variance-covariance components); (2) to investigate the effects of individual characteristics on crime, controlling for relevant features of the environment (i.e., "controlling out" clustering); (3) to examine the effects of environmental factors on crime, controlling for compositional differences across contexts (i.e., contextual effects); and (4) to estimate the effects of variables at one level of analysis on relationships occurring at another level (i.e., moderating or cross-level interaction effects). The growing consensus in the discipline is that a full understanding of crime ultimately requires the simultaneous examination of individual- and community-level characteristics as well as a consideration of how these factors interact to explain offending.

Future Work and Theoretical and Methodological Challenges

Although current research is wrestling with understanding linkages across levels of the social structure, important challenges remain. Theoretically, criminological and sociological inquiry must focus on linking individual- and community-level processes rather than "controlling out" the variance of one level of analysis when studying the other. Although some research examining cross-level moderating effects has made strides in this direction (also see Situational Action Theory, Wikström 2010), criminologists need to *theorize* about how selection processes and neighborhood-level influences act in concert to structure the observed residential landscape of communities.

Perhaps the most formidable impediment to methodological progress is the paucity of data sources that take into account the naturally occurring hierarchical social structure. This issue was recognized by Bursik and Grasmick (1993) almost 20 years ago, when they argued that any test of the systemic model of crime's framework requires information on relational networks across neighborhoods, information that is usually not readily available in commonly used secondary data sources such as the US Census.

Although few datasets measure individual and contextual characteristics simultaneously, their popularity is increasing. For example, the Project on Human Development in Chicago Neighborhoods (PHDCN) combines longitudinal data from youth and parent interviews with neighborhood surveys, systematic observations of neighborhoods, and the US census (see Sampson et al. 1997). The National Longitudinal Survey of Adolescent Health (Add Health) combines a comprehensive psychological and behavioral inventory of youths with rich peer network and school-level data (see Bearman, Jones, and Udry 1997). And most recently, the Los Angeles Family and Neighborhood Survey (L.A. FANS) (see Narayan et al. 2003) and the Peterborough Adolescent and Young Adult Development Study (PADS+) (see Wikström, Treiber, and Hardie 2011) were developed to allow for the simultaneous study of how person, family, peer, school, and neighborhood characteristics influence criminal behavior. The development of data sets taking into account the hierarchical social structure, along with the increased availability of multilevel modeling software, should allow researchers to investigate the complex ways in which individual and contextual factors contribute to offending behavior.

Other "Neighborhood Effects"

Multilevel research has also begun to uncover new kinds of "neighborhood effects." For example, Zimmerman and Messner (2011) interpreted a cross-level interaction between neighborhood disadvantage and violent peer exposure not as a "moderating effect" as commonly understood in the literature, but instead as a "contextual effect" of disadvantage on peer violence combined with an underlying "nonlinear" individual-level effect of violent peer exposure on violence. In addition, Zimmerman and Vásquez (2011) uncovered a multilevel process whereby the functional form of an individual-level predictor of crime depended on neighborhood context. These studies highlight the continued need to investigate the *indirect* ways in which neighborhood context can influence offending.

Research has also recognized that social characteristics in one neighborhood can influence social processes in another. That is, neighborhoods are not "islands unto themselves" (Sampson et al. 1999, 637); rather, neighborhoods share borders (and variance) and are nested within broader social aggregates such as cities. The fact that neighborhoods overlap within a larger socioeconomic system has led to the study of spatial dynamics (Massey and Denton 1993), which emerge because neighborhoods are inextricably linked, share similar characteristics, and can influence one another socially, economically, and politically (Morenoff and Sampson 1997; Sampson et al. 1999). Research in this budding area of inquiry indicates that individuals are nested within neighborhoods, which are themselves situated near other theoretically strategic neighborhoods within a broader social context.

Finally, researchers have theorized about and empirically examined reciprocal relationships and feedback processes among social structural variables, social process variables, and crime rates (e.g., Bellair 2000; Liska and Bellair 1995; Markowitz et al. 2001; Sampson 2006). The possibility of reciprocal causal processes calls for the reconsideration of an issue in the study of neighborhood effects that has typically been viewed in purely methodological terms, that is, the issue of "selection bias." Researchers have long recognized that correlations between features of neighborhoods and levels of crime can be produced both by the impact of the neighborhood conditions on the residents residing therein ("context effects") and by choices of individuals to live in neighborhoods with different characteristics ("selection effects"). Although selection processes are often regarded as a "statistical nuisance" to be controlled in order to evaluate accurately the importance of neighborhood context (Sampson 2008, 227), Sampson (2008, 217) has observed that "neighborhood selection is part of a process of stratification that situates individual decisions within an ordered, yet constantly changing, residential landscape." It is thus necessary to continue to work toward disentangling the causal structure of neighborhood mechanisms and particularly, reciprocal and selection processes.

Conclusions

We have provided a general overview of contemporary research that has identified theoretically relevant neighborhood mechanisms through which the structural factors central to social disorganization theory influence offending. We have also highlighted the growing awareness that persons and contexts do not exist in isolation and that the interconnections among individual- and neighborhood-level factors are complex. Examining the connections between different levels of analysis, however, presents both theoretical and methodological challenges. Criminological and sociological inquiry needs to focus on linking individual-level and community-level processes, rather than "controlling" the variance of one level of analysis when studying the other. Methodologically, researchers need to continue to develop analytical programs and data sets that take into account the hierarchical social structure. Only through such advancements will we be able to disentangle the complex relationships between individuals and the social contexts in which they are embedded, as David Farrington astutely anticipated decades ago.

Note

1. Our discussion in this chapter is adapted from Messner and Zimmerman (forthcoming).

References

Anderson, Elijah. 1999. *Code of the Streets: Decency, Violence, and the Moral Life of the Inner City*. New York: Norton.

Bearman, Peter S., J. Stephen Jones, and J. Richard Udry. 1997. The National Longitudinal Study of Adolescent Health. www.unc.edu/projects/addhealth/design.

Bellair, Paul E. 1997. "Social Interaction and Community Crime: Examining the Importance of Neighbor Networks." *Criminology* 35: 677–703.

Bellair, Paul E. 2000. "Informal Surveillance and Street Crime: A Complex Relationship." *Criminology* 38: 137–170.

Browning, Christopher, Seth L. Feinberg, and Robert D. Dietz. 2004. "The Paradox of Social Organization: Networks, Collective Efficacy, and Violent Crime in Urban Neighborhoods." *Social Forces* 83: 503–534.

Bursik, Robert J., and Harold G. Grasmick. 1993. *Neighborhoods and Crime*. New York: Lexington Books.

Farrington, David P. 1992. "Explaining the Beginning, Progress, and Ending of Antisocial Behavior from Birth to Adulthood." In *Advances in Criminological Theory*, vol. 3: *Facts, Frameworks, and Forecasts*, edited by Joan McCord, 253–286. New Brunswick, NJ: Transaction.

Farrington, David P. 1993. "Have Any Individual, Family or Neighbourhood Influences on Offending Been Demonstrated Conclusively?" In *Integrating Individual and Ecological Aspects of Crime* (BRÅ-report 1993), edited by David P Farrington, Robert J Sampson, and Per-Olof H. Wikström, 23–48. Stockholm: Fritzes.

Farrington, David P. 1999. "A Criminological Research Agenda for the Next Millennium." *International Journal of Offender Therapy and Comparative Criminology* 43: 154–167.

Farrington, David P. 2000. "Explaining and Preventing Crime: The Globalization of Knowledge—The American Society of Criminology 1999 Presidential Address." *Criminology* 38: 1–24.

Farrington, David P. 2002. "Are Within-Individual Causes of Delinquency the Same as Between-Individual Causes?" *Criminal Behaviour and Mental Health* 12: 53–68.

Hampton, Keith N., and Barry Wellman. 2003. "Neighboring in Netville: How the Internet Supports Community and Social Capital in a Wired Suburb." *City and Community* 2: 277–311.

Kubrin, Charis E., and Ronald Weitzer. 2003. "New Directions in Social Disorganization Theory." *Journal of Research in Crime and Delinquency* 40: 374–402.

Liska, Allen E., and Paul E. Bellair. 1995. "Violent-Crime Rates and Racial Composition: Convergence over Time." *American Journal of Sociology* 101: 578–610.

Markowitz, Fred E., Paul E. Bellair, Allen E. Liska, and Jianhong Liu. 2001. "Extending Social Disorganization Theory: Modeling the Relationships between Cohesion, Disorder, and Fear." *Criminology* 39: 293–320.

Massey, Douglas S., and Nancy Denton. 1993. *American Apartheid: Segregation and the Making of the Underclass*. Cambridge: Harvard University Press.

Messner, Steven F., and Gregory M. Zimmerman. In press. "Community-Level Influences on Crime and Offending." In *The Oxford Handbook on Crime Prevention*, edited by Brandon C. Welsh and David P. Farrington. New York: Oxford University Press.

Morenoff, Jeffrey D., and Robert J. Sampson. 1997. "Violent Crime and the Spatial Dynamics of Neighborhood Transition: Chicago, 1970–1990." *Social Forces* 76: 31–64.

Morenoff, Jeffrey D., Robert J. Sampson, and Stephen Raudenbush. 2001. "Neighborhood Inequality, Collective Efficacy, and the Spatial Dynamics of Homicide." *Criminology* 39: 517–560.

Narayan, Sastry, Bonnie Ghosh-Dastidar, John Adams, and Anne R. Pebley. 2003. *The Design of Multilevel Survey of Children, Families, and Communities: The Los Angeles Family and Neighborhood Survey*. Working Papers 03–21, RAND Corporation Publications Department.

Pattillo-McCoy, Mary E. 1999. *Black Picket Fences: Privilege and Peril among the Black Middle Class*. Chicago: University of Chicago Press.

Raudenbush, Stephen W., and Anthony S. Bryk. 2002. *Hierarchical Linear Models: Applications and Data Analysis Methods*. 2nd ed. London: Sage.

Sampson, Robert J. 2006. "Collective Efficacy Theory: Lessons Learned and Directions for Future Inquiry." In *Advances in Criminological Theory*, vol. 15: *Taking Stock: The Status of Criminological Theory*, edited by Francis T. Cullen, John Paul Wright, and Kristie R. Blevins, 149–167. New Brunswick, NJ: Transaction.

Sampson, Robert J. 2008. "Moving to Inequality: Neighborhood Effects and Experiments Meet Social Structure." *American Journal of Sociology* 114: 189–231.

Sampson, Robert J., Jeffrey D. Morenoff, and Felton Earls. 1999. "Beyond Social Capital: Spatial Dynamics of Collective Efficacy for Children." *American Sociological Review* 64: 633–660.

Sampson, Robert J., Stephen Raudenbush, and Felton Earls. 1997. "Neighborhoods and Violent Crime: A Multilevel Study of Collective Efficacy." *Science* 277: 918–924.

Sampson, Robert J., and William J. Wilson. 1995. "Toward a Theory of Race, Crime, and Urban Inequality." In *Crime and Inequality*, edited by John Hagan and Ruth D. Peterson, 37–54. Stanford, CA: Stanford University Press.

Shaw, Clifford, and Henry D. McKay. 1931. *Social Factors in Delinquency*. Chicago: University of Chicago Press.

Shaw, Clifford, and Henry D. McKay. 1942. *Juvenile Delinquency and Urban Areas*. Chicago: University of Chicago Press.

Tonry, Michael H., Lloyd E. Ohlin, and David P. Farrington. 1991. *Human Development and Criminal Behavior*. New York: Springer.

Warner, Barbara D. 2003. "The Role of Attenuated Culture in Social Disorganization Theory." *Criminology* 41: 73–97.

Warner, Barbara D., and Pamela Rountree. 1997. "Examining Informal Social Ties in a Community and Crime Model: Questioning the Systemic Nature of Informal Social Control." *Social Problems* 44: 520–536.

Wikström, Per-Olof H. 2004. "Crime as Alternative: Towards a Cross-level Situational Action Theory of Crime Causation." In *Beyond Empiricism*, edited by Joan McCord. New Brunswick, NJ: Transaction.

Wikström, Per-Olof H. 2010. "Situational Action Theory." In *Encyclopedia of Criminological Theory*, edited by Francis T Cullen and Pamela Wilcox. Beverly Hills, CA: Sage.

Wikström, Per-Olof H., and Rolf Loeber. 2000. "Do Disadvantaged Neighborhoods Cause Well-Adjusted Children to Become Adolescent Delinquents? A Study of Male Juvenile Serious Offending, Individual Risk and Protective Factors, and Neighborhood Context." *Criminology* 38: 1109–1142.

Wikström, Per-Olof H., and Robert J. Sampson. 2003. "Social Mechanisms of Community Influences on Crime and Pathways in Criminality." In *Causes of Conduct Disorder and Juvenile Delinquency*, edited by Benjamin B. Lahey, Terrie E. Moffitt, and Avshalom Caspi. New York: Guildford Press.

Wikström, Per-Olof H, Kyle Treiber, and Beth Hardie. 2011. "Examining the Role of the Environment in Crime Causation: Small-Area Community Surveys and Space-Time Budgets." In *The SAGE Handbook of Criminological Research Methods*, edited by David Gadd, Susanna Karstedt, and Steven Messner, 111–127. Los Angeles: Sage.

Wilson, William J. 1987. *The Truly Disadvantaged: The Inner City, the Underclass, and Public Policy*. Chicago: University of Chicago Press.

Zimmerman, Gregory M., and Steven F. Messner. 2011. "Neighborhood Context and Nonlinear Peer Effects on Adolescent Violent Crime." *Criminology* 49: 873–903.

Zimmerman, Gregory M., and Bob Edward Vásquez. 2011. "Decomposing the Peer Effect on Adolescent Substance Use: Mediation, Nonlinearity, and Differential Nonlinearity." *Criminology* 49: 1235–1273.

10

Risk and Protective Factors in the Assessment of School Bullies and Victims

Maria M. Ttofi and Peter K. Smith

David Farrington has made many outstanding contributions to knowledge, especially on the development of offending and antisocial behavior, and on the effectiveness of interventions in reducing offending and antisocial behavior. Within this framework, one may highlight his research on intragenerational and intergenerational continuity of school bullying as well as his contributions regarding the effectiveness of bullying prevention programs. His scholarly articles are especially pioneering, noteworthy, and influential. In his elegant 1993 paper in *Crime and Justice*, David Farrington offered a comprehensive and exhaustive review that initiated his current position as one of the leading world experts in the area of school bullying. An empirical part, based on longitudinal analyses from the Cambridge Study in Delinquent Development, complemented the review part of the paper and emphasized the importance of incorporating longitudinal data in examining this form of externalizing behavior. Many of the suggestions for future research put forward in his 1993 manuscript have been addressed to date, but many others (especially those concerning longitudinal research) have not been fully addressed so far.

In 2011, David Farrington played a crucial role in initiating new longitudinal data analyses from major prospective longitudinal studies across the world. This was a major task leading into two special issues (in *Criminal Behaviour and Mental Health* and in the *Journal of Aggression, Conflict and Peace Research*)[1] regarding the long-term adverse consequences (i.e., internalizing and externalizing problems) of school bullying. All the above considered, it is highly appropriate for us to focus in this chapter on the importance of (*a*) incorporating prospective longitudinal data in examining school bullying and (*b*) investigating risk and protective factors for the assessment of school bullies and victims. Implications arising from these new directions of research for future antibullying initiatives are discussed.

Current Research on School Bullying

Bullying is a serious problem plaguing school youth in both developed and developing countries (Smith et al. 1999). Thirty years of research have nevertheless been completed to date with distinct directions of interest and with subsequent contributions to the understanding of this phenomenon (Smith 2011). Reviews on individual and family correlates of school bullying have been conducted, synthesizing data from (primarily) cross-sectional studies. These reviews are not detailed here because of space limitations.

A substantial body of research has already been conducted in the area of bullying prevention. A thorough systematic review and meta-analysis on the effectiveness of bullying prevention programs was completed under the aegis of the Campbell Collaboration (Farrington and Ttofi 2009). A total of 622 reports concerned with bullying prevention were found, and 89 of these reports (describing 53 different program evaluations) were included in the review. It was found that, overall, school-based antibullying programs are effective. On average, bullying decreased by 20–23 percent and victimization decreased by 17–20 percent. Many challenges still remain within the area of bullying prevention, as detailed in the Campbell Report, and interested readers should consult the relevant work. What has not been discussed so far is the importance of incorporating risk and protective factors in the assessment of school bullies and their victims.

Risk and Protective Factors for the Assessment of Bullying and Its Negative Effects

School bullying uniquely contributes to internalizing and externalizing problems after taking into account preexisting adjustment problems and other major childhood risk factors (Ttofi et al. 2011a; 2011b). However, not all children involved in school bullying go on to experience adjustment difficulties. Some "resilient" children function better than would be expected (Bowes et al. 2010).

Various questions subsequently arise: First, what protective factors interrupt the continuity from school bullying to later adverse outcomes? What are the intervening mechanisms that nullify the effect of school bullying on a given outcome? Second, what factors give resiliency to children from multiproblem milieus, enabling them to avoid being involved in school bullying as either perpetrators or victims? In other words, what protective factors buffer the effects of risk factors for bullying perpetration and victimization? These questions can be more adequately addressed using data from prospective longitudinal studies and also by focusing on both risk and protective factors.

Risk-focused prevention has become very popular, based on the idea that offending and other externalizing problems can be reduced by targeting and alleviating risk factors (Farrington 2000). Following the traditional risk factors approach, an interventionist could investigate risk factors that are related to both childhood bullying and adult offending. It would be expected that the removal of relevant risk factors should reduce the probability of offending (or other adverse outcomes) later in life. To give an example, a recent systematic review and meta-analysis on risk factors predicting children's involvement in school bullying (Cook et al. 2010) found that the typical school bully is one who exhibits significant externalizing behavior, has both social competence and academic challenges, possesses negative attitudes and beliefs about others, has negative self-related cognitions, has trouble resolving problems with others, and comes from a family environment characterized by conflict and poor parental monitoring. Notably, many of the above risk factors are also related to juvenile delinquency and offending (Farrington in press). Subsequently, following the traditional risk factors approach, interventionists and practitioners would argue that removal of these risk factors could reduce both bullying and offending and enable children to live well-adjusted lives in the long run.

Although the above approach is scientifically sound, it has more recently become clear that prevention and intervention initiatives should, for various methodological and practical reasons, expand this traditional approach in such a way that protective factors are also taken into account. Focusing on building resilience of children at risk is a more positive approach, and more attractive to communities, than reducing risk factors, which emphasizes deficits and problems (Pollard et al. 1999).

As early as 1993, researchers have emphasized the methodological reasons for using longitudinal data in investigating school bullying (Farrington 1993). In order to examine whether a risk factor is a predictor or possible cause for a given outcome, the risk factor needs to be measured before the outcome. Therefore, prospective longitudinal designs are needed to investigate risk factors and especially whether causal effects can be identified (Murray et al. 2009). Future research on school bullying should examine risk and protective factors related to school bullying based on longitudinal studies. Longitudinal research is needed on careers of bullying and victimization: when they begin, how long they persist, and when they end. In addition, variables that influence onset, persistence, and desistance within this longitudinal framework should be studied. The vast majority of current research is based on cross-sectional data, which does not allow examination of whether any given (individual, family or social) factor is a correlate, a predictor, or a possible cause of bullying. This problem has important implications for new antibullying initiatives. Program planners need to effectively target causes of bullying behavior and not merely risk markers that are symptoms of this type of problem behavior.

Protective Factors in New Antibullying Initiatives: Some Examples

Significant research attention has been directed toward identifying risk factors for bullying and victimization, so that we can now sketch a fairly accurate profile of the characteristics of childhood perpetrators and victims of school bullying (Cook et al. 2010). However, this picture is incomplete and it is time that researchers started investigating what protective factors may moderate the relations between risk factors and the likelihood of children becoming victims and bullies (Bollmer et al. 2005, 702). Researchers should also examine protective factors that interrupt the continuity from bullying to later adverse outcomes based on longitudinal studies.

In a short-term longitudinal study, Smith and his colleagues (2004) found that "escaped victims" (those who were no longer victims after a period of two years) did not differ substantially in terms of their profiles from nonvictims and reported a number of successful strategies for dealing with the experience of being bullied, such as talking to someone about incidents or making efforts to find new friends. These victims were less likely than continuing victims to blame themselves for being bullied. A high-quality friendship has been identified as a protective factor that significantly moderates the relationship between bullying behavior and externalizing problems (Bollmer et al. 2005) and further research on the matter is warranted.

Bijttebbier and Vertommen (1998) found that victims of school bullying were more likely to use internalizing coping strategies (e.g., avoiding facing the problem or remaining passive) in dealing with peer relationships. School bullies, on the other hand, were more likely to use externalizing coping strategies such as aggression and blaming others. It is possible that good reasoning and problem-solving skills may be a protective factor against school bullying, although no research has examined this topic so far. Findings in similar areas of research are nevertheless suggestive. Werner and Smith (1992), for example, found that good reading, reasoning, and problem-solving skills at age 10 were important protective factors among high-risk children who did not develop serious behavioral problems by age 18. A high IQ, which is related to good reasoning and problem-solving skills, has also been identified as a protective risk factor. In the E-risk study, Jaffee and her colleagues (2007) concluded that maltreated children who did not become antisocial tended to have high intelligence and to live in low crime neighborhoods with high social cohesion and informal social control.

Future research on school bullying also needs to examine the extent to which bonding to significant others is a protective factor against school bullying. Findings in similar areas of research are suggestive. Based on data from the Rochester Youth Development Study, Carolyn Smith and her colleagues (1995) found that high-risk children who were resilient (i.e., nondelinquent) tended to receive good parental supervision and good attachment to parents. Within the area of school bullying, existing research has found that families protect against the negative effects of bullying victimization (Bowes et al. 2010).

Conclusions

Within various fields, such as criminology, protective factors have started to receive increased attention and are considered a key challenge for the next generation of risk assessment research (Farrington 2007). Research findings on protective factors are even more scattered within the area of school bullying. In future, bullying agencies need to adopt a risk- and protection-focused prevention approach as their framework to guide new antibullying initiatives.

It is necessary to develop an assessment instrument that can provide data on empirically identified risk and protective factors for school bullying based on findings from prospective longitudinal research and following guidelines from relevant research in other fields. Possible differences in measurement reliability and validity across gender, age, and racial/ethnic groups of such an instrument should also be examined. Such an instrument would have important applications in prevention need assessment and strategic prevention planning. The time is ripe to mount a new program of international collaborative research on risk and protective factors against school bullying and its long-term consequences based on prospective longitudinal studies from across the world.

References

Bijttebbier, Patricia, and Hans Vertommen. 1998. "Coping with Peer Argument in School-Aged Children with Bully/Victim Problems." *British Journal of Educational Psychology* 68: 387–394.

Bollmer, Julie M., Richard Milich, Monica J. Harris, and Melissa A. Maras. 2005. "A Friend in Need: The Role of Friendship Quality as a Protective Factor in Peer Victimization and Bullying." *Journal of Interpersonal Violence* 20: 701–712.

Bowes, Lucy, Barbara Maughan, Avshalom Caspi, Terrie E. Moffitt, and Louise Arsenault. 2010. "Families Promote Emotional and Behavioural Resilience to Bullying: Evidence of an Environmental Effect." *Journal of Child Psychology and Psychiatry* 51: 809–817.

Cook, Clayton R., Kirk R. Williams, Nancy G. Guerra, Tia E. Kim, and Shelly Sadek. 2010. "Predictors of Bullying and Victimization in Childhood and Adolescence: A Meta-analytic Investigation." *School Psychology Quarterly* 25: 65–83.

Farrington, David P. 1993. "Understanding and Preventing Bullying." In *Crime and Justice: A Review of Research*, vol. 17, edited by Michael Tonry, 381–458. Chicago: University of Chicago Press.

Farrington, David P. 2000. "Explaining and Preventing Crime: The Globalization of Knowledge—The American Society of Criminology 1999 Presidential Address." *Criminology* 38: 1–24.

Farrington, David P. 2007. "Advancing Knowledge about Desistance." *Journal of Contemporary Criminal Justice* 23: 125–134.

Farrington, David P. In press. "Childhood Risk Factors for Young Adult Offending: Onset and Persistence." In *Young Adult Offenders and the Criminal Justice System*, edited by Friedrich Lösel, Anthony E. Bottoms, and David P. Farrington. Cullompton, Devon, UK: Willan.

Farrington, David P., and Maria M. Ttofi. 2009. School-Based Programs to Reduce Bullying and Victimization. Campbell Systematic Reviews. http://www.campbellcollaboration.org.

Jaffee, Sara R., Avshalom Caspi, Terrie E. Moffitt, Monika Polo-Tomas, and Alan Taylor. 2007. "Individual, Family, and Neighborhood Factors Distinguish Resilient from Non-resilient Maltreated Children: A Cumulative Stressors Model." *Child Abuse and Neglect* 31: 231–253.

Murray Joseph, David P. Farrington, and Manuel P. Eisner. 2009. "Drawing Conclusions about Causes from Systematic Reviews of Risk Factors: The Cambridge Quality Checklists." *Journal of Experimental Criminology* 5: 1–23.

Pollard, John A., J. David Hawkins, and Michael W. Arthur. 1999. "Risk and Protection: Are Both Necessary to Understand Diverse Behavioural Outcomes in Adolescence?" *Social Work Research* 23: 145–158.

Smith, Carolyn A., A. J. Lizotte, Terence P. Thornberry, and Marvin D. Krohn. 1995. "Resilient Youth: Identifying Factors That Prevent High-Risk Youth from Engaging in Delinquency and Drug Use." In *Delinquency and Disrepute in the Life Course*, edited by John L. Hagan, 217–247. Greenwich, CT: JAI Press.

Smith, Peter K. 2011. "Bullying in Schools: Thirty Years of Research." In *Bullying in Different Contexts: Commonalities, Differences and the Role of Theory*, edited by Iain Coyne and Claire Monks, 36–59. Cambridge: Cambridge University Press.

Smith, Peter K., Yohji Morita, Josine Junger-Tas, Dan Olweus, Richard Catalano, and Peter Slee. 1999. *The Nature of School Bullying: A Cross-national Perspective*. London: Routledge.

Smith, Peter K., Lorenzo Talamelli, Helen Cowie, Paul Naylor, and Preeti Chauhan. 2004. "Profiles of Non-victims, Escaped Victims, Continuing Victims and New Victims of School Bullying." *British Journal of Educational Psychology* 74: 565–581.

Ttofi, Maria M., David P. Farrington, Friedrich Lösel, and Rolf Loeber. 2011a. "Do the Victims of School Bullying Tend to Become Depressed Later in Life? A Systematic Review and Meta-analysis of Longitudinal Studies." *Journal of Aggression, Conflict and Peace Research* 3: 63–73.

Ttofi, Maria M., David P. Farrington, Friedrich Lösel, and Rolf Loeber. 2011b. "The Predictive Efficiency of School Bullying versus Later Offending: A Systematic/Meta-analytic Review of Longitudinal Studies." *Criminal Behaviour and Mental Health* 21: 80–89.

Werner, Emmy E., and Ruth S. Smith. 1992. *Overcoming the Odds: Children from Birth to Adulthood*. Ithaca, NY: Cornell University Press.

11

Adult Onset Offending

PERSPECTIVES FOR FUTURE RESEARCH

Georgia Zara

Talent perceives difference, Genius Unity

—WILLIAM B. YEATS, 1887

David Farrington's scientific contribution to criminological research is timeless. It is not accidentally that he is recognized as the *Renaissance man in criminology* (Walston 2009, 66). His emphasis on within-individual differences over time and on the effects of psychological and mental problems on later maladjustment has proven to be beneficial to the comprehension of adult onset offending (Farrington 2003).

An adult onset is the beginning of a criminal career at age 21 or afterward. The choice of 21 as the best cut-off age for adult onset intertwines with the legal concept of full responsibility in Western society (Gulotta 2009), and with the psychological and social scope of adulthood.

The Scientific Relevance of Adult Onset Offending

Researchers have prevalently explored early onset, and this interest has overshadowed the fact that adult offenders constitute a more substantial proportion of the offending population (Harris 2010). It was Farrington (1986) who stated that "offending is not predominantly a teenage phenomenon" (235) and that, to a significant degree, offending behavior can be predicted as early as childhood. International research seems to have supported this view.

A Delayed Criminal Career

Early-in-life psychological and mental problems can take the forms of internalized manifestations (Mervielde et al. 2005), but few studies have linked internalized problems to later criminal behavior (Elander et al. 2000; Kerr et al. 1997).

Five issues should be addressed when tackling future criminality:

1. Risk factors do not always have an immediate and direct impact: the extent and timing of their impact depends on the combination of individual characteristics, their sensitivity, and their exposure to hazardous circumstances at a vulnerable time. Their *sleeper effects* may only be seen later in life (Loeber 1990).
2. Early predictors may have a long-term impact and a stronger effect as time goes by. Perhaps, as in a *ripple effect*, the longer the temporal interval, the sturdier the influence (Zara and Farrington 2010).
3. Many factors that play a protective or inhibitory role in childhood or adolescence may fail to protect throughout adult life, thus transforming their protective impact into a risk influence in adulthood, as in a *switch effect* (Zara 2010).
4. Psychological insulation or resilience toward antisocial influences may not last, but rather may contribute to a sort of heightened sensitivity or *kindling effect* (Kendler, Thornton, and Gardner 2000) that places individuals at greater risk when rechallenged.
5. Delinquency abstention is not necessarily and always "a sign of good adolescent adjustment" (Moffitt 1993, 690). A history of antisocial abstinence in childhood or adolescence, when rebelling or risk taking are most typical, appears to become a critical factor in the emergence of adult onset offending. When antisocial abstinence is the result of avoidance or of psychological internalization problems, the risk of future maladjustment in the form of mental problems, life failure, and offending is intensified (Ollendick, Seligman, and Butcher 1999).

These issues lead to the concept of a *delayed criminal career* so that the external manifestation of criminal problems is more likely to emerge late in time. The assumption is that late onset offenders are likely to have psychological characteristics that provide early, but temporary, insulation against antisocial influences.

Who Are the First-Time Adult Onset Offenders?

In the Cambridge Study in Delinquent Development (CSDD), out of the 411[1] London males originally involved in the study, 403 (eight males were excluded from the analysis because of death and emigration) were followed from ages 8–10 to ages 48–50, and were divided, on the basis of conviction records and using the cutoff point of 21 years of age, into late onset offenders ($n = 38$), early onset offenders ($n = 129$), and nonoffenders ($n = 236$) (Farrington 2003).

Late onset offenders constituted 22.75 percent of the CSDD offending population. The average age of late antisocial onset was 21.80 versus age 10.00 for early onset, with an average criminal career length (defined as the time between the first and the last offenses) of 3.28 years. The average criminal career duration, excluding those with a single offense (who had a career duration of 0), was 8.30 years. Almost 40 percent of late onset offenders were recidivist, against almost 80 percent of early onset offending ($p < .0001$). On average, late onset offenders committed two offenses, while early onset offenders committed on average six offenses.

Late onset offenders differed from early onset offenders in the type of offenses they committed, which most commonly included sex offenses (46 percent), theft from work (27.3 percent), vandalism (23.5 percent), and fraud (19.3 percent) (McGee and Farrington 2010). All these offenses except vandalism are most likely to be committed by adult offenders. Regarding sex crime, for which most of the late onset offenders were involved, further investigation is paramount, insofar as the late onset offenders were more likely to admit sexual inhibition, and to have never experienced sexual intercourse by age 18.

How Early Can Adult Criminality Be Predicted?

Numerous multivariate analyses (Farrington, Coid, and West 2009; Piquero et al. 2010; Zara and Farrington 2010) performed with the CSDD show that mental health and quality of housing, along with family stability, as measured since ages 8–10, are crucial for a well-adjusted adult life.

Investigating retrospectively the life of the CSDD late onset offenders, and analyzing prospectively the impact of the different risk factors upon their development, it emerged that their adult criminality was not a sudden event. It was possible to track an underlying pattern of risk factors that anticipated and intensified their vulnerability to late antisocial influences. Figure 11.1 shows the pattern[2] of internalized, familial, and social problems in the life of a CSDD late onset offender that seem to have affected his development and social functioning.

Up to adulthood, the adult onset offenders shared many behavioral and temperamental similarities with nonoffenders. However, late onset offenders were more likely at ages 8–10 to come from poor housing (e.g., neglected accommodation, poor decoration and interior, inadequate and old furniture, etc.) (Odds Ratio or OR = 3.1, CI = 1.5–6.4) and have a low nonverbal IQ (OR = 2.3, CI = 1.1–5.1). At age 14 they were more anxious (OR = 2.8, CI = 1.0–7.9), and at age 18 they reported a higher level of neuroticism (OR = 2.4, CI = 1.2–5.1) and a more unstable employment pattern (OR = 2.3, CI = 1.0–5.5). Whereas these features sustained the avoidance of antisocial involvement up to adulthood, they had, however, hampered the development of their psychological resilience.

In comparison with early onset offenders, they were more likely at ages 8–10 to be nervous (OR = .38, CI = .16–.88), withdrawn and with few, if any, friends (OR = .29, CI = .09–.95). At age 14 they were less likely to be aggressive (OR = 3.5, CI = 1.5–8.1) and to self-report delinquency (OR = 8.4, CI = 2.4–28.9). At age 18 they were more likely to have never experienced sexual intercourse (based on

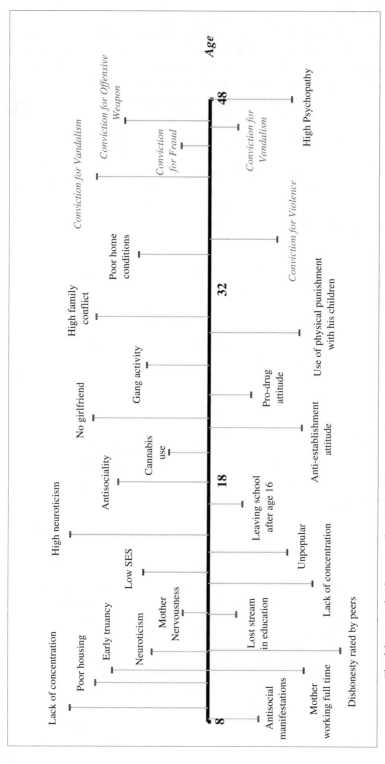

FIGURE 11.1   *The delinquent development of a CSDD adult onset offender.*

self-reported information) (OR = .15, CI = .05–.39). They were less likely than early onset offenders to be involved in gang activity, gambling, and self-reported violence.

Despite a different beginning, overall, late onset offenders became more similar to early onset offenders by age 32. In a recent study (Zara and Farrington 2009), late onset offenders were more unsuccessful than nonoffenders in many aspects of their lives; 40.6 percent of them were leading unsuccessful lives, in comparison with 12.2 percent of nonoffenders (OR = 4.9, CI = 2.2–11.1). Interestingly, no differences were found between late and early onset offenders regarding life success.

Psychopathy and Late Onset Offending

To explore further the psychological implication of adult onset offending over the criminal career, a current exploration of the CSDD is analyzing how adult onset offending could be related to psychopathy. Psychopathy has always been studied in association with persistent and chronic offending, but not to late onset offending. Psychopathy as operationalized by Cooke and colleagues (2004) is recognized as composed of traits of an arrogant and deceitful interpersonal style (ADI), a deficient affective experience (DAE), an impulsive and irresponsible life style (IIB), and the facet of antisocial behavior (ANT) as an additional component.

At age 48, 365 CSDD men out of the 394 still alive completed a social interview, and 304 of them (83 percent) also completed a medical interview that included the PCL:SV and the SCID-II (Farrington 2007). Scores on the 12-item PCL:SV ranged from 1 to 12 for late onset offenders (M = 4.0; SD = 2.9), and from 1 to 16 for early onset offenders (M = 6.7; SD = 4.3). *Factor 1* was combined by ADI and DAE to create an affective interpersonal dimension (AI), and *factor 2* included IIB and ANT, so as to create a broad impulsive and antisocial dimension (IA).

Among early onset offenders in the CSDD, 32 percent scored high on psychopathy versus 8 percent of late onset offenders. High levels of psychopathy were related to early offending (OR = 5.5). Table 11.1 also shows relationships between the four facets and onsets.

Late onset offending was better characterized by a higher risk of affective deficiency than by impulsivity and antisociality, suggesting that affective and emotional difficulties play a significant impact in determining antisocial involvement at some later point in life. Previous multivariate analyses are concordant with this result: emotional and psychological difficulties are likely to put an individual at a delayed risk for offending, acting early in life as inhibitory factors against antisociality. Anxiety at ages 12–14 was the only psychological problem that was significantly correlated to the affective/interpersonal factor of psychopathy (r = .276, p < .002). Empirical studies (Casey et al. 2011) indicate that adolescence reflects a period of increased rates of anxiety. Anxiety may act as a moderator of antisocial

TABLE 11.1   PCL:SV scores versus onset offending

	PCL:SV	% Late onset offenders	% Early onset offenders	Risk	
Scores	%	High	High	OR	CI 95%
Total PCL:SV	26.4	7.7	31.6	5.5*	1.23–24.97
Factor 1: AI	19.8	7.7	23.2	3.6	.792–16.52
Factor 2: IA	33.9	11.5	40.0	5.1*	1.43–18.22
Facet 1: ADI	22.3	7.7	26.3	4.3	.944–19.46
Facet 2: DAE	30.6	19.2	33.7	2.1	.736–6.18
Facet 3: IIB	28.9	11.5	33.7	3.9*	1.09–13.95
Facet 4: ANT	41.3	15.4	48.4	5.2*	1.65–16.12

Notes: As reported in the chapter file.
Notes: OR: Odds Ratios (all $p < .05$). In this analysis, PCL:SV scores for all facets and factors were dichotomized. *Factor 1—AI*: Affective/interpersonal factor. *Factor 2—IA*: Impulsive/antisocial factor.
Facet 1—ADI: Arrogant and Deceitful Interpersonal. Facet 2—DAE: Deficient Affective Experience. Facet 3—IIB: Impulsive and Irresponsible Behavior. Facet 4—ANT: Antisocial Behavior.
High score on PCL:SV = 10 or more out of 24; high score on ADI, DAE and IIB = 2 or more out of 6; high scores on ANT = 4 or more out of 6. High score on the affective and interpersonal factor = 3 or more out of 8, the highest score reached in this study for this factor. High score on impulsive and antisocial factor = 6 or more out of 11, the highest score reached in this study for this factor.
For total PCL:SV, area under ROC curve = .692, SE = .055, $p < .003$. For the *AI* factor, area under ROC curve = .628, SE = .057, $p < .045$. For the *IA* factor, area under ROC curve = .700, SE = .057, $p < .002$.

manifestation in adolescence, and yet it may put individuals at risk of future affective deficiency. That there is a link between affective and interpersonal deficiency and late onset offending is a proposition needing investigation.

The affective/interpersonal factor was not significant in discriminating early onset from late onset offending in the CSDD, whereas early onset offending was more likely to be related to the impulsive/antisocial factor; that is, in those individuals who show high impulsivity and antisocial features the risk of becoming an early offender was 5.1 times higher than for those who are lower on this factor.

The pattern of delinquent onset in adulthood is likely to be made up of a process of cumulative *wear and tear*, caused by repeated struggles with psychosocial stressors. These results, explored over a period of 40 years, suggest a *degree of heterotypic continuity*, in that children and adolescents with psychological problems who were socially isolated had higher rates of adult onset.

Research and Dissemination

Psychological and familial early factors emerged as crucial and independent predictors of late maladjustment. In their longitudinal study, Beyers and Loeber (2003) reported that sadness and depressive moods displayed unexpected effects, appeared to predict an increased rate in delinquency, and reduced the odds of criminal abstention. In a meta-analysis of childhood predictors of adult criminality, Leschied and colleagues (2008) found that dynamic risks as opposed to static predictors are better and more significantly related to later adult criminality. Remarkably, emotional difficulties, consistent with depression, and including withdrawal, anxiety, and social alienation, were significant, even if modest predictors of future criminality (ES = .22; CI = .009–.43; Z_c = 2.04, p <. 05).

More studies are necessary to explore the continuity effect of internalized problems upon development, and also the *switch effect* of protective factors, when individuals get older and when other development demands and life circumstances require a different pattern of coping responses. As Borum (2000) suggests, precision in predictive accuracy increases as our appreciation of the development context, where risk factors occur, increases.

Early Prevention for Late Criminality

Two main points have emerged from late onset research. One is related to risk assessment. The other is related to early prevention.

Research on adult onset offenders has started to demonstrate that because different factors are responsible for promoting early or late delinquent onsets, it is paramount to include psychological dynamic factors in the assessment of risk. Bayer and colleagues (2011) argue that reducing "internalizing problems early in life holds potential to subsequently narrow cumulative disparities in mental health and related disadvantage across people's lifetime" (55). Early prevention, which lessens adult offending, will also reduce mental problems, drinking, family dysfunction, marital conflicts, school failure, unemployment, and life failure. Understanding and preventing late onset offending urgently requires early intervention.

Notes

1. An example of timeline offending was presented at the American Society of Criminology Conference in St. Louis (November 11–15, 2008) by T. R. McGee and D. P. Farrington in their communication entitled "Are There Any True Adult Onset Offenders?"

2. The life success index is a combined measure based on nine criteria: unsatisfactory accommodation; unsatisfactory cohabitation; unsuccessful with children; unsatisfactory employment history; involved in fights in the last five years; substance use in the last five years; self-reported offenses (other than theft from work or tax fraud) in the last five years; unsatisfactory mental health (scoring five or more on the General Health Questionnaire); convictions in the last five years (Farrington et al. 2006).

References

Bayer, Jordana K., Ronald M. Rapee, Harriet Hiscock, Obioha C. Ukoumunne, Catherine Mihalopoulos, and Melissa Wake. 2011. "Translational Research to Prevent Internalizing Problems Early in Childhood." *Depression and Anxiety* 28: 50–57.

Beyers, Jennifer M., and Rolf Loeber. 2003. "Untangling Developmental Relations between Depressed mood and Delinquency." *Journal of Abnormal Child Psychology* 31(3): 247–266. DOI 10.1002/da.20743.

Borum, Randy 2000. "Assessing Violence Risk among Youth." *Journal of Clinical Psychology* 56: 1263–1288.

Casey, B. J., Erika J. Ruberry, Victoria Libby, Charles E. Glatt, Todd Hare, Fatima Soliman, Stephanie Duhoux, Helena Frielingsdorf, and Nim Tottenham. 2011. "Transitional and Translational Studies of Risk for Anxiety." *Depression and Anxiety* 28: 18–28. DOI 10.1002/da.20783.

Cooke, David J., Christine Michie, Stephen D. Hart, and Daniel A. Clark. 2004. "Reconstructing Psychopathy: Clarifying the Significance of Antisocial and Socially Deviant Behavior in the Diagnosis of Psychopathic Personality Disorder." *Journal of Personality Disorders* 18: 337–357. DOI: 10.1521/pedi.2004.18.4.337.

Elander, James, Michael Rutter, Emily Simonoff, and Andrew Pickles. 2000. "Explanations for Apparent Late Onset Criminality in a High-Risk Sample of Children Followed up in Adult life." *British Journal of Criminology* 40: 497–509. DOI: 10.1093/bjc/40.3.497.

Farrington, David P. 1986. "Stepping Stones to Adult Criminal Careers." In *Development of Antisocial and Prosocial Behaviour: Research, Theories and Issues*, edited by Dan Olweus, Jack Block, and Marian R. Yarrow, 359–384. New York: Academic Press.

Farrington, David P. 2003. "Key Results from the First Forty Years of the Cambridge Study in Delinquent Development." In *Taking Stock of Delinquency: An Overview of Findings from Contemporary Longitudinal Studies*, edited by Terence P. Thornberry and Marvin D. Krohn, 137–183. New York: Kluwer Academic / Plenum.

Farrington, David P. 2007. "Social Origins of Psychopathy." In *International Handbook on Psychopathic Disorders and the Law*, vol. 1: *Diagnosis and Treatment*, edited by Alan R. Felthous and Henning Sass, 319–334. New York: Wiley.

Farrington, David P., Jeremy W. Coid, Louise Harnett, Darrick Jolliffe, Nadine Soteriou, Richard Turner, and Donald J. West. 2006. *Criminal Careers up to Age 50 and Life Success up to Age 48: New Findings from the Cambridge Study in Delinquent Development*. Home Office Research Study No. 299. London: Home Office.

Farrington, David P., Jeremy W. Coid, and Donald J. West. 2009. "The Development of Offending from Age 8 to Age 50: Recent Results from the Cambridge Study in Delinquent Development." *Monatsschrift für Kriminologie und Strafrechtsreform* 92: 160–173.

Gulotta, Guglielmo. 2009. "La responsabilità penale nell'era delle neuroscienze" [Criminal responsibility in the era of neuroscience]. In *Manuale di Neuroscienze Forensi [Manual of forensic neuroscience]*, edited by Angelo Bianchi, Guglielmo Gulotta, and Giuseppe Sartori, 3–14. Milan: Giuffrè.

Harris, Patricia M. 2010. "The First-Time Adult-Onset Offender: Findings from a Community Corrections Cohort." *International Journal of Offender Therapy and Comparative Criminology* 14: 1–33. DOI: 10.1177/0306624X10372110.

Kerr, Margaret, Richard. E. Tremblay, Linda Pagani, and Frank Vitaro. 1997. "Boys' Behavioral Inhibition and the Risk of Later Delinquency." *Archives of General Psychiatry* 54: 809–816.

Leschied, Alan, Debbie Chiodo, Elizabeth Nowicki, and Susan Rodger. 2008. "Childhood Predictors of Adult Criminality: A Meta-analysis Drawn from the Prospective Longitudinal Literature." *Canadian Journal of Criminology and Criminal Justice* 50: 435–467. DOI: 10.3138/cjccj.50.4.435.

Loeber, Rolf. 1990. "Development and Risk factors of Juvenile Antisocial Behavior and Delinquency." *Clinical Psychology Review* 10: 1–41.

McGee, Tara R., and David P. Farrington. 2010. "Are There Any True Adult-onset Offenders?" *British Journal of Criminology* 50: 530–549. DOI: 10.1093/bjc/azq008.

Mervielde, Ivan, Barbara De Clercq, Filip De Fruyt, and Karla Van Leeuwen. 2005. "Temperament, Personality, and Developmental Psychopathology as Childhood Antecedents of Personality Disorders." *Journal of Personality Disorders* 19: 171–201.

Moffitt, Terrie E. 1993. "Adolescence-Limited and Life-Course-Persistent Antisocial Behaviour: A Development Taxonomy." *Psychological Review* 100: 674–701.

Ollendick, Thomas H., Laura D. Seligman, and A. Timothy Butcher. 1999. "Does Anxiety Mitigate the Behavioral Expression of Severe Conduct Disorder in Delinquent Youths." *Journal of Anxiety Disorders* 13: 565–574. DOI: 10.1016/S0887-6185(99)00023-7.

Piquero, Alex R., David P. Farrington, Daniel S. Nagin, and Terrie E. Moffitt. 2010. "Trajectories of Offending and Their Relation to Life Failure in Late Middle Age: Findings from the Cambridge Study in Delinquent Development." *Journal of Research in Crime and Delinquency* 47: 151–173. DOI: 10.1177/0022427809357713.

Walston, Catharine, ed. 2009. *Challenging Crime: A Portrait of the Cambridge Institute of Criminology*. London: Third Millennium.

Zara, Georgia. 2010. "Persistenza e recidivismo criminale: Il risk-assessment in psicologia criminologica [Persistence and criminal recidivism: Risk-assessment in criminological psychology]. In *Mente, Società e Diritto [Mind, society and the law]*, edited by Guglielmo Gulotta and Antonietta Curci, 555–603. Milan: Giuffrè.

Zara, Georgia, and David P. Farrington. 2009. "Childhood and Adolescent Predictors of Late Onset Criminal Careers." *Journal of Youth and Adolescence* 38: 287–300. DOI: 10.1007/s10964-008-9350-3.

Zara, Georgia, and David P. Farrington. 2010. "A Longitudinal Analysis of Early Risk Factors for Adult Onset Offending: What Predicts a Delayed Criminal Career?" *Criminal Behaviour and Mental Health* 20: 257–273. DOI: 10.1002/cbm.763.

12

The Next Generation of Longitudinal Studies

Magda Stouthamer-Loeber

Longitudinal studies, with their repeated measurements spanning decades, by their nature are very expensive and should be used only for those research questions that require the study of between-individual and within-individual changes over time. Thus, they should only be used when a developmental approach to offending will yield information for questions that cannot be answered by cross-sectional studies.

One of the problems in executing longitudinal studies is that the management skills and practical experience needed to conduct such studies are rarely taught during graduate training in universities, and need to be acquired by researchers by mentors or through books (Stouthamer-Loeber and van Kammen 1995). Moreover, information on how to run such studies is rarely found in articles published in scientific journals. Although we can now learn from a fair number of longitudinal studies dealing with antisocial and delinquent behavior (summarized in Loeber et al. 2008, 20; Killias, Redondo, and Sarnecki in press), it is of great help to have a mentor who has hands-on experience.

David Farrington has fulfilled that role for me and for our team. I met him first in the early eighties and we were fortunate enough to involve him in the Pittsburgh Youth Study (PYS). Apart from his profound influence on the content of the study and his extensive list of papers and several books on the PYS data, which he wrote or on which he collaborated, he was invaluable as a sounding board on practical matters such as training, contacting participants, and the general management of a large study. This knowledge was derived from his experience in the Cambridge Study in Delinquent Development, in which the participants have been followed up until age 48 and their offspring are currently being interviewed as well (Farrington 2003; Piquero et al. 2010). Especially important was David's conviction that investigators needed to be involved in all matters of data collection and management and not count on staff to run a study for them. Before researchers can withdraw behind their desks to write papers, they have to be entirely assured that the data are as good as they can possibly be. David taught us that involvement in the daily running of a study is not a distraction, but a necessity.

Since David's initial involvement with the PYS, longitudinal studies have changed in method of data collection and storage. Issues of consent and confidentiality as well as research conditions have changed as well. Changes in the content of longitudinal studies will be discussed elsewhere in this volume (see chapter 2, by Loeber).

Method of Data Collection

One of the questions confronting the researcher early on is whether to contract out the sample selection and data collection or whether to keep these tasks "in house." There are pros and cons for either decision. If the research team has no specialized knowledge of sample selection and data collection, it may be easier to use a survey organization. Also, if data collection needs to take place across the country it may make sense to use an existing network of interviewers affiliated with a survey organization. In addition, some researchers may not have the inclination or the time to be involved in data collection and prefer to receive the data "ready made." There are also several arguments that can be made against the use of a survey organization. First, the expense is generally larger than is necessary for in-house data collection. More important, however, is that the researchers do not have direct control over the number of contact attempts with potential participants and the quality and completeness of the data and how the participants have been treated. Survey organizations generally do their own quality control, which leaves the researchers to take the quality of the final product on faith. It would be better if researchers would take some of the quality control in their own hands to ensure that the product they receive is as good as it should be.

Data collection has largely moved away from unstructured interviews that required extensive training and coding afterward to interviewing with structured answer formats. The advantage of the latter method is that the questions are more likely to be asked in a uniform manner of each participant and that there is less coding to be done after the interview is completed. Other changes have to do with the recording of the interviews. Most surveys now use electronic data collection, avoiding data entry (Groves et al. 2009). An additional change has been that most studies now use multiple rather than single informants to ensure a more complete picture of the participant and his or her environment. The frequency of repeated measures has increased and studies cover longer periods of time, allowing a larger portion of development of offending to be studied and to move from studying persistence to also taking into account desistance. In these studies desistance from offending can be better estimated if the time window for desistance is sufficiently large to measure stable desistance. These studies also allow for the detection of cases with a late onset.

Method of Data Storage

We have gone from mainframe storage with backup tapes that seem to go out of date continuously to in-office servers or just desktop computers.

Consent and Confidentiality

Robins (1976) remarked on the change that the informed consent procedures had brought to research in the United States. Databases that in the past could have been used to select potential participants became off bounds because prior consent was required. The more recent HIPAA law, enacted in 1996, has further restricted access to health and health care information. Consent forms are now complicated documents.

Research Conditions

The increased use of answering telephone machines and the availability of the caller number has impeded the contacting of participants. Also the extensive use of cell phones makes contacting more difficult since phone numbers are not listed and cell phone numbers tend to change more rapidly than landlines. On the other hand, ways of electronic searching for people have multiplied. For instance, many states have extensive online databases of incarcerated individuals.

The success of longitudinal studies depends very much on the sustained cooperation of the participants. In order for a participant to cooperate, the participant first needs to be found and contacted and to agree to another round. Although there are well-developed methods of imputation of missing data, they work best for analyzing group data (McCartney, Burchinal, and Bub 2006). However, longitudinal studies also allow the study of the developmental paths of individual participants over time, and actual data are far to be preferred over imputation. In many studies the group of most interest (e.g., families of conduct disordered boys) requires the most attempts to find, contact, and interview (see Cotter et al. 1995). Curtailing search and contact attempts does in general yield a biased subject loss. Different search and contact methods are described, for example, in Cotter et al. (2002) and Stouthamer-Loeber and van Kammen (1995).

What Will the Future Bring?

Since longitudinal studies are expensive and the topic of antisocial behavior and crime may be in or out of favor with funding agencies over time, it is not possible to anticipate when new longitudinal studies can be started. Also, in our experience, funds available for existing or planned longitudinal studies may fluctuate over time.

Method of Data Collection

Although face-to-face interviewing will always have the advantage of ensuring a person's identity, the ease and the reduction in cost of web-based data collection will increase over time when more people have access to online electronic devices (e.g., Celio et al. 2011; Gosling et al. 2004). Such devices do not necessarily have to be a computer but may be a phone as long as it can connect to a survey program that can provide the questions and can store the data. Various devices may also collect motion or sleep data or can alert the participant to provide some specific information (Anokwa et al. 2009). Web-based data collection makes it easier for participants to continue to participate in a study from practically all over the world. However, electronically assisted interviewing still has at least three problems: getting the participant to do it, completing the survey in a confidential manner, and ascertaining the identity of the participant. Thus, face-to-face interviewing, even though it is costly, may still be the most certain way of collecting data.

Method of Data Storage

Changes in data storage are likely to take place. Cloud storage and computing will make it possible to use one's desktop computer just as a typing device with all the software and data stored somewhere else (Armbrust et al. 2010). Although security problems still have to be worked out, this may also be a way to make data available to certified users. Sharing data collected in large, expensive longitudinal studies is now often a requirement for obtaining funds in the first place. Cloud computing may be a way to deal with the technical end of data sharing.

Consent and Confidentiality

The consent and confidentiality requirements have become stricter over the years, and researchers, at least in the United States, have to go to great length to explain procedures and reasons for data collection and how the data will be kept confidential. Data sharing provides a challenge for the promise of confidentiality. Even if the most obvious identifiable information is removed from a file, it may still be possible to identify a participant through a combination of variables (called deductive discovery). This puts a participant at risk of being identified and information being misused. In addition, it also puts the original investigators at risk for having to pay a fine for a breach in confidentiality.

In our experience, the safest way of dealing with these confidentiality problems is to have each person wanting to use data write a small proposal that is approved by his or her university and has the appropriate IRB approval, shifting the responsibility of confidentiality to the "new" researcher who was not involved in the original data collection. Since data sharing is now more or less the norm, I expect that procedures for deidentifying data and for certifying that "new" investigators will protect the confidentiality of the data will become standard soon. Deidentifying a data set, however, will reduce the number of questions that can be answered after sensitive data has been removed.

Research Conditions

Longitudinal surveys, by their nature, cannot provide extensive feedback to the participants or provide help or treatment. Thus, in general, a participant may not directly benefit from participating. The reason that people do participate in these studies is because they are curious, they are made to feel special, they are civic-minded, or they are paid for their time. Further factors that may influence participation are the time it takes to participate, the ease of participation, and participants' earlier experience in being interviewed.

Collaboration within Studies

With most studies aspiring to cover many disparate areas such as genetics and environmental influences, future studies will require a team of collaborators with a lead investigator willing and able to commit a large portion of his or her professional life to keeping such a study going and attract collaborators who are experts in specific fields to work with over many years.

Since the academic system values principal investigatorship rather than co-investigatorship, a structure needs to be found that makes it worthwhile to be part of a larger team. One way to do this is to devise substudies each with its own principal investigator and funding. However, such a solution presupposes a stable line of funding for the main study.

Collaboration across Studies or Study Sites

It is expected that in the future there will be a better integration of biological and environmental and individual factors. This will probably be accomplished by pooling data from different studies in order to make sure the sample is large enough for small effects to show. Data pooling is often more complicated than it sounds. Presumably "comparable" data may have a slightly different format, or different collection sites may have left some questions out, leading to a cumbersome process of making a combined data set.

Funding agencies are at present the driving force for data pooling and data transfer to agencies set up to deal with data storage and data requests from researchers outside of the original group of investigators. The advantage of wider collaboration, apart from a larger sample size, is that more extensive use is made of the large investment needed for longitudinal studies. The original investigators cannot be experts on all questions that could potentially be examined with the collected data. However, the danger is that regardless of how well the data are documented, "new" researchers may misinterpret the meaning of some variables. It is, therefore, always useful to be in contact with the original investigators.

Agency Involvement

The size of future studies and the range of variables that should be included may require funding from several agencies. Collaboration between agencies and the acceptance of new thoughts in the field will require that the investigators play a very active role in preparing agencies for the scope of the planned research and for the idea of funding from different agencies. Researchers cannot wait for a request for proposals to come out that just fits their plans or expect agencies to take the lead role in searching for collaborations with other agencies. Instead, prospective investigators need to work together with agency staff to develop a blueprint for future longitudinal studies and for finding the necessary funding.

Secondary Data Analyses

Secondary data analysis, whether it is by pooling data from different studies or analyzing data from one study for a new purpose, is a great way to increase the yield of the research investment. It is useful, however, to keep a record of secondary research projects so that researchers do not compete with each other on the same topic. That is not to say that it would not be useful to have two different views on the same research question, but researchers should be aware of other projects using the same data bordering on their areas of interest.

In summary, the complex art and science of longitudinal studies continues to be exciting and challenging. New questions can be pursued, and new data collection tools spring up regularly. David Farrington has taught us much over many years and he continues to be an example to follow.

References

Anokwa, Yaw, Carl Hartung, Waylon Brunette, Gaetano Borriello, and Adam Lerer. 2009. "Open Source Data Collection in the Developing World." *Computer* 42.10: 97–99. http://dx.doi.org/10.1109/MC.2009.328.

Armbrust, Michael, Armando Fox, Rean Griffith, Anthony D. Joseph, Randy Katz, Andy Konwinski, Gunho Lee, David Patterson, Ariel Rabkin, Ion Stoica, and Mate Zahara. 2010. "A View of Cloud Computing." *Communication of the ACM* 53: 50–58.

Celio, Mark A., Courtney S. Vetter-O'Hagan, Stephen A Lisman, Gerard E. Johanson, and Linda P. Spear. 2011. "Integrating Field Methodology and Web-Based Data Collection to Assess the Reliability of the Alcohol Use Disorders Identification Test (AUDIT)." *Drug and Alcohol Dependence.* doi:10.10.1/j.drugalcdep.2011.05.035.

Cotter, Robert B., Jeffrey D. Burke, Rolf Loeber, and Judith L. Navratil. 2002. "Innovative Retention Methods in Longitudinal Research: A Case Study of the Development Trends Study." *Journal of Child and Family Studies* 11: 485–498.

Cotter, Robert B., Jeffrey D. Burke, Magda Stouthamer-Loeber, and Rolf Loeber. 2005. "Contacting Participants for Follow-up: How Much Effort Is Required to Retain Participants in Longitudinal Studies?" *Evaluation and Program Planning* 28: 15–21.

Farrington, David P. 2003. "Developmental and Life-Course Criminology: Key Theoretical and Empirical Issues—The 2002 Sutherland Award Address." *Criminology* 41: 201–235.

Gosling, Samuel D., Simine Vazire, Sanjay Srivastava, and Oliver P. John. 2004. "Should We Trust Web-Based Studies?" *American Psychologist* 59: 93–104.

Groves, Robert M., William D. Mosher, James M. Lepkowski, and Nicole G. Kirgis. 2009. "Planning and Development of the Continuous National Survey of Family Growth." *Vital Health Statistics* 1: 1–64.

Killias, Martin, Santiago Redondo, and Jerzy Sarnecki. In press. "European Perspectives." In *Transitions from Juvenile Delinquency to Adult Crime: Criminal Careers, Justice Policy and Prevention*, edited by Rolf Loeber and David P. Farrington. New York: Oxford University Press.

Loeber, Rolf, David P. Farrington, Magda Stouthamer-Loeber, and Helene R.White. 2008. *Violence and Serious Theft: Development and Prediction from Childhood to Adulthood.* New York: Routledge.

McCartney, Kathleen, Margaret R. Burchinal, and Kristen L. Bub. 2006. *Best Practices in Quantitative Methods for Developmentalists.* Boston: Blackwell.

Piquero, Alex R., David P. Farrington, Daniel S. Nagin, and Terrie E. Moffitt. 2010. "Trajectories of Offending and Their Relation to Life Failure in Late Middle Age: Findings from the Cambridge Study in Delinquent Development." *Journal of Research in Crime and Delinquency* 47: 151–173.

Robins, Lee N. 1976. "Problems in Follow-up Studies." *American Journal of Psychiatry* 134: 904–907.

Stouthamer-Loeber, Magda, and Welmoet B. Van Kammen. 1995. *Data Collection and Management: A Practical Guide.* Newbury Park, CA: Sage.

PART II

Criminal Careers and Justice

13

Research on Criminal Careers, Part 1

CONTRIBUTIONS, OPPORTUNITIES, AND NEEDS

Alfred Blumstein

The richness and longevity of the Cambridge Study in Delinquent Development (CSDD) has been a remarkable achievement reflecting David Farrington's intense persistence in following through on a project once initiated, in providing access to a major research resource to many other criminologists, and in yielding an impressive array of publications by Farrington and his colleagues and students that represent major contributions to knowledge about risk factors, protective factors, intergenerational offending, and so many other factors in delinquent development (see, for example, Farrington et al. 2010). The research covers a cohort of over 400 London boys from age eight until well into their fifties so far, and is still going strong. Aside from the impressive performance in the CSDD with about 200 publications, Farrington's intellectual contributions go well beyond that with hundreds of other publications based on research aside from the CSDD.

An important theme that runs throughout Farrington's impressive bibliography is the theme of criminal careers. Obviously, the CSDD allows him to carefully track the development of the criminal careers of his London cohort, but in light of its limited sample size, he has gone far afield into the issue of criminal careers more broadly. This is an area in which his contributions have been most important, and they provide the take-out point for this chapter dedicated to David Farrington that examines research on criminal careers, explores some of the rich knowledge that has been accumulated over the past decades, pays some attention to the needs for further development to clarify some regions of ambiguity, and explores opportunities for further research.

Data Sources

The data to estimate the parameters of criminal careers are of two major kinds. The first is self-reports of individual offending and many other life characteristics derived from diligent researchers like David Farrington in pursuing the information for his CSDD. The self-reports from the individuals interviewed periodically provide information on their individual offenses as well as on the many other events and experiences going on in their lives that could possibly be affecting their criminal activity. The second approach involves use of official records like arrest histories or "rap sheets" maintained by most jurisdictions. The rap sheets provide a record only of the offenses for which an arrest occurred, and typically include basic demographic information like age, race, and sex, but little more about the life circumstances of the offender that might have been a factor contributing to the commission of the offense. On the other hand, rap sheets are available in the millions, whereas self-report studies typically involve at most a few thousand respondents and require diligent pursuit of those respondents over the longitudinal period of the study. Finding means of linking the two kinds of records would be of considerable value in generating the benefits of each. For example, having an estimate of the probability of arrest following commission of a crime (Blumstein et al. 2011) could facilitate estimation of true offending frequency from information on the arrest frequency derived from rap sheets (see also Farrington et al. 2007).

Criminal Careers

A "criminal career" provides the means of focusing on individual offending and the patterns of that offending by individuals (Blumstein et al. 1986). It does not attempt to represent an individual's primary mode of earning a living, but rather to characterize some of the features of how that individual engages in crime. It attempts to say something about the process of initiation in criminal activity, the age at which it occurs, and something about the precipitating events. Also, it should convey information about the other end of the career, something about the process of termination or reduction in criminal activity. In particular, the time between initiation and termination, or the duration of the criminal career, is of interest. Perhaps of even greater interest, especially to a sentencing judge, is the "residual duration" or the interval from any particular intervention until the termination of the career. Between the starting and ending points are the details of the individual's criminal activity, including most importantly the kinds of crimes he commits, the frequency with which he commits them, and any trends in seriousness of the offenses committed or trends in specialization by moving from a generic mix of offenses to a more narrow mixture, perhaps reflecting the development of expertise in that particular area.

The Envelope of the Criminal Career: Initiation and Termination Initiation

Initiation of a criminal career most typically occurs during the early or mid teenage years, probably at the instigation of a somewhat older recruiter who provides the incentive and the guidance for the early illegal acts. Recording of the initial event is, of course, likely to occur at a somewhat earlier age if it is based on self-reports (the first "crime") than if based on an official record (the first "arrest," which could well have been preceded by other crimes for which no arrest occurred).

Most research on criminal careers indicates the saliency of early initiation: younger initiation is likely to be associated with a longer career and more likely to involve more serious offenses.

Termination

In contrast to initiation, termination is a much more complex process to describe and analyze. Where initiation is marked by an explicit event, termination is presumably marked by the absence of such anticipated events. Thus, to the extent that the career has been marked by a steady stream of offenses followed by a recurrent gap in offending, that could be an indication of a significant reduction in the offending frequency, and possibly a drop to a zero rate, or termination. On the other hand, many criminal careers can be characterized by a general decline with age in their offending frequency, and so that pattern can complicate any estimate of when the career terminated. To the extent that the decline was fairly steady, one might make an estimate of the rate of decline and an associated projection of when the pattern would be expected to reach zero. The issue of termination is made even more complicated by the potential for intermittency discussed in the next section; it is entirely possible for an individual to demonstrate a clear pattern of termination, followed by a period of no further offending, which is later followed by a reinitiation of an offending pattern that may or may not be similar to the previous one.

It is, of course, interesting and important to develop information on the duration of criminal careers and the distribution of that duration as a function of individual demographic and social characteristics, age at initiation, crime types involved in the career, and other aspects of the career. A particularly interesting question is the degree to which a period of incarceration changes the career duration. It is possible that the incarceration effect is criminogenic, and so serves to extend the career for an interval, perhaps as long as or even longer than the period of incarceration, thereby nullifying at least that aspect of the incapacitative effect of the incarceration; on the other hand, for at least some people, the effect of the incarceration could be rehabilitative or deterrent, and thereby shorten the career. It is impressive how little we know about the magnitudes and directions of these effects, and especially of the interaction of these effects on individuals of different characteristics.

An important variant on the measure of total career duration is the *residual* duration, or the remaining career length at some point of an involvement with the criminal justice system. In particular, such information is especially important in deciding a sentence to be imposed on an individual whose prior criminal career is known. If that residual duration is short, then imposing a long sentence would be wasteful of limited prison capacity. Here again, we have only limited information in order to generate estimates of residual career duration.

Offending Frequency

Perhaps one of the most interesting and important parameters of an individual's criminal career and of the distribution within an offending population is the frequency, or crimes committed per year, often designated by the Greek letter lambda (λ), reflecting its standard use as a rate perimeter in statistical analysis. Obviously individuals with higher values of λ represent a greater threat to public safety and become strong candidates for incarceration. In some important work over 30 years ago, researchers at RAND (Chaiken, Chaiken, and Peterson 1982) interviewed prisoners to estimate their individual values of λ. Perhaps one of the most interesting observations deriving from those interviews was the extreme skewness of the distribution of offending frequency among those who indicated that they had engaged in that particular kind of offense. For those who did burglary, the median offending frequency was about 4 events per year, but the 90th percentile was over 150; similarly, for those who did robbery, the medium was about 3, and the 90th percentile was 37. This clearly provides a strong incentive to provide a means for estimating those individual offending frequencies, since the high-λ individuals represent strong candidates for incarceration in order to maximize an incapacitative effect.

Recognizing this opportunity, Peter Greenwood (1982) developed an algorithm for estimating individual values of λ based on information on prior offending history, and proposed using that approach to achieve what he called "selective incapacitation." Those proposals were met with considerable opposition, partly because of concern about the "disparity" that would be introduced thereby (i.e., people convicted of the same offense would receive different sentences) and because of a concern of the inevitable false positives that would be associated with any such prediction. It is ironic that by 2011, virtually all the states in the United States, faced with severe budget constraints and looking to reduce their prison populations, but without increasing risks to public safety, are developing improved methods of "risk assessment" to identify individuals most appropriate to send to prison or to keep imprisoned. Of course, this introduces considerable "disparity" in the sentencing process, but other more pressing needs are being served.

One of the continuing questions about offending frequency is how it varies over the course of the career. There have been some who argue that that information is totally contained in the aggregate age-crime curve (typically represented as the ratio of arrests—or crimes—at age A divided by the population of age A). This curve typically rises quickly during early adolescence, reaches a peak at about age

18 (and the age of that peak will vary by crime type), and then declines steadily, but at different rates depending on the crime type; for example, the decline for burglary is relatively rapid, declining to a value half the peak by age 24, whereas the decline for aggravated assault is typically appreciably slower (i.e., more older people engage in aggravated assault than in burglary), not reaching its half-peak value until the early 30s. This highlights the variation across crime types, but the more important consideration precluding the use of the age-crime curve is the recognition that its curvature is a function not only of the changing offending frequency with age, but also the initiation of criminal careers (primarily but not exclusively during the rise portion of the age-crime curve) and the termination of careers (again, primarily but not exclusively during the decline portion of the curves).

Changing Patterns over the Course of the Career

As soon as one considers the multiplicity of crime types over the course of an individual criminal career, one is struck by the considerable complexity of career patterns. It is clearly important to know whether the offending frequency is a measure of the number of shopliftings or the number of murders, and certainly a high-λ shoplifter is of far less concern than a low-λ murderer. Thus, there needs to be attention directed at the relative seriousness of the different kinds of offenses. There was a period when that was given some attention (e.g., Wolfgang et al. 1985; Blumstein 1974), and efforts at developing such weights would certainly seem warranted, especially in the developing context of risk assessment, where "recidivism" (without much attention to the crime type of the recidivist event) is the dominant measure.

One approach that has been used for exploring the mix of offenses in a criminal career is the "crime-switch matrix," which provides an opportunity to estimate the probability of somebody whose last crime was of type i next committing a crime of type j. The diagonal of the matrix represents the probability of repeating crime-type i, and the diagonal does usually tend to be somewhat elevated, but not dramatically so. Most offenders, especially at younger ages, seem to be generalists rather than specialists, covering a reasonably broad mix of crime types over their criminal careers.

Another related issue is the degree to which we see a growth in seriousness of the offenses committed (for example, a typical pattern is one of increasing seriousness, moving from larceny to burglary to robbery); this escalation pattern is common in the juvenile years but much more difficult to pin down in later years.

Another related issue that links the duration of a career with the offending frequency is the potential for intermittency. In a pair of papers using CSDD data (Barnett, Blumstein, and Farrington 1987 and 1989), we found a way to distinguish between high-frequency and low-frequency offenders and also to get a measure of their career durations. It turned out that about 18 percent of the high-frequency offenders had a very visible gap in their offending patterns. We were not able to discern such gaps in the low-frequency offenders because the normal interval between their offenses was too long to enable us to identify clearly a period of diminished offending activity.

Many other issues that characterize criminal careers warrant extended discussion, Piquero et al. (2007) have provided some rich discussion in that direction.

Needs

Given the importance of generating useful knowledge about criminal careers, both for basic understanding of offending patterns and for use in a wide variety of policy arenas, is impressive how limited that knowledge is and how little effort seems to be currently directed at building that knowledge. In the United States, there were major efforts over 30 years ago to build a knowledge base, and there was considerable progress during that time, but there has been very little more recent effort to update the older results, which have aged over an interval during which many aspects of offending patterns could well have changed.

Most criminal career knowledge is parochial in the sense that it derives from studies of a particular longitudinal cohort at a particular site or is based on official record data from some single or small number of jurisdictions. Very little effort has been directed at identifying robust information about key criminal career parameters that prevail at multiple sites. Some longitudinal studies have been initiated at multiple sites with the hope of generalizable results, but the great majority of the efforts have been directed at findings from the individual sites, with relatively little attention to the identification of generic findings.

An even greater gap exists in the comparative literature on criminal careers in different countries. Given the general commonality in the methods used, it would appear to be particularly desirable to make some richer comparisons than have been attempted so far, say, between the criminal career findings in the CSDD and in those of Rolf Loeber's Pittsburgh Youth Study.

As indicated earlier in this chapter, it is important that we generate good estimates of the various criminal career parameters, but also to understand the factors affecting those parameters. In particular it is important that we get better knowledge about the effects of criminal justice policies and actions—particularly incarceration—on those parameters.

Some longitudinal studies have run 25 years or more, and they provide excellent opportunities for studying the intergenerational relationship in criminal careers, as they have begun tracking the children of those in the initial cohort. It might be particularly intriguing if one could follow not only the children being raised by the first- generation cohort, but also those who have been adopted or moved into other family settings in order to separate genetic and environmental transmission

Opportunities

One approach to the analysis of criminal careers that is different in many respects from many of the aspects highlighted here is the trajectory method developed and championed by Daniel Nagin (2005). That approach integrates information from a large number of individual trajectories into a handful of aggregate trajectories that capture much of the content. Looking at the trajectories of a cohort at different ages allows one to examine transition processes as individuals move from assignment to one particular aggregate trajectory to another. One can also examine the covariates associated with the different trajectories as a means of identifying prospective risk or protective factors.

One other important area for the study of criminal careers is in the realm of co-offending. Particularly at young ages, when co-offending is much more common than individual offending, it becomes important to be able to identify the criminal career parameters that cut across the joint participants. Particularly in an environment where there is a more senior "recruiter" initiating a "recruit," the subsequent criminal career of the recruit could become of considerable interest. This is an area with considerable interest, but the major difficulties in penetrating the area are associated with the need to maintain records on all possible co-offenders. The Add Health project at the Carolina Population Center of the University of North Carolina has some promise of making some significant headway in this area by drawing their samples within individual schools, thereby enhancing the likelihood that data on all the co-offenders would be captured.

Much of criminal career research has been dominated by research on longitudinal cohorts like those of CSSD, some having sample sizes perhaps even as much as an order of magnitude larger, but not dramatically larger. As modern information sharing within the criminal justice system becomes more widespread in formats that are more standardized, there will be richer information collected from official records. That will make it all the more important to find effective means for linking the large numbers of such records to the rich data available in the cohort studies. An important approach to enhancing those connections will be associated with estimates of the probability of arrest following a crime, and those estimates will vary with type of crime, offender characteristics, and jurisdictions. Research in those directions is very likely to be productive.

Another major realm of new opportunities should be associated with the rapidly growing attention being paid to two major areas of biotechnology—brain imaging and genetics. It is reasonable to anticipate that at least a significant subset of offenders will demonstrate very different dynamic fMRI brain patterns under various stimuli than others; it would be very surprising if their criminal careers were not similarly anomalous. To the extent that this distinctive subpopulation is found but found to be very small, then that information would still be interesting, but not very helpful for policy or operations. If, however, it is sufficiently sizable and if it represents the end of the offender distribution that is of primary concern, then that could be most useful.

We are also seeing major advances in understanding gene-environment interactions, and that understanding is likely to contribute to much better understanding of the nature of criminal careers. The pathbreaking work of Caspi et al. (2002) in highlighting the interaction of a particular gene (AMOA) with maltreatment of a child dictating whether that maltreatment would lead to violence as an adult provides an ideal example of how both factors need to be taken into account in understanding the nature of criminal careers. Each of the many longitudinal cohort studies—even those that were completed some time ago—could augment their data collection by taking a DNA sample of each of their cohort members. The research team is not likely to become genetic specialists, but retention of the data could open the possibility of pursuing further gene-environment interaction studies, as was done with the New Zealand cohort studied by Caspi et al. (2002).

It should be clear that there are many exciting opportunities for enhancing research on criminal careers, and that research is bound to be extremely valuable for generating understanding and for affecting public policy. What is needed is far more funding than has typically been available—and much more continued involvement by David Farrington in providing his typical leadership to those research endeavors.

References

Barnett, Arnold, Alfred Blumstein, and David P. Farrington. 1987. "Probabilistic Models of Youthful Criminal Careers." *Criminology* 25: 83–107.

Barnett, Arnold, Alfred Blumstein, and David P. Farrington. 1989. "A Prospective Test of a Criminal Career Model." *Criminology* 27: 373–388.

Blumstein, Alfred. 1974. "Seriousness Weights in an Index of Crime." *American Sociological Review*, 39: 854–864.

Blumstein, Alfred, Jacqueline Cohen, Alex Piquero, and Christy Visher. 2011. "Linking the Crime and Arrest Process to Measure Individual Crime Rates: Variations in Individual Arrest Risk per Crime (Q)" *Journal of Quantitative Criminology* 26: 533–548.

Blumstein, Alfred, Jacqueline Cohen, Jeffrey Roth, and Christy A. Visher. 1986. *Criminal Careers and "Career Criminals"*. Report of the National Academy of Sciences Panel on Research on Criminal Careers. Washington, DC: National Academy Press.

Caspi, Avshalom, Joseph McClay, Terrie E. Moffitt, Jonathan Mill, Judy Martin, Ian W. Craig, Alan Taylor, and Richie Poulton. 2002. "Role of Genotype in the Cycle of Violence in Maltreated Children." *Science* 2: 851–854.

Chaiken, Jan M., Marcia R. Chaiken, and Joyce E. Peterson. 1982. *Varieties of Criminal Behavior*. RAND Corporation Report No. R-2814/1-NIJ.

Farrington, David P., Jeremy W. Coid, and Donald J. West. 2009. "The Development of Offending from Age 8 to Age 50: Recent Findings from the Cambridge Study in Delinquent Development." *Monatsschrift fur Kriminologie und Strafrechtsreform* 92: 160–173.

Farrington, David P., Derek Jolliffe, Rolf Loeber, and Donni Lynn Homish. 2007. "How Many Offenses Are Really Committed per Juvenile Court Offender?" *Victims and Offenders* 2: 227–249.

Greenwood, Peter. 1982. *Selective Incapacitation*. RAND Corporation Report No. R-2815/1 NIJ.

Nagin, Daniel. 2005. *Group-Based Modeling of Development*. Cambridge: Harvard University Press.

Piquero, Alex, David P. Farrington, and Alfred Blumstein. 2007. *Key Issues in Criminal Career Research: New Analyses of the Cambridge Study in Delinquent Development*. Cambridge: Cambridge University Press.

Wolfgang, Marvin E., Robert M. Figlio, Paul E. Tracy, and Simon I. Singer. 1985. *National Survey of Crime Severity*. US Department of Justice Bureau of Justice Statistics Report No. NCJ 096017.

14

Research on Criminal Careers, Part 2

LOOKING BACK TO PREDICT AHEAD

Alex R. Piquero

What do Keith Richards, Jimmy Page, and David P. Farrington have in common? Aside from the fact that they are all British and enjoy rock and roll: they are all Officers of the British Empire. Such individuals are recognized for playing a distinguished role in any field and whose achievements are recognized nationally. David P. Farrington, of course, is recognized for his seminal work in the area of criminal careers, the topic of this chapter. Herein, I provide a brief overview of what is known about criminal careers and most importantly what I believe the future will bring. Throughout the chapter, I comment on how Farrington's work has made major contributions to aspects of theory, methods, and policy within the criminal careers area.

Brief History of Criminal Careers

The theoretical and empirical study of the longitudinal patterning of criminal careers has long been of interest to criminologists. This line of work has produced several insights into criminal careers, its onset, persistence, and eventual desistance, as well as the risk and protective factors associated with these and other criminal career dimensions (Blumstein et al. 1986; Piquero, Farrington, and Blumstein 2003; Wolfgang, Figlio, and Sellin 1972). Several well-established findings have been produced (Farrington 2003a: 2): (1) age of onset of offending is most typically between 8 and 14, earlier with self-report data and later with official records, while the age of desistance from offending (measured with official records) is most typically between 20 and 29; (2) prevalence of offending peaks in the late teenage years—between 15 and 19; (3) an early age of onset predicts a relatively long criminal career duration and the commission of relatively more offenses; (4) there is marked continuity in offending and antisocial behavior from childhood to the teenage years and to adulthood; (5) a small fraction of the population ("chronic offenders") commits a large fraction of all crimes; chronic offenders tend to have an early onset, a high individual offending frequency, and a long criminal career; (6) offending is more versatile than specialized (but specialization may increase with age); (7) the types of acts defined as offenses are elements of a larger syndrome of antisocial behavior that includes heavy drinking, reckless driving, promiscuous sex, and so on; (8) as people enter adulthood, they change from group to lone offending; (9) the reasons given for offending up to the late teenage years are quite variable, including excitement/enjoyment, escape from boredom, and emotional or utilitarian reasons, while after age 20 utilitarian motives become increasingly dominant; and (10) different types of offenses tend to be first committed at distinctively different ages.

These findings have led to the respecification of some criminological theories, but also have been instrumental in developing a strand of frameworks and theories that have come to be known as developmental / life course criminology (DLC). DLC focuses on how antisocial and criminal activity waxes and wanes across the life course, with specific attention being paid to age-graded risk/protective factors, the effect of life events on persistence/desistance, and the potential differences within individuals and across offending trajectories (Loeber and Le Blanc 1990; Piquero 2008).

Taken together, the theoretical and empirical research on criminal careers has also produced several relevant policy implications. One set of these implications stresses prevention/intervention efforts to be applied during the first decade of life. Evidence-based programs in this stage of the life course have concentrated efforts on family/parent training, altering cognitive and decision-making styles among offenders, both of which are aimed at improving a child's self-control (Piquero et al. 2009; 2010). A second set of policy proscriptions makes use of the criminal career data as information to be consulted when making sentencing decisions. Research on career length, for example, shows that on average, careers are not typically longer than 10 years, suggesting that long-term sentences that focus on severity to the exclusion of certainty are wasteful decisions and should be reconsidered (Blumstein and Piquero 2007).

The Cambridge Study in Delinquent Development

The Cambridge Study in Delinquent Development is a prospective longitudinal survey of over 400 London males that started when the males were about age eight and continues to this day. The main impetus behind the study was to trace the development of antisocial behavior among these men but also to assess as many risk and protective factors as early as possible in the life course. To date, the CSDD has produced almost 200 articles and several books summarizing many important theoretical issues and empirical questions (Farrington 2003b; Piquero, Farrington, and Blumstein 2007).

Space does not permit a review of the many questions investigated and findings uncovered with the CSDD data, but a few stand out. First, analyses have demonstrated the predictive power of variables at ages 8 to 10, and have also provided important insight into the effect of life events, like getting married or becoming unemployed, on crime. Second, data have also demonstrated continuity and discontinuity over time, not only in offending but in several areas related to offending such as overall health, employment, and substance use. Third, data have showed that getting convicted for the first time was followed by an increase in self-reported offending. Fourth, about 5 percent of families account for 50 percent of all convictions of all family members (mothers, fathers, sons, and daughters). Fifth, data show highly replicable risk factors over time and place, for example, low family income, low school achievement, and having convicted parents. Sixth, data on criminal convictions show that there is great variation in the longitudinal trajectory of criminal offending, with different groups of males following different pathways (in terms of shape and time-trend) of offending. The costs of their criminal offending has also been found to vary significantly, with the most high-rate chronic offenders exerting a significant "crime tax." Seventh, these offending trajectories also exhibit different health outcomes in midadulthood, with the most chronic offenders experiencing the most life-failure across many life domains including relationships, accidents, and overall health. Finally, the males engage in a great many delinquent/antisocial behaviors, the majority of which do not come to the attention of the formal criminal justice authorities. The future study of the males as they enter their fifties is certain to provide an even further description of their lives generally, as well as how crime and its outcomes manifest to their siblings, spouses, and children.

Contentious and Unresolved Issues

Although there have been many important discoveries about the nature and progression of criminal careers generally and with the CSDD in particular, there remain many contentious and unresolved issues that set the stage for an exciting research agenda going forward. Some of these contentious issues include (1) whether individual offending frequency varies with age; (2) whether the seriousness of offending escalates up to a certain age and then de-escalates, or whether it is much more stable with age; (3) whether early onset offenders differ in both risk/protective factors as well as offending frequency/seriousness over the life course; (4) whether the offenses among chronic offenders are more serious on average or whether chronic offenders differ in degree or in kind from nonchronic offenders; (5) whether crime-specific onset sequences are merely age-appropriate behavioral manifestations of some common underlying theoretical construct or if the onset of one type of behavior facilitates or acts as a stepping stone toward the onset of another; (6) whether the findings of offense versatility uncovered by the early twenties holds as some offenders transition into early and middle adulthood; and (7) whether the findings of positive marriage effects for altering crime trajectories is replicable for other life events.

Moving forward, there are many under- and uninvestigated issues that need much attention, and a few of these are listed here. First, research is needed on sorting out whether theories and key findings that have emerged on mainly white subjects (and mainly males) hold across other demographic profiles. Second, research is needed on expanding the types of life events that influence persistence/desistance in/from crime. Third, research is needed on policy-relevant offending populations in particular, to include longitudinal studies that track these offenders after criminal justice contact to determine whether and how such contacts influence offending trajectories. Fourth, research is needed on an expanded array of risk/protective factors that make use of recent discoveries in the areas of biology and genetics. Fifth, research is needed on further modification and respecification of classic criminological theories that are in need of updating to make use of recent criminal career findings. Sixth, research is needed on disentangling intermittency (the stops and starts within an offending career) and desistance. Seventh, research is needed on the contributions of situations and their attendant social context influences on criminal offender decision-making. Eighth, research is needed on the development and scrutiny of new methodological and statistical techniques as they are applied to criminal career data and the interpretations of study estimates.

Aside from these theoretical and methodological issues, research needs to devote considerable time on policy questions that emerge directly from criminal career research. For example, more and better knowledge of criminal career patterns and the risk/protective factors that relate to them can provide (*a*) data on average and residual career lengths, which, in turn, can help formulate more rational sentencing and punishment policies (Blumstein and Piquero 2007) and (*b*) knowledge of the factors that emerge early in life that influence criminal and other adverse behaviors so as to pinpoint targets for prevention/intervention programs. When considered together and with a focus on making cost-effective, evidence-based policies dealing with crime and its consequences, criminal career research is both basic *and* applied, and certainly of relevance as cities, states, and countries encounter strained budgets.

Closing Comments

Few criminologists have made the kind of contribution that has shaped the life course of the discipline. David P. Farrington is one of those individuals. He has been involved in some pioneering data collections throughout the world, including, of course, the CSDD. He has been instrumental in developing theory and research on the nature and patterning of criminal offending over the life course. He has unselfishly trained a cadre of undergraduate and graduate students. He has been involved in a large array of professional, national, and international study groups and projects. He has served as president of several major professional societies. And of course, he is one of the most prolific and highly cited criminologists. Yet one aspect of David Farrington's career and his legacy sometimes escapes notice: his archiving of—and collaborative provision of—the CSDD data. By providing criminologists access to the data he has spent a lifetime collecting with very little extramural funding, Farrington has given criminologists unique access to a data source that permits the study criminal career questions.

It goes without saying that David's research on criminal careers has shed important light on criminal careers and has also stimulated criminological theory as it continues to focus on the development of criminal offending over the life course. But what may be the more person-oriented contribution of his career is the man behind the scholar. To share one personal story, David recently took the time to write me an email indicating that I "was a great contributor." Of course, receiving this note from David was one of the most touching professional experiences of my life. David was one of the few scholars who took the time out of his busy schedule at the American Society of Criminology meetings when I was a beginning graduate student to talk with me about my training and interests. That gesture served as an example of what one should be like at that stage of one's career. Yet I think that David had that email slightly wrong. Instead, it is me and the field of criminology who should be thanking him as a "great contributor" for sharing his data, his intellect, and his passion for criminology to us all.

Looking back, Farrington did not predict that he would be a high-rate publisher in the area of criminal careers, but hard work, dedication, and collaboration with CSDD pioneer Donald West positioned him well. Looking forward, there is no doubt that David will continue his pursuit of important research topics, with a zest for scientific inquiry that is rare among the many colleagues who retire. David is a case exemplar of when and where a high-rate chronic offender is a good thing!

References

Blumstein, Alfred, Jacqueline Cohen, Jeffrey A. Roth, and Christy A. Visher. 1986. *Criminal Careers and "Career Criminals"*. Washington, DC: National Academy Press.

Blumstein, Alfred, and Alex R. Piquero. 2007. "Criminal Careers Research and Rational Sentencing Policy." *Criminology & Public Policy* 6: 679–688.

Farrington, David P. 2003a. "Developmental and Life-Course Criminology: Key Theoretical and Empirical Issues—The 2002 Sutherland Award Address." *Criminology* 41: 221–255.

Farrington, David P. 2003b. "Key Results from the First Forty Years of the Cambridge Study in Delinquent Development." In *Taking Stock of Delinquency: An Overview of Findings from Contemporary Longitudinal Studies*, edited by Terence P. Thornberry and Marvin D. Krohn, 147–184. Boston: Kluwer.

Loeber, Rolf, and Marc Le Blanc. 1990. "Toward a Developmental Criminology." In *Crime and Justice: A Review of Research*, vol. 12, edited by Michael Tonry and Norval Morris, 375–473. Chicago: University of Chicago Press.

Piquero, Alex R. 2008. "Taking Stock of Developmental Trajectories of Criminal Activity over the Life Course." In *The Long View of Crime: A Synthesis of Longitudinal Research*, edited by Akiva Liberman, 23–78. New York: Springer.

Piquero, Alex R., David P. Farrington, and Alfred Blumstein. 2003. "The Criminal Career Paradigm." In *Crime and Justice: A Review of Research*, vol. 30, edited by Michael Tonry, 359–506. Chicago: University of Chicago Press.

Piquero, Alex R., David P. Farrington, and Alfred Blumstein. 2007. *Key Issues in Criminal Career Research: New Analyses of the Cambridge Study in Delinquent Development*. New York: Cambridge University Press.

Piquero, Alex R., David P. Farrington, Brandon C. Welsh, Richard Tremblay, and Wesley Jennings. 2009. "Effects of Early Family/Parent Training Programs on Antisocial Behavior and Delinquency." *Journal of Experimental Criminology* 5: 83–120.

Piquero, Alex R., Wesley Jennings, and David P. Farrington. 2010. "On the Malleability of Self-Control: Theoretical and Policy Implications Regarding a General Theory of Crime." *Justice Quarterly* 27: 803–834.

Wolfgang, Marvin E., Robert M. Figlio, and Thorsten Sellin. 1972. *Delinquency in a Birth Cohort*. Chicago: University of Chicago Press.

15

Harvesting of Administrative Records

NEW PROBLEMS, GREAT POTENTIAL

Howard N. Snyder

Beginning in the early 1980s I directed a research team responsible for reporting national statistics of juvenile court activity in the United States. When this work began in the 1920s there was a short-lived attempt to collect detailed statistical information on each case processed by courts with juvenile responsibility nation-wide. The goal was impractical at that time. The data collection effort quickly reverted to courts reporting simple counts of cases processed in a year. In the late 1950s a new attempt was made to collect detailed case-level data from a sample of courts. The federal agency responsible for the data collection at the time developed a standardized case-level data collection form and asked courts to complete a form for each case processed and ship the completed forms back to Washington. This effort too was short-lived and once again the data collection system reverted back to courts' reporting annual case counts. When the federal government decided to contract out the data collection effort, our nongovernmental research organiza-tion was instructed to continue the current data collection procedures and also to explore yet again the feasibility of case-level data collection.

One possibility quickly presented itself. Now that the request for data was not coming directly from the federal government, many juvenile courts determined that they did not have time to complete the single-page annual form. Instead, they offered to provide our team with a copy of the data files underlying their auto-mated case management systems, suggesting that we could develop the needed case counts by analyzing the data files ourselves. It did not take long to realize the value of these administrative data files. They contained more detailed information on each case processed than any case-level data collection form would ever have attempted to collect. The data also had been used by the courts to support their ongoing case processing, management, reporting, and evaluation activities so we had more confidence in the quality of these data than we had in the information captured on aggregate reporting forms that had little relevance to the courts.

There were problems to be addressed. Each file was constructed to reflect the nature of local court policies and practices. Also, each administrative data file had its own unique data structures, variables, and coding values. However, we gradually learned to write programs to extract and standardize similar data from these files. The standardized data mimicked in many ways the data that would have been generated by the case-level data collection form developed in the late 1950s if it had ever been successfully implemented. In the early 1980s, with the development of automated management information systems in juvenile courts, we were at the beginning of an era when a new method of data collection to support national juvenile court statistics had become possible. For several years our team explored the practicality and utility of harvesting existing administrative databases as the foundation of a national statistical system.

Some were uncertain that a national statistical effort could be based on administrative data, including the US Department of Justice (DOJ), which was legislatively mandated to collect these statistics and was the source of our funding. So DOJ established an advisory committee to review our work and determine the feasibility of our novel model of data collection. The four members of the advisory committee were Alfred Blumstein, Malcolm Klein, Daniel Kasprzyk, and David Farrington. Over a multiyear period the advisory committee worked closely with the research team to develop a detailed understanding of the work, the problems encountered, and the outcomes. In the end the committee strongly endorsed our new method for collecting juvenile court information, saying that it was the most practical and cost-efficient mode to achieve our goals. David Farrington was an ardent supporter. Not only did he use and promote the detailed national estimates of case characteristics flowing from the work, he used the harvested administrative databases as the basis of his own research, displaying their benefits beyond the production of national statistics. David's support (and that of the other advisors) enabled our research team to continue expanding our collection of administrative databases and to develop the techniques to facilitate their use and exploitation. These techniques and the example set by this work established the precedent of using administrative data as the basis of national statistical efforts.

Growing Need for Administrative Databases

Many national statistical systems are facing serious challenges. Established data collection methods are increasing in cost, are becoming less effective, and are not meeting the changing demands of policymakers and the public. The problems faced by the National Criminal Victimization Survey (NCVS) in the United States are typical of some of these issues. The NCVS is a large household survey that asks residents about the property and violent victimizations they have experienced. Funding for this effort has not kept up with the cost of data collection; as a result, the sample size has declined and standard errors have grown to the point where it is difficult to document moderate changes in crime from year to year. For the NCVS this problem has been exacerbated with the large decline in crime rates in the United States. That is, while it is beneficial for society, the declining crime rates mean that a growing proportion of households contacted by the NCVS report no crime, decreasing the efficiency of the sample. All self-reported crime surveys (including the NCVS) are dogged with criticisms that certain crimes are underreported (e.g., domestic violence), that changes in relatively rare events (e.g., sexual assaults) cannot be monitored, and that certain crime types are missed completely by the survey (e.g., crimes against young children). National statistical efforts based on obtaining responses from a large sample of entities (whether they be persons, households, or institutions) are encountering more difficulty maintaining the integrity of the sample as voluntary response rates decline and respondent fatigue increases. Added to these concerns, policymakers and the public are asking or expecting national statistical efforts to generate subnational (e.g., state or city) statistics that require far larger samples. They are also asking these efforts to produce more current information (e.g., last month's crime rates) that requires rapid data collection and analysis.

Some of these weaknesses could be addressed with more funding. However, whenever more funds are requested, funding agencies rightfully ask for alternative solutions; but viable alternatives are becoming harder to find. For example, household panel surveys such as the NCVS could be replaced by less expensive cross-sectional efforts in which the sample members change for each wave of the survey. For years many national cross-sectional data collection efforts have successfully employed random digit dialing (RDD) techniques. RDD is relatively easy to implement and the statistical parameters of the data (at least in the past) could be determined. However, RDD is losing support in the statistical community. The transition from landlines to cellular telephones with number portability has greatly diminished the capability of RRD samples to generate geographically representative samples (especially for certain segments of the population). For many national statistical efforts to address their criticisms and meet their growing demands, new data collection options must be considered and tested.

Tapping the Potential of Administrative Data

One data collection alternative that can cost-effectively address many of described weaknesses of national statistical efforts while providing both detailed information at subnational levels and current statistics is the harvesting of administrative datasets. Administrative data, by definition, are not collected to support national statistics. They are collected to meet daily information needs of the entities that host them. In the areas of crime and justice, such data sets include those from law enforcement, the courts, and probation/correction agencies, as well as those housed in criminal history repositories. Data from these management information systems overcome many of the concerns raised about current national collection efforts. These systems capture detailed attribute data on all (i.e., a census, not a sample of) matters handled—including rare events. They hold the most current information possible on these matters and the activities of the agency. Users of these data can have confidence in their general validity because the data are used to support the daily activities of the agency or agencies involved. Finally, these data are collected by local entities, so they are able to support the development of local and subnational estimates with a detail that is impossible via most (if not all) other practical means of data collection.

Considerable effort must be expended prior to the analysis of administrative data. This work \involves (1) establishing data transfer agreements with the administrative agencies, (2) developing a detailed understanding of the structure, logic, and content of the administrative database, and (3) creating programs able to extract the needed statistical information from the administrative databases. Traditional statistical systems obtain the consent of their subjects before the data are collected; administrative data collectors must seek the approval of the cooperating agencies before that data will be transmitted. This agreement between the administrative agency (i.e., the original data collector) and the statistical team wishing to harvest these data should be formalized in a Memorandum of Understanding (MOU). A typical MOU should detail what data will be harvested, how these data will be used, how they will be protected from misuse, how the personally identifiable information will be secured, and what will happen to the data at the end of the project period. MOUs should be thought through carefully by each party involved. Each party has its own issues and concerns, and a clear statement of how they will be addressed should be clearly specified before the data are transmitted.

Users of administrative data must develop a detailed understanding of the data they are to receive. Administrative data are not originally collected to support statistical efforts so their internal structures, logic, and coding options are often problematic for statisticians. Most administrative data systems are designed to support the handling of a single case and not to facilitate the summarization of many cases. For example, many fields in a law enforcement administrative data-set are free-text fields that are easily understood by someone reviewing the case. That is, it is not uncommon for the offense fields with such data sets to contain scores of spellings for a single charge. This problematic characteristic of administrative data-sets is magnified when data sets from multiple agencies are combined for statistical analysis. Before statisticians can extract their information from administrative data-sets, they must write relatively complex data extraction programs that understand the structure and logic of the data sets. These programs must be carefully tested to ensure that the information is accurately distilled from the administrative data and that the programs deal successfully with the many nuisances (i.e., inconsistencies, historical changes, and logical errors) that are always an integral part of administrative data.

With the MOU in place, with an understanding of raw data, and with the extract programs written and tested, the statistician can begin the harvesting the administrative data. The simplest approach is to request a copy of the complete administrative data-set. This requires the minimal level of effort from the administrative agency. However, for various reasons, both parties may be more comfortable transmitting a portion of the data set (e.g., all court cases disposed in a single year). Either way, statisticians quickly obtain a substantial quantity of information that details the matters handled by the administrative agency. The actual cost of administrative data collection and processing is typically far less than original statistical data collection efforts, with the relative cost diminishing with each subsequent request for data from the same administrative agency.

It is instructive to speculate on the ways administrative data could be used to support national statistical efforts. The juvenile court work discussed earlier has attempted to collect data from the universe of juvenile courts in the nation. A more practical data collection model is to select a representative of entities and harvest their administrative data. Using this approach, if some members of the sample do not have administrative data, funds could be provided to support their development—an outcome that would serve the needs of both the local agency and the statistical project. Under another model, administrative data could be used to supplement the data collection activities of a traditional system. For example, the cost of statistical systems based on prison inmate interviews increases as items are added to the interview protocol. Administrative data could be used to reduce the cost of such interviews by providing information (e.g., arrest and conviction histories) that would otherwise have to be collected directly from the inmate during the interview. Finally, administrative data could be used to improve the efficiency of a sampling design. For example, the NCVS could tap local law enforcement administrative records to identify neighborhoods with a high victimization rate and then oversample households in these areas to yield a more productive sampling frame.

As administrative data-sets continue to expand in coverage and quality, statisticians will become more and more aware of their potential and their value. To take advantage of these data, statisticians (and their students) must develop a new set of skills (e.g., designing data extraction software) and new tools for accessing the accuracy and completeness of these data (i.e., new measures of error and response bias). With relatively low cost and the capability to provide detailed and recent information from large samples, administrative information systems will become a major source of raw data for many national statistical efforts. As an example of this potential, it is an interesting academic exercise to consider how an effort as large and complex as a national census might be accomplished using only administrative data. In the United States there are several large national administrative data-sets that capture information on overlapping portions of the US population (e.g., birth records, school records, tax records, Social Security records, welfare records, and death records). If the numerous privacy concerns could be successfully addressed, these administrative data resources could yield detailed information on an extremely high proportion of the US population. If records on an individual could be linked across data sets and duplicated records eliminated (both complex data-processing tasks), the resulting information would likely produce a respectable national census. While a national census based on administrative data may be far in the future, it is clear that many national statistical systems will soon be exploiting the great potential of administrative data.

16

Twenty-five Years of Developmental Criminology

WHAT WE KNOW, WHAT WE NEED TO KNOW

Marc Le Blanc

In 1980, during part of a sabbatical in Montreal, David Farrington was very active in preparing publications. If a criminal career specialist had assessed his onset and frequency, he could have predicted a massive contribution to criminology and the diversity of the subjects that he would master. I thank him for his inspiring example and his influence on our thinking.

Developmental criminology describes within-individual changes, along the life course, for all forms of deviant behavior and explains their development (onset, continuity, and extinction). It shares many constructs and empirical results with the criminal career paradigm and, particularly, a preference for longitudinal data (Blumstein et al. 1986; Piquero, Farrington and Blumstein 2007). It adopts concepts from developmental psychology and the chaos-order paradigm in science. This chapter sets out to answer two key questions about the development of deviant behavior: What do we know? and What do we need to know? The full data, literature reviews, and arguments for the developmental criminology paradigm have been stated in several papers (Le Blanc and Fréchette 1989; Loeber and Le Blanc 1990; Le Blanc and Loeber 1998; Le Blanc 2002; 2006; 2009).

The Construct of Deviant Behavior

The key phenomenon to be studied by developmental criminology is the course of conformity to conventional standards of behavior during the life of an individual. This notion of conformity is the classical position (Hirschi 1969). It is defined by population behavioral norms for a particular society at a specific historical period. Laws delimit many of these behavioral norms, including crimes that are defined by the criminal code, school attendance, and many other deviant behaviors. All the behaviors of the deviant behavior syndrome can be measured through a self-reported questionnaire, and many forms of deviant behavior can be assessed with official records: criminal, driving, school, medical, and so on.

Over the last 40 years, the vast majority of criminologists have accepted the proposition that all types of deviant behaviors are part of a latent construct. Theorists such as Gottfredson and Hirschi (1990) state that all forms of deviant behaviors are equivalent to crime. That position has received support from numerous empirical studies of self-reported deviance as well as officially recorded crime (Le Blanc and Bouthillier 2003). In addition, researchers have identified metadimensions such as overt and covert antisocial behaviors, and authority conflict (Loeber, Keenan, and Zhang 1998).

Le Blanc and Bouthillier (2003) proposed and tested the idea that the construct of deviant behavior is a hierarchical domain of behaviors. This model states that deviant behavior is composed of four subconstructs: covert, overt, authority conflict, and reckless behaviors. The subconstructs are composed of 12 forms of deviant behavior: motor vehicle use, sex, drugs, disorderly conduct, gambling, authority conflict at home and school, vandalism, violence, fraud, theft, and sexual aggression.

The deviant behavior syndrome manifests itself in different ways along the life span. It is a heterotypic phenomenon, and, as a consequence, there is continuity and change in the nature of the deviant behaviors that compose the syndrome through the life course. Le Blanc (2006) illustrates this phenomenon using the ages of onset and offset from self-reported data for a sample of adjudicated males of the 1960s generation.

The Course of Deviant Behavior

Developmental criminology states that the course of deviant behavior is a cycle that takes the form of an inverse U-shape for every individual during their life course (in criminology known as the age-crime curve). It remains to be tested that this statement applies to all forms of the deviant behavior syndrome. In addition, criminologists now agree on the static and dynamic measures of offending (Le Blanc and Loeber 1998; Piquero, Farrington, and Blumstein 2003). The static measures are participation, frequency, lambda, seriousness, variety, and crime mix. The dynamic measures are age of onset, age of termination, duration, and crime switching. It is hypothesized that they can be applied to describe the course of all forms of deviant behavior in the hierarchical structure of this latent construct.

Since individuals vary in the timing and the height of their inverse U-shape trajectory of deviant behavior, a task of criminology is to identify the mechanisms that create the form of this trajectory, and the mechanisms that influence quantitative and qualitative changes on that trajectory along the life course

Quantitative changes. These are defined in terms of growth and decline in deviant behavior. First, quantitative changes are manifested by the degree of change in participation. Second, quantitative changes correspond to the direction of change; they manifest themselves in the form of progression or regression in frequency of the behaviors. Third, quantitative changes refer to the rate of change or the velocity, primarily in the form of the degree of change over time (lambda). In addition, the growth can be inferred from the relationships between the onset of deviant behavior and its frequency (acceleration), variety (diversification), and duration (stabilization).

Finally, there is a gradual desistance from deviant behavior. This process is observable through deceleration (decrease in frequency), specialization (decrease in variety), and reaching a ceiling (stabilizing seriousness). Our theoretical position is that these kinds of quantitative changes, which have been demonstrated for offending, can be replicated for all other types of deviant behavior.

Qualitative changes. These changes refer to something new, something that is different from what went on before, and something that is more complex according to Werner's (1957) ontogenetic principle, which stated that "whenever development occurs it proceeds from a state of relative globality and lack of differentiation to a state of increasing differentiation, articulation, and hierarchic integration" (126).

The changes in the nature of the behavior tend to be subdivided into a developmental sequence that comprises a certain number of hierarchical stages. There is a developmental sequence in criminal activity represented by different stages of crime seriousness between the age of onset and offset of criminal activity. Le Blanc and Loeber's (1998) review indicates that there is clearly a developmental sequence for some other types of deviant behavior, such as violence (Loeber and Hay 1997) and drug use (Kandel 2002). It is hypothesized that future research will demonstrate such sequences for all other forms of deviant behaviors.

The qualitative changes can be analyzed in terms of escalation to de-escalation on a developmental sequence. Escalation implies conservation of the behaviors that are part of a person's repertory (innovation, the introduction of a new behavior; retention, maintaining a less serious type of behavior while moving to more serious behaviors), synchrony of the development of different types of deviant behavior (simultaneity, attaining the same level of seriousness on two or more types of behavior); and adjacency, the embedding of deviant behavior of different types, and paths (going through parts or the whole sequence). The escalation hypothesis for criminal activity is well established. However, it is not the case now for the de-escalation hypothesis (Le Blanc 2002). I propose that escalation and de-escalation apply to all forms of deviant behaviors.

Trajectories. The quantitative and qualitative changes constitute an individual's trajectory of deviant behavior. Individual trajectories vary in timing (onset and offset) and degree (frequency, seriousness) and nature (behavioral content, synchrony, conservation). As a consequence, each individual displays a specific reverse U-shaped course of development.

Following Wolfgang, Figlio, and Sellin's (1972) landmark study, criminologists have identified developmental trajectories of criminal activity. To do so, they have used different methodologies (Le Blanc 2002), starting with transition matrices. Later on, they employed ad hoc dynamic classification (cross-tabulation of measures of deviant behaviors at two or more times). This led to the use of group detection methods (cluster analysis, group-based modeling, growth curve modeling, latent trajectory modeling, and others). All the studies using different methodologies have detected between 3 and 10 trajectories, ranging from the abstinent trajectory to the major persistent trajectory over time. The number and the nature of the trajectories varied with the nature of the sample (representative samples or justice system samples, including arrestees and adjudicated males), the racial and gender composition of the samples, the age span of the study, and other sample characteristics.

I propose that there are three metatrajectories for all types of deviant behaviors, which can be divided into more specific trajectories. The three metatrajectories are called persistent, transitory, and common. Research shows that each of these trajectories can be described with the static and dynamic parameters and in terms of the quantitative and qualitative changes mentioned above.

The persistent trajectory (Le Blanc and Fréchette 1989) or life course trajectory (Moffitt 1993) is well known. The individuals that follow this trajectory represent a small fraction of the population that commits a large proportion of all deviant behaviors. Individuals in this trajectory start during childhood; the growth of deviant behavior is rapid; their deviant behavior peaks toward the end of adolescence; they maintain a high level of deviance until the middle of their twenties; and their deviant behavior declines and ends on average by their midthirties. The persistent trajectory also applies to many other forms of deviant behavior and crime.

The transitory or temporary trajectory (Le Blanc and Fréchette 1989) or adolescence-limited trajectory (Moffitt 1993) is also well known. The individuals who follow this trajectory represent an important percentage of the deviant population. They start during adolescence; the growth is rapid and significant during the middle of adolescence; the decline is at the end of adolescence; and they often display an episode of relatively minor deviant behavior in their early twenties. This metatrajectory is also observable during adulthood for a late onset group. In addition, the temporary deviant adopts a similar trajectory for some forms of deviant behavior and crime.

The last trajectory is common deviant behavior. Behaviors in this trajectory are occasional in an otherwise law-abiding existence. The deviant behaviors in this trajectory occur mainly around the middle of adolescence, and are manifested by acts of vandalism, minor theft, drugs, and public mischief. This metatrajectory is an epiphenomenon of adolescence. I expect that future research will show that these three metatrajectories also apply to the development of other forms of deviant behaviors.

The Self-Regulation of Deviant Behavior

Criminology is well equipped to describe the course of deviant behavior and has identified many of the mechanisms explaining its course. However, deviant behavior has never been presented as a self-organizing phenomenon. Drawing from the developmental perspective in psychology and the chaos-order paradigm in science, Le Blanc (2006, 2009) proposed that deviant behavior, and all its forms, can be partly characterized as a self-regulating phenomenon. From this perspective,

I adopt the following principles that extend the developmental paradigm: the contextuality of the development of deviant behavior, the orthogenic principle, the sensitivity to the initial condition, the principle of probabilistic epigenesis, and that development is interactional. Deviant behavior tends to be in a state of chaos when there is a low probability of the behavior. This situation is common during adolescence when the deviant syndrome tends to attains its peak. In accordance with the principle of self-similarity, I am proposing that the same tools can be used to understand the developmental sequence of all the forms of deviant behavior.

Self-organization is a characteristic of systems, as well as all living and human beings. Developmentalists recognize the importance of the self-regulating process and that individuals are active in their development. An individual gives shape to his or her experience by activating or deactivating environments. Self-organization in the chaos-order paradigm means that "human beings can control their own control parameters, giving them the capability to make bifurcations within their own dynamical schemes and complex dynamical systems. Sentient beings can thus learn their own response diagrams, so to speak, can learn to navigate them, and can imagine extrapolations of those diagrams and test a new universe of self" (Abraham 1995, 41). Latent trajectory modeling is a tool to test self-organization of forms of deviant behaviors (Le Blanc 2009).

There are two metamechanisms of the personal control of deviant behavior in our generic control theory (Le Blanc 1997): self-control and social control. Each is modulated by the social status and the biological capacity of the individual. Self and social controls synthesize numerous factors that have been identified in the empirical literature as having a potential impact on deviant behavior. Le Blanc (2006) reviewed knowledge of the course of self-control and social control. From a developmental criminology perspective, their courses should interact with the course of deviant behavior.

The Course of Self-Control

In 1990, Gottfredson and Hirschi provided a new impetus to criminological research by restating that the psychological dimension is a crucial explanatory factor of crime. Low self-control theory was increasingly tested with cross-sectional and longitudinal data. There have been attempts to assess the construct validity of low self-control as a multidimensional construct. This theory has two major postulates: low self-control is the most important causal factor in explaining antisocial behaviors and it remains stable in antisocial individuals. Since it was proposed that the course of deviant behavior should be described in terms of quantitative and qualitative changes and developmental trajectories, I propose that these analytical tools apply to the development of self-control.

Quantitative changes. The literature on the development of personality has documented the growth and decline in individuals' self-control. It recognizes that growth is governed by the aging-stability law. Accordingly, self-control tends to stabilize and become less likely to change as a person grows older.

Specialists of personality indicate that both stability and change are observable in the development of self-control (Morizot and Le Blanc 2003). On the one hand, estimates of the rank-order continuity show that individual differences in self-control tend to become more stable across time. On the other hand, the assessment of the mean-level continuity reveals a nontrivial maturational trend toward a better psychological adjustment. This indicates that self-control traits are not developmentally static predispositions. Moreover, measurement invariance across groups and across time suggests that the self-control structure of traits is a meaningful model for studying very different types of individuals' self-control. However, adjudicated males and men in the general population show clear differences in self-control development. As a consequence, Gottfredson and Hirschi's (1990) position that low self-control remains stable across the life course is a gross statement of its development of self-control.

Qualitative changes and trajectories. Even if the results of the quantitative change studies support the hypothesis of a normative maturation in the direction of a better self-control, there is still no evidence for discrete stages. However, the marked slowing of the maturation rate after age 30 may be an indication that individuals have reached some sort of qualitatively distinct psychological adaptation.

The quantitative and qualitative changes that take place in the course of the development of self-control constitute a general trajectory. However, few scientists have identified trajectories of personality development. Morizot and Le Blanc (2003b; 2005), using a representative sample of men, identified four self-control developmental trajectories: Overcontrolled, Undercontrolled, Resilients, and Anomics. The level of antisocial behavior increased from the better to the less mature trajectories. In addition, they identified similar self-control developmental trajectories in the adjudicated sample and each of them was differentially related to antisocial behavior across time.

I conclude that the data on the development of self-control shows that there is ample knowledge of the quantitative and qualitative changes in the course self-control during the life span. In addition, there is an emerging knowledge of the trajectories of self-control in the general population and for low self-control groups. All these results challenge Gottfredson and Hirschi's (1990) view that low self-control remains stable across the life course for antisocial individuals.

The Course of Social Control

Criminologists have made considerable conceptual efforts in defining social controls and studying their interactions with various forms of deviant behavior. The notion of social control involves three constructs that are modulated by social status: bonds to society (attachment and commitment), internal and external constraints, and models and lifestyles. There are some rare indications in the criminological literature about continuity and change in social controls during the life course (Le Blanc 2006). Bonds, models, and constraints seem to be evolving according to the maturational hypothesis. However, there is little evidence on developmental sequences except for peer relations and play. In addition, descriptions of developmental trajectories of social controls have not been published.

The Developmental Interactions between the Courses of Self-Control, Social Control, and Deviant Behavior

Le Blanc (2006) proposed a theoretical model of the developmental interactions between controls and deviant behavior. Latent trajectory modeling is a statistical procedure that allows the analysis of these developmental interactions. However, little work has been done yet in this area (Morizot and Le Blanc 2007).

Conclusion

Over the years, criminologists have been creative with the measurement of deviant behavior, and have been imaginative in proposing explanatory constructs such as self-control and social control and their components. In addition, criminologists have been effective in testing interactional models of various complexities.

Developmental criminology, starting in the 1980s, focused on individual changes in deviant behavior along the life course. Deviant behavior was conceived and tested as a hierarchical domain of behaviors. Along with the criminal career paradigm, developmental criminology used common static and dynamic descriptive measures of deviant behavior. Developmental criminology's contribution was based on developmental psychology and the chaos-order paradigm, and proposed an understanding of the processes that support continuity and change in the cycle of deviant behavior as a self-regulating phenomenon. These processes manifest themselves as quantitative and qualitative mechanisms of change that construct developmental trajectories. The fundamental argument of developmental crimi-nology is that the operationalization of the development of deviant behavior can be applied to the explanatory constructs of self- and social control.

The challenge for criminologists is the complexity of the developmental explana-tion of deviant behavior. They accept that deviant behavior is the result of multiple influences along the life course: biological, psychological, social, cultural, and others at the levels of crime, criminal, and criminality. However, criminologists' ability to describe how these influences interact is limited. There is a large gap between the perception of the complexities of these interactions, their discursive statements, the operational models describing them, and the results of the empirical tests of these models. The discursive statements and models of criminology are often characterized by oversimplification, and this is evident, for example, in the study of low self-control. There are numerous explanations for that gap: the limited cognitive capacity to consider simultaneously many factors from different levels of explanation in continuous interactions, the limited ability to communicate the perceptions of these interactions, and the unavailability of an appropriate technology to model them. Criminology is inefficient in characterizing developmental interactions because theories and models are linear, even if they are sometimes interactional and recursive or if they consider multiple levels of explanations. Particularly, these models do not take completely into account numerous and complex interactions and the random component that is part of development. This is independent of the limits of the available statistical tools.

The theories and models suffer from two difficulties: considering the maximum possible number of interactions that can be perceived and integrating a random component in the development of behavior and self- and social controls. To overcome these difficulties, I used Briggs and Peat's (1989) "phase space map" to expose the hidden complexities of system changes over time. Beyond that understanding of developmental interactions, there is a need for more appropriate statistical tools to test complex self-regulating explanatory models.

Acknowledgments

The Montreal Two-Sample Two-Generation Longitudinal Study (MTSTGLS) was supported over the years by the Social Sciences and Humanities Research Council of Canada (SSHRC), the Fonds Québécois pour la Recherche Sociale (FQRS), and the Fonds pour la Formation des Chercheurs et L'action Concertée du Québec (FCACQ).

References

Abraham, Frederick D. 1995. "Introduction to Dynamics: A Basic Language: A Basic Metamodeling Strategy." In *Chaos Theory in Psychology*, edited by Frederick D. Abraham and Albert R. Gilgen, 31–52. Westport, CT: Greenwood Press.

Blumstein, Alfred, Jacqueline Cohen, Jeffrey A. Roth, and Christy A. Visher. 1986. *Criminal Careers and "Career Criminals"*. Washington, DC: National Academy Press.

Briggs, John, and F. D. Peat. 1989. *Turbulent Mirror*. New York: Harper and Row.

Gottfredson, Michael A., and Travis Hirschi. 1990. *A General Theory of Crime*. Stanford, CA: Stanford University Press.

Hirschi, Travis. 1969. *Causes of Delinquency*. Berkeley: University of California Press.

Kandel, Denise. 2002. *Stages and Pathways of Drug Involvement*. Cambridge: Cambridge University Press.

Le Blanc, Marc. 1997. "A Generic Control Theory of the Criminal Phenomenon, the Structural and the Dynamical Statements of an Integrative Multilayered Control Theory." *Advances in Theoretical Criminology* 7: 215–286.

Le Blanc, Marc. 2002. "The Offending Cycle, Escalation and De-escalation in Delinquent Behavior: A Challenge for Criminology." *International Journal of Comparative and Applied Criminal Justice* 26: 53–84.

Le Blanc, Marc. 2006. "Self-Control and Social Control of Deviant Behavior in Context: Development and Interactions along the Life Course." In *The Explanation of Crime: Context, Mechanisms, and Development*, edited by Per-Olof Wikström and Robert Sampson, 195–242. Cambridge: Cambridge University Press.

Le Blanc, Marc. 2009. "The Development of Deviant Behavior, Its Self-Regulation." *Monatsschrift fuer Kriminologie und Strafrechtsreform* 91: 117–136.

Le Blanc, Marc, and Christiane Bouthillier. 2003. "A Developmental Test of the General Deviance Syndrome with Adjudicated Girls and Boys Using Hierarchical Confirmatory Factor Analysis." *Criminal Behavior and Mental Health* 13: 81–105.

Le Blanc, Marc, and Marcel Fréchette. 1989. *Male Criminal Activity: Its Development from Childhood to Adulthood.* New York: Springer.

Le Blanc, Marc, and Rolf Loeber. 1998. "Developmental Criminology Upgraded." In *Crime and Justice: A Review of Research*, vol. 23, edited by Michael Tonry, 149–232. Chicago: University of Chicago Press.

Loeber, Rolf, and Dale Hay. 1997. "Key Issues in the Development of Aggression and Violence from Childhood to Early Adulthood." *Annual Review in Psychology* 48: 371–410.

Loeber, Rolf, Kate Keenan, and Quan Zhang. 1998. "Boys' Experimentation and Persistence in Developmental Pathways toward Serious Delinquency." *Journal of Child and Family Studies* 6: 321–357.

Loeber, Rolf, and Marc Le Blanc. 1990. "Toward a Developmental Criminology." In *Crime and Justice: A Review of Research*, vol. 12, edited by Michael Tonry and Norval Morris, 375–473. Chicago: University of Chicago Press.

Moffitt, Terri E. 1993. "Adolescence-Limited and Life-Course Persistent Antisocial Behavior: A Developmental Taxonomy." *Psychological Review* 100: 674–701.

Morizot, Julien, and Marc Le Blanc. 2003a. "Continuity and Change in Personality from Mid-adolescence to Mid-life: A 25-Year Longitudinal Study Comparing Conventional and Adjudicated Men." *Journal of Personality* 71: 705–755.

Morizot, Julien, and Marc Le Blanc. 2003b. "Searching for a Developmental Typology of Personality in an Adjudicated Men's Sample and Its Relations to Antisocial Behaviors from Adolescence to Midlife: A 25-Year Longitudinal Study." *Criminal Behavior and Mental Health* 13: 241–277.

Morizot, Julien, and Marc Le Blanc. 2005. "Searching for Developmental Types of Personality and Their Relation to Antisocial Behaviors: A 25-Year Longitudinal Study Comparing Conventional and Adjudicated Men from Adolescence to Midlife." *Journal of Personality* 73: 139–182.

Morizot, Julien, and Marc Le Blanc. 2007. "Behavioral, Self, and Social Control Predictors of the Normative Process of Desistance from Criminal Activity: A Test of the Launch- and Contemporaneous-Effect Models." *Journal of Contemporary Criminal Justice* 21: 50–71.

Piquero, Alex R., David P. Farrington, and Alfred Blumstein. 2003. "The Criminal Career Paradigm." In *Crime and Justice: A Review of Research*, vol. 30, edited by Michael Tonry, 359–506. Chicago: University of Chicago Press.

Piquero, Alex R., David P. Farrington, and Alfred Blumstein. 2007. *Key Issues in Criminal Career Research.* Cambridge: Cambridge University Press.

Werner, Heinz. 1957. "The Concept of Development from a Comparative and Organismic Point of View." In *The Concept of Development*, edited by Dale B. Harris, 125–148. Minneapolis: University of Minnesota Press.

Wolfgang, Marvin E., Robert M. Figlio, and Thorsten Sellin. 1972. *Delinquency in a Birth Cohort*. Chicago: University of Chicago Press.

17

Pushing Back the Frontiers of Knowledge on Desistance from Crime

Lila Kazemian

Over the course of the past four decades, David Farrington's research has significantly enhanced our understanding of crime. His seminal study (in collaboration with Donald West), the Cambridge Study in Delinquent Development, has been particularly important in advancing knowledge on criminal careers and desistance. The current chapter provides a brief overview of the state of knowledge on desistance from crime, underlines some of the most significant developments in this area of research, and highlights David Farrington's key contributions.

What Have We Learned about Desistance from Crime?

The value and importance of studying desistance, particularly for postonset intervention efforts, have been stressed abundantly in the literature and will not be reiterated here (see Kazemian 2007; Laub and Sampson 2001). Predictors of desistance highlighted in the literature include, among others, the strength and quality of bonds to sources of informal social control (Bersani, Laub, and Nieuwbeerta 2009; Farrington and West 1995; Laub and Sampson 2003), human agency and the development of a prosocial identity (Maruna 2001), interactions with deviant peers (Warr 1998) or prosocial coworkers (Wright and Cullen 2004), substance use (Giordano et al. 2002; Maruna 2001), exposure to strain (Eitle 2010), and stigmatization resulting from contacts with the criminal justice system (Maruna 2001). Some key developments in the growing literature on desistance are noteworthy.

First, many researchers have acknowledged the relevance of perceiving desistance as a process rather than an event (Bottoms et al. 2004; Bushway et al. 2001; Loeber and Le Blanc 1990). It has been acknowledged that the cessation of offending activities is unlikely to occur suddenly, especially among individuals who have been highly active in offending from a young age. The failure to study the progressive changes that occur throughout the criminal career may overlook the distinct pathways to termination from crime that characterize different individuals.

Second, many researchers agree that desistance is likely to occur as a result of the combined influence of social and cognitive factors (Bottoms et al. 2004; Giordano et al. 2002; LeBel et al. 2008). Farrall and Bowling (1999, 261) highlighted the importance of integrating both human agency and situational circumstances in the analysis of desistance, and warned researchers about the inaccuracy of regarding individuals as either "super-agents" (i.e., with perfect free will) or "super-dupes" (whose actions are solely determined by wider social forces). LeBel et al. (2008) found support for a "subjective-social model," suggesting that subjective states exert direct and indirect effects on recidivism through their impact on social circumstances. Individuals with a positive mindset and supportive social networks are better equipped to face problems, resist temptations, and avoid setbacks, provided that the obstacles are not excessive. Desistance is thus regarded as a system of interactions between various internal and external factors.

Third, it has been suggested that offender classifications in desistance research, namely, the contrast between desisters and persisters, may not be accurate (Laub and Sampson 2003; Maruna 2001). Maruna (2001) argued that desisting and persisting offenders are similar individuals at different stages of the process of change, and not inherently distinct individuals. In addition, some prior research has underlined the difficulties in making accurate long-term predictions about desistance based on early risk factors (Kazemian, Farrington, and Le Blanc 2009; Laub and Sampson 2003). These findings suggest that individuals are capable of change, and that life events may attenuate the impact of factors traditionally associated with delayed desistance.

Challenges pertaining to the definition and measurement of desistance have been highlighted elsewhere (Kazemian 2007; Laub and Sampson 2001). These issues include the lack of consensus on the operationalization of desistance, varying lengths of observation periods, intermittency in criminal careers and false desistance, and selection effects. Reviews of the literature have suggested that when prospective longitudinal data are not available, observation periods are short, and dichotomous measures of desistance are employed, desistance is likely to indicate a temporary lull in the behaviors of interest (e.g., offending) as opposed to the permanent cessation of these behaviors (see Kazemian 2007). This is not to say that cross-sectional data should not be used in desistance research. Cross-sectional data may be helpful in understanding variables that trigger the desistance process.

The Future of Desistance Research

Despite the substantial progress in desistance research, some important issues warrant more attention. First, we need to operationalize desistance beyond a single-parameter outcome and integrate several criminal career parameters in the measure of desistance (i.e., frequency, seriousness, and versatility) in order to better capture the changes occurring in the dynamics of offending. Such a conceptualization was suggested by Le Blanc and Fréchette (1989) and Loeber and Le Blanc (1990) over two decades ago, but remains underutilized in desistance research. In addition, the assessment of desistance should extend beyond the traditional measure of offending. Additional outcome measures for successful desistance may include improvements in mental and physical health outcomes, social bonds and integration, personality traits, and behavioral variables other than offending (e.g., substance use and routine activities).

Second, efforts should be undertaken to better integrate knowledge generated in desistance and prisoner reentry research. While desistance research has primarily emphasized theoretical advancements, research on offender reintegration has focused on the practical implications of the desistance process of formerly incarcerated individuals as they return to the community. Findings drawn from desistance research have obvious implications for reentry practices, but these two areas of study often appear to be disjointed. Recent studies have successfully bridged this gap by examining the predictive value of criminal history records on redemption and desistance (e.g., Blumstein and Nakamura 2009; Bushway, Nieuwbeerta, and Blokland 2011). The obstacles faced by formerly incarcerated individuals upon release from prison share many similarities with the impediments to desistance identified in the literature, namely strains on family relationships, physical and mental health issues, substance abuse, housing issues, lack of marketable skills, restrictive laws and policies, and unemployment (Burnett 2004; Laub and Sampson 2001; Maruna 2001; Petersilia 2003; Travis 2005).

Third, desistance research has, for the most part, failed to integrate the concept of resilience (for exceptions, see Born, Chevalier, and Humblet 1997; Lösel and Bender 2003). In the psychological literature, resilient individuals refer to those who are exposed to life stresses but who "defy expectation by developing into well-adapted individuals" (Luthar 1991, 600). In the context of desistance research, better knowledge about resilience would shed some light on the factors that contribute to the success of individuals who, theoretically and statistically, may be less likely to desist given their exposure to influential risk factors. Resilience shares some similarities with the concept of protective factors. Farrington (2007) has stressed the importance of identifying factors that may accelerate the desistance process and inform interventions after the onset of criminal careers.

Fourth, given the relatively limited participation rates of women in crime, studies investigating the desistance process of female offenders have been more limited in number and scope when compared to studies using male samples. Specifically, longitudinal studies of female offending have been particularly scarce (for exception, see Giordano 2010). A better understanding of the desistance process of female offenders would also offer insight about the relevance of gender-specific intervention programs.

Fifth, research on subjective accounts of desistance (such as emotions, motivations, and self-enforced goals) is relatively underdeveloped, possibly because there is a tendency to regard subjective dimensions of human experiences as "unscientific" (Maruna 2001, 8). With the exception of qualitative studies, the input of desisting offenders has seldom been documented. When investigating why offenders desist from crime, quantitative researchers tend to overlook the viewpoints of the concerned actors. We generally document several social and psychological indicators, and conduct statistical analyses to identify factors that significantly predict desistance. While this approach has generated a wealth of knowledge on desistance, self-assessments of conditions needed to successfully desist and reintegrate into the community are also important in the explanation of desistance, and these dimensions are generally overlooked in appraisals carried out by external observers (e.g., researchers, criminal justice professionals, etc.).

Sixth, data collected within short time intervals and over various periods of the life course are needed to investigate patterns of intermittency in criminal careers and better explain "false desistance" (i.e., temporary lulls in offending). There is a need to better understand the cognitive and social factors that promote desistance at particular points in the criminal career.

Finally, it has often been argued that the use of longitudinal data is useful in disentangling the sequencing of social and cognitive predictors in the explanation of desistance, but it remains unclear whether this issue is crucial to our understanding of desistance. Several authors have discussed the complexity of establishing the temporal order between cognitive processes, situational circumstances, and desistance from crime (Bottoms et al. 2004; LeBel et al. 2008), even with the use of more sophisticated statistical methods. Situational and cognitive changes are often interdependent and may occur simultaneously. Given that desistance is believed to be optimal when both cognitive and social conditions are fulfilled, resolving the sequencing issue may not add any additional insight to our understanding of desistance.

David Farrington's Contributions to Desistance Research

David Farrington's work has made significant contributions to criminal career and desistance research and generated a wealth of knowledge on the development of crime over the life course. With Al Blumstein and Jacqueline Cohen, David Farrington engaged in a debate with Gottfredson and Hirschi regarding the value of criminal career research (Blumstein, Cohen, and Farrington 1988a; 1988b). In these publications, the authors highlighted the importance of distinguishing between different criminal career parameters in order to develop more focused policies and further argued that the predictors of the onset of delinquency may be different from those of desistance from crime. Perhaps most importantly, the authors questioned Gottfredson and Hirschi's claim of age-crime invariance, and suggested that declines in aggregate crime rates may reflect changes in prevalence rather than lambda (i.e., individual crime rate of active offenders). This was an important assertion for desistance research as it suggested that progress toward termination from crime does not occur at the same rate for all individuals, thereby igniting a large body of research that sought to examine factors that explained these differences. David Farrington's work has also brought attention to the fact that the indicators explaining differences *between* individuals may differ from factors explaining changes in offending *within* individuals (Farrington 2002; Kazemian, Farrington, and Le Blanc 2009). He has, in several publications, emphasized the crucial importance of studying within-individual changes in offending behavior across the life course. With Donald West, he contrasted the crime-inhibiting effects of marriage and cohabitation with a partner (Farrington and West 1995). He has also been involved in analyses of criminal career parameters (including desistance) using international samples (e.g., Farrington and Wikström 1994; Loeber et al. 1991). He has made significant contributions to various longitudinal studies (e.g., Pittsburgh Youth Study) and has offered valuable recommendations to other researchers engaged in the area of criminal career and desistance research (e.g., see Farrington 2007). His and others' recommendations for future research include the expansion of the definition and operationalization of desistance, the bridging of the gap between desistance and reentry research, further inquiry into the factors that may accelerate the desistance process or contribute to the resilience of some individuals to reoffending, increased efforts in better understanding the desistance process of female offenders, additional attention to the subjective dimensions of desistance, and more comprehensive data collected over various periods of the life course.

David Farrington's work has truly, in his own words, "pushed back the frontiers of knowledge" on criminal career and desistance research. The discipline is greatly indebted to him for his contributions to the study of crime, as are the fortunate students who have had the privilege of working with him and benefiting from his extensive knowledge and kindness.

References

Bersani, Bianca E., John H. Laub, and Paul Nieuwbeerta. 2009. "Marriage and Desistance from Crime in the Netherlands: Do Gender and Socio-Historical Context Matter?" *Journal of Quantitative Criminology* 25: 3–24.

Blumstein, Alfred, Jacqueline Cohen, and David P. Farrington. 1988a. "Criminal Career Research: Its Value for Criminology." *Criminology* 26: 1–36.

Blumstein, Alfred, Jacqueline Cohen, and David P. Farrington. 1988b. "Longitudinal and Criminal Career Research: Further Clarifications." *Criminology* 26: 57–74.

Blumstein, Alfred, and Kiminori Nakamura. 2009. "Redemption in the Presence of Widespread Criminal Background Checks." *Criminology* 47: 327–359.

Born, Michel, Vinciane Chevalier, and Ilse Humblet. 1997. "Resilience, Desistance and Delinquent Careers of Adolescent Offenders." *Journal of Adolescence* 20: 679–694.

Bottoms, Anthony, Joanna Shapland, Andrew Costello, Deborah Holmes, and Grant Muir. 2004. "Towards Desistance: Theoretical Underpinnings for an Empirical Study." *Howard Journal of Criminal Justice* 43: 368–389.

Burnett, Ros. 2004. "To Reoffend or Not to Reoffend? The Ambivalence of Convicted Property Offenders." In *After Crime and Punishment: Pathways to Offender Reintegration*, edited by Shadd Maruna and Russ Immarigeon, 152–180. Cullompton, Devon: Willan.

Bushway, Shawn D., Paul Nieuwbeerta, and Arjan Blokland. 2011. "The Predictive Value of Criminal Background Checks: Do Age and Criminal History Affect Time to Redemption?" *Criminology* 49: 27–60.

Bushway, Shawn D., Alex R. Piquero, Lisa M. Broidy, Elizabeth Cauffman, and Paul Mazerolle. 2001. "An Empirical Framework for Studying Desistance as a Process." *Criminology* 39: 491–515.

Eitle, David. 2010. "General Strain Theory, Persistence, and Desistance among Young Adult Males." *Journal of Criminal Justice* 38: 1113–1121.

Farrall, Stephen, and Benjamin Bowling. 1999. "Structuration, Human Development and Desistance from Crime." *British Journal of Criminology* 39: 253–268.

Farrington, David P. 2007. "Advancing Knowledge about Desistance." *Journal of Contemporary Criminal Justice* 23: 125–134.

Farrington, David P., Rolf Loeber, Yamming Yin, and Stewart J. Anderson. 2002. "Are Within-Individual Causes of Delinquency the Same as Between-Individual Causes?" *Criminal Behavior and Mental Health* 12: 53–68.

Farrington, David P., and Donald J. West. 1995. "Effects of Marriage, Separation, and Children on Offending by Adults Males." In *Current Perspectives on Aging and the Life Cycle*, edited by Zena S. Blau and John Hagan, 249–281. Greenwich, CT: JAI Press.

Farrington, David P., and Per-Olof H. Wikström. 1994. "Criminal Careers in London and Stockholm: A Cross-National Comparative Study." In *Cross-National Longitudinal Research on Human Development and Criminal Behavior*, edited by Elmar G. M. Weitekamp and Hans-J. Kerner, 65–89. Dordrecht: Kluwer.

Giordano, Peggy L. 2010. *Legacies of Crime: A Follow-up of the Children of Highly Delinquent Girls and Boys*. New York: Cambridge University Press.

Giordano, Peggy L., Stephen A. Cernkovich, and Jennifer L. Rudolph. 2002. "Gender, Crime, and Desistance: Toward a Theory of Cognitive Transformation." *American Journal of Sociology* 107: 990–1064.

Kazemian, Lila. 2007. "Desistance from Crime: Theoretical, Empirical, Methodological, and Policy Considerations." *Journal of Contemporary Criminal Justice* 23: 5–27.

Kazemian, Lila, David P. Farrington, and Marc Le Blanc. 2009. "Can We Make Accurate Long-Term Predictions about Patterns of De-escalation in Offending Behavior?" *Journal of Youth and Adolescence* 38: 384–400.

Laub, John H., and Robert J. Sampson. 2001. "Understanding Desistance from Crime." In *Crime and Justice: A Review of Research*, vol. 28, edited by Michael Tonry, 1–69. Chicago: University of Chicago Press.

Laub, John H., and Robert J. Sampson. 2003. *Shared Beginnings, Divergent Lives: Delinquent Boys to Age 70*. Cambridge: Harvard University Press.

Le Blanc, Marc, and Marcel Fréchette. 1989. *Male Criminal Activity from Childhood through Youth: Multilevel and Developmental Perspectives*. New York: Springer.

LeBel, Thomas P., Ros Burnett, Shadd Maruna, and Shawn Bushway. 2008. "The 'Chicken and Egg' of Subjective and Social Factors in Desistance from Crime." *European Journal of Criminology* 5: 130–158.

Loeber, Rolf, and Marc Le Blanc. 1990. "Toward a Developmental Criminology." In *Crime and Justice: A Review of Research*, vol. 12, edited by Michael Tonry and Norval Morris, 375–473. Chicago: University of Chicago Press.

Loeber, Rolf, Magda Stouthamer-Loeber, Welmoet Van Kammen, and David P. Farrington. 1991. "Initiation, Escalation and Desistance in Juvenile Offending and Their Correlates." *Journal of Criminal Law & Criminology* 82: 36–82.

Lösel, Friedrich, and Doris Bender 2003. "Protective Factors and Resilience." In *Early Prevention of Adult Antisocial Behaviour*, edited by David P. Farrington and Jeremy W. Coid, 130–204. Cambridge: Cambridge University Press.

Luthar, Suniya S. 1991. "Vulnerability and Resilience: A Study of High-Risk Adolescents." *Child Development* 62: 600–616.

Maruna, Shadd. 2001. *Making Good: How Ex-Convicts Reform and Rebuild Their Lives*. Washington, DC: American Psychological Association.

Petersilia, Joan. 2003. *When Prisoners Come Home: Parole and Prisoner Reentry*. New York: Oxford University Press.

Travis, Jeremy. 2005. *But They All Come Back: Facing the Challenges of Prisoner Reentry*. Washington, DC: Urban Institute Press.

Warr, Mark. 1998. "Life-Course Transitions and Desistance from Crime." *Criminology* 36: 183–216.

Wright, John Paul, and Francis T. Cullen. 2004. "Employment, Peers, and Life-Course Transitions." *Justice Quarterly* 21: 183–205.

18

Does Psychopathy Appear Fully Only in Adulthood?

Raymond R. Corrado

A key theme of Farrington's more recent research on psychopathy is psychopathic traits as a key correlate of serious and violent young offenders and long-term criminal trajectories (Farrington 2005; Farrington, Ullrich, and Salekin 2010). Importantly, many of the traits associated with low self-control are either identical or conceptually close to the various measures of psychopathy. At present, however, it remains unclear whether psychopathy is readily distinguishable from other personality disorders, and whether antisocial behavior should be considered a primary or defining feature. There is even more uncertainty regarding if psychopathy exists and can be measured in childhood and adolescence.

This latter concern is the central theme of each of the chapters in the recently published *Handbook of Child and Adolescent Psychopathy* (Salekin and Lynam 2010) including the Farrington, Ullrich, and Salekin chapter. In responding to the specific concerns raised by current psychopathy instruments utilized for children and adolescents, Farrington and colleagues made two key recommendations. First, they stated that "more effort should be directed toward integrating the personality constructs underlying psychopathy, especially arrogant and deceitful interpersonal life-style and deficient affective experience, with larger personality constructs" (Farrington, Ullrich, and Salekin 2010, 221). Second, they asserted that "research is required on the development of more unbiased, valid, and reliable instruments to measure psychopathy, particularly in children and adolescents . . . and it is desirable to have measures that are not contaminated by anti-social behavior, and that do not rely on open-ended questions" (222).

This chapter addresses several of Farrington's specific concerns about the concept of psychopathy regarding adolescents generally, and serious and violent offenders specifically. Unfortunately, the most common instrument utilized for incarcerated serious and violent offenders—the PCL:YV—does not solve these problems. This "gold standard" instrument has been criticized—like the PCL-R, from which it was derived—as being both too narrow in content and too heavily saturated with antisocial behavior (Corrado et al. 2004; Vincent et al. 2008). I will present preliminary research concerning the PCL:YV and the new Comprehensive

Assessment of Psychopathic Personality Disorder (CAPP) based on large samples of incarcerated serious and violent young offenders, which arguably overcomes the problems of the PCL:YV (Dawson et al. in press).

The Debate: Basic Issues Concerning Psychopathy and Youth

Research on psychopathy in adolescence was stimulated by the Psychopathy Checklist: Youth Version (PCL:YV), Forth, Kosson, and Hare's (2003) adaptation of the Hare Psychopathy Checklist-Revised (PCL-R), a test designed for use with adults. Patrick (2010), however, has pointed out that there are many fundamental theoretical problems with the PCL-R itself, which also affect tests developed from or based on the PCL-R. Among the most important and most basic issues was the theoretical stipulation of the hierarchical structure of essential or underlying dimensions of psychopathy.

One of the themes that has emerged regarding the predictive validity of the PCL:YV regarding serious and violent young offender recidivism is the predominance of the antisocial behavioral dimension over the affective and or deceitful/interpersonal factors (Corrado et al. 2004). This concern raises the more general question of whether or not the meanness dimension can be separated from antisocial behavior, particularly criminality. Patrick and colleagues (2007) maintain that this distinction is critical and that both meanness and boldness can be distinguished from disinhibition or impulsive antisociality. Similarly, they argue for the need to disassociate callous-aggressive from externalizing behavior such as anger, impulsivity, and high negative emotionality.

A theme related to the predominance of behavior in conceptualizing and measuring psychopathy in youth is the importance of including anxiety directly into the underlying key constructs of disinhibition and/or boldness. There is sufficient empirical research, to date, that indicates a substantial difference between adults and adolescents concerning the centrality of anxiety in the latter age stage compared to the former. Developmentally, youth generally undergo more intense socialization as they adapt to age-related expectations and new social opportunities; therefore, theoretically, anxiety is not precluded as a dimension of psychopathy. In effect, while low to moderate anxiety, as opposed to very little or no anxiety, typically has not been central to most common conceptualizations of adult psychopathy, it tentatively appears important for adolescent conceptualizations (Salekin et al. 2005). As well, anxiety is central to the developmental attachment perspective, and, therefore, other dimensions of the broader construct of attachment also need to be incorporated into adolescent conceptualizations of psychopathy. Another key difference is that, for youth, narcissism is highly correlated with impulsivity, while, for adults, narcissism is highly correlated with the callous-unemotional dimension (Kotler and McMahon 2010).

The general theme, therefore, that emerges from the discussion and debates is that, while there are commonalities in the existence of psychopathic traits between adolescents and adults, there are also important differences in terms of the patterns of these traits and even the hierarchy of underlying dimensions. Most importantly, according to Lynam (2010), compared to adults, youth are more "mildly stress reactive." He argues further that conceptualizations such as the PCL-based adolescent measures are inherently incapable of providing valid measures of the basic dimensions of this complex personality disorder.

Regarding the etiology of adolescent psychopathy, Blair's (2004; 2007) "integrated emotions systems" model of psychopathy is a genetically derived developmental model that implicates brain neuroanatomy and chemistry with specified and related cognitive and emotional processes in explaining this personality disorder. Both recent genetic and cohort research have provided considerable support for this model; however, Blair has cautioned against the use of simple conceptual models of psychopathy, as the conceptualization of psychopathy needs to include cognitive items regarding avoidance of sadness and fear dimensions, in addition to "pain in others," that is, the difficulty in recognizing and responding emotionally to typical facial and other indicators of an individual experiencing pain. In effect, it is unlikely that a single or simple theoretical model will be able to respond to the multifinality and equifinality that is already evident in the relatively few studies of adolescent psychopathy.

Measuring Adolescent Psychopathy with an Emphasis on Personality Traits

In an effort to remain consistent with current research findings, and to address concerns surrounding the measurement of psychopathy in adolescents, attention has primarily focused on the development and use of personality-based, as opposed to behaviorally based, measures. Several instruments have been proposed or employed; however, I limit discussion to the most prominent measures, specifically the Five Factor Model (FFM), as assessed via the Neuroticism Extroversion Openness–Personality Inventory Revised (NEO-PI-R), the Psychopathic Personality Inventory (PPI), and the more recently developed Comprehensive Assessment of Psychopathic Personality Disorder (CAPP). I draw on the similarities and distinctions between the FFM, PPI, and CAPP to address the two main concerns previously outlined by Farrington and colleagues.

The FFM was developed as a self-report psychopathy assessment for use, primarily, with noncriminal samples (Skeem et al. 2005). This model posits that personality, and subsequently personality dysfunction, is structured by five broad domains, each with six specific facets or traits. Similar to the FFM, Lilienfeld and Andrews (1996) created the PPI, which emphasizes the importance of traits such as fearlessness, egocentricity, the inability to form close attachments, and a lack of anxiety; however, it moves away from the five-factor approach and suggests that psychopathy may be best represented by two primary factors, Fearless Dominance (FD) and Self-Centered Impulsivity (SCI), and a third subscale referred to as the Coldheartedness Scale.

At both the adult and youth levels, considerable research supports the validity and usefulness of the FFM (NEO-PI-R) and PPI (see Lynam 2010). However, the reliance on self-report psychopathy assessment and community-based samples has limited the applicability of these instruments in clinical and institutional settings. This is of particular concern when assessing psychopathy in target samples, such as serious and violent young offenders.

Taking into account the strengths and limitations presented by both personality-based (FFM and PPI) and behaviorally based (PCL-R and PCL:YV) measures, Cooke, Hart, and Logan (2005) developed the CAPP. This instrument is a six-dimensional hierarchical model of psychopathic personality disorder that expands on the PCL's conceptualization of psychopathy by introducing personality domains related to attachment, cognition, and self-concept while still retaining important behavioral, interpersonal, and affective traits represented by the domains of behavior, dominance, and emotion.[1]

Like the FFM and PPI, the CAPP follows a straightforward lexical, elemental approach. A series of detailed indicators represent more broadly defined latent factor/domain constructs. In addition, as depicted in table 18.1, the FFM and CAPP contain many similar traits/elements. The CAPP, however, places greater emphasis on elements of an individual's sense of self, attachments to significant others, particularly the ability to form lasting emotional connections, and cognitive processes, as opposed to traits of stress and anxiety. Utilizing information from clinical and institutional interviews, Cooke and colleagues (2005) were able to include reference to all clinically relevant items, as outlined by Lilienfeld and Andrews (1996), and Patrick (2010), while simultaneously reducing or eliminating emphasis on the importance of behaviors and emotions that are considered to be normative in institutional settings. For example, high anxiety and behavioral issues are more common in institutional samples than in community samples. This is especially the case with youth samples. In addition, the CAPP encompasses a larger number of facets, such as the Self domain's Sense of Entitlement and the Emotion domain's Lacks Emotional Depth. As a result, the CAPP appears to better address the full scope and complexity of psychopathic personality disorder.

New Directions: The Advantages and Disadvantages of the CAPP

The CAPP is currently being assessed globally as a potential assessment instrument for psychopathic personality disorder among incarcerated adult and youth populations, as well as in forensic settings. Preliminary results from both quantitative and qualitative studies reveal that the CAPP demonstrates strong internal consistency, fair/good to excellent interrater reliability, promising predictive validity, and a comprehensive

TABLE 18.1 Comparison of CAPP and FFM Traits/Elements

		Symptom	Indicator Corresponding to Symptom	FFM Scale and Corresponding Factor
Attachment	A1	*Detached*	Remote, Cold, Distant	Warmth (E)
	A2	*Uncommitted*	Unfaithful, Undevoted, Disloyal	Tendermindedness (A)
	A3	*Unempathic*	Uncompassionate, Cruel, Callous	Modesty (A)
	A4	*Uncaring*	Inconsiderate, Thoughtless, Neglectful	Altruism (A
Behavioral	B1	*Lacks Perseverance*	Idle, Undisciplined, Unconscientious	Self-Discipline (C)
	B2	*Unreliable*	Undependable, Untrustworthy, Irresponsible	Competence (C)
	B3	*Reckless*	Rash, Impetuous, Risk-Taking	Deliberation (C)
	B4	*Restless*	Overactive, Fidgety, Energetic	Excitement Seeking (E)
	B5	*Disruptive*	Disobedient, Unruly, Unmanageable	Activity (E)
	B6	*Aggressive*	Threatening, Violent, Bullying	Assertiveness (E)
Cognitive	C1	*Suspicious*	Distrustful, Guarded, Hypervigilant	Trust (A)
	C2	*Lacks Concentration*	Distractable, Inattentive, Unfocused	Impulsiveness (N)
	C3	*Intolerant*	Narrow-minded, Bigoted, Hypercritical	Values (O), Hostility (N)
	C4	*Inflexible*	Stubborn, Rigid, Uncompromising	Compliance (A) Fantasy (O)
	C5	*Lack Planfulness*	Aimless, Unsystematic, Disorganized	Dutifulness, Order, Achievement Striving (C)
Dominance	D1	*Antagonistic*	Hostile, Disagreeable, Contemptuous	Positive Emotion (E)
	D2	*Domineering*	Arrogant, Overbearing, Controlling	Assertiveness (E)
	D3	*Deceitful*	Dishonest, Deceptive, Duplicitous	
	D4	*Manipulative*	Devious, Exploitative, Calculating	
	D5	*Insincere*	Superficial, Slick, Evasive	Straightforwardness (A)
	D6	*Garrulous*	Glib, Verbose, Pretentious	Gregariousness (E)
Emotional	E1	*Lacks Anxiety*	Unconcerned, Unworried, Fearless	Anxiety (N)
	E2	*Lacks Pleasure*	Pessimistic, Gloomy, Unethusiastic	Depression (N)
	E3	*Lacks Emotional Depth*	Unemotional, Indifferent, Inexpressive	
	E4	*Lacks Emotional Stability*	Temperamental, Moody, Irritable	Vulnerability (N)
	E5	*Lacks Remorse*	Unrepentant, Unapologetic, Unashamed	Tendermindedness (A)

(continued)

		Symptom	Indicator Corresponding to Symptom	FFM Scale and Corresponding Factor
Self	S1	*Self-Centred*	Egocentric, Selfish, Self-Absorbed	
	S2	*Self-Aggrandizing*	Self-Important, Conceited, Condescending	
	S3	*Sense of Uniqueness*	Extraordinary, Exceptional, Special	
	S4	*Sense of Entitlement*	Demanding, Persistent, Sense of being Deserving	
	S5	*Sense of Invulnerability*	Invincible, Indestructible, Unbeatable	
	S6	*Self-Justifying*	Minimizing, Denying, Blaming	
	S7	*Unstable Self-Concept*	Labile, Incomplete, Chaotic Sense of Self	Self-Consciousness (N)

Agreeablement: A, C: Conscientiousness, E: Extraversion, N: Neuroticism, O: Openness

profile of psychopathic personality disorder (see Dawson et al. in press; Hoff et al. in press; Kreis et al. in press; McCormick, Corrado, and Hart 2008; Pedersen et al. 2010).

In addition, the CAPP appears to have a number of advantages over other assessment instruments. First, the CAPP was designed to be a bottom-up lexical approach, allowing for increased focus on elemental personality traits and the conceptualization of types of personality. This is important considering the multifaceted and heterotypic nature of psychopathic personality disorder, particularly for serious and violent young offenders. Second, by ensuring the six domains are mutually exclusive and exhaustive, the CAPP serves to broaden the scope of psychopathy, while simultaneously avoiding complications including compound traits and suppressor effects. Finally, as opposed to the self-report assessment tools, the CAPP is designed to be utilized by trained/expert personnel. Provided that many of the subjects under consideration may present with psychopathic symptoms, which include pathological lying and the inability to experience true emotion, it is generally preferred to utilize an instrument whereby a professional is responsible for gathering and assessing the information.

Although it appears to be a promising instrument, there are still a number of issues regarding the design and implementation of the CAPP. Of primary concern is the time required to complete a CAPP rating. Not only does the CAPP have a large number of domains and corresponding traits (six and 33 respectfully), it requires the rater to consider both the strength and functional impairment of each symptom. Further, although the CAPP provides a comprehensive list of personality traits, the validity and necessity of all items have yet to be determined. According to Hoff and colleagues (in press) and Kreis and colleagues (in press), certain items, such as Lacks Concentration on the Cognitive domain and Restless on the Behavior domain may not be highly representative of the construct of psychopathy.

Conclusions

If psychopathy remains an elusive construct in adulthood, it is both immature and elusive in childhood and adolescence. I believe that our research using the CAPP may help to make progress on Farrington's two key concerns regarding the applicability of this construct in early developmental stages. Specifically, we conclude:

1. Psychopathy can be *reliably* assessed (i.e., in terms of interrater reliability and internal consistency) in adolescence using the PCL:YV and the CAPP since the reliabilities obtained in adolescents are similar to those others have obtained in adults.[2]
2. Psychopathy can be *validly* assessed (in terms of association with past and future delinquency) in adolescence using the PCL:YV and CAPP since the postdictive and predictive validities obtained in adolescents are similar to those others have obtained in adults.[3]
3. The CAPP may have greater utility than the PCL:YV for assessing psychopathy in adolescence since it provides more specific information about symptoms.
4. The CAPP appears to assess a broad range of psychopathic symptoms free from contamination by official delinquency, something that will help researchers to understand the role of psychopathy in the complex, heterogeneous manifestations of serious and violent offending in adolescents.

Acknowledgments

Stephanie Dawson contributed to the section on the advantages and disadvantages of the CAPP instrument and Evan McCuish created table 18.1. Stephan Hart provided insightful suggestions and Adrienne Peters edited several versions in response to reviewer comments. This research is supported by four successive Social Science and Humanities Council of Canada Research Grants.

Notes

1. See Cooke, Hart, and Logan (2005) for a more detailed description of each of these domains.

2. Reliabilities for the CAPP were about the same as those for the PCL:YV.

3. Validities for the CAPP were about the same as those for the PCL:YV (at least, for the interpersonal, affective, and behavioral facets—lower than for the antisocial facet).

References

Blair, R. J. R. 2004. "The Roles of Orbitofrontal Cortex in the Modulation of Antisocial Behavior." *Brain and Cognition* 55: 198–208.

Blair, R. J. R. 2007. "Empathic Dysfunction in Psychopathic Individuals." In *Empathy in Mental Illness*, edited by Tom F. D. Farrow and Peter W. R. Woodruff, 3–16. Cambridge: Cambridge University Press.

Cooke, David, Stephen Hart, and Caroline Logan. 2005. *Comprehensive Assessment of Psychopathic Personality Disorder: Institutional Rating Scale, Version 1.1.* Unpublished manual.

Corrado, Raymond R., Gina M. Vincent, Stephen D. Hart, and Irwin M. Cohen. 2004. "Predictive Validity of the Psychopathy Checklist: Youth Version for General and Violent Recidivism." *Behavioral Sciences & the Law* 22: 5–22.

Dawson, Stephanie E., Evan C. McCuish, Raymond R. Corrado, and Stephen D. Hart. In press. "Assessing Psychopathy with the CAPP and PCL:YV: Utilizing a Case Study to Understand the Manifestation of Psychopathic Traits in Youth." *International Journal of Forensic Mental Health.*

Farrington, David P. 2005. "The Importance of Child and Adolescent Psychopathy." *Journal of Abnormal Child Psychology* 33: 489–497.

Farrington, David P., Simone Ullrich, and Randall T. Salekin. 2010. "Environmental Influences on Child and Adolescent Psychopathy." In *Handbook of Child and Adolescent Psychopathy*, edited by Randall T. Salekin and Donald R. Lynam, 251–283. New York: Guilford Press.

Forth, Adelle E., David S. Kosson, and Robert D. Hare. 2003. *The Psychopathy Checklist: Youth Version.* Toronto: Multi-Health Systems.

Hoff, Helge A., Knut Rypdal, Arnstein Mykletun, and David J. Cooke. In press. "A Prototypicality Validation of the Comprehensive Assessment of Psychopathic Personality (CAPP) Model." *Journal of Personality Disorders.*

Kotler, Julie S., and Robert J. McMahon. 2010. "Assessment of Child and Adolescent Psychopathy." In *Handbook of Child and Adolescent Psychopathy*, edited by Randall T. Salekin and Donald R. Lynam, 79–109. New York: Guilford Press.

Kreis, Mette K. F., David J. Cooke, Christine Michie, Helge A. Hoff, and Caroline Logan. In press. "The Comprehensive Assessment of Psychopathic Personality (CAPP): Content Validation Using Prototypical Analysis." *Journal of Personality Disorders.*

Lilienfeld, Scott O., and Brian P. Andrews. 1996. "Development and Preliminary Validation of a Self-Report Measure of Psychopathic Personality Traits in Noncriminal Population." *Journal of Personality Assessment* 66: 488–524.

Lynam, Donald R. 2010. "Child and Adolescent Psychopathy and Personality." In *Handbook of Child and Adolescent Psychopathy*, edited by Randall T. Salekin and Donald R. Lynam, 179–201. New York: Guilford Press.

McCormick, Amanda, Raymond R. Corrado, and Stephen D. Hart. 2008. "Interrater Reliability and Internal Consistency Reliability of the Comprehensive Assessment of Psychopathic Personality Disorder among Incarcerated Young Offenders." Paper presented at the Eight International Association of Forensic Mental Health Services (IAFMHS) Annual Conference, Vienna.

Patrick, Christopher J. 2010. "Conceptualizing the Psychopathic Personality: Disinhibited, Bold, . . . or Just Plain Mean?" In *Handbook of Child and Adolescent Psychopathy*, edited by Randall T. Salekin and Donald R. Lynam, 15–48. New York: Guilford.

Patrick, Christopher J., Brian M. Hicks, Penny E. Nichol, and Robert F. Krueger. 2007. "A Bifactor Approach to Modeling the Structure of the Psychopathy Checklist-Revised." *Journal of Personality Disorder* 21: 118–141.

Pedersen, Liselotte, Camilla Kunz, Peter Elsass, and Kirsten Rasmussen. 2010. "Psychopathy as a Risk Factor for Violent Recidivism—Investigating the Psychopathy Checklist Screening Version (PCL:SV) and the Comprehensive Assessment of Psychopathic Personality (CAPP) in a Forensic Psychiatric Setting." *International Journal of Forensic Mental Health* 9: 308–315.

Salekin, Randall T., Anne-Marie Leistico, Krista K. Trobst, Crystal L. Schrum, and John E. Lochman. 2005. "Adolescent Psychopathy and Personality Theory—the Interpersonal Circumplex: Expanding Evidence of a Nomological Net." *Journal of Abnormal Child Psychology* 33: 445–460.

Salekin, Randall T., and Donald R. Lynam. 2010. "Child and Adolescent Psychopathy: The Road Ahead." In *Handbook of Child and Adolescent Psychopathy*, edited by Randall T. Salekin and Donald R. Lynam, 401–420. New York: Guilford.

Skeem, Jennifer L., Joshua D. Miller, Edward Mulvey, Jenny Tiemann, and John Monahan. 2005. "Using a Five-Factor Lens to Explore the Relation between Personality Traits and Violence in Psychiatric Patients." *Journal of Consulting and Clinical Psychology* 73: 454–465.

Vincent, Gina M., Candice L. Odgers, Amanda V. McCormick, and Raymond R. Corrado. 2008. "The PCL:YV and Recidivism in Male and Female Juveniles: A Follow-up into Young Adulthood." *International Journal of Law and Psychiatry* 31: 287–296.

PART III

Prevention

19

Preventing Delinquency by Putting Families First

Brandon C. Welsh

Delinquency prevention spans many domains, including the individual, community, school, and family. Some are more relevant and more important depending on the age of the child. The transition from childhood to adolescence is particularly salient. David Farrington's lifework has made a major contribution to our understanding of which factors in these domains are the best predictors of delinquency and later criminal offending, the cumulative and interactive effects of risk factors, and the most effective interventions to target these factors to prevent children from embarking on a life of crime (Farrington and Welsh 2007).

While one may be hard pressed to identify from David's voluminous writings which domain he views as the most important to delinquency and its prevention, there is one that I am inclined to nominate. It is the family. This is derived in part from his early work with Donald West on the pioneering Cambridge Study in Delinquent Development to his present-day directorship of the study and its almost 50 years of follow-up, not to mention his continued return to and elaboration of this subject (Farrington 2011). It also comes from a long-standing research collaboration that David and I have pursued on family-based crime prevention, which began as part of my Ph.D. training at Cambridge (Farrington and Welsh 1999). Whatever the source, David Farrington has been at the forefront in demonstrating that families matter and by putting families first we can go a long way toward improving the effectiveness of delinquency prevention.

The Research Base

Family-based prevention programs and policies target risk factors for delinquency and offending that are associated with the family. After decades of rigorous study— using prospective longitudinal studies—a great deal is known about family risk factors. Farrington (2011) organized these factors into six main categories: (1) criminal and antisocial parents and siblings; (2) large family size; (3) child-rearing methods (poor supervision, inconsistent discipline, parental coldness and rejection, low parental involvement with the child); (4) abuse (physical or sexual) or neglect; (5) parental conflict and disrupted families; and (6) other parental features (especially young parents, substance abuse, stress, or depression of parents). The strongest family factor that predicts offending is usually criminal or antisocial parents. Other quite strong and replicable family factors that predict offending are large family size, poor parental supervision, parental conflict, and disrupted families (Derzon 2010; Farrington and Welsh 2007).

Broadly speaking, family-based prevention programs have developed in two major fields of study: psychology and public health. When delivered by psychologists, these programs are often classified into parent management training, functional family therapy, or family preservation (Wasserman and Miller 1998). Typically, they attempt to change the social contingencies in the family environment so that children are rewarded in some way for appropriate or prosocial behaviors and punished in some way for inappropriate or antisocial behaviors. Family-based programs delivered by health professionals such as nurses are typically less behavioral, mainly providing advice and guidance to parents or general parent education. Home visiting with new parents is one of the more popular forms of this type of family intervention (Olds, Sadler, and Kitzman 2007).

Within these fields of study, there is an emerging evidence base on the effectiveness of early family-based programs designed to address some of the most important familial risk factors for delinquency. Systematic reviews and meta-analyses incorporating the highest-quality studies have shown that a number of program models are effective in preventing delinquency and later offending, including nurse home visits and parent management training.

Two recent reviews capture the broad-scale effectiveness of family-based prevention programs. Manning, Homel, and Smith (2010) carried out a meta-analysis of the effects of early developmental prevention programs for children up to age five years on delinquency and other outcomes in adolescence. Eleven high-quality studies were included that covered a variety of program modalities: structured preschool, center-based developmental day care, home visitation, family support services, and parental education (improvement of core parenting skills). Results show significant effects across a number of important domain outcomes, including educational achievement (mean effect size $d = 0.53$), delinquency/deviance (0.48), cognitive development (0.34), involvement in the justice system (0.24), and family well-being (0.18). Interestingly, program duration and intensity were associated with larger effect sizes, but not multicomponent programs.

Piquero and his colleagues (2009) carried out a systematic review and meta-analysis of the effects of early family/parent training programs for children up to age five years on antisocial behavior and delinquency. The review, which included 55 randomized controlled experiments, investigated the full range of these programs, including home visits, parent education plus day care, and parent management training. Results indicate that early family/parent training is an effective intervention for reducing antisocial behavior and delinquency, with a mean effect size d = 0.35. These programs also produce a wide range of other important benefits for families, including improved school readiness and school performance on the part of children and greater employment and educational opportunities for parents.

Maximizing the Influence of Family

There are a number of key opportunities to build upon this research base to improve the effectiveness of family-based delinquency prevention programs and, importantly, to further advance the relevance of prevention in US crime policy.

NURSE-FAMILY PARTNERSHIP PROGRAM

Perhaps the most important early family-based delinquency prevention program is the Nurse-Family Partnership (NFP) developed by David Olds (Olds et al. 2007). At its core is the provision of nurse home visits for new parents. Home visits focus on educating parents to improve the life chances of children from a very young age, often beginning at birth or the final trimester of pregnancy. Other goals include the prevention of preterm or low weight births, the promotion of healthy child development or school readiness, and the prevention of child abuse and neglect. Home visits also seek to improve parental well-being, linking parents to community resources to help with employment, education, or addiction recovery.

NFP was first tested in Elmira, New York, in the early 1980s. Four hundred first-time mothers were randomly assigned to receive home visits from nurses during pregnancy, or to receive visits both during pregnancy and during the first two years of life, or to a control group who received no visits. Each visit lasted just over one hour and the mothers were visited on average every two weeks. The home visitors gave advice about prenatal and postnatal care of the child, about infant development, and about the importance of proper nutrition and avoiding smoking and drinking during pregnancy.

The evaluation showed that the program caused a significant decrease in recorded child physical abuse and neglect during the first two years of life, especially by poor, unmarried, teenage mothers, and in a 15-year follow-up, significantly fewer experimental than control group mothers were identified as perpetrators of child abuse and neglect. At the age of 15, children of the higher-risk mothers who received home visits incurred significantly fewer arrests than controls (Olds et al. 2007). In the latest follow-up at age 19, compared to their control counterparts, girls of the full sample of mothers had incurred significantly fewer arrests and convictions and girls of the higher-risk mothers had significantly fewer children of their own and less Medicaid use; few program effects were observed for the boys (Eckenrode et al. 2010). Benefit-cost analyses have repeatedly shown that for every dollar spent on the program, benefits are about three to four times greater (Welsh and Farrington 2011). Large-scale replications in Memphis and Denver are also showing a range of positive effects for children and mothers (Olds et al. 2007).

Today, NFP operates in 400 counties in 32 states, serving more than 21,000 families each year. Crucial to each of these sites and the program's continued expansion is a commitment by local providers to ensure fidelity to the model. As programs are implemented in new settings or scaled-up for wider public use, there is the very real threat that the program will become diluted and its effectiveness greatly reduced. As a sign of the importance of this concern, a national office was established to work with local providers to make sure that NFP programs are implemented and operated as planned and to help address local needs. This marks a crucial advancement in the local delivery of evidence-based prevention programs.

SUPPORTING FAMILIES

Another powerful story that concerns the importance of families is currently playing out in some of the most impoverished neighborhoods in New York City. It concerns a program that was not explicitly designed with the prevention of delinquency in mind. It also concerns a program that is not centered on the family domain. Instead, the program, known as the Harlem Children's Zone (HCZ), is comprehensive in nature, addressing key needs across many domains. Set up by Geoffrey Canada in the late 1990s, HCZ is designed to improve the life chances of children faced with poverty by providing them with a wide range of programs that follow them from infancy through adolescence, a safety net of sorts (Tough 2008, 5). Efforts to improve academic achievement figure most prominently in HCZ.

What makes this program relevant to the present discussion is that Canada realized from the outset that the best education for children means nothing at all if they must return every day to a home where there is parental conflict, sometimes violence, and little or no parental interest in or support for what they are learning in school. To help address these and other family issues, Canada designed a range of services for parents, including parent training classes and a program called Baby College to help parents cope with newborns. Strengthening community resources is another important feature of HCZ.

Family support services figure prominently in many multimodal or comprehensive social programs, including some that have measured delinquency and later offending. But the lesson here could very well be that family support should play a prominent and long-lasting role alongside efforts to improve educational achievement. Support for this view comes from the highly effective Chicago Child-Parent Center program (Reynolds et al. 2011). Future research including an evaluation of HCZ is needed to explore the family support–educational achievement link.

FAMILY PROGRAMS FOR SYSTEM-INVOLVED YOUTH

Importantly, the future of family-based delinquency prevention extends beyond the early years of the life course and involves working with adjudicated youth. Three of the most important evidence-based delinquency prevention programs target serious juvenile offenders. These are functional family therapy (FFT), multidimensional treatment foster care (MTFC), and multisystematic therapy (MST) (Greenwood 2006). FFT involves modifying patterns of family interaction—by modeling, prompting, and reinforcement—to encourage clear communication of requests and solutions between family members, and to minimize conflict. MTFC involves individual-focused therapeutic care (e.g., skill building in problem solving) for the young person in an alternative, noncorrectional environment (foster care) and parent management training. In the case of MST the particular type of treatment is chosen according to the needs of the young person, with family support playing a central role.

The intensity of these programs, their well-developed implementation proto-cols, and a focus on high-risk youthful offenders stand out as key features. But perhaps the unique element of these programs is their focus on the family—even alternative families in the case of MTFC—as an element of change at a time in a young person's life when family influence is giving way to friends and other inter-ests. The roll-out of these programs in many states across the country marks an important opportunity for family-based crime prevention.

Conclusion

There is much to celebrate in the area of delinquency prevention, and family-based programs are playing a major role. The future of delinquency prevention, whether delivered during the early years of the life course or targeted at serious juvenile offenders, will benefit from even greater integration of family interventions and support services. As David Farrington discovered in his early research and con-tinues to show today, the family domain is front and center in improving the life chances of at-risk children and building a safer society.

References

Derzon, James H. 2010. "The Correspondence of Family Features with Problem, Aggressive, Criminal, and Violent Behavior: A Meta-analysis." *Journal of Experimental Criminology* 6: 263–292.

Eckenrode, John, Mary Campa, Dennis W. Luckey, Charles R. Henderson, Robert Cole, Harriet J. Kitzman, Elizabeth Anson, Kimberly Sidora-Arcoleo, Jane Powers, and David L. Olds. 2010. "Long-Term Effects of Prenatal and Infancy Nurse Home Visitation on the Life Course of Youths: 19-Year Follow-up of a Randomized Trial." *Archives of Pediatrics and Adolescent Medicine* 164: 9–15.

Farrington, David P. 2011. "Families and Crime." In *Crime and Public Policy*, edited by James Q. Wilson and Joan Petersilia, 130–157. New York: Oxford University Press.

Farrington, David P., and Brandon C. Welsh. 1999. "Delinquency Prevention Using Family-Based Interventions." *Children and Society* 13: 287–303.

Farrington, David P., and Brandon C. Welsh. 2007. *Saving Children from a Life of Crime: Early Risk Factors and Effective Interventions*. New York: Oxford University.

Greenwood, Peter W. 2006. *Changing Lives: Delinquency Prevention as Crime-Control Policy*. Chicago: University of Chicago Press.

Manning, Matthew, Ross Homel, and Christine Smith. 2010. "A Meta-analysis of the Effects of Early Developmental Prevention Programs in At-Risk Populations on Non-health Outcomes in Adolescence." *Children and Youth Services Review* 32: 506–519.

Olds, David L., Lois Sadler, and Harriet J. Kitzman. 2007. "Programs for Parents of Infants and Toddlers: Recent Evidence from Randomized Trials." *Journal of Child Psychology and Psychiatry* 48: 355–391.

Piquero, Alex R., David P. Farrington, Brandon C. Welsh, Richard E. Tremblay, and Wesley G. Jennings. 2009. "Effects of Early/Family Parent Training Programs on Antisocial Behavior and Delinquency." *Journal of Experimental Criminology* 5: 83–120.

Reynolds, Arthur J., Judy A. Temple, Suh-Ruu Ou, Irma A. Arteaga, and Barry A. B. White. 2011. "School-Based Early Childhood Education and Age-28 Well-Being: Effects by Timing, Dosage, and Subgroups." *Science* 333: 360–364.

Tough, Paul. 2008. *Whatever It Takes: Geoffrey Canada's Quest to Change Harlem and America*. Boston: Houghton Mifflin.

Wasserman, Gail A., and Laurie S. Miller. 1998. "The Prevention of Serious and Violent Juvenile Offending." In *Serious and Violent Juvenile Offenders: Risk Factors and Successful Interventions*, edited by Rolf Loeber and David P. Farrington, 197–247. Thousand Oaks, CA: Sage.

Welsh, Brandon C., and David P. Farrington. 2011. "The Benefits and Costs of Early Prevention Compared with Imprisonment: Toward Evidence-Based Policy." *Prison Journal* 91(3S1): 120–137.

20

The Future of Preventive Public Health

IMPLICATIONS OF BRAIN VIOLENCE RESEARCH

Frederick P. Rivara

I came to know and work with David Farrington in a roundabout way. I had been involved with research on one of the most important public health problems in the United States, that of gun violence. This led me to think about the problem of violence more generally, and since I am a pediatrician, the problem of youth violence. In searching for a mentor for a sabbatical project, all roads pointed toward David Farrington as the most knowledgeable person in the world. David was (and is) incredibly generous. He took me under his wing, taught me a tremendous amount, introduced me to the field and the people working in it, and created opportunities all along the way. I owe him an enormous debt of gratitude.

Population Prevalence of Risk Factors for Violence

The public health model of prevention is qualitatively different from the models used by other social sciences such as criminology, psychology, and sociology. This public health model seeks to improve the health and welfare of the largest proportion of the population with an intervention and does not necessarily focus on those at greatest risk, those who might benefit the most, or interventions that have the greatest chance of success in an individual. Public health is population health.

On a population level, the most prevalent risk factors for later violent behavior are those falling under the term "adverse childhood experiences" or ACEs (Anda et al. 2010). This concept arose from a combined retrospective-prospective longitudinal study of 17,337 individuals enrolled in a health insurance plan in San Diego, California, and has now evolved into ongoing surveys in a number of US states and other countries. These studies have examined a broad array of experiences in childhood such as abuse, neglect, maltreatment, poverty, and parental mental illness, and demonstrated their link to a host of unhealthy behaviors, violence, chronic disease, and disability in adulthood. At least one ACE was reported by 64 percent of respondents in the initial study, and 22 percent of respondents had three or more ACEs (Anda et al. 2006). In the original sample, 6 percent of adults grew up with mental illness in the household and 6 percent with criminal behavior by one or more of the adults in the household. In Washington State, 17 percent of adults report being physically abused and 17 percent of women and 7 percent of men report sexual abuse during childhood (Anda and Brown 2010). One-third of adults reported growing up with substance abuse in the household.

These ACEs represent a cumulative burden of exposure to chronic adversities that are not randomly distributed in the population. Having one ACE markedly increases the likelihood of having one or more additional adverse exposures. For example, 81 percent of those reporting growing up with household substance abuse reported at least one additional ACE. A great deal of research has shown a dose-response relationship between the number of ACEs and subsequent behavioral, mental, and physical problems as adults (Anda et al. 2010). The sum of these ACEs—the ACE score—is a reproducible index of the impact of stress during childhood.

Toxic Stress

The National Scientific Council on the Developing Child has classified stress experiences into positive, tolerable, and toxic, based on the body's response to stress (National Scientific Council on the Developing Child 2005). Positive stress, such as learning to deal with normal separation from parents, is an important part of healthy development. Tolerable stress is distinguished by serious events that are time limited and can be met by normal physiologic homeostatic responses. In contrast, toxic stress refers to repetitive and/or prolonged stress that overwhelms the organism's chance to cope. Those who experience it are the children who grow up in poverty, live in dangerous neighborhoods, are exposed to violence both inside and outside the home, and face personal and familial substance abuse and a peer group of similarly exposed individuals. Farrington's body of work has clearly outlined the factors associated with the development of violent and criminal behavior.

As shown by physiological, psychological, and imaging studies of neuro-functioning in the last two decades, these risk factors exert their effect through direct and lasting effects on brain structure and function. Early effects of stress on the brain can have profound effects on functions that develop later in childhood and adolescence, such as those that mediate emotional responses or social interaction. For example, childhood sexual abuse is associated with reduction in hippocampus and amygdale volume, leading to mood disturbance and impaired memory (Bremner et al. 2003). Chronic exposure to poverty is associated with reduction in volume of the prefrontal cortex, leading to impaired executive function (Gianaros et al. 2007). More recent research indicates that the brain continues to develop during adolescence and into young adulthood, thereby increasing the window for long-term effects of stress.

These effects on the brain can be permanent and even passed on to the next generation through the phenomenon of epigenetics, in which there are environmentally induced changes in gene expression, through processes such as methylation and acetylation (Weaver et al. 2004). For example, maternal depression during pregnancy increases methylation of *GR* 1F promoter DNA in infants, which in turn is associated with increased salivary cortisol at three months of age (Oberlander et al. 2008). In a study of suicide victims, those with a history of child abuse had decreased GR expression in the brain and elevated GR 1F promoter methylation (McGowan et al. 2009), indicating the long-term effects of ACEs on the brain and life course. Evidence from studies in animals indicate that the effects of maternal neglect can be passed on to the next generation, through the transmission of methylated DNA (Champagne and Meaney 2007).

Implications for Prevention

Future public health efforts to prevent violence at the population level must start early with prevention of toxic stress to this large group of children. The persistent social class disparities in health and educational achievement, as well as crime and violence, among individuals of different race/ethnicities and socioeconomic backgrounds have their roots in the exposure of past generations to disparate levels of adverse environmental exposures. The concept of child maltreatment should be broadened, based on the research of the last two decades, to include the various experiences that contribute to toxic stress, damage to the individual, and ultimately violence. This includes poverty first of all. Natural experiments in the United States, such as development of new sources of revenue for impoverished communities, demonstrate that addressing widespread poverty decreases the risk of mental, emotional, and behavioral disorders in children (but not for those who were older at the time of the intervention) as well as when these individuals reach adulthood (Costello et al. 2010).

Evidence-based interventions are available to improve parenting skills, reduce child maltreatment, and lessen the amount of toxic stress to which children, especially young children, are exposed. The Triple P program, developed by Sanders in Australia, reduced substantiated child maltreatment and child out-of-home placement when examined in a community-wide intervention in South Carolina (Prinz et al. 2009). This public health approach to improving parenting skills is a complement to more intensive interventions, such as Parent Child Interaction Therapy, for selected dysfunctional families.

Because the household environment is grossly suboptimal for so many children, out-of-home child care and early childhood education are critically important. A wealth of data indicates that these interventions are effective and cost-effective. However, such programs must be of high quality; low-quality programs are not only a waste of scarce resources, they can be harmful to the children in them.

Future Research

The science of the biological effects of environmental exposures and stress on the developing brain is only beginning and many key questions remain, the answers to which are important in guiding public policy. The past research has underscored the complexities of the various interdependent interactions. The effect of stress on the brain is moderated by the genome, yet the understanding of which genes moderate these effects and how they do so is very limited at present. This complex interaction of environmental experiences, genes, and neurobiological development is poorly understood. The epigenetic effects of environmental exposures have mostly been conducted in animals and the need to develop methods to study such effects in living humans, for example, with peripheral blood cells, must be developed.

While we know that the brain continues to develop during adolescence and young adulthood, the ways stress during these times affects brain biology, development, and function are unknown and need to be investigated. For example, how does being bullied during adolescence affect brain function and structure in young adulthood? Advances in brain imaging, both in humans and in animals, hold great promise for identifying these structural and functional changes in the brain. Most importantly, can such changes in the brain be ameliorated or reversed, and if so, what is the critical period for doing so and what types of interventions are needed? Are there biomarkers of the level of toxic stress experienced, on the one hand, and the degree of pronutrient experiences, on the other?

The US National Institutes of Health is undertaking a large and very costly study to track a cohort of 100,000 children from the prenatal period into adulthood. The impetus for this study is in great part driven by the search for the effects of physical toxins in the environment on the developing child, and to find the multifactorial causes for common disorders such as autism, now estimated to affect as many as 1 of every 110 children. Those interested in the etiology and prevention of violence should be as vocal as their environmental health colleagues in ensuring that the data are collected in the National Children's Study to investigate the effects of toxic stress on the brain and the development of violent and aggressive behavior. This study offers the opportunity to study how environmentally induced short-term effects can have long-term outcomes.

How to Fund These Efforts?

As I write this, all the economies in the Western world are still suffering under an economic recession and cutbacks have been made everywhere, but perhaps most of all in educational and social service programs. How are the interventions outlined above to be funded then? While all of us may believe that new funds should be expended, this is highly unlikely in the immediate future.

I believe the most lasting way to do so is to make public health interventions a normal part of doing business in various sectors of society. The health care industry should take the lead, since it accounts for the single largest industry in many countries. In 2008, health care in the United States cost $2.3 trillion and accounted for 16.2 percent of the GDP. In the European Union, health care spending averaged 6.7 percent of GDP in 2006, and accounted for 12–15 percent of government outlays. As mentioned above, children and families are seen early and frequently by the health care system and effective, evidence-based interventions are available that can be implemented in these settings. Much of what is done during well-child care, with the exception of immunizations, is not evidence-based and is probably worthless, and more worthwhile activities can and should be substituted without increasing health care or societal costs. Health information technology is rapidly spreading and can be used to better screen and track high-risk children and facilitate referral for the small percentage of children who need specialty care for their emotional and behavioral problems.

Children's protective services should also be reexamined. A recent follow-up of children in the Longitudinal Studies of Child Abuse and Neglect found that the 27.6 percent of households that were evaluated by children's protective services for possible child maltreatment were no better off when the child was eight years old in terms of social support, child behavior, or family functioning than the households that were at risk but not investigated, and in fact mothers in investigated households had more depressive symptoms (Campbell et al. 2010). The investigative functioning of CPS perhaps can be better conducted by the police, while the home-visiting roles have been shown to be well implemented by home health nurses. The same if not a lower expenditure of money might be much better spent in a different way.

Easy answers are not available for how the educational system can best interact to reduce the level of toxic stress on children. While funding reductions are almost certainly harmful, funding increases may not necessarily result in the expected degree of improved outcome that is anticipated. However, emphasis must be given to quality early childhood education for all children, not just non-poor children (who are most likely to receive it but probably the least likely to need it).

David Farrington has done a tremendous job in pointing out to all of us the causes of violence. The time is now for us to use this information to improve the health and welfare of the public.

References

Anda, Robert F., and David W. Brown. 2010. *The Face of a Chronic Public Health Disaster: Results from the 2009 Behavioral Risk Factor Surveillance System*. Olympia, WA: Washington State Family Policy Council.

Anda, Robert F., Alexander Butchart, Vincent J. Felitti, and David W. Brown. 2010. "Building a Framework for Global Surveillance of the Public Health Implications of Adverse Childhood Experiences." *American Journal of Preventive Medicine* 39: 93–98.

Anda, Robert F., Vincent J. Felitti, J. Douglas Bremner, John D. Walker, Charles Whitfield, Bruce D. Perry, Shanta R. Dube, and Wayne H. Giles. 2006. "The Enduring Effects of Abuse and Related Adverse Experiences in Childhood: A Convergence of Evidence from Neurobiology and Epidemiology." *European Archives of Psychiatry and Clinical Neuroscience* 256: 174–186.

Bremner, J. Douglas, Meena Vythilingam, Eric Vermetten, Steven M. Southwick, Thomas McGlashan, Ashan Nazeer, Sarfraz Khan, L. Viola Vaccarino, Robert Soufer, Pradeep K. Garg, Chin K. Ng, Lawrence H. Staib, James S. Duncan, and Dennis S. Charney. 2003. "MRI and PET Study of Deficits in Hippocampal Structure and Function in Women with Childhood Sexual Abuse and Posttraumatic Stress Disorder." *American Journal of Psychiatry* 160: 924–932.

Campbell, Kristine A., Lawrence J. Cook, Bonnie J. LaFleur, and Heather T. Keenan. 2010. "Household, Family, and Child Risk Factors after an Investigation for Suspected Child Maltreatment: A Missed Opportunity for Prevention." *Archives of Pediatrics & Adolescent Medicine* 164: 943–949.

Champagne, Frances A., and Michael J. Meaney. 2007. "Transgenerational Effects of Social Environment on Variations in Maternal Care and Behavioral Response to Novelty." *Behavioral Neurosience* 121: 1353–1363.

Costello, E. Jane, Alaattin Erkanli, William Copeland, and Adrian Angold. 2010. "Association of Family Income Supplements in Adolescence with Development of Psychiatric and Substance Use Disorders in Adulthood among an American Indian Population." *Journal of the American Medical Association* 303: 1954–1960.

Gianaros, Peter J., Jeffrey A. Horenstein, Sheldon Cohen, Karen A. Matthews, Sarah M. Brown, Janine D. Flory, Hugo D. Critchley, Stephen B. Manuck, and Ahmad R. Hariri. 2007. "Perigenual Anterior Cingulate Morphology Covaries with Perceived Social Standing." *Social Cognitive Affective Neuroscience* 2: 161–173.

McGowan, Patrick O., Aya Sasaki, Ana C. D'Alessio, Sergiy Dymov, Benoit Labonte, Moshe Szyf, Gustavo Turecki, and Michael J. Meany. 2009. "Epigenetic Regulation of the Glucocorticoid Receptor in Human Brain Associates with Childhood Abuse." *Nature Neuroscience* 12: 342–348.

National Scientific Council on the Developing Child. 2005. "Excessive Stress Disrupts the Architecture of the Developing Brain." Working paper No. 3. Retrieved May 23, 2011, from http://developingchild.harvard.edu/library/reports_and_working_papers/working_papers/wp3/.

Oberlander, Tim F., Joanne Weinberg, Michael Papsdorf, Ruth Grunau, Shaila Misri, and Angela M. Devlin. 2008. "Prenatal Exposure to Maternal Depression, Neonatal Methylation of Human Glucocorticoid Receptor Gene (NR3C1) and Infant Cortisol Stress Responses." *Epigenetics* 3: 97–106.

Prinz, Ronald J., Matthew R. Sanders, Cheri J. Shapiro, Daniel J. Whitaker, and John R. Lutzker. 2009. "Population-Based Prevention of Child Maltreatment: The U.S. Triple P System Population Trial." *Prevention Science* 10: 1–12.

Weaver, Ian C., Nadia Cervoni, Frances A. Champagne, Ana C. D'Alessio, Shakti Sharma, Jonathan R. Seckl, Sergiy Dymov, Moshe Szyf, and Michael J. Meaney. 2004. "Epigenetic Programming by Maternal Behavior." *Nature Neuroscience* 7: 847–854.

21

"Own the Place, Own the Crime" Prevention

HOW EVIDENCE ABOUT PLACE-BASED CRIME SHIFTS THE BURDEN OF PREVENTION

John E. Eck and Rob T. Guerette

When police focus on small high-crime areas—hot spots—they can reduce crime (Braga 2005), at least in the short term (Sherman 1990). But what about interventions that alter the physical and social environment of the place and do not necessarily involve police? In this chapter we examine the effectiveness of these types of place interventions to reduce crime. We first define proprietary places—the sites of the interventions. Next we show why places are important. We then present findings of a systematic review of place-based crime prevention evaluations. Our final section explores the implications of our findings: the need to tailor-make interventions and the use of what we call "own the place, own the crime" prevention.

Defining Place

A *place is small* (Sherman, Gartin, and Buerger 1989) because a place must be of a size that allows an offender to control the target and manage the immediate situation. Places have four other features (Eck 1994, 10). They have a *known geographical location*. They have *boundaries* so we can locate events as occurring inside or outside of them. Places have a *principal function*—such as living, recreation, work, and transport. Places with the same function are called "facilities" (Eck, Clarke, and Guerette 2007). Places are *legally controlled by a person or organization* that manages them. Because the term place is not used consistently, Madensen and Eck (in press) suggest that locations with these five characteristics be called *proprietary* places, to differentiate them from *proximal* places (street segments), and *pooled* places (larger areas such as neighborhoods). This chapter only discusses proprietary places.

The utility of a place-based prevention method depends on the type of facility within which it is applied: CCTV is feasible in stores and parking areas, but not in public restrooms, for example. Homes operate differently than bars, so comparing them to bars is inappropriate, but comparisons among residences or among bars can be meaningful. We will focus on five very common facilities: residential, public, retail, transportation, and recreation.

Importance of Places for Crime

There are four reasons proprietary places are important (Eck and Guerette 2012). First, a few places contain a very large proportion of crime. This is so common that Wilcox and Eck (2011, 476) call it the "iron law of troublesome places." Second, spatial displacement of crime following prevention is not a serious threat. The evidence for this is now established: displacement happens on occasion but it never fully overwhelms prevention benefits (Guerette and Bowers 2009). Third, reducing crime at high-crime proprietary places often reduces crime at nearby locations (Guerette and Bowers 2009). Finally, there are owners responsible for the management of proprietary places.

Managers are place owners (Eck 1994). They make decisions about the physical and social environment of proprietary places and in this way control crime at their locations. At places, managers organize the physical environment; they regulate conduct; they control access; and they acquire resources (Madensen 2007). *The crime prevention aspects of place management grow out of these decisions.*

All crime prevention at proprietary places—locks, lights, signage, CCTV (closed-circuit television), rules of conduct, space reconfiguration, most guardianship, and any form of crime prevention through environmental design (CPTED)—requires the consent of place managers. There are legal methods for compelling place managers to implement measures to reduce crime. This is sometimes called "third party policing" (Mazerolle and Ransley 2005), though nonpolice actors can also mobilize civil law through the threat of suits against owners of the crime places. To avoid this, place managers implement many crime prevention techniques (Eck 1996). Threatening owners of high-crime places with civil sanctions reduces drug dealing and crime at their places (Green 1995; Mazerolle, Roehl, and Kadleck 1998; Eck and Wartell 1998). Most efforts to control disorder and crime in bars necessitate getting place managers involved (Madensen and Eck 2008). So it is likely that most proprietary places have little or no crime because their managers are doing things differently than the few place managers with substantial crime problems. But what sorts of things work to reduce what sorts of crime at propriety places?

Interventions That Prevent Crime at Places

We conducted a systematic review of which situational interventions prevent crime at places (for details on the methods used, see Eck and Guerette 2012 ; Guerette and Bowers 2009). We found a total of 149 evaluations across the five facilities. Table 21.1 presents the overall conclusions reported by the evaluations' authors. We see variation in effectiveness among place types, though for no facility did reported effectiveness dip below 60 percent. All recreational interventions appear successful, but the number of these evaluations is small. Interventions in public outdoor settings and in residences had the most failures, but even in these settings ineffective interventions were uncommon compared to successes and mixed successes.

There are several possible explanations for the lower success rate at public places compared to other settings: they are more open and less contained; they may have a wider variety of deviance; or implementation may be weaker. In the next section we will consider a fourth hypothesis: use of off-the-shelf techniques.

Our positive assessment of the utility of place-based interventions should be tempered by the nature of the evaluation methods used. Evaluations of place-based interventions are, on average, modest in terms of their rigor. The strongest evaluations are rare and have been applied only to residential and retail settings. Weak evaluations are distributed over most types of settings. Nevertheless, the consistency of the findings gives us reason to be optimistic about the use of place-based interventions.

Future Implications

Place-based prevention works in a variety of facilities and against a variety of common crimes (Eck and Guerette 2012). Although place-based prevention is effective, we cannot say precisely how useful it is. There are a number of reasons for this, including the methods used to evaluate these interventions. A more important

TABLE 21.1 Effectiveness of place-based intervention evaluations by facility

Facility	Percent of authors' conclusions (n)			
	Effective	Not effective	Mixed findings	Inconclusive
Residential (39)	77 (30)	10 (4)	10 (4)	3 (1)
Public ways (52)	62 (32)	12 (6)	19 (10)	8 (4)
Retail (25)	88 (22)	4 (1)	4 (1)	4 (1)
Transport (26)	88 (23)	0 (0)	8 (2)	4 (1)
Recreational (7)	100 (7)	--	--	--
Total (149)	77 (114)	7 (11)	11 (17)	5 (7)

reason is that proprietary places are quite varied—we examined only five facility types—and the range of possible interventions is enormous. This suggests two implications, aside from conducting more research, for future crime prevention efforts.

First, prevention practitioners will need to understand the crime problem at their places, and only then pick solutions that fit. This is in keeping with the principles of situational crime prevention (Clarke 1992) and problem-oriented policing (Goldstein 1990). The importance of this can be seen by looking at the success rate of commonly selected interventions. Table 21.2 ranks interventions in decreasing order of use (totals column) and shows (in the rows) the percentage of each intervention type that had various outcomes. Seven interventions account for 79 percent of the 149 evaluations. Though all interventions listed in table 21.2 were more effective than not, perversely the least effective interventions are the most commonly used. These findings suggest that broad-scale use of any place prevention technique will be less effective than using "tailor-made" interventions.

If this conclusion is correct, then evidence-based practitioners will need to ask, "Given the specific conditions at my places, what is likely to work to reduce the crime I am most concerned with?" General evidence about effectiveness should be applied in the context of specific evidence about a place's crime problem. This means that it is critical to strengthen the capacity of practitioners to analyze problems, form partnerships with other stakeholders, and find situationally specific solutions.

The second suggestion we make is that government policymakers will need to consider who is responsible for proprietary places, and hold those people and organizations accountable for the crimes occurring at their locations. Crime has traditionally been thought of as a public concern that the public tax dollar should address. Once we start considering crime opportunities, we must bear in mind that the owners of proprietary places control these crime opportunities, and no one else has the authority to control these opportunities without first getting place managers' compliance.

TABLE 21.2 Effectiveness of the most used interventions

| Intervention | Totals | Authors' conclusions | | | |
		Effective	Not effective	Mixed	Inconclusive
CCTV	25 (37)	59 (22)	14 (5)	24 (9)	3 (1)
Lighting	14 (20)	55 (11)	15 (3)	15 (3)	15 (3)
CPTED	11 (16)	94 (15)			6 (1)
Mixed / other	10 (16)	93 (14)	7 (1)		
Access control	9 (14)	92 (13)			8 (1)
Place management	6 (9)	89 (8)		11 (1)	
Street redesign	4 (6)	67 (4)		17 (1)	17 (1)
Total	79 (118)	74 (87)	7 (8)	12 (14)	6 (7)

If instead of having government agencies implement crime prevention practices at proprietary places, we shifted prevention responsibility to place owners, then they and their customers would bear the costs of prevention. Perhaps governments' principal role in crime prevention at proprietary places is to set limits for crime that place managers cannot exceed, and then hold managers accountable for staying under these limits. Place managers can then choose the interventions (within broad legal bounds) that work best for them, in their situation. We call this a policy of "If you own the place you own the crime." Most place managers will have no trouble taking control—they do not own much crime (Payne and Eck 2007). The few place managers who own most of the crime would bear the burden of such a policy.

References

Braga, Anthony A. 2005. "Hot Spots Policing and Crime Prevention: A Systematic Review of Randomized Controlled Trials." *Journal of Experimental Criminology* 1: 317–342.

Clarke, Ronald V., ed. 1992. *Situational Crime Prevention: Successful Case Studies.* Albany, NY: Harrow and Heston.

Eck, John E. 1994. "Drug Markets and Drug Places: A Case-Control Study of the Spatial Structure of Illicit Drug Dealing." Ph.D. dissertation, University of Maryland.

Eck, John E. 1996. "Do Premises Liability Suits Promote Business Crime Prevention?" In *Business and Crime Prevention*, edited by Ronald V. Clarke and Marcus Felson, 125–150. Monsey, NY: Criminal Justice Press.

Eck, John E., Ronald V. Clarke, and Rob T. Guerette. 2007. "Risky Facilities: Crime Concentration in Homogeneous Sets of Establishments and Facilities." In *Imagination for Crime Prevention*, edited by Graham Farrell, Kate J. Bowers, Shane D. Johnson, and Michael Townsley, 225–264. Monsey, NY: Criminal Justice Press.

Eck, John E., and Rob T. Guerette. 2012. "Place-Based Crime Prevention: Theory, Evidence, and Policy." In *The Oxford Handbook of Crime Prevention*, edited by Brandon C. Welsh and David P. Farrington, 354–383. New York: Oxford University Press.

Eck, John E., and Julie Wartell. 1998. "Improving the Management of Rental Properties with Drug Problems: A Randomized Experiment." In *Civil Remedies and Crime Prevention*, edited by Lorraine Mazerolle and Jan Roehl, 161–185. Monsey, NY: Criminal Justice Press.

Goldstein, Herman. 1990. *Problem-Oriented Policing.* New York: McGraw-Hill.

Green, Lorraine. 1995. "Policing Places with Drug Problems: The Multi-agency Response Team Approach." In *Crime and Place*, edited by John E. Eck and David Weisburd, 199–215. Monsey, NY: Criminal Justice Press.

Guerette, Rob T., and Kate J. Bowers. 2009. "Assessing the Extent of Crime Displacement and Diffusion of Benefits: A Systematic Review of Situational Crime Prevention Evaluations." *Criminology* 47: 1331–1368.

Madensen, Tamara D. 2007. "Bar Management and Crime: Toward a Dynamic Theory of Place Management and Crime Hotspots." Ph.D. dissertation, University of Cincinnati.

Madensen, Tamara D., and John E. Eck. 2008. "Violence in Bars: Exploring the Impact of Place Manager Decision-Making." *Crime Prevention and Community Safety* 10: 111–125.

Madensen, Tamara D., and John E. Eck. In press. "Crime Places and Place Management." In *Oxford Handbook of Criminological Theory*, edited by Pamela Wilcox and Francis Cullen. New York: Oxford University Press.

Mazerolle, Lorraine, and Janet Ransley. 2005. *Third Party Policing*. New York: Cambridge University Press.

Mazerolle, Lorraine G., Jan Roehl, and Colleen Kadleck. 1998. "Controlling Social Disorder Using Civil Remedies: Results from a Randomized Field Experiment in Oakland, California." In *Civil Remedies and Crime Prevention*, edited by Lorraine Green Mazerolle and Jan Roehl, 141–159. Monsey, NY: Criminal Justice Press.

Payne, Troy, and John E. Eck. 2007. "Who Owns Crime?" Paper presented at the annual conference of the American Society of Criminology, Atlanta, November 14–17.

Sherman, Lawrence W. 1990. "Police Crackdowns: Initial and Residual Deterrence." In *Crime and Justice: A Review of Research*, vol. 12, edited by Michael Tonry and Norval Morris, 1–48. Chicago: University of Chicago Press.

Sherman, Lawrence W., Patrick R. Gartin, and Michael E. Buerger. 1989. "Hot Spots of Predatory Crime: Routine Activities and the Criminology of Place." *Criminology* 27: 27–55.

Wilcox, Pamela, and John E. Eck. 2011. "The Criminology of the Unpopular: Implications for Policy Aimed at Payday Lending Facilities." *Criminology and Public Policy* 10: 473–482.

22

Community Approaches to Preventing Crime and Violence

THE CHALLENGE OF BUILDING PREVENTION CAPACITY

Ross Homel and Tara Renae McGee

David Farrington has had an enormous influence on the theory and practice of crime prevention. One publication in particular (Farrington 1994), which highlighted the long-term effects of a range of early-in-life prevention programs, changed the life of the first author of this chapter. In a context where early prevention was largely absent from the policy landscape in Australia, this article inspired a vision for the widespread adoption of social policies for children, families, and communities based on developmental prevention. A federal government report (Homel et al. 1999) led, in turn, to the establishment in 2001 of the Pathways to Prevention Project (Homel et al. 2006), a community-based early prevention project in a socially disadvantaged area of Brisbane. Pathways, although differing in significant ways from the projects reviewed in Farrington (1994), drew inspiration none the less from Professor Farrington's ideas on community prevention (Farrington 1996).

In this chapter we pay tribute to Professor Farrington's indefatigable efforts to put crime prevention onto a scientific foundation by offering some reflections on the emerging shape of community approaches to the prevention of crime, aggressive behavior, and violence. Our larger goal is to support, but also to critique and expand, the agenda for a comprehensive national prevention strategy put forward by Professors Farrington and Welsh most recently in their book *Saving Children from a Life of Crime* (2007). We propose the use by prevention-oriented criminologists, in addition to the familiar research-to-practice or prevention science literatures, of developmental systems theory (Lerner and Castellino 2002) for its emphasis on relations or connections among individuals, organizations, and settings within human ecology and the need therefore to make these the focus of preventive efforts; community-centered models for insights into issues such as community engagement and strengthening community capacity (Flaspohler et al. 2008); and implementation science as a way of strengthening organizational capacity and governance arrangements for prevention (Homel and Homel 2012).

We also wish to suggest that the early prevention approach that is the focus of *Saving Children*, while critically important, is not on its own sufficient for building community prevention capacity within a national framework. We appreciate of course that this was not Farrington and Welsh's specific purpose, but since there is so much good material in their proposals that bears on community approaches, it would in our view be useful to expand the agenda from early prevention to the overall prevention of child, youth, and young adult crime, violence, and substance misuse. Our main reason for arguing that not all eggs should be put in the early years basket (say, up to age seven) is that while these programs produce consistently positive results across a range of life domains in adolescence, reductions in crime or substance abuse are not necessarily maintained into late adolescence or early adulthood, especially for males (e.g., Eckenrode et al. 2010). Earlier positive effects may be overwhelmed by situational and other processes characteristic of the emerging adulthood life phase, necessitating the use of situational, regulatory, or (possibly) criminal justice preventive approaches as well as developmental interventions at various times beyond the early years ("early in the pathway, not necessarily early in life" was one of the key points of the 1999 Pathways to Prevention report). Developmental approaches in the early years can easily be defended and should properly be valued, on the basis of their multiple benefits across childhood, adolescence, and beyond, but a national crime and violence prevention strategy should rely on all ethical approaches that work. In practice, effective and sustainable community strategies will increasingly be based on multiagency collaborations that implement, at several points in the life course, programs that are an eclectic mix of situational, criminal justice, regulatory, and developmental approaches within a community framework.

A key problem that Farrington and Welsh (2007) identify is that there is little agreement on the definition of community prevention. We opt with them for Hope's definition as "actions intended to change the social conditions that are believed to sustain crime in residential communities" (21). However, interventions that really do attempt to change social conditions are rarely evaluated to the standard that Farrington and Welsh rightly demand. An exception is Communities That Care, an extremely promising risk-focused community mobilization model (Hawkins et al. 2008). Another well-evaluated model aimed at changing social conditions was the Fighting Back community empowerment initiative designed to support communities in tackling drugs, delinquency, and violence (discussed by Embry 2004). Unfortunately, the evaluation showed that Fighting Back had no effect on child or youth outcomes and actually had a significant negative effect on adult substance abuse, perhaps supporting Embry's conclusion (577) that "the findings soundly refuted the community-empowerment model."

Other examples in the literature illustrate that community approaches can be well evaluated and can be effective. However, the generally poor state of scientific knowledge about community prevention, especially when attempted at scale, suggests that the field needs better concepts and a broader array of tools. We have found in creating and implementing the Pathways to Prevention Project that developmental systems theory (DST) has provided an invaluable framework for organizing our thinking about the focus of preventive activities, which should, as we have noted, be on changing the relations or connections between the different levels of organization in the developmental system (Freiberg, Homel, and Branch 2010). The relational emphasis of DST has profound implications for prevention theory and practice since children, families, schools, community agencies, and residents have to be thought about simultaneously in terms of their reciprocal interactions with each other within a dynamic (time varying) system.

One practical interpretation of DST is that to strengthen the developmental system and achieve sustainable improvements in child and youth outcomes, service providers or community agencies need to forge trusting relationships with families and children, and form respectful power-sharing alliances with local organizations such as schools, churches, child care centers, kindergartens, or youth organizations. They also need ideally to operate within a framework of integrated or collaborative practice, characterized by a blurring of the boundaries between organizations and by harmonious, mutually supportive practices in families, schools, community agencies, and other key settings. Collaborative practice has always been a primary goal of the Pathways to Prevention Project but remains as yet largely out of reach, consistent with the experience of nearly all those who have engaged in cognate endeavors.

The practices that fit naturally within the developmental systems framework—building trust and respectful relationships, engaging families, and striving for collaborative practice between services and enduring developmental institutions such as schools—have a close affinity with community-centered or collaborative community action models of intervention. In these models the focus is on the evolution of practice in local contexts and on the improvement of existing practice over the introduction of something new, with the practitioner taking center stage rather than being the recipient of an innovation developed through external research. Empowerment, capacity building, and engagement are the hallmarks of these approaches, but as Bowen, Gwiasda, and Brown (2004, 356) observe in reporting the results of two community engagement projects, community residents and the prevention field are in "vastly different places with respect to primary violence prevention." There is a huge gap between what often happens in community-centered approaches and what prevention science demands in terms of careful measurement, use of randomized controlled trials, and program fidelity.

Straddling this gap has been a primary goal of the Pathways to Prevention Project, which has aimed simultaneously to use existing models of family support and school and community engagement while introducing where possible program approaches based explicitly on research, underpinning the whole enterprise with as much systematic measurement of patterns of participation and child and family outcomes as is possible within the hurly-burly of the daily routines of schools and a busy community agency. Our optimism that a genuine scientific synthesis between the research-to-practice and community-centered models is possible is based both on our experience in Pathways and on the generally sanguine outlook of others in the field. How this dialectic plays out will certainly be one of the defining features of the community prevention field over the next few years.

Talk of community engagement and related issues raises the important issue of community capacity and its links with prevention capacity (Flaspohler et al. 2008). The community, whether viewed as the locality or in broader terms (such as city entertainment areas that attract adolescents and young adults), provides a potentially rich context for modifying person-environment interactions central to crime and violence prevention. However, a critical missing element is rigorous quantitative analysis that establishes the likely causal effects on child and youth outcomes of well-conceptualized and theoretically grounded dimensions of community capacity. There are actually good grounds for dismissing community or locality altogether as a causal risk factor for crime and antisocial behavior, since when individual and family factors are controlled, standard measures of community characteristics such a social disadvantage often disappear, as in a recent analysis by McGee and colleagues (2011) of antisocial behavior by Brisbane adolescents. Of course this does not rule out community-based prevention strategies, but the target of such strategies would be individual and family risk factors, not social conditions.

Support for strategies that explicitly aim to build community capacity comes from recent work by Odgers and her colleagues (2009), who conceptualized community capacity in terms of collective efficacy. They demonstrated with UK data that collective efficacy exerts an effect on antisocial behavior at school entry over and above individual and family factors, but only in disadvantaged neighborhoods. If replicated this finding gives clear direction to those who argue for prevention based on building community capacity, but the challenge then for the field will be to devise strategies that actually improve collective efficacy in challenging disadvantaged areas, and to demonstrate rigorously consequential reductions in crime and violence.

So far in this chapter we have highlighted the value of some ambitious new directions for community prevention, and to some extent thrown out a challenge to entrenched thinking based on the typical research-to-practice model. Implementation science, which has arisen largely within the human services and health fields, is one response to the challenge of getting scientific evidence into routine practice (Fixsen et al. 2009). Systematic reviews of implementation processes suggest that implementation is a recursive process with six functional stages: exploration, installation, initial implementation, full implementation, innovation, and sustainability. These are elaborated by Ross and Peter Homel (2012), who demonstrate their applicability to crime prevention through a series of case studies and also outline the core components of effective implementation: staff recruitment, training, coaching, and performance evaluation, supported by data systems, a facilitative administration, and a responsive system. Homel and Homel view these core components as part of a governance model for human service agencies and argue that the crime prevention field can make a distinctive contribution to implementation science through the governance systems for multiorganizational partnerships with which crime prevention practitioners have such familiarity. Such partnership approaches have been largely ignored so far within the implementation science literature.

Regardless of scientific or ideological persuasion, there is plenty in the agenda we have adumbrated in this chapter for all those concerned with community crime prevention. Those wedded to traditional prevention science will find much to attract them, but also many challenges, in its young cousin, implementation science. Similarly, those committed to community-centered approaches, including working with services already established in the community, need to demonstrate using quantitative measurement and rigorous research designs that such approaches really prevent crime and violence. All could be enriched in their thinking and practice by drawing on relational developmental systems theory into which, for example, established theories of social bonding and newer concepts of community capacity neatly fit. But all of these complicated theories and ambitious plans for community change will founder unless they are grounded in the gritty empirical realities of crime and violence so brilliantly analyzed by David Farrington throughout his long career.

Acknowledgments

Aspects of the research reported in this chapter were supported by the Australian Research Council (LP0560771 and DP0984675), the Criminology Research Council, the Australian Government Attorney-General's Department, the Charles and Sylvia Viertel Foundation, and the Queensland Department of Communities. We also acknowledge the intellectual input of Kate Freiberg and Sara Branch in their work on the Pathways to Prevention Project.

References

Bowen, Linda K., Victoria Gwiasda, and M. Mitchell Brown. 2004. "Engaging Community Residents to Prevent Violence." *Journal of Interpersonal Violence* 19: 356–367.
Eckenrode, John, Mary Campa, Dennis W. Luckey, Charles R. Henderson Jr., Robert Cole, Harriet Kitzman, Elizabeth Anson, Kimberly Sidora-Arcoleo, Jane Powers, and David Olds. 2010. "Long-Term Effects of Prenatal and Infancy Nurse Home Visitation on the Life Course of Youths: 19-Year Follow-up of a Randomized Trial." *Archives of Pediatrics and Adolescent Medicine* 164: 9–15.
Embry, Dennis D. 2004. "Community-Based Prevention Using Simple, Low-Cost, Evidence-Based Kernels and Behavior Vaccines." *Journal of Community Psychology* 32: 575–591.
Farrington, David P. 1994. "Early Developmental Prevention of Juvenile Delinquency." *Criminal Behaviour and Mental Health* 4: 209–227.

Farrington, David P. 1996. *Understanding and Preventing Youth Crime.* York: Rowntree.

Farrington, David P., and Brandon C. Welsh. 2007. *Saving Children from a Life of Crime: Early Risk Factors and Effective Interventions.* Oxford: Oxford University Press.

Fixsen, Dean L., Karen A. Blase, Sandra F. Naoom, and Frances Wallace. 2009. "Core Implementation Components." *Research on Social Work Practice* 16: 531–540.

Flaspohler, Paul, Jennifer Duffy, Abraham Wandersman, Lindsey Stillman, and Melissa A. Maras. 2008. "Unpacking Prevention Capacity: An Intersection of Research-to-Practice Models and Community-Centered Models." *American Journal of Community Psychology* 41: 182–196.

Freiberg, Kate, Ross Homel, and Sara Branch. 2010. "Circles of Care: The Struggle to Strengthen the Developmental System through the Pathways to Prevention Project." *Family Matters* 84: 28–34.

Hawkins, J. David, Eric C. Brown, Sabrina Oesterle, Michael W. Arthur, Robert D. Abbott, and Richard F. Catalano. 2008. "Early Effects of Communities That Care on Targeted Risks and Initiation of Delinquent Behavior and Substance Use." *Journal of Adolescent Health* 43: 15–22.

Homel, Ross, Jacqueline J. Goodnow, Linda Gilmore, Marie Leech, Judy Cashmore, Alan Hayes, Jeanette Lawrence, Ian O'Connor, Tony Vinson, Jackob Najman, and John Western. 1999. *Pathways to Prevention: Developmental and Early Intervention Approaches to Crime in Australia (Full Report, Summary and Appendices).* Canberra: Australian Government Publishing Service.

Homel, Ross, and Peter Homel. 2012. "Implementing Crime Prevention: Good Governance and a Science of Implementation." In *The Oxford Handbook of Crime Prevention,* edited by Brandon C. Welsh and David P. Farrington, 423–445. New York: Oxford University Press.

Lerner, Richard M., and Domini R. Castellino. 2002. "Contemporary Developmental Theory and Adolescence: Developmental Systems and Applied Developmental Science." *Journal of Adolescent Health* 31: 122–135.

McGee, Tara Renae, Rebecca Wickes, Jonathon Corcoran, William Bor, and Jackob Najman. 2011. "Antisocial Behaviour: An Examination of Individual, Family, and Neighbourhood Factors." *Trends and Issues in Crime and Justice* 410: 1–6.

Odgers, Candice L., Terrie E. Moffitt, Laura M. Tach, Robert J. Sampson, Alan Taylor, Charlotte L. Matthews, and Avshalom Caspi. 2009. "The Protective Effects of Neighbourhood Collective Efficacy on British Children Growing Up in Deprivation: A Developmental Analysis." *Developmental Psychology* 45: 942–957.

23

Taking Effective Crime Prevention to Scale

FROM SCHOOL-BASED PROGRAMS TO COMMUNITY-WIDE PREVENTION SYSTEMS

J. David Hawkins, Richard F. Catalano, Karl G. Hill, and Rick Kosterman

We are indebted to David Farrington and his pioneering longitudinal study, the Cambridge Study in Delinquent Development, which identified early risk factors in the individual and the environment for later delinquent and criminal behavior (Farrington and West 1982). This work and the work of Del Elliott and his colleagues in the National Youth Study (Elliott, Huizinga, and Ageton 1985) provided the foundation for the Social Development Research Group's efforts to develop risk- and protection-focused prevention approaches.

Farrington's identification of childhood predictors of adolescent delinquency stimulated our efforts in developmental crime prevention focused on reducing empirically identified family, school, and individual risk factors in order to prevent later criminal behavior. We thought that if crime could be predicted from family, school, and other developmental factors, it could be prevented by targeting and changing those factors. We looked to David's longitudinal study of 411 London boys to identify malleable predictors for preventive intervention.

David has been a steadfast proponent of developmental and life course criminology to understand risk factors at different stages of life and within-individual change over the life course (Farrington 2003). He has stressed the importance of prospective longitudinal surveys for this research. Inspired by his thinking, we began the Seattle Social Development Project (SSDP) in 1980 both to test our theory of delinquent behavior, the social development model (Catalano and Hawkins 1996), and to test interventions seeking to reduce risk factors and enhance protective factors specified in the theory.

David also reinforced our vision of the value of nesting interventions in longitudinal studies to facilitate greater understanding of both intervention effectiveness and etiological processes. During the early 1990s, he advocated the integration of experimental tests of programs to prevent antisocial behavior into a longitudinal framework, noting that this design capitalizes on the advantages of both forms of research (Farrington 1992). As a realization of this vision, the SSDP study continues more than 30 years later, tracking changes in developmental trajectories and testing the long-term effects of childhood intervention into adulthood.

The Seattle Social Development Project (SDDP)

The SSDP is a longitudinal preventive intervention study that sought both to understand the etiology of delinquent behavior and to test interventions to prevent delinquent behavior. Prior to the study, there had been nine experimental trials in the United States seeking to prevent delinquency, but none had demonstrated significant effects. Over the next 30 years, this changed dramatically due to two advances. First, longitudinal studies of development like the Cambridge Study in Delinquent Development identified factors that predict delinquent behavior. Longitudinal analyses in the SSDP study itself have produced over 100 publications examining the course, predictors, and consequences of a broad range of youth health and behavior outcomes. Second, preventive interventions designed to reduce risk factors and bolster protective factors have been tested in controlled studies and have been found to be effective in preventing substance abuse, delinquency, and violence (Welsh and Farrington 2006). The SSDP intervention is among these (Hawkins et al. 1999).

The SSDP intervention was developed as a theory-guided, universal preventive intervention that sought to promote positive social development during the elementary school years in order to prevent later delinquency and other problem behaviors. We hypothesized that if we could help children get on a positive developmental trajectory between the ages of 6 and 12 years, they would be less likely to risk their stake in academic, social, and economic success by engaging in behaviors such as delinquency and drug abuse that could compromise their health and future educational and occupational prospects.

The SSDP intervention was guided by the social development model (SDM), a developmental theory that specifies etiological pathways to antisocial and prosocial outcomes. The SDM has demonstrated to be a good fit across studies and samples, predicting substance use and misuse, school misbehavior, violence, and depression through adolescence to age 21 (Catalano et al. 2005; Huang et al. 2001; Lonczak et al. 2001). The SDM provides a framework for preventive intervention because it addresses empirically determined risk and protective factors across multiple life domains.

The SDM hypothesizes that social development is influenced by important social structural factors, including external social constraints (social norms, rules, and laws), by one's position in the social structure (socioeconomic status, race, gender), and by individual characteristics (such as temperament differences that affect responses to the environment). In this context, the social developmental

environment is defined by perceived opportunities for involvement in both prosocial interactions and antisocial interactions, by one's actual involvement, by one's
skills to perform in these pro- or antisocial interactions, and by the perceived
rewards or costs one experiences as a consequence of involvement with prosocial
or antisocial others. When opportunities lead to involvement, and that involvement is skillful and rewarded, a social bond of emotional attachment and commitment develops to the individual or group with whom one is interacting, whether
prosocial or antisocial. Bonding, in turn, creates motivation in the individual to
adopt and conform to the norms and values of the individual or group to whom
the individual feels bonded, whether involved in prosocial or antisocial activities.
In sum, the SDM hypothesizes both a "prosocial pathway" leading to positive
outcomes and an "antisocial pathway" leading to problem behaviors.

In developing the SSDP intervention, we hypothesized that parents and
teachers, equipped with the principles of the SDM, could guide the developmental
trajectories of children and improve outcomes. We thought that by helping
teachers use better methods of instruction and classroom management and
helping parents improve their family management skills in order to increase opportunities and recognition for prosocial behavior in the classroom and home
environments, it would be possible to promote better long-term outcomes. In
families, our work sought to reduce empirically identified risk factors such as poor
family management and family conflict and strengthen protective factors including opportunities for active involvement in the family and parental reinforcement for children's prosocial involvement, improvement, and achievement. We
hypothesized that targeting these factors would strengthen children's bonds of attachment and commitment to family, and that, if children's bonds to family were
strong and parents explicitly communicated prosocial and health-promoting
standards for behavior, children would be more likely to follow prosocial standards and avoid delinquency and other problem behaviors.

Similarly, we sought to reduce empirically identified risk factors related to
school, including academic failure and low commitment to schooling, by strengthening protective factors including opportunities for active involvement in the
classroom and teacher and peer reinforcement for children's prosocial involvement, improvement, and achievement at school. By improving opportunities and
rewards at school and thereby strengthening children's bond of commitment and
attachment to school, we hypothesized that children would be more likely to seek
success in life by completing high school, furthering their education and finding
gainful employment, and would be less likely to risk this success by engaging in
delinquent or other problem behaviors. We helped teachers and parents achieve
these changes during the elementary grades and compared the children's outcomes to a comparison group that did not receive the intervention.

Early results examining intervention efficacy found significant intervention
effects on targeted outcomes. Hawkins and colleagues (1992) found that, after the
first four years of receiving the intervention, youths in the full intervention

reported significantly less delinquency and alcohol initiation than control students. We also examined the effects of the intervention on theoretically targeted mediators of their intervention logic model and found that youths in the full-intervention condition reported better family communication, family involvement, attachment to family, and family management; as well as better school rewards, attachment, and commitment compared to controls. O'Donnell and colleagues (1995) found that at the end of the sixth grade (age 12), girls in the full-intervention group from low-income families reported significantly less cigarette use initiation than their control counterparts, and less alcohol and marijuana initiation. Boys in the full-intervention condition from low-income families were significantly more likely to report improved social skills, schoolwork, and commitment to school, to have better achievement test scores and grades, and were less likely to have antisocial peers than their control counterparts.

Intervention effects continued to be demonstrated in developmentally appropriate domains into adulthood. By age 18 (six years postintervention), compared to controls, youths in the full intervention had significantly reduced school misbehavior, lifetime violence, and heavy alcohol use, and improved school commitment, school attachment, and achievement (Hawkins et al. 1999). Also by age 18, youths in the full intervention had significantly lower lifetime prevalence of sexual intercourse, early pregnancy (or causing pregnancy), and multiple sex partners than controls (Hawkins et al. 1999). Lonczak and colleagues (2002) replicated these risky sex findings at age 21, and also found a significantly increased probability of condom use during last intercourse (among single individuals), and decreased incidence of lifetime sexually transmitted infections (STI) diagnosis in the full-intervention group compared with controls. By age 21, the full-intervention group, compared to controls, showed significantly better outcomes with respect to education, employment, and mental health, as well as reduced crime (Hawkins et al. 2005). By ages 24–27, the full-intervention group, compared with controls, showed significantly better socioeconomic attainment and mental health (Hawkins et al. 2008).

Examining intervention effects on the onset of STI through age 30, Hill and colleagues (2010) found significant main effects of the intervention. Additionally, significant ethnicity-by-intervention effects were found for those in the full-intervention condition such that reduction in STI was significantly stronger for African Americans than for Caucasians. Meditational analyses of these intervention effects among the African American participants found that prosocial adolescent family environment, school bonding, and delayed initiation of sexual behavior mediated intervention effects on STI hazard.

As we were developing and testing the SSDP preventive intervention, effective preventive interventions were being developed and tested throughout the United States and abroad. Interventions focused on preventing the initiation of substance use during early adolescence have shown prolonged effects in reducing the use and abuse of substances later in adolescence (Botvin et al. 1995; Chou et al. 1998). These

results suggest that preventing the initiation of substance use during early adolescence by addressing risk and protective factors salient during this developmental
period is a viable prevention approach. Yet many schools and communities use
prevention approaches with little or no evidence of effectiveness (Gottfredson,
Wilson, and Najaka 2002). Further, even when schools and communities select a
tested, effective prevention approach, they often fail to implement it with fidelity
to the standards delineated by program designers (Gottfredson and Gottfredson
2002). The development and testing of strategies for disseminating effective preventive interventions and improving the quality of implementation has emerged
as a priority for prevention research.

Communities That Care (CTC)

In 1987, we began to work on a strategy to empower communities to use the
advances of prevention science to identify elevated risks in their community and
to address them by choosing and implementing tested and effective preventive
interventions that sought to reduce those risk factors. We developed CTC, a
community prevention operating system consisting of processes and tools that
guide community leaders and stakeholders in effective prevention. Through
demonstrations and implementations for over 20 years we continued to develop
this operating system that has been improved by community input and formative
evaluation. The CTC system teaches steps for forming coalitions of diverse community stakeholders, assessing levels of malleable risk and protective factors in
the community, and choosing and implementing tested and effective preventive
interventions to address elevated risks and depressed protective factors in the
community. Thus, different communities target different risk and protective factors and choose different interventions to address them. CTC has been tested in
a randomized community trial and has produced community-wide reductions
in delinquent behavior, tobacco use, and alcohol use among young people
(Hawkins et al. 2009).

The Future: Universal School-Based Intervention
and Community-Wide Prevention Systems

The future will be characterized by local collection and utilization of epidemio-
logic data on levels of risk and protection exposure in the local youth populations. School personnel will recognize that risk factors for delinquency and
substance abuse also predict academic difficulties and school failure and that the
protective factors identified in the SDM promote academic and economic success as well as prevent crime and substance abuse. In light of this information,
schools will broaden their view of their mission to promote both academic

success and positive social and emotional development. Schools will promote academic success and prevent crime, substance abuse, unwanted pregnancies, and other problem behaviors by implementing tested and effective policies, programs, and curricula to reduce risk factors and strengthen protective factors affecting their students. Schools and community stakeholders will work collaboratively to routinely assess levels of risk and protective factors affecting youth through surveys of students and will use these data to guide prevention and youth development efforts. Communities will choose and implement with fidelity tested and effective preventive interventions to reduce risk and strengthen protection across development from pregnancy through young adulthood. Using the tools of prevention science, schools and communities will systematically monitor levels of risk and protection periodically and will adjust preventive interventions to maximize effects.

The emergence of data on shared risk factors for adolescent mental, emotional, and behavior problems and academic failure and on shared protective factors that promote healthy prosocial development, and the identification of preventive interventions that reduce risk, enhance protection, and lead to better outcomes in multiple domains are major breakthroughs. This new knowledge has the potential to empower communities and increase civic engagement. Local control and the "democratization of prevention" will increase as invested community members and service providers select strategies from menus of policies and programs that have been tested and shown to be effective in addressing elevated risks and strengthening protection. Community involvement, investment, and ownership of tested and effective prevention and youth development interventions will generate *sustainable* local preventive interventions that work. The emergence of communities that promote behavioral health and successful development of all their children could create the conditions for true social justice in society.

References

Botvin, Gilbert J., Eli Baker, Linda Dusenbury, Elizabeth M. Botvin, and Tracy Diaz. 1995. "Long-Term Follow-up Results of a Randomized Drug Abuse Prevention Trial in a White Middle-Class Population." *Journal of the American Medical Association* 273: 1106–1112.

Catalano, Richard F., and J. David Hawkins. 1996. "The Social Development Model: A Theory of Antisocial Behavior." In *Delinquency and Crime: Current Theories*, edited by J. David Hawkins, 139–197. New York: Cambridge University Press.

Catalano, Richard F., Jisuk Park, Tracy W. Harachi, Kevin P. Haggerty, Robert D. Abbott, and J. David Hawkins. 2005. "Mediating the Effects of Poverty, Gender, Individual Characteristics, and External Constraints on Antisocial Behavior: A Test of the Social Development Model and Implications for Developmental Life-Course Theory." In *Integrated Developmental and Life-Course Theories of Offending*, edited by David P. Farrington, 93–124. New Brunswick, NJ: Transaction.

Chou, Chih Ping, Susanne Montgomery, Mary Ann Pentz, Louise A. Rohrbach, C. Anderson Johnson, Brian R. Flay, and David P. MacKinnon. 1998. "Effects of a Community-Based Prevention Program in Decreasing Drug Use in High-Risk Adolescents." *American Journal of Public Health* 88: 944–948.

Elliott, Delbert S., David Huizinga, and Suzanne S. Ageton. 1985. *Explaining Delinquency and Drug Use.* Beverly Hills, CA: Sage.

Farrington, David P. 1992. "The Need for Longitudinal-Experimental Research on Offending and Antisocial Behavior." In *Preventing Antisocial Behavior*, edited by Joan McCord and Richard E. Tremblay, 353–376. New York: Guilford.

Farrington, David P. 2003. "Developmental and Life-Course Criminology: Key Theoretical and Empirical Issues—the 2002 Sutherland Award Address." *Criminology* 41: 221–255.

Farrington, David P., and Donald J. West. 1982. "The Cambridge Study in Delinquent Development." In *Prospective Longitudinal Research: An Empirical Basis for the Primary Prevention of Psychosocial Disorders*, edited by Sarnoff A. Mednick and André E. Baert, 137–145. Oxford: Oxford University Press.

Gottfredson, Denise C., and Gary D. Gottfredson. 2002. "Quality of School-Based Prevention Programs: Results from a National Survey." *Journal of Research in Crime and Delinquency* 39: 3–35.

Gottfredson, Denise C., David B. Wilson, and Stacy S. Najaka. 2002. "School-Based Crime Prevention." *Evidence-Based Crime Prevention*, edited by Lawrence W. Sherman, David P. Farrington, Brandon C. Welsh, and Doris L. MacKenzie, 56–164. New York: Routledge.

Hawkins, J. David, Richard F. Catalano, Rick Kosterman, Robert D. Abbott, and Karl G. Hill. 1999. "Preventing Adolescent Health-Risk Behaviors by Strengthening Protection During Childhood." *Archives of Pediatrics and Adolescent Medicine* 153: 226–234.

Hawkins, J. David, Richard F. Catalano, Diane M. Morrison, Julie O'Donnell, Robert D. Abbott, and Edward L. Day. 1992. "The Seattle Social Development Project: Effects of the First Four Years on Protective Factors and Problem Behaviors." In *Preventing Antisocial Behavior: Interventions from Birth through Adolescence*, edited by Joan McCord and Richard E. Tremblay, 139–161. New York: Guilford Press.

Hawkins, J. David, Rick Kosterman, Richard F. Catalano, Karl G. Hill, and Robert D. Abbott. 2005. "Promoting Positive Adult Functioning through Social Development Intervention in Childhood: Long-Term Effects from the Seattle Social Development Project." *Archives of Pediatrics and Adolescent Medicine* 159: 25–31.

Hawkins, J. David, Rick Kosterman, Richard Catalano, Karl G. Hill, and Robert D. Abbott. 2008. "Effects of Social Development Intervention in Childhood Fifteen Years Later." *Archives of Pediatrics and Adolescent Medicine* 162: 1133–1141.

Hawkins, J. David, Sabrina Oesterle, Eric C. Brown, Michael W. Arthur, Robert D. Abbott, Abigail A. Fagan, and Richard F. Catalano. 2009. "Results of a Type 2 Translational Research Trial to Prevent Adolescent Drug Use and Delinquency: A Test of Communities That Care." *Archives of Pediatrics and Adolescent Medicine* 163: 789–798.

Hill, Karl G., Jennifer A. Bailey, J. David Hawkins, Richard F. Catalano, Rick Kosterman, Sabrina Oesterle, and Robert D. Abbott. 2010. *Effects and Mediators of the Seattle Social Development Project Intervention on the Onset of STI Diagnosis through Age 30.* Unpublished manuscript. Social Development Research Group, University of Washington, Seattle.

Huang, Bu, Rick Kosterman, Richard F. Catalano, J. David Hawkins, and Robert D. Abbott. 2001. "Modeling Mediation in the Etiology of Violent Behavior and Adolescence: A Test of the Social Development Model." *Criminology* 39: 75–107.

Lonczak, Heather S., Robert D. Abbott, J. David Hawkins, Rick Kosterman, and Richard F. Catalano. 2002. "Effects of the Seattle Social Development Project on Sexual Behavior, Pregnancy, Birth, and Sexually Transmitted Disease Outcomes by Age 21 Years." *Archives of Pediatrics and Adolescent Medicine* 156: 438–447.

Lonczak, Heather S., Bu Huang, Richard F. Catalano, J. David Hawkins, Karl G. Hill, Robert D. Abbott, Jean A. M. Ryan, and Rick Kosterman. 2001. "The Social Predictors of Adolescent Alcohol Misuse: A Test of the Social Development Model." *Journal of Studies on Alcohol* 62: 179–189.

O'Donnell, Julie, J. David Hawkins, Richard F. Catalano, Robert D. Abbott, and Edward L. Day. 1995. "Preventing School Failure, Drug Use, and Delinquency among Low-Income Children: Long-Term Intervention in Elementary Schools." *American Journal of Orthopsychiatry* 65: 87–100.

Welsh, Brandon C., and David P. Farrington. 2006. "Evidence-Based Crime Prevention." In *Preventing Crime: What Works for Children, Offenders, Victims, and Places*, edited by Brandon C. Welsh and David P. Farrington, 1–20. New York: Springer.

PART IV

Intervention and Treatment

24

The Human Experiment in Treatment

A MEANS TO THE END OF OFFENDER RECIDIVISM

Doris Layton MacKenzie and Gaylene Styve Armstrong

Forty years ago, dramatic events combined to create an environment conducive to major social changes in the United States. People began to question the legitimacy of our social institutions. Recognizing the inequities in society for minorities and women led many to support civil and women's rights. Additionally, a movement mostly driven by youthful citizens questioned the mores of the times. They demanded more sexual freedom and insisted on freedom of choice in things such as clothes and hairstyles. The social chaos was further fueled by conflicts over the war in Vietnam. Antiwar advocates displayed their disagreement, demonstrating social disobedience through antiwar marches and draft dodging. Taken as a whole, times were ripe for a change, and major transformations occurred in US social institutions (Cullen and Gilbert 1982).

Along with the general social chaos of the time, corrections faced some additional issues. For one, the experiences of prison inmates led to prison riots where both staff and inmates were injured or killed. Sentencing research revealed extreme discretion and disparity in sentencing and the negative consequences for many minorities. The watershed event was a major research report evaluating the effectiveness of correctional programs by Martinson and his colleagues, which was interpreted to show that "nothing works" to change offenders (Martinson 1974; Lipton, Martinson, and Wilks 1975). The authors did not say that nothing could work. What they did say was that considering the substandard research designs examining poorly implemented programs, it was impossible to tell what could potentially work to reduce future offending. But times were ripe for a change, and "nothing works" became the mantra within corrections. At the same time, crime rates were increasing and illegal drug use was becoming common. These issues led both liberals and conservatives to argue for, and implement, change in the existing correctional policy.

With the philosophical shift from an emphasis on rehabilitation, which had existed for the first seven decades of the twentieth century, to a philosophy of incapacitation and deterrence, policy changes were quickly apparent and had a major impact on US corrections. Sentencing guidelines and mandatory minimums were designed to limit discretion in sentencing. The "War on Drugs" increased sentence lengths and the number of prison sentences for drug offenders. A philosophical change away from rehabilitation to incapacitation and deterrence meant more retributive sentences were initiated. The idea was that if nothing worked to rehabilitate prisoners then maybe it was better to keep them in prison or give them onerous punishments so they would not continue to commit crimes.

The impact of these correctional policies on the size of the correctional population was also quickly evident. From 1930 until about 1975 incarceration rates remained about 100 for every 100,000 in the population, leading Blumstein and Cohen (1973) to propose a theory of the stability of punishment. Yet by 1985 the incarceration rate had risen to 313 per 100,000, and it continued to grow so that by 2009 there were well over 2 million offenders incarcerated in federal and state prisons and local jails. The incarceration rate at this point had reached 748 per 100,000 US residents. Furthermore, the shift in correctional policies not only impacted the number of persons incarcerated, but also the number of individuals who were on community supervision. In 1980, 1.1 million offenders were on probation and another 220,438 were on parole, but by 2009 these numbers had grown to over 4.2 million on probation and 819,308 on parole.

Correctional programs and policies built upon incapacitation and deterrence became the prevailing perspective. As a result, less time and money were made available for offender programs, which became compounded by budgetary challenges associated with overcrowded prisons. Rehabilitation became a prohibited word. Correctional interventions focused on control (e.g., urine testing, intensive supervision) and punishment (e.g., boot camps). Correctional staff members had more of a policing mentality and were relatively uninterested in supporting the provision of services and treatment, instead being forced to center their attention on basic warehousing and control of incarcerated offenders. Confinement became ruled by a belief that if "nothing works," the only reason for treatment in prison is to keep prisoners active and healthy.

While many accepted the mantra that nothing worked to change offenders, as well as the changes in correctional policy, others continued to try to understand the causes of crime, how to change offenders, and what research techniques would enable us to successfully identify effective programs and policies. David Farrington was one such voice (Farrington, Ohlin, and Wilson 1986). Addressing the issues found in the Martinson report, he argued that more rigorous research of better-implemented programs would successfully demonstrate what was effective in preventing or reducing the criminal behavior of delinquents and offenders.

Farrington was far ahead of others when he began extolling the benefits of randomized experiments. In an early paper, Farrington identified 35 randomized experiments published between 1957 and 1981 that examined the impact of crime and justice interventions on offending outcomes (Farrington 1983). In concluding his paper, Farrington argued for an increase in the quality of the research used in criminology, especially stronger methodological designs. Farrington's statements had an important impact on the field. Without doubt, his emphasis on using more rigorous research methods bolstered the quality of research in criminology. A more recent review by Farrington and Welsh (2005) demonstrated this improvement, finding an additional 83 experiments with offending outcomes conducted since Farrington's earlier review.

Both in his emphasis on the quality of research and support for the importance of evaluating correctional programming, David Farrington was a driving force in bringing about changes in the field of criminology and criminal justice. In his words, "evaluation research has tended to be a 'poor relation' in criminology" (2006, 335). As Farrington goes on to note, evaluation has never had high status within criminology: traditional criminology has valued more academic, theoretical studies of the causes of crime. Applied, policy-oriented research was looked down upon. Reflecting this viewpoint is the fact that until the founding of the *Journal of Experimental Criminology* in 2005 no journal focused on criminological evaluation, although *Criminal Justice and Behavior* and more recently *Criminology and Public Policy* have published interesting policy-relevant studies.

In addition to the lack of outlets for evaluation research, no criminological organization focused on evaluations until the relatively new Campbell Collaboration, the Academy of Experimental Criminology, and the Division on Experimental Criminology in the American Society of Criminology. The existence of these groups enabled Farrington and colleagues to create additional awareness of, and advocate for, the need for an increased quantity of *quality* research in criminology. These recent developments also indicate a dramatic change in the prominence and value placed on evaluation research in criminology.

The emphasis on increased evaluations and the quality of these evaluations had several valuable outcomes. First, the existing incapacitation and deterrence interventions were submitted to rigorous tests to determine whether programs operating under these philosophies were effective. Evaluations of the popular correctional interventions, such as boot camp prisons, intensive probation and parole supervision, and drug testing, found they were not effective in reducing criminal behavior. Some programs, such as Scared Straight, even appeared to increase future criminality (MacKenzie 2006). Existing policies such as long prison sentences also were found to do little to deter criminal behavior and were suggested to even be criminogenic (Nagin, Cullen, and Jonson 2009). Additionally, studies discovered many unintended consequences of existing policies in that the large number of youth being sent to prison decimated some urban communities, and further had unintended consequences on many living in the devastated communities. Moreover, it was determined that a large proportion of those suffering under these draconian policies were young minorities from inner cities.

Improved statistical techniques along with systematic reviews and meta-analyses provided evidence of what was effective in preventing and reducing criminal behavior (MacKenzie 2006). As had been argued by Farrington and many others working in criminology from a psychological perspective, individual-level differences in attitudes and thinking are important determinants of criminal activity. Effective programs must follow certain principles of effective practice (Andrews and Bonta 2003). In a summary of her examination of correctional treatment programs, management strategies, and interventions, MacKenzie found programs such as cognitive skills, vocational and academic education, and drug treatment are effective in reducing later recidivism, while incapacitation and deterrence-based programs (e.g. supervision, boot camps) were not. According to her, effective programs are those that address cognitive change as a component of the program. From this perspective, effective programs must bring about a transformation in individuals' thinking before they are ready to take advantage of services and opportunities. The disappointing research findings of the ineffectiveness of many reentry programs may be because the interventions seldom combine the focus on work opportunities with programs to address the criminogenic thinking of the participants.

We are now on the brink of another major paradigm change in corrections. Again, a combination of factors has impinged on corrections, and these factors appear to be leading to a major transformation in correctional policy and practice. Research evidence has demonstrated the failure of incapacitation and deterrence policies while increasing evidence shows rehabilitation and services that create cognitive change in criminal thinking can effectively prevent or reduce criminal behavior. Policymakers, correctional administrators, and researchers search for ways to use this scientific knowledge to reduce correctional populations without producing a corresponding increase in crime. There is a new emphasis on "evidence-based" interventions, interventions that have been shown to be effective when tested with rigorous research designs and advanced statistical techniques (MacKenzie 2001; 2005).

Many other factors are also aligning to prime this shift in correctional philosophy. A growth in research that demonstrates programs that follow treatment protocols are effective is evident. Broad-based awareness of the "revolving door" as well as the impact of deinstitutionalization of the mentally ill on the correctional population, especially jails, is now commonplace. Recognition of specialized needs for subpopulations such as female offenders and those with co-occurring disorders has developed, along with an understanding of challenges posed by sentencing guidelines that provide little flexibility and do not consider how to integrate treatment into guidelines so some can be diverted from prison. Numerous methodological and statistical advancements also accompany these areas of substantive growth, such as an emphasis on measuring fidelity and on appropriate modeling of myriad services now provided to some offenders.

The downturn in the economy is perhaps the most significant factor generating an interest in changing corrections. Various levels of governments are searching for ways to reduce expenditures, and the correctional system is an appealing target. Policymakers are recognizing the high cost associated with a large incarcerated population and are seeking politically palatable methods of reducing the population without appearing "soft" on crime, even utilizing the mantra "smart on crime."

The motivating forces in corrections today appear to be "evidence-based" interventions and being "smart on crime." This new perspective will require close working relationships among policymakers, practitioners, and researchers if the goals of more successful and cost-effective correctional interventions are to be realized. Decisions must be made about which offenders will benefit most from treatments, which are appropriate candidates for alternative correctional strategies, and who can safely be released from prisons or jails without jeopardizing public safety.

In our opinion, some of the most pressing issues are the identification and management of special populations such as the mentally ill, women, those with dual diagnoses, and drug-involved offenders. Furthermore, these interventions must be done "smartly" so recommended programs and management of offenders become neither prohibitively expensive nor a threat to public safety. Decision-making will require valid and reliable tools to guide evidence-based decisions about the risks offenders present to the community and their treatment needs. Research clearly demonstrates that these tools substantially improve predictions when compared to clinical judgment alone in predicting reoffending and violent crime. In an effort to reduce costs, some jurisdictions are examining how to incorporate risk and needs assessments into all phases of justice decision-making from pretrial through sentencing and release. These instruments will assist decision-makers in determining appropriate candidates for alternative treatment or management with the benefit of reducing the costly use of incarceration when more effective evidence-based alternatives are possible.

Another pressing issue for correctional research is the determination of effective treatment models for offenders with mental illness. In both prisons and jails, there are staggering numbers of people who struggle with mental health issues. While some screening processes are in place, many inmates are still not appropriately diagnosed or treated for their conditions. Upon release, many of these same individuals experience ongoing challenges in the reentry process, including maintaining compliance with medication and meeting their own basic needs. Pioneering work in the area of offenders with mental illness has led to an important distinction regarding the offenders themselves. Contrary to previous opinion, a fundamental assumption growing in the literature is that mental illness is not necessarily the cause of criminal behaviors resulting in incarceration. Instead, the same risk factors for the perpetuation of violence and other criminal acts such as an established criminal history, antisocial personality, antisocial cognitions, and a tendency toward antisocial associates are shared by both those with and those without mental illness. Moreover, these factors are generally stronger predictors of recidivism than mental illness diagnoses themselves, although psychological conditions appear to be related to the poor functioning of the mentally ill in the community (Skeem, Manchak, and Peterson 2011). Correctional agencies must recognize that these offenders are working with two deficits—criminal and mental health components. Accordingly, agencies, therapists, and program developers must work to address the treatment of underlying criminogenic needs of offenders, along with mental illness in order to facilitate successful reintegration into their community. While offenders with mental health or other issues have been used as an example here, the message from the literature clearly indicates the need to work within a multidimensional treatment environment, which may require improved planning and coordination efforts.

While research has successfully identified therapeutic programs that are effective in reducing recidivism, much less is known about how to ensure these programs are delivered with fidelity and therapeutic integrity, or the extent to which interventions conform to the manner of service intended by the developers of the service. Criminology in general has been criticized by Petersilia (2003) for its lack of focus on what goes on inside corrections programs. Despite increasing knowledge and statistical precision, correctional research continues to fail to question the "black box" itself. The lack of precision in understanding program content and processes has been noted within correctional approaches in general (see Bonta et al. 2008). When programs appropriately adhere to the principles of risk, need, and responsivity, they can effectively reduce recidivism, but many do not follow these principles (Andrews and Bonta 2006). Consequently, an ideal component of any correctional program evaluation is a relatively thorough, yet unobtrusive assessment of program delivery, especially when a program is adopted from another jurisdiction or population, since portability of a promising program does not always follow (see Armstrong 2003). The next generation of correctional programs and related policies is poised to include a careful, rigorous evaluation of both content and outcome, given the increased interest of policymakers and practitioners alike in evidence-based practices that hold promise for increased economic efficiency.

In summary, we are on the cusp of a new age in corrections. At this point, we do not know what the future will bring. What is clear is that the old paradigm has failed and changes are on the way. Certainly, we must address the problems created by the old philosophy as we move toward smarter ways to address crime problems with evidence-based solutions.

References

Andrews, Donald A., and James Bonta. 2003. *The Psychology of Criminal Conduct*. 3rd ed. Cincinnati: Anderson.

Andrews, Donald A., and James Bonta. 2006. *The Psychology of Criminal Conduct*. 4th ed. Cincinnati: Anderson.

Armstrong, Todd. 2003. "The Effect of Moral Reconation Therapy on the Recidivism of Youthful Offenders: A Randomized Experiment." *Criminal Justice and Behavior* 30: 668–687.

Blumstein, Alfred, and Jacqueline Cohen. 1973. "A Theory of the Stability of Punishment." *Journal of Criminal Law and Criminology* 64: 198–207.

Bonta, James, Tanya Rugge, Terri L. Scott, Guy Bourgon, and Annie Yassine. 2008. "Exploring the Black Box of Community Supervision." *Journal of Offender Rehabilitation* 47: 248–270.

Cullen, Francis T., and Karen Gilbert. 1982. *Reaffirming Rehabilitation*. Cincinnati: Anderson.

Farrington, David P. 1983. "Sex, Sentencing, and Reconviction." *British Journal of Criminology* 23: 229–248.

Farrington, David P. 2006. "Methodological Quality and the Evaluation of Anti-crime Programs." *Journal of Experimental Criminology* 2: 329–337.

Farrington, David. P., Lloyd E. Ohlin, and James Q. Wilson. 1986. *Understanding and Controlling Crime: Toward a New Research Strategy*. New York: Springer.

Farrington, David P., and Brandon C. Welsh. 2005. "Randomized Experiments in Criminology: What Have We Learned in the Last Two Decades." *Journal of Experimental Criminology* 1: 9–38.

Lipton, Douglas S., Robert Martinson, and Judith Wilks. 1975. *The Effectiveness of Correctional Treatment: A Survey of Treatment Evaluation Studies*. New York: Praeger.

MacKenzie, Doris Layton. 2001. "Corrections and Sentencing in the 21st Century: Evidence-Based Corrections and Sentencing." *Prison Journal* 81: 299–312.

MacKenzie, Doris Layton. 2005. "The Importance of Using Scientific Evidence to Make Decisions about Correctional Programming." *Criminology and Public Policy* 4: 249–258.

MacKenzie, Doris Layton. 2006. *What Works in Corrections? Reducing the Criminal Activites of Offenders and Delinquents*. New York: Cambridge University Press.

Martinson, Robert. 1974. "What Works?—Questions and Answers about Prison Reform." *Public Interest* 35: 22–54.

Nagin, Daniel S., Francis T. Cullen, and Cheryl Lero Jonson. 2009. "Imprisonment and Reoffending." In *Crime and Justice: A Review of the Research*, vol. 38, edited by Michael Tonry, 115–200. Chicago: University of Chicago Press.

Petersilia, Joan. 2003. *When Prisoners Come Home: Parole and Prisoner Reentry*. New York: Oxford University Press.

Skeem, Jennifer L., Sarah Manchak, and Jullian K. Peterson. 2011. "Correctional Policy for Offenders with Mental Illness: Creating a New Paradigm for Recidivism Reduction." *Law and Human Behavior* 35: 110–126.

25

Toward a Third Phase of "What Works" in Offender Rehabilitation

Friedrich Lösel

Writing an essay in honor of David Farrington is both easy and difficult. It is easy because he has addressed so many topics that one can smoothly relate one's own research to his work. On the other hand, it is difficult because David has published so much that one may simply replicate what he has already written somewhere. This is a particular risk for me as my research interests are similar to David's, ranging from risk and protective factors in the development of crime and violence over school bullying and football hooliganism to early prevention and offender rehabilitation. No other criminologist has inspired my research as much as David.

This essay addresses offender rehabilitation. In this field David was a pioneer in delinquent behavior modification (Farrington 1979). Later he evaluated many programs in primary studies and meta-analyses, addressed practical issues such as program implementation, and dealt with cost-benefit issues. He also promoted experiments and quality standards for evaluation and founded the Campbell Collaboration Crime and Justice Group to provide the best evidence on "what works." Within this context, I will briefly address the "what works" movement in correctional treatment, actual controversies about it, and future perspectives.

A First Phase of "What Works" in Correctional Treatment

In the late 1980s, we published a German book on social therapy in prisons that contained an early meta-analysis on offender rehabilitation (Lösel and Köferl 1989). We stated a pendulum swing from therapeutic optimism in the 1960s to Martinson's "nothing works" conclusion in the 1970s, which was mainly due to a lack of sound evaluations and simple significance counting. We pleaded for a more continuous development of knowledge on reducing reoffending and revealed a small positive treatment effect: This was in accordance with early North American meta-analyses (e.g., Andrews et al. 1990; Lipsey 1992).

Since then, many systematic reviews contributed to a renaissance of correctional treatment. They show not only a mean positive effect ($d \approx 0.20$), but also clear differences between types of programs (Aos, Miller, and Drake 2006; Lipsey and Cullen 2007; Lösel and Schmucker 2005; McGuire 2002; MacKenzie 2006; Tong and Farrington 2007). Cognitive behavioral treatment (CBT), structured therapeutic communities, multisystemic approaches, and basic education showed mostly positive outcomes. Relatively strong effects were observed in programs that followed the Risk-Need-Responsivity (RNR) principles (Andrews and Bonta 2010). Low structured casework, counseling, mentoring, or psychodynamic approaches were less successful. Purely punitive or deterrent measures showed zero or even negative effects.

A Second Phase of "What Works" in Correctional Treatment

After the research-oriented first phase followed a strong increase of program implementation. This was not only triggered by the scientific evidence but also by media reports on extreme cases of sexual and violent offending that raised serious public concern. In many countries, policy reacted punitively, but also invested in correctional treatment. Countries such as England and Wales, the Netherlands, Norway, Scotland, Sweden, and some US states and (temporarily) Canada introduced program accreditation as part of an evidence-guided policy. In England and Wales the Correctional Services Accreditation Panel (CSAP) applied criteria that were based on RNR and other research: (1) clear model of change, (2) thorough selection of offenders, (3) targeting dynamic risk factors, (4) effective learning and teaching methods, (5) skill orientation, (6) appropriate sequence and duration, (7) promotion of offender motivation, (8) continuity of services, (9) ensuring program integrity, and (10) ongoing evaluation.

Within a few years, approximately 40 programs for general, violent, sexual, drug-addicted, alcohol-misusing, road traffic, and domestic violence offenders were accredited for use in prisons and/or the community. More than 25,000 offenders participated in programs per year. Intensive assessment, staff training, supervision, and audits were carried out to ensure quality. Overall, this is probably the world's most ambitious example of transforming "what works" research into policy. However, the fast rollout led to practical problems and deficits in sound evaluation (Maguire et al. 2010). Some findings were promising; others revealed mixed results and led to controversial discussions (e.g., Harper and Chitty 2005; Hollin 2008).

More recent data suggest indirectly that the policy was not unsuccessful. For example, reconviction rates dropped for offenders with prison sentences of more than one year—these are the typical recipients of programs. There are also some encouraging results on community treatment programs. Most recently, Travers and colleagues (2010) compared more than 17,000 participants of the custodial Enhanced

Thinking Skills program with offenders from a national cohort who were matched for risk level and sentence length. Overall, there was a reduction in reoffending of more than 12 percent. Positive effects have also been observed in a similar study on sexual offender treatment (Ruth Mann, personal communication).

Current Discussions and Controversies

In spite of encouraging findings, the "what works" movement has been put under question (Brayford, Cowe, and Deering 2010; Farrall 2006; Ward and Brown 2004). It has been criticized that the prevailing approaches (*a*) promote too much centralization and top-down administration; (*b*) contain demanding processes of program accreditation and audit; (*c*) reduce diversity and creativity in practice; (*d*) place too much emphasis on quantitative data; (*e*) give too much weight to standardized CBT programs; (*f*) focus primarily on characteristics of the individual; (*g*) adhere to a risk- and deficit-oriented image of the offender; and (*h*) ignore systems and institutional issues. Some arguments (a, b, c, d) derive from typical reaction to accreditation and evidence-oriented policies (Maguire et al. 2010). Others (e, f, g, h) reflect stereotypes of the "what works" approach that do not acknowledge the broad range of programs and also expansions of RNR (Andrews et al. 2011; Lipsey and Cullen 2007).

A part of the current discussions relates to the Good Lives Model (GLM; Ward and Brown 2004) that puts more emphasis on treatment alliances, offender strengths, and other issues. However, Andrews and colleagues (2011) show that the GLM goes not much beyond an extended RNR model and that its empirical evidence is yet meager. Other publications plead for a switch from "what works" to a "desistance paradigm" (Brayford et al. 2010; McNeill 2006). Here the focus shifts from specific programs to social institutions and natural protective factors. Marriage or stable employment is a typical example of such turning points in life (e.g., Maruna 2001; Sampson and Laub 1993), but many other personal and social resources may also play a role (Bottoms and Shapland 2011; Lösel and Bender 2003). The focus on desistance is not at all in conflict with the "what works" question. Although there is more weight given to community services and social and individual resources, "what works in reducing reoffending" can easily be translated into "what works in promoting desistance" (Lösel in press; Porporino 2010). In both perspectives treatment programs can contribute to a desirable outcome, but do not determine it.

Toward a Third Phase of "What Works"

In physics one counts only seven new paradigms in 500 years, whereas social scientists seem to like more frequent discussions about paradigm shifts. In offender rehabilitation this bears the risk of abandoning methodological standards (Farrington

2003) and the achievements over the last two decades. Without doubt, there are many organizational issues and creative activities that go beyond the mainstream of "what works" (e.g., Brayford et al. 2010). They are relevant for the "culture" of criminal justice and offenders' well-being, however, we know little about their effect on reoffending. Therefore, we need more systematic research on "what else works."

In particular, it is necessary to expand our knowledge about the many factors that contribute to reducing reoffending (or increasing desistance). These go far beyond the mere program contents but are not yet well investigated (Lösel 2011). Much more research is needed on "what works" with whom, in what contexts, under what conditions, and with regard to what outcomes. To achieve progress in this direction, I propose 10 strategies:

1. More "systems" instead of "silo" approaches: In the "what works" literature programs are seen as isolated entities. However, in practice offenders may not only participate in a specific CBT program but also get education, vocational training, and social services in the community. These interventions are not randomly allocated and will not exert simple additive effects. As clinical pharmacology and technology show, the effects of one measure can increase or decrease depending on the context of others. Similar thoughts underlie multisystemic programs and the National Offender Management Service's pathways to reducing reoffending: accommodation; education, training and employment; mental and physical health; drugs and alcohol; finance and debt; children and families; and attitudes, thinking, and behavior.

2. More controlled evaluations of routine practice: The above-mentioned systems- and multiagency approaches are less suitable for standard (quasi-) experimental evaluations of single programs. This should not lead to a fallback into noninterpretable designs. On the one hand, randomized controlled trials can address systematic variations of intervention elements. On the other hand, large cohort studies with matching procedures can be used to evaluate patterns of interventions.

3. More systematic process evaluation: In addition to the program content its quality of implementation is relevant for effectiveness. Although this sounds trivial, most outcome studies on rehabilitation provide no, or only rudimentary, data on integrity. Audit systems have limited value for this purpose because they mainly address organizational features and reveal not much variation. Process analyses are also necessary to answer practical questions such as the impact of fixed groups versus a rolling format.

4. More links between programs and the institutional context: Since the early work of Moos it has been shown that the institutional climate is important. Such factors are related to the well-being of clients and prison suicides (Liebling and Arnold 2005). More research is needed on

the moderating or mediating effects of institutional contexts on treatment programs.

5. More emphasis on relationship issues: In psychotherapy mutual cooperation, reinforcement, and bonding between client and therapist are very important for the outcome (Orlinsky et al. 1994). Although correctional programs are often more structured and educative, Ward's plea for more attention to therapeutic alliances is appropriate. This does not mean that "what works" is replaced by "who works" (as sometimes suggested), because unstructured casework has not shown strong effects (Andrews and Bonta 2010).

6. More differentiation and individualization: Many current offending behavior programs are fully standardized. There is not much evidence on this issue, but in sexual offender treatment some individualized elements seem to be more effective (Schmucker and Lösel 2009). Of course, correctional programs should not move too far toward individual delivery. This would be very expensive and abandon the strengths of learning in groups. However, rehabilitation programs should provide enough free space to deal with intimate personal problems or minority issues that are difficult to address in standard programs.

7. More integration of natural protective factors: The RNR concept focused on dynamic risk factors, and its expansions also include the assessment of strengths (Andrews et al. 2011). In agreement with the GLM and desistance research, this approach should be intensified. However, protective factors are only the opposite pole of risk factors, and many offenders show an accumulation of the latter. As both effects depend on dose-response functions (Lösel and Bender 2003), one should not rely too much on strengthening single factors on one side of the balance.

8. More direct comparisons of custodial and community measures: Imprisonment seems to have no deterrent but even a small criminogenic effect (Durlauf and Nagin 2011). Although the respective studies did not address the impact of custodial treatment, other research also showed some advantage of community programs (Lipsey and Cullen 2007; Lösel and Schmucker 2005). However, there are only few direct experimental comparisons of custodial and ambulatory programs and therefore more studies should investigate what levels of offender risk and harm can be most effectively addressed in both contexts.

9. More links between offender treatment and neurobiology: Neurobiological research on personality-disordered offenders has made clear progress (Glenn and Raine 2008). Therefore, this field should receive more attention in treatment. For example, there are some promising findings on antiandrogen treatment for specific sexual

offenders and on selective serotonin reuptake inhibitors (SSRIs) for subgroups of impulsive clients. In both fields more evaluation is needed (also on side effects). Neurobiology must not necessarily lead to more pharmacotherapy but can help to differentiate psychosocial measures (e.g., in combinations with CBT).

10. More attention to national and cultural differences: The current evidence on "what works" is mainly based on North American studies. Systematic reviews do not only show a lack of controlled research in Asia, South America, and Africa, but also in Europe (Koehler et al. 2011). Research and practice need to address in more detail the problems of transferring and adapting Anglo-American correctional programs to other justice systems and local needs.

I hope that these proposals will help to continue "what works" in the spirit of David Farrington and support offenders in desisting from crime and living a law-abiding "good life" (whatever this may be in their own view).

Note

This essay is based on an invited plenary lecture at the Fourth International Conference on Psychology and Law of the American Psychology and Law Society, Australian and New Zealand Association of Psychiatry, Psychology and Law, and European Association of Psychology and Law, held in March 2011 in Miami, Florida.

References

Andrews, Donald A., and James Bonta. 2010. *The Psychology of Criminal Conduct.* 5th ed. Cincinnati: Anderson.

Andrews, Donald A., James Bonta, and Steve Wormith. 2011. "The Risk-Need-Responsivity (RNR) Model: Does Adding the Good Lives Model Contribute to Effective Crime Prevention?" *Criminal Justice and Behavior* 38: 735–755.

Andrews, Donald A., Ivan Zinger, Robert D. Hoge, James Bonta, Paul Gendreau, and Francis T. Cullen. 1990. "Does Correctional Treatment Work? A Clinically Relevant and Psychologically Informed Meta-analysis." *Criminology* 28: 369–404.

Aos, Steve, Marna Miller, and Elizabeth Drake. 2006. *Evidence-Based Adult Corrections Programs: What Works and What Does Not.* Olympia: Washington State Institute of Public Policy.

Bottoms, Anthony, and Joanna Shapland. 2011. "Steps towards Desistance among Young Male Adult Offenders." In *Escape Routes*, edited by Stephen Farrall, Mike Hough, Shadd Maruna and Richard Sparks, 43–80. Milton Park, UK: Routledge.

Brayford, Jo, Francis Cowe, and John Deering. 2010. *What Else Works? Creative Works with Offenders.* Cullompton, UK: Willan.

Durlauf, Steven N., and Daniel S. Nagin. 2011. "Imprisonment and Crime: Can Both be Reduced?" *Criminology and Public Policy* 10: 13–54.

Farrall, Stephen. 2006. "Rolling Back the State: Mrs. Thatcher's Criminological Legacy." *International Journal of the Sociology of Law* 34: 256–277.

Farrington, David P. 1979. "Delinquent Behaviour Modification in the Natural Environment." *British Journal of Criminology* 19: 353–372.

Farrington, David P. 2003. "Methodological Quality Standards for Evaluation Research." *Annals of the American Academy of Political and Social Science* 587: 49–68.

Glenn, Andrea L., and Adrian Raine. 2008. "The Neurobiology of Psychopathy." *Psychiatric Clinics of North America* 31: 463–475.

Harper, Gemma, and Chloe Chitty. 2005. *The Impact of Corrections on Re-offending: A Review of "What Works"*. Home Office Research Study 291. London: Home Office.

Hollin, Clive R. 2008. "Evaluating Offending Behaviour Programmes: Does Only Randomization Glister?" *Criminology and Criminal Justice* 8: 89–106.

Koehler, Johann, Thomas Akoensi, David Humphries, and Friedrich Lösel. 2011. *A Systematic Review and Meta-analysis on the Effects of Young Offender Treatment in Europe*. Report of the STARR Project. Cambridge: Institute of Criminology.

Liebling, Alison, and Helen Arnold. 2005. *Prisons and Their Moral Performance*. Oxford: Oxford University Press.

Lipsey, Mark W. 1992. "The Effect of Treatment on Juvenile Delinquents: Results from Meta-analysis." In *Psychology and Law: International Perspectives*, edited by Friedrich Lösel, Doris Bender, and Thomas Bliesener, 131–143. Berlin: de Gruyter.

Lipsey, Mark W., and Francis T. Cullen. 2007. "The Effectiveness of Correctional Rehabilitation: A Review of Systematic Reviews." *Annual Review of Law and Social Science* 3: 297–320.

Lösel, Friedrich. In press. "What Works in Correctional Treatment and Rehabilitation for Young Adults?" In *Young Adult Offenders: Lost in Transition?* edited by Friedrich Lösel, Anthony E. Bottoms, and David P. Farrington. Milton Park, UK: Routledge.

Lösel, Friedrich, and Doris Bender. 2003. "Protective Factors and Resilience." In *Early Prevention of Adult Antisocial Behaviour*, edited by David P. Farrington and Jeremy Coid, 130–204. Cambridge: Cambridge University Press.

Lösel, Friedrich, and Peter Köferl. 1989. "Evaluation Research on Correctional Treatment in West Germany: A Meta-Analysis." In *Criminal Behavior and the Justice System*, edited by Hermann Wegener, Friedrich Lösel, and Jochen Haisch, 234–237. New York: Springer.

Lösel, Friedrich, and Martin Schmucker. 2005. "The Effectiveness of Treatment for Sexual Offenders: A Comprehensive Meta-analysis." *Journal of Experimental Criminology* 1: 117–146.

MacKenzie, Doris L. 2006. *What Works in Corrections? Reducing the Criminal Activities of Offenders and Delinquents*. Cambridge: Cambridge University Press.

Maguire, Mike, Don Grubin, Friedrich Lösel, and Peter Raynor. 2010. "'What Works' and the Correctional Services Accreditation Panel: Taking Stock from an Inside Perspective." *Criminology and Criminal Justice* 10: 37–58.

Maruna, Shadd. 2001. *Making Good: How Ex-convicts Reform and Rebuild Their Lives*. Washington, DC: American Psychological Association Books.

McGuire, James. 2002. "Integrating Findings from Research Reviews." In *Offender Rehabilitation and Treatment*, edited by James McGuire, 3–38. Chichester, UK: Wiley.

McNeill, Fergus. 2006. "A Desistance Paradigm for Offender Management." *Criminology and Criminal Justice* 6: 39–62.

Orlinsky, David E., Klaus Grawe, and Barbara K. Parks. 1994. "Process and Outcome in Psychotherapy." In *Handbook of Psychotherapy and Behavior Change*, 4th ed., edited by Allen E. Bergin and Sol L. Garfield, 270–376. New York: Wiley.

Porporino, Frank. 2010. "Bringing Sense and Sensitivity to Corrections: From Programmes to 'Fix' Offenders to Services to Support Desistance." In *What Else Works?* edited by Jo Brayford, Francis Cowe and John Deering, 61–86. Cullompton, UK: Willan.

Sampson, Robert J., and John H. Laub. 1993. *Crime in the Making: Pathways and Turning Points through Life*. Cambridge: Harvard University Press.

Schmucker, Martin, and Friedrich Lösel. 2009. "A Systematic Review of High-Quality Evaluations of Sexual Offender Treatment." Paper presented at the Ninth Conference of the European Society of Criminology, Ljubljana, Slovenia, September 9–12.

Tong, L. S. Joy, and David P. Farrington. 2006. "How Effective Is the Reasoning and Rehabilitation Programme in Reducing Offending? A Meta-analysis of Evaluations in Four Countries." *Psychology, Crime and Law* 12: 3–24.

Travers, Rosie, Helen C. Wakeling, Ruth E. Mann, and Clive R. Hollin. 2010. *Reconviction following a Cognitive Skills Intervention*. London: National Offender Management Service.

Ward, Tony, and Mark Brown. 2004. "The Good Lives Model and Conceptual Issues in Offender Rehabilitation." *Psychology, Crime and Law* 10: 243–257.

26

Raising the Bar

TRANSFORMING KNOWLEDGE TO PRACTICE FOR CHILDREN IN CONFLICT WITH THE LAW

Leena K. Augimeri and Christopher J. Koegl

It is impossible to sum up the enormous influence Professor David Farrington has had on the fields of criminology and psychology—especially in expanding our understanding of child delinquency. His broad vision has extended the boundaries of knowledge and has played a significant role in our own professional development for more than 30 years. He has been a wonderful colleague and mentor, first when we were students studying crime, deviance, and human behavior, and later on in our professional careers as scientists, practitioners, and program developers. His research, knowledge, and forward thinking has played a pivotal role in *raising the bar* in terms of our understanding of child delinquency and bullying, as well as the critical elements needed to develop and evaluate interventions to meet the needs of high-risk children, families, and communities. His work greatly influenced the creation of our own crime prevention strategy for young children in conflict with the law, which includes police-community referral protocols, structured risk/need assessments, and gender-sensitive programs (Augimeri et al. 2011; Koegl et al. 2008). He inspires our thinking and continues to push us to *raise the bar* in regards to risk and promotive factors, self-control, intervening early in the lives of high-risk children, and methodological issues in evaluating effectiveness of crime prevention models. This journey of learning and sharing began over 20 years ago when one of us (LKA) had the honor of meeting David in Reno, Nevada, at the annual meeting of the American Society of Criminology. Over the intervening years, we have been fortunate to have had many stimulating discussions, for example, about the importance of randomized controlled trials; how to define and measure treatment success; understanding outliers; addressing risk factors; and incorporating scientist-practitioner ideals into our work.

Current Knowledge and Practice with Antisocial Children in Conflict with the Law

Over the past three decades, there have been some significant accomplishments in research on the early causes of crime and programmatic approaches for antisocial children and their families. From our perspective, five books stand out as landmark publications for their depth, breadth, and quality of work in this area: *Serious and Violent Juvenile Offenders: Risk Factors and Successful Interventions* (Loeber and Farrington 1998), *Child Delinquents: Development, Intervention, and Service Needs* (Loeber and Farrington 2001), *Saving Children from a Life of Crime: Early Risk Factors and Effective Interventions* (Farrington and Welsh 2007), *Tomorrow's Criminals: The Development of Child Delinquency and Effective Interventions* (Loeber et al. 2008), and *Preventing and Reducing Juvenile Delinquency: A Comprehensive Framework* (Howell 2003). Each of these publications provide clinicians, researchers, and policymakers with a wealth of information in identifying the early causes of crime and highlighting promising programs and strategies for antisocial children. In summary, the collective body of this knowledge demonstrates the following:

1. Whether true *causes*, *moderators*, or *correlates*, a number of child and family risk factors are fairly consistently associated with future antisocial behavior.
2. Relatively more is known about risk factors than protective and promotive factors, and accordingly, more is known about the causes of crime than desistence from crime.
3. It is advantageous to intervene early with high-risk antisocial children and to target interventions according to their identified risk and need.
4. There are treatment modalities that are effective, and some very promising programs have been created. However, relative to the wide body of risk factor research, much less has been done to create, implement, and evaluate effective programs designed specifically for antisocial children in conflict with the law.
5. Referral mechanisms to direct at-risk youth to appropriate services are needed. In practice, however, such initiatives are typically ad hoc due to a lack of resources, unclear roles, and service gaps between societal institutions spanning sectors such as education, child protection, health care, police services, and children's mental health.

We would go one step further to summarize the preceding propositions to make two additional points. With some limited exceptions, we estimate that the field is currently in a better position to predict the future behavior of antisocial children than it is to predict how systems of care will respond to them. We also believe that monitoring and accountability are undeveloped areas within these systems. Although there are some evidence-based programs that have been in existence for a number of years, mechanisms need to be put in place to ensure model adherence and to measure treatment fidelity. In other words, we know relatively more about the *knowledge* side of the equation (e.g., about the causes and correlates of crime) than we do about the *practice* end (e.g., how the system responds and monitors) when it comes to antisocial children. It is important to note that this imbalance does *not* exist within the broader discipline of criminology, which devotes considerable attention to the study of the administration of justice and the behavior of legal and penal institutions for adults engaging in antisocial behavior.

At least in Canada, part of the problem stems from a gap in law and policy that does not *require* the timely referral of high-risk antisocial children to appropriate programs and services that are developmentally geared toward addressing their behavior. While some provinces and territories have child protection statutes containing specific provisions that make childhood antisocial behavior a sufficient condition for formal state intervention, these provisions are typically not used in practice. When we last surveyed child protection authorities in Canada about 10 years ago (Goldberg et al. 1999), we learned that they typically prioritize child protection over the prevention of antisocial behavior per se, leaving an identifiable service gap for antisocial children and their families.

Why is the system not rallying around children with conduct problems? Part of this issue is related to the enormous stigma that still surrounds mental illness and, in particular, children with mental health problems engaged in antisocial behavior (Pescosolido et al. 2007). In our experience, children with conduct problems suffer additional stigma due to their disruptive activities at home, in school, and out in the community. This makes them relatively unattractive not only to school personnel, neighbors, peers, and others, but also to the average service provider because, like their male adult offender counterparts, they are typically difficult to engage and require resource-intensive treatment. In the educational context, we have also witnessed a rise in "zero-tolerance" policies that facilitate the automatic suspension of disruptive children by school personnel, sometimes for minor infractions such as using foul language. To this we would respond by saying that, while it is not acceptable, for these children swearing is the least of their problems. More can and should be done to keep high-risk youths in school to minimize premature school dropout and further difficulties at home and in the community.

One of the greatest challenges facing the field at the moment is the relative shortage of mental health programs geared toward antisocial children. Despite the prevalence and seriousness of antisocial behavior in society, at the time of this publication, there are only a handful of "model programs" under the "Blueprints for Violence Prevention" (www.colorado.edu/cspv/blueprints/modelprograms. html) and "Promising and Model Crime Prevention Programs—Volume 1" (National Crime Prevention Centre 2008) schemes. Many of these programs have not been disseminated universally, and, therefore, we wonder about the nature of the current service landscape and what the true magnitude of unmet need is for children and their families in need of such specialized services across Canada and the United States. What is the system capacity to treat children with early conduct problems? Where do the many undocumented programs stand in terms of their measured effectiveness and their applicability to children with mild, moderate, and severe levels of conduct problems?

Tolan and Dodge's (2005) analysis of the children's mental health system in the United States indicates to us that much still needs to be done to reform the mental health system for children and youth and that a significant step in this regard would be to reframe the problem as a key health care priority. We are in agreement with this line of thinking, and we lend our voice to the call for prioritizing children's mental health particularly when the *poor* mental health of children can have pervasive and long-lasting effects over their life course.

Because most children will grow out of their antisocial behaviors, the issue of reliably identifying *tomorrow's criminals* has become a focus of psychological and criminological research. We embarked on this task over 10 years ago with the development of the Early Assessment Risk Lists for Boys (EARL-20B; Augimeri et al. 2001) and Girls (EARL-21G; Levene et al. 2001). Research on these tools demonstrates that they can be used to predict future antisocial behavior, criminal offending (Augimeri et al. 2010), health system encounters, disease and illness, and monetary costs to both the criminal justice and the health care systems (Koegl 2011). The intended purpose of the instruments is to assist professionals in clinical risk management and service planning, not merely statistical prediction. Although these instruments were designed to frame the assessment in neutral-to-positive terms, we would concede that they do not do enough to explicitly delineate strengths-based or promotive factors for treatment. This problem is not unique to the EARLs but germane to criminological risk factor research in general. As we continue to revise the tools, we will be incorporating more protective factors into the assessment frame, much in the same way that has been recently accomplished for adults (e.g., Vogel et al. 2009) and further develop a corresponding EARL service plan that will link identified risk factors to clinical risk management strategies (de Ruiter and Augimeri in press).

The Future for Research and Practice with Antisocial Children in Conflict with the Law

The fields of criminology and psychology are currently moving toward an increased focus on evidence-based practice. We see this as a positive development that will be well received by organizations that have a research-receptive culture and that embrace quality assurance and monitoring activities. Our sense is that many organizations still need to make this transition. Fortunately, there are a number of ways to move to an evidence-based model of practice that is inclusive and respectful of a wide range of approaches and traditions (Brown, Rounthwaite, and Barwick 2011). We foresee that establishing fidelity and integrity frameworks and ensuring the ongoing monitoring of such activities will constitute the next major challenge to the field as we move the vast body of criminological and psychological research into practice. In this regard, having in-house research support and access to web-based data collection and management systems (e.g., to centralize research activities) will be essential. This could have the added benefit of facilitating multisite evaluations and the collection of a larger number of cases for statistical analysis. Such has been done with Multisystemic Therapy for adolescents (Schoenwald 2008) and SNAP for latency-aged children (Augimeri, Walsh, and Slater 2011).

As evidence-based programs and practices are improved, effective models will become candidates for wider dissemination. This leads to what we see as the next major challenge for the field: abandoning unproven or less promising programs in favor of new approaches that have a measurable impact. To return to a point made earlier: the literature on program implementation and the transportability of such programs is relatively small in comparison to the research on the causes and correlates of crime. As a result, less attention has been paid to which clinician and/or service organizational characteristics are conducive to long-lasting, positive effects. In fact, we think there should be a temporary shift in focus *away* from the attributes of the target population(s) of antisocial children and, instead, toward an analysis of the attributes of the population(s) of service providers adopting evidence-based programs. This could generate novel research questions that are relevant to the early identification, engagement, and effective treatment of antisocial children. Some of these might be, for example: What interpersonal or clinical skills are associated with the consistent engagement of conduct-disordered children and their families? What is the most effective model for ensuring that clinicians are up-to-date with changes in the knowledge base and treatment innovations? Is the organization committed and competent to implement an evidence-based program? We think that research into questions like these could make treatment more client-focused and could bring greater accountability to children's mental health and community-based services. This would include a focus on staff skills, factors that affect clinical competency such as supervision, training, and consultation, and organizational implementation standards and principles (Augimeri, Walsh, and Slater 2011).

A greater emphasis on factors influencing the receptiveness of antisocial children and their families to treatment would be most certainly beneficial. It is well known that children with persistent conduct problems drop out of treatment at a fairly high rate (e.g., Luk et al. 2001), and therefore, a greater understanding of how to engage high-risk cases, particularly those antisocial families that might be most resistant to participating in treatment, is essential. In addition, knowing more about promotive factors would help to situate services within a positive context—something that would greatly enhance client participation by moving treatment away from a deficit-based framework (Farrington and Welsh 2007).

In this regard, we see an enormous potential to involve multiple systems simultaneously, which is why over a decade ago we recommended the establishment of Community Teams for Children under 12 Committing Offences

(Goldberg et al. 1999). Such teams could include, for example, representatives from the criminal justice system such as the police, child welfare, school personnel, health, and children's mental health. The mandate of the community team would be to establish police-community referral protocols, manage a centralized referral intake line, conduct comprehensive risk and needs assessments, and allocate appropriate gender-sensitive services to at-risk children and their families. From a national perspective, and to further advance knowledge and practices for children in conflict with the law, lead members from community teams could form a National Advisory Working Group for Children and Youth Involved in Offending Behavior. The mandate of this group would be to create a knowledge-based resource hub dedicated to disseminating and supporting research and cutting-edge practices tailored to the needs of high-risk children and their families. This would provide the much needed mechanism to *raise the bar* with respect to knowledge, practice, and accountability by keeping treatment providers current with respect to the latest innovations in research, and vice versa. This is at the heart of evidence-based practice.

References

Augimeri, Leena K., Pia Enebrink, Margaret Walsh, and Depeng Jiang. 2010. "Gender-Specific Childhood Risk Assessment Tools: Early Assessment Risk Lists for Boys (EARL-20B) and Girls (EARL-21G)." In *Handbook of Violence Risk Assessment Tools*, edited by Randy K. Otto and Kevin S. Douglas, 43–62. New York: Routledge.

Augimeri, Leena K., Christopher J. Koegl, Christopher D. Webster, and Kathy S. Levene. 2001. *Early Assessment Risk List for Boys (EARL-20B): Version 2*. Toronto: Child Development Institute.

Augimeri, Leena K., Margaret Walsh, Angela D. Liddon, and Carla R. Dassinger. 2011. "From Risk Identification to Risk Management: A Comprehensive Strategy for Young Children Engaged in Antisocial Behavior." In *Juvenile Justice and Delinquency*, edited by David W. Springer and Albert R. Roberts, 117–140. Sudbury, MA: Jones and Bartlett.

Augimeri, Leena K., Margaret Walsh, and Nicola Slater. 2011. "Rolling Out SNAP®, an Evidence-Based Intervention: A Summary of Implementation, Evaluation and Research." *International Journal of Child, Youth and Family Studies* 2: 330–352.

Blueprints for Violence Prevention, 2011. "Model Programs." www.colorado.edu/cspv/blueprints/modelprograms.html.

Brown, Jacquie, Jane Rounthwaite, and Melanie Barwick. 2011. "Implementing Evidence-Based Practices: A Transformational Organizational Change Process." *International Journal of Knowledge, Culture and Change Management* 10: 33–53.

de Ruiter, Corine, and Leena K. Augimeri. In press. "Making Prevention Work: From Risk Assessment to Effective Interventions in Children and Adolescents Committing Offences." In *Managing Clinical Risk: A Practitioner's Guide*, edited by Caroline Logan and Lorraine Johnstone. London: Routledge.

Farrington, David P., and Brandon C. Welsh. 2007. *Saving Children from a Life of Crime: Early Risk Factors and Effective Interventions*. Oxford: Oxford University Press.

Goldberg, Kenneth, Leena K. Augimeri, Christopher J. Koegl, and Christopher D. Webster. 1999. *Canadian Children under 12 Committing Offences: Legal and Treatment Approaches.* Toronto: Earlscourt Child and Family Centre.

Howell, James C. 2003. *Preventing and Reducing Juvenile Delinquency: A Comprehensive Framework.* Thousand Oaks, CA: Sage.

Koegl, Christopher J. 2011. "High-Risk Antisocial Children: Predicting Future Criminal and Health Outcomes." Ph.D. dissertation, Institute of Criminology, Cambridge University.

Koegl, Christopher J., Leena K. Augimeri, Paola Ferrante, Margaret Walsh, and Nicola Slater. 2008. "A Canadian Programme for Child Delinquents." In *Tomorrow's Criminals: The Development of Child Delinquency and Effective Interventions*, edited by Rolf Loeber, N. Wim Slot, Peter van der Laan, and Machteld Hoeve, 285–300. Burlington, VT: Ashgate.

Levene, Kathy S., Leena K. Augimeri, Debra J. Pepler, Margaret Walsh, Christopher J. Koegl, and Christopher D. Webster. 2001. *Early Assessment Risk List for Girls (EARL-21G): Version 1.* Consultation ed. Toronto: Child Development Institute.

Loeber, Rolf, and David P. Farrington, eds. 1998. *Serious and Violent Juvenile Offenders: Risk Factors and Successful Interventions.* Thousand Oaks, CA: Sage.

Loeber, Rolf, and David P. Farrington, eds. 2001. *Child Delinquents: Development, Intervention, and Service Needs.* Thousand Oaks, CA: Sage.

Loeber, Rolf, N. Wim Slot, Peter van der Laan, and Machteld Hoeve, eds. 2008. *Tomorrow's Criminals: The Development of Child Delinquency and Effective Interventions.* Burlington, VT: Ashgate.

Luk, Ernest. S. L., Petra K. Staiger, John Mathai, Lisa Wong, Peter Birleson, and Robert Adler. 2001. "Children with Persistent Conduct Problems Who Dropout of Treatment." *European Child & Adolescent Psychiatry* 10: 28–36.

National Crime Prevention Centre. 2008. "Promising and Model Crime Prevention Programs—Volume 1." www.publicsafety.gc.ca/res/cp/res/2008-pcpp-eng.aspx.

Pescosolido, Bernice A., Danielle L. Fettes, Jack K. Martin, John Monahan, and Jane D. McLeod. 2007. "Perceived Dangerousness of Children with Mental Health Problems and Support for Coerced Treatment." *Psychiatric Services* 58: 619–625.

Schoenwald, Sonja K. 2008. "Toward Evidence-Based Transport of Evidence-Based Treatments: MST as an Example." *Journal of Child & Adolescent Substance Abuse* 17: 69–91.

Tolan, Patrick H., and Kenneth A. Dodge. 2005. "Children's Mental Health as a Primary Care and Concern: A System for Comprehensive Support and Service." *American Psychologist* 60: 601–614.

Vogel, Vivienne, Corine de Ruiter, Yvonne Bouman, and Makelaardij de Vries Robbé. 2009. *Structured Assessment of Protective Factors for Violence Risk (SAPROF): English Version 1.* Utrecht: Forum Educatief.

27

Intervening with Violence

PRIORITIES FOR REFORM FROM A PUBLIC HEALTH PERSPECTIVE

Jonathan P. Shepherd

Reflecting its impact on global health, particularly on the health of youth and young adults, violence is recognized as a public health issue by the World Health Organization and some national governments, nongovernmental organizations, and public health professionals (Krug et al. 2002). While distinctive public health contributions to violence prevention are emerging, a barrier to this approach is a lack of delineation between public health and criminological violence measures and solutions. This reflects uncertainty about what constitutes a health as opposed to a crime and justice outcome, and about how public health differs from other health disciplines. The development of public health contributions to violence prevention depends on clarification of these issues.

Public health is concerned with risks to health on a population but not an individual level. Therefore, public health approaches to violence are to do with the incidence of violence (rates of incidents per unit population) and with violent injury or injurer prevalence (rates of injured or injurers per unit population). Injury can of course be physical or of a mental health nature. Thus, a public health approach to violence is not concerned with victimization or offending or issues of culpability, intent, or punishment (Shepherd and Farrington 1993).

This brief consideration of the future of public health as it relates to violence is concerned not only with violence prevention but also with another public health role: the organization and commissioning of research in and for health services. This perspective is proving particularly useful since it allows comparisons between, on the one hand, the development of research and, on the other, research infrastructure in health and in crime and justice and points to reforms that could usefully be made.

From this public health perspective, criminology should move toward a better balance between qualitative and quantitative approaches; from a largely observational and reflective role to a wider experimental and interventionist role in addition; and from a position distant from crime and justice services to a much closer relationship both with services and with the training of crime and justice professionals.

David Farrington, resolutely, tirelessly, and generously over many decades has championed this route. His quantitative, statistical approach and values, his openness to the new perspectives and language of disciplines like public health, which were beyond the frontiers of criminology, his discriminating, cumulative approach to evidence, which has contributed in large part to an exponential increase in systematic evidence reviews, and his enduring vocation for mentorship have all been influential. Like a good public health doctor, he is keenly interested in the future of populations (see e.g., Langan and Farrington 1998), including the global criminology community.

An important goal is a continuum of knowledge production from theory through innovation, evaluation, evidence synthesis, and implementation and vice versa (Shepherd 2007). Public health models of this process need to be applied in criminology. The following developments could achieve this.

University Crime and Justice Schools and Institutes

University crime and justice schools and institutes are needed to provide the applied research foundations of crime and justice services (e.g., police, offender management, victim, crime analysis services). These new learning communities would bridge current gaps between theoretical and applied criminology and integrate innovation, research, services, and the training of professionals. University medical and dental schools provide a suitable (but not the only) model for these, in which practitioner academics in public health, primary care, surgery, and other disciplines lead applied research and teaching and also practice, thus providing evidence conduits—often in the same person—among practice, evaluation, and training.

Professionalize Crime and Justice Services

Professions are characterized by self-funded professional bodies dedicated to advancing practice standards whose examinations and assessments are the basis of professional qualifications, critical self-regulation, and a thirst for knowledge of intervention effectiveness. This has resulted within medicine, city and town planning, and business, for example, in profession-generated funding streams, as well as charitable arrangements for research, determined and successful advocacy for foundations in first-rank universities, and headquarters that are entirely separate from the offices of profession trades unions.

Crime and justice provides a mixed picture viewed from this perspective. Law meets all these criteria, though it might be argued that legal professional training should be integrated more closely with law research so that results find their way more easily into professional practice (Shepherd 2010). There are clear signs in policing of a transition in this direction, though, even where they are present, there are gaps. In the Netherlands, policing has solid foundations in established universities, but in the United States policing is still very largely a blue-collar business. In the United Kingdom, only one front-rank university, Cardiff, has a police institute (www.upsi.org.uk; there is a virtual institute in Scotland). Probation is surprisingly weak from this point of view and not differentiated from social work to the extent that it is developing its own professional identity. Crime analysis, compared, say, with the academic disciplines of epidemiology and public health, is hugely undeveloped. One of the results of this is that crime analysis is particularly vulnerable to funding cuts in the international economic downturn. This is important in a variety of ways, not least that targeted policing depends on knowing on a continuous basis where and when crime is concentrated. Although these concentrations tend to be in the same districts over time (Weisburd 2011), precise locations and times vary according, for example, to changes in alcohol licensing, retail activity, development of the built environment, and changes in traffic flow.

Criminology therefore has much to gain from encouraging and facilitating this professionalization process among crime and justice practitioner groups—greater and better-managed research funding, links in their own universities to police and offender management researchers, greater credibility as opportunities for influencing and improving services, and access to more and higher-quality service data.

Integrate Victim Services with Mental Health Services

The integration of victim services with mental health services could have major benefits. It could tear down the funding wall between victim and mental health services and result in integrated provision—as has occurred in prisoner health as a result of transferring governmental responsibility from crime and justice to the health sector. It would also focus mental health research and development resources on victim health and well-being, raise the status of victims, and could improve service outcomes as victim services come under greater scientific scrutiny. This is not, however, to propose that crime and justice should be medicalized. The core issues in crime and justice (e.g., offending, intent, guilt, punishment, and reparation) are different from those in health, which is concerned with illness, injury, disease, and medical and surgical treatment (Shepherd and Farrington 1993). Offending often has mental and physical health consequences and offenders often suffer from mental health problems and organic disease, but this is no reason to conclude that offending constitutes an illness or an array of illnesses. This biological model of offending has largely been rejected, though care is needed to ensure that relevant models of research organization and research designs developed or refined in medicine are not rejected on the same grounds. Any discussion about the merits or otherwise of a medical model needs to start with a definition of the model in question.

Develop the Epidemiology of Violence

From a health perspective, it seems extraordinary that population-level crime analysis has not yet achieved identity as a criminology discipline and that there is no equivalent to public health in crime and justice. The impact of environmental, transport, and education interventions on health is well known and continues to be investigated but there are far fewer evaluations of the impact of crime and justice interventions on health.

For years it has been known that a great deal of violence is not ascertained (to use a public health term) by the police and why this is (see e.g., Clarkson et al. 1994); for decades national and international crime surveys have been carried out to understand violence levels and risk factors. Furthermore, ever since the 1998 UK Crime and Disorder Act brought about statutory crime reduction partnerships in the UK, there have been partnership analysts to synthesize crime data from multiple sources. But all this has yet to prompt the genesis of such a discipline. From a medical perspective, perhaps this reflects a lack of scientific background in the crime and justice arena or overdependence on central governments to provide this role, perhaps a lack of convincing stories of how population-level data have identified and been used to solve local and regional crime problems. A casualty has surely been public understanding of crime levels and therefore of crime risk. In the absence of annual authoritative, statistically sound reports about violence and other crime, as are commonplace on infectious disease, for example, local media and an anxious public are usually left to draw conclusions only from sensationalized accounts of individual cases. The pity is that these data are often produced but, reflecting concern that they might stigmatize cities and regions with relatively high crime levels, they are not published. In the UK, for example, comparative data about crime are carefully collated according to a range of town- and city-level social and economic variables, and distributed to police forces and community safety partnerships, but not published. Among other uses, publication could motivate crime reduction agencies to do more and provide a means of holding them accountable.

Figure 27.1 demonstrates two important influences on citywide police recording of violence: first, the impact of the adoption of a universal police crime-recording standard in England and Wales in 2002, which increased recording in all cities; and, second, the impact of information sharing (implemented in 2003) by Cardiff's sole emergency department with Cardiff police through an analyst in the local statutory partnership in which clinicians who

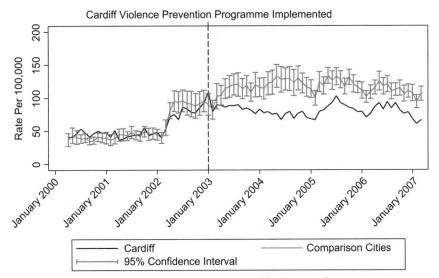

FIGURE 27.1 *Wounding assault rates by month, Cardiff and mean of comparison cities*

Source: Florence et al. (2011). Note: The National Crime Recording Standard (NCRS) was implemented January 1999 in Birmingham and Coventry, October 1999 in Stoke-on-Trent, August 2000 in Preston, October 2000 in Bristol, February 2002 in Leeds and Lincoln, and April 2002 in Cardiff, Derby, Leicester, Newcastle-upon-Tyne, Northampton, Plymouth, Reading, and Sheffield.

treat victims participate, which decreased violence in Cardiff compared to other cities (Florence et al. 2011).

This carefully controlled, time series evaluation paves the way for replication of this population-level experiment, which involves collaboration between crime and justice and health agencies, in other regions and countries—replication that is under way in the United States, facilitated by the Centers for Disease Control and Prevention. This is an example of how criminology could and should join forces with public health to evaluate collaborative interventions across the two sectors.

Develop Science-Based Care Pathways for Victims and Offenders

The most important result of a public health perspective on violence should be reductions in the burden of illness and injury achieved at a population level by means of science-based interventions delivered in a coherent, organized program, for example, according to a care pathway. Such a pathway, developed in Cardiff, is summarized in figure 27.2. It incorporates initial treatment, when physical injuries are treated; subsequent wound care, when sutures are removed and dressings are changed; and mental health service provision, when the psychological and psychiatric impacts of violence are identified and treated. At each stage of treatment, there is an important prevention element. Thus, when the injured person first

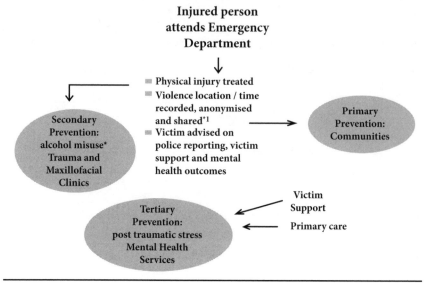

EVIDENCE BASED
CARE PATHWAY: COMBINING
TRAUMA CARE WITH PREVENTION

Injured person
attends Emergency
Department

- Physical injury treated
- Violence location / time recorded, anonymised and shared[*1]
- Victim advised on police reporting, victim support and mental health outcomes

Secondary Prevention: alcohol misuse[*] Trauma and Maxillofacial Clinics

Primary Prevention: Communities

Tertiary Prevention: post traumatic stress Mental Health Services

Victim Support

Primary care

---

[*]**Royal College treatment standard**
[1]**UK Government commitment**

Source: Violence and Society Research Group, Cardiff University www.vrg.cf.ac.uk
Prototype pathway developed with and in Cardiff and Vale University Health Board and the Safer Capital Partnership

Implementation: Welsh Assembly Government, UK Home Office, Department of Health and WHO Violence Prevention Alliance

FIGURE 27.2   *A victim care pathway that incorporates physical and mental health treatment and violence prevention at each stage of care*

Source: Adapted from Shepherd (2005). *Note:* The Royal College treatment standards constitute guidance for surgeons, emergency physicians, and nurses on the treatment of alcohol misuse among trauma patients (Royal College of Surgeons 2010), and guidance for emergency physicians on information sharing for violence prevention (College of Emergency Medicine 2009). For evidence of UK Government commitment, see HM Government (2010).

attends the emergency department, anonymized information germane to policing (precise violence location, time, and weapon) are collected and shared with a community crime analyst for the purpose of targeting police and city government prevention resources. This is an example of effective primary prevention (Florence et al. 2011). Next, when the injured person attends a trauma clinic for wound care, screening for alcohol misuse (a key risk factor) is carried out, and those screening positive for misuse according to a valid and reliable measure are treated using a brief motivational intervention: a psychological intervention known on the basis of at least three meta-analyses to be effective (Smith et al. 2003). This constitutes secondary prevention. Third, mental health needs assessments are used to identify people at risk of developing post-traumatic stress disorder so that preemptive interventions can be used to limit the development of this condition (Bisson et al. 2004). This is an example of tertiary prevention.

Conclusion

The principal conclusion of this short description of the current state and attractive future of violence as a public health issue is, perhaps, that continuing on this course will link theory with practice and will connect and motivate criminologists, policymakers, and practitioners as never before. As at the start of one of David Farrington's longitudinal studies, however, there is much to learn, and quantum leaps in understanding are not predictable, as the contributors to this book can all attest. But such leaps are far more likely if there are learning communities of investigators from disparate disciplines and cultures, drawn together, refreshed and sustained by selfless, tolerant, yet discriminating scholars, among whom Farrington is a peerless example.

References

Bisson, Jonathan I., Jonathan P. Shepherd, Deborah Joy, Rachel Probert, and Robert G. Newcombe. 2004. "Early Cognitive-Behavioural Therapy for Post-traumatic Stress Symptoms: Randomised Controlled Trial." *British Journal of Psychiatry* 184: 63–69.

Boyle, Adrian, Jonathan P. Shepherd, and David Sheehan. 2009. *Guideline for Information Sharing to Reduce Community Violence*. London: College of Emergency Medicine.

Clarkson, Chris, Antonia Cretney, Gwynn Davis, and Jonathan P. Shepherd. 1994. "Assaults: The Relationship between Seriousness, Criminalisation and Punishment." *Criminal Law Review January*: 4–19.

Florence, Curtis, Jonathan P. Shepherd, Lain Brennan, and Thomas Simon. 2011. "Effectiveness of Anonymised Information Sharing and Use in a Health Service, Police and Local Government Partnership for Preventing Violence Related Injury: Experimental Study and Time Series Analysis." *British Medical Journal* 342: d3313. doi:10.1136/bmj.d3313.

HM Government. 2010. *The Coalition: Our Programme for Government*. London: HM Government.

Krug, Etienne G., Linda L. Dahlberg, James A. Mercy, Anthony B. Zwi, and Rafael Lozano. 2002. *World Report on Violence and Health*. Geneva: World Health Organization.

Langan, Patrick A., and David P. Farrington. 1998. *Crime and Justice in the United States and in England and Wales, 1981–96*. Washington, DC: US Department of Justice, Bureau of Justice Statistics.

Royal College of Surgeons of England. 2010. *Position Statement: Reducing Alcohol Misuse in Trauma and Other Surgical Patients*. London: Royal College of Surgeons of England.

Shepherd, Jonathan P. 2005. "Victim Services in the National Health Service: Combining Treatment with Violence Prevention." *Criminal Behaviour and Mental Health* 15: 75–80.

Shepherd, Jonathan P. 2007. "The Production and Management of Evidence for Public Service Reform." *Evidence and Policy* 3: 231–251.

Shepherd, Jonathan P. 2010. "Why Separate Law Research, Practice and Professional Train-
    ing?" *The Times* (London), August 26.
Shepherd, Jonathan P., and David P. Farrington. 1993. "Assault as a Public Health Problem."
    Journal of the Royal Society of Medicine 86: 89–94.
Smith, Alison J., Ray Hodgson, and Jonathan P. Shepherd. 2003. "Randomised Controlled
    Trial of a Brief Intervention after Alcohol-Related Facial Injury." *Addiction* 98: 43–52.
Weisburd, David. 2011. "Shifting Crime and Justice Resources from Prisons to Police: Shift-
    ing Police from People to Places." *Criminology and Public Policy* 10: 153–164.

28

How to Reduce the Global Homicide Rate to 2 per 100,000 by 2060

Manuel Eisner and Amy Nivette

The current average global homicide rate is about 8 per 100,000 per year. This means, that in the first decade of the twenty-first century an estimated 5 million people lost their lives due to interpersonal violence, making murder a more important source of violent death than war. In many countries it is a leading cause of death among 15- to 44-year-olds (Geneva Declaration Secretariat 2008).

Can this loss of human lives be significantly reduced in the coming decades? And if so: By what means? Only recently have researchers and policymakers started to address this issue, most prominently through the World Health Organization and its Violence Prevention Alliance (Krug et al. 2002). However, developing the knowledge base to effectively reduce homicide across the world remains a huge challenge. To highlight these challenges, and ways to address them, we reflect about the kind of criminology needed to reduce the global homicide rate to a level close to that of contemporary pacified societies, namely about 2 per 100,000, over the next 50 years.

Is Such a Reduction Possible?

Is a worldwide reduction of homicide rates to about 2 per 100,000 within the next 50 years imaginable? We developed a simple scenario to explore this question: Derived from the 2004/5 international homicide data collected by UNODC (United Nations Office on Drugs and Crime 2011), we split the country-level data into quartiles (see table 28.1). This shows, for example, that the average homicide rate in the 25 percent of countries with the highest homicide rates is 26.9 per 100,000. Almost one-fifth (18.6 percent) of the world population lives in these countries, which account for 56.8 percent of all homicides worldwide. In contrast, 12.2 percent of the world population currently lives in the 46 countries with the lowest homicide rates. In these countries, the average rate was 1.2 per 100,000, thus accounting for 1.5 percent of all homicides worldwide.

TABLE 28.1 A Scenario for a Global Reduction of Homicide Rates by 75% by 2060

Quartile	Situation 2004/5			Target for 2060		
	Mean Homicide Rate	% of World Population	% of homicides	Annual Reduction	HR by 2060	Total Reduction
Highest (1)	26.9	18.6	56.8	−4%	3.5	−87%
2	11.9	14.2	19.2	−3%	2.6	−78%
3	3.7	53.5	22.4	−2%	1.3	−65%
Lowest (4)	1.2	12.2	1.5	−1%	0.7	−42%

Sources: Homicide: WHO estimates compiled by UNODC (2011); Population: World Bank World Development Indicators (2011).

We use these data to understand how a global homicide rate of 2 per 100,000 could be achieved over the coming 50 years. Following the logic of prevention science, we assume that it would be desirable to focus efforts on those countries that suffer most from lethal interpersonal violence. We therefore modeled an average decline of 4 percent per year in the highest quartile and of 1 percent in the lowest quartile. By 2060 this decline would result in homicide rates of between 0.7 and 3.5, and the global homicide rate (weighted by current country size) would be 1.8 per 100,000. On the basis of the present world population this means about 430,000 fewer victims of homicide per year.

Empirical evidence suggests that declines of this size are within reach: There are many historical and contemporary examples where individual countries have experienced similar falls in homicide rates over several decades (LaFree 1999). Thus, a nonsystematic sample of countries across the globe suggests that during periods of society-wide pacification the annual rates of decline range between 2 percent and 8 percent (table 28.2).

A worldwide drop by 75 percent over five decades would hence be ambitious, but within the range of patterns that have been observed in the past. But how would criminology have to advance in order to make research-based recommendations to the global community about how to achieve this goal?

A Takeoff of Global Violence Prevention

The past 10 years have seen an astonishing development in global violence prevention efforts, many of which build on research by David Farrington: Their cornerstones are good basic research on the causal risk-factors for violence (Farrington 1998, 2003), experimental research on the effectiveness of interventions (Farrington 1983, 2006b), and meta-analyses as a principled way to summarize knowledge across studies (Farrington and Welsh 2007). These principles first had an enormous influence on the spread of evidence-based crime prevention in the United States, spreading to Western Europe over the past 15 years.

TABLE 28.2 Some Historically Documented Major Drops in Homicide Rates

Country	Peak (Year)	Trough (year)	No of years	Mean annual decline
Sweden (Stockholm)	26.0 (1650s)	1.4 (1750s)	100	−2.9%
Italy	8.0 (1880)	2.2 (1930)	50	−2.8%
Hong Kong	6.9 (1921)	0.7 (1961)	40	−5.6%
Japan	3.5 (1955)	0.9 (1990)	35	−3.8%
United States	9.8 (1991)	5.0 (2009)	18	−3.7%
Washington DC	80.6 (1991)	24.0 (2009)	18	−6.5%
Colombia	83.0 (1991)	35.2 (2009)	18	−4.5%
South Africa	60.0 (1995)	34.2 (2010)	16	−4.0%
Italy	3.3 (1991)	1.0 (2008)	17	−6.8%

Sources: Sweden and Italy: Eisner (2003); Japan: Johnson (2008); Hong Kong and Colombia: Pan American Health Organization (2011); South Africa: South Africa Police Service (2002/2003, 2009/2010).

Since 2002 the World Health Organization has made these principles a cornerstone of its global campaign for violence prevention. This is reflected in three major reports: The *World Report on Violence and Health* (Krug et al. 2002), the *Preventing Violence* report (World Health Organization 2004), and the *Violence Prevention: The Evidence* report (World Health Organization 2010). They are complemented by the World Violence Prevention Alliance, a network of WHO member states, international agencies, and civil society organizations working to prevent violence, and the Violence Prevention website maintained by the Centre for Public Health at Liverpool John Moores University, in collaboration with WHO (http://www.preventviolence.info). Among others, it provides access to high-quality evaluations of the effectiveness of interventions to prevent violence from across the world.

These initiatives are a big step toward a coordinated, evidence-based global strategy. However, while the road map laid out by Farrington and others is currently the most promising path to pursue, criminology will need to address several unresolved issues to significantly contribute to a global sustained decline of serious violence and homicide. We sketch out three topics that would make this goal more realistic.

The Cross-Cultural Universality of Causal Risk Factors

Good basic science on the epidemiology and the causes of violent crime is an important basis for effective prevention. Longitudinal studies, in particular, provide key information on the predictors of serious offending and violence, and that should hence be at the center of risk-focused intervention: "The basic idea of risk-focused prevention is very simple: Identify the key risk factors for offending and implement prevention methods designed to counteract them" (Farrington 2006a).

In the developed world a large body of research has been accumulated over the past 50 years on individual, family, school, and situational causal risk factors associated with serious violence. Many of these risk factors appear to be similar in different Western countries. However, the evidence is much more limited for the rest of the world. This raises the question of whether the same parenting styles and the same life-skills are universally associated with the risk of violence everywhere in the world (World Health Organization 2010). The evidence is thin and the verdict on the weight of universal risk factors relative to culturally specific factors is still out. Some risk factors like low self-control seem to be universally associated with violence (Rebellon et al. 2008). But others are probably not. For example, a recent study by Boakye (2011) on delinquency in Ghana found that some risk factors such as poor parental supervision, physical punishment, and large family size—featuring prominently in many prevention programs—were unrelated to delinquency in Ghana, although they were associated with crime in Pittsburgh and London. Also, individual risk factors for attacking other people's lives may differ significantly between societies with different overall levels of interpersonal violence. For instance, rational violent self-help in the absence of law enforcement and organized violent entrepreneurs may be highly relevant in high-homicide countries, while individual pathologies may account for more variation in low-homicide contexts.

If criminology is to make good recommendations on how to reduce serious violence and homicide across the globe, cross-cultural comparative research on causal risk factors will have to advance significantly. It will need good empirical evidence on what risk and protective factors are most relevant in different cultures or economic and political contexts. In particular—besides good cross-sectional studies—criminologists will need cross-culturally comparative longitudinal studies, which enhance the knowledge base needed for the advancement of effective violence reduction in different contexts.

Scaling up the Evidence Base

For the developed world, meta-analyses and lists of recommended interventions now help practitioners to improve services and implement more effective interventions. The recently initiated WHO prevention website has started to develop a similar knowledge-base on a global scale. We examined the 131 studies on this website by WHO region (table 28.3). The results illustrate the challenge of creating an evidence-base for a globally relevant violence prevention strategy.

It demonstrates that 98 percent of all studies on promising interventions come from the Americas (mainly from the United States and Canada) and Europe (mainly Western Europe). A finer geographic analysis would probably reveal that more than 95 percent of all program evaluations relate to about 12 percent of the global population, while less than 5 percent of evaluations worldwide relate to the remaining 90 percent of the global population.

TABLE 28.3   Number of Studies on Effective Violence Prevention by WHO Region

WHO Region	Number of Studies		World Population	
	N	%	In Millions	%
Africa	3	2	805	12
Americas	120	92	915	14
Eastern Mediterranean Region	0	0	1760	26
European Region	8	6	889	13
South East Asia Region	0	0	580	9
Western Pacific Region	0	0	1787	27

Note: Number of studies included on the WHO Violence Prevention Website, http://www.preventviolence.info

Developing a broader knowledge basis that adequately reflects the major regions of the world and that would allow interventions to have a genuine impact on macro-level trends will be a major challenge. This will not only be an issue of conducting experimental replication studies of the same interventions in different contexts across the world and solving the issue of taking interventions to scale— these two challenges are known and will likely be addressed by an emerging global prevention science (Krug et al. 2002). Rather, criminology and related disciplines (education science, prevention science, and public health research) will have to develop a much broader range of research-based strategies, processes, and programs that can be tailored to the needs of different populations.

Understanding the Pacification of Societies

A future criminology that wants to create knowledge useful for a global reduction in homicide rates will also need to advance and integrate macro-level institutional analyses. Countries with high homicide rates only partly suffer from a lack of evidence-based parent training programs, and initiatives exclusively aimed at improving individuals and their immediate environment are unlikely to do the job. Both historical and cross-national comparative analyses suggest that the process of pacifying societies requires more.

Societies with the highest levels of homicide in Latin America (e.g., El Salvador, Colombia), Africa (e.g., South Africa, Congo), or Asia (e.g., Kazakhstan, Russia) suffer from a syndrome of characteristics (e.g., Nivette 2011). These include high state corruption, low investments into public health and education, low state stability, ethnic, ideological, or religious cleavages, and high inequality. Low-homicide societies, in contrast, tend to have a functioning and stable state that is accountable to its citizens, effective public health, education and criminal justice systems, relatively low social inequality, and citizens that actively engage in matters of shared concern.

Levels of homicide, it seems, are influenced by whether societies are ruled by law, whether elites are trusted, whether corruption is under control, and whether services are provided; in short, they are influenced by social institutions. Historical research suggests, for example, that establishing faith in the government and confidence that its legal and judicial institutions are fair and will redress wrongs and protect lives and property are among the most important requirements for homicide rates to fall (LaFree 1998; Roth 2009).

The implications of macro-level research for effective prevention have remained largely unexplored, although the reports by the World Health Organization recognize the need for a better integration. The public health perspective that dominates much current thinking is important. But violence prevention, in order to be effective, needs to address both sides: Change the way people lead their lives and change the wider structures so that more civilized patterns of life become worthwhile and attractive.

We believe that the chances of a successful reduction of homicide rates can be greatly increased by making broader institutional change an integral part of prevention efforts. Currently, the links between macro-level research on institutional contexts and prevention science are poorly developed. Better and more conclusive research is needed on the ways in which specific components of state building are associated with violence. Building states with an effective and legitimate police force, a noncorrupt public administration, and accepted mechanisms to solve conflicts between groups may turn out to be a critical component of the long-term decline of homicide.

Conclusion

We can observe that major long-term declines in homicide rates have happened in the past, but we lack the knowledge to make them happen. Developing this knowledge base will require a more encompassing criminology that overcomes its traditional limitation to Western, highly developed societies, and that develops a much broader knowledge base on the patterns and causes of violence across the globe. It will also need a significant expansion of experimental, quasi-experimental, and observational studies on the effects of programs and processes on violence in different settings and for various groups. And finally, it will require an integration of knowledge on macro-level dynamics into strategies to reduce violence. If these advances, which have already started, are transported into actual policymaking, a significant reduction of homicide rates is a realistic goal.

References

Boakye, Kofi. 2011. "Juvenile Delinquency in Ghana: A Cross-Cultural Comparative Study of Offenders and Non-offenders." Ph.D. dissertation, Institute of Criminology, Cambridge University.

Eisner, Manuel. 2003. "Long-Term Historical Trends in Violent Crime." *Crime and Justice: A Review of Research*, vol. 30, edited by Michael Tonry, 83–142. Chicago: University of Chicago Press.

Farrington, David P. 1983. "Randomized Experiments on Crime and Justice." In *Crime and Justice: An Annual Review of Research*, vol. 4, edited by Michael Tonry and Norval Morris, 257–308. Chicago: University of Chicago Press.

Farrington, David P. 1998. "Early Predictors of Adolescent Aggression and Adult Violence." *Violence and Victims* 4: 79–100.

Farrington, David P. 2003. "Developmental and Life-Course Criminology: Key Theoretical and Empirical Issues—the 2002 Sutherland Award Address." *Criminology* 41: 221–225.

Farrington, David P. 2006a. "Childhood Risk Factors and Risk-Focussed Prevention." In *Oxford Handbook of Criminology*, edited by Mike Maguire, Rod Morgan, and Robert Reiner, 602–640. Oxford: Oxford University Press.

Farrington, David P. 2006b. "Key Longitudinal-Experimental Studies in Criminology." *Journal of Experimental Criminology* 2: 121–141.

Farrington, David P., and Brandon C. Welsh. 2007. *Saving Children from a Life of Crime: Early Risk Factors and Effective Interventions*. Oxford: Oxford University Press.

Geneva Declaration Secretariat. 2008. *Global Burden of Armed Violence*. Geneva: Geneva Declaration Secretariat.

Johnson, David T. 2008. "The Homicide Drop in Postwar Japan." *Homicide Studies* 12: 146–160.

Krug, Etienne G., James A. Mercy, Linda L. Dahlberg, and Anthony B. Zwi. 2002. *World Report on Violence and Health*. Geneva: World Health Organization.

LaFree, Gary D. 1998. *Losing Legitimacy: Street Crime and the Decline of Social Institutions in America*. Boulder, CO: Westview.

LaFree, Gary D. 1999. "Declining Violent Crime Rates in the 1990s: Predicting Crime Booms and Busts." *Annual Review of Sociology* 25: 145–168.

Nivette, Amy. 2011. "Cross-National Predictors of Homicide: A Meta-analysis." *Homicide Studies* 15: 103–131.

Pan American Health Organization. 2011. Indicator Trend Chart. Retrieved July 2, 2011, from http://new.paho.org/hq/index.php?option=com_content&task=.

South African Police Service. 2002–2003. Annual Report. Retrieved July 2, 2011, from http://www.saps.gov.za/saps_profile/strategic_framework/annual_report/index.htm.

South African Police Service. 2009–2010. Annual Report. Retrieved July 2, 2011, from http://www.saps.gov.za/saps_profile/strategic_framework/annual_report/index.htm.

Rebellon, Cesar J., Murray A. Straus, and Rose Medeiros. 2008. "Self-Control in Global Perspective: An Empirical Assessment of Gottfredson and Hirchi's General Theory within and across 32 National Settings." *European Journal of Criminology* 5: 331–361.

Roth, Randolph. 2009. *American Homicide*. Cambridge: Belknap Press, Harvard University Press.

United Nations Office on Drugs and Crime. 2011. International Homicide Statistics (IHS). Available online at http://www.unodc.org/unodc/en/data-and-analysis/ihs.html.

World Bank. 2011. *World Development Indicators*. Retrieved July 2, 2011, from http://data.worldbank.org/.

World Health Organization. 2004. *Preventing Violence: A Guide to Implementing the Recommendations of the World Report on Violence and Health*. Geneva: World Health Organization.

World Health Organization. 2010. *Violence Prevention: The Evidence*. Geneva: World Health Organization.

PART V

Public Policy Strategies

29

The Problem with Macrocriminology

James Q. Wilson

David Farrington has done extraordinary work in helping us understand the individual differences in the likelihood that people will commit crimes. His longitudinal study of boys growing up in London is a pioneering piece of research from which we have learned a great deal.

Think about what we thought we knew in 1950 about crime. Criminal behavior was learned from "differential association"; we acquired it, so to speak, by being with people who were already criminal. This raised the interesting question of how the people with whom we hung out learned their criminal proclivities. The answer, I suppose, was from the people with whom they had earlier been associated. The idea created an infinite regress tracing back to some bad person (Adam in the Garden of Eden?) who started the whole process.

Because social class affects the people with whom we associate, class conflict is important to explaining criminal attitudes. Social class also helps us understand white-collar crime. But people who started writing about white-collar crime tended to emphasize the high status and social respectability of these offenders. When empirical research began to look at people who had been convicted of the various offenses that might constitute white-collar crimes, they learned that some were affluent college graduates (if they had been found guilty of antitrust violations), but were only middle-class high-school graduates if they had been convicted of bribery, tax fraud, or credit fraud (Simpson and Weisburd 2009).

Today our knowledge of individual differences in offending (what I call microcriminology) is vastly more sophisticated. Offenders differ from nonoffenders in self-control, intelligence, family background, pulse rate, personality factors, and educational achievement as well as in income and gang affiliations. These factors have been found in studies such as the one Farrington and his predecessor have conducted as well as in other longitudinal inquiries and in clinical and group surveys.

But we have made very little progress in macrocriminology. We are not much better at explaining why the crime rate goes up or goes down than we were in 1950. This is not a problem just for criminology. Microeconomics (the study of how people distribute their resources among competing alternatives) has made remarkable progress. But ask economists if we have become much better at macro-economics, or at least that part of it that predicts changes in and cures for the business cycle, and they are likely to change the subject.

The central challenge facing criminology is to see if it can say anything that is useful and true about changes in the crime rate. I once told a class that criminology did no better at explaining changes in the crime rate than meteorologists did in predicting the weather. I now realize I was being unfair to meteorology. In June it can confidently say that six months from then the temperature will be lower.

By contrast ask yourself how many criminologists knew that the crime rate was going to go up in the 1960s and down in the late 1990s. A few probably did that, but it was a matter of making a lucky guess. Knowing a lot about microcriminology is only a modest help. Crime rates do not go up because the genetic makeup of young people has suddenly been altered and they do not go down because far fewer children live in single-parent families.

During the recession that hit the United States in 2008 the unemployment rate soared, but the crime rate fell. Since the late 1960s the conventional argument was that, other things being equal, more illegal work would be done if there was less legal work to do. In 1968, Gary Becker of the University of Chicago created a powerful theory suggesting that crime was rational: it resulted from people choosing among leisure, legitimate work, and crime. Becker argued that a person commits a crime if the expected utility to him exceeds the utility he would get by using his time and resources for other activities, such as leisure or legal work. Some people are risk-averse but others prefer risk; for the first group, an increase in the risk of punishment deters crime more than a similar change for the second group (Becker 1968).

During the Great Depression, when unemployment hit 25 percent, the crime rate in many cities went down. There were not very useful national crime statistics early in the 1930s, but studies of local police records and individual citizens by scholars such as Glenn Elder generally found less, not more, crime (Elder 1974).

Among the explanations for this puzzle is this one: unemployment and poverty were so common that people were drawn closer to their families. They devoted their energies to mutual support and were urged to take whatever poor or part-time jobs that existed. In the family or the workplace, young people were under adult supervision. Of course in those days children below the age of 16 were legally able to take jobs. Today many families are weaker and children are more independent and so we do not see the same effect.

Another puzzle is that when we compare periods of rising crime rates, such as the 1960s, with those of declining crime rates, such as late 1990s and early 2000s, the unemployment rate in both periods is essentially the same. Between 1960 and 1970, the unemployment rate averaged 4.8 percent; between 1995 and 2005, it averaged 5.0 percent. Yet in the first period the robbery rate tripled while in the second it was cut nearly in half.

Most criminologists today think that the evidence for a link between crime and unemployment is, at best, mixed. Some suggest that a 1 percent increase in the unemployment rate should produce no more than a 2 percent increase in property crime rates. One dollar more in legal earnings per month, one study found, leads to a seven-cent decrease in illegal earnings (Bushway 2011). But when during the recent recession the unemployment rate doubled—from roughly 5 percent to nearly 10 percent—there should have been a 10 percent increase in the crime rate. There wasn't.

Instead the FBI reported during 2009 an 8 percent drop in rate for robbery and a 17 percent drop for auto theft. In the first six months of 2010, the property crime rate fell another 2 percent. Much the same story can be found in big-city reports. Between 2008 and 2010, New York City had a 4 percent decline in robberies and a 10 percent drop in burglaries. Boston, Chicago, and Los Angeles showed similar declines.

To deal with this problem, some scholars have said that the unemployment rate is too crude a measure. It is, after all, only an estimate of the proportion of people looking for work who have not found it. There are, they suggest, better measures. One is the labor force participation rate: that is, the proportion of people not in school, not at work, and not looking for work. These individuals are detached from the labor force and so are especially vulnerable to criminal opportunities. In 2008, about half of men ages 16 to 24 were in the labor force, down from over two-thirds in 1988. There was a comparable decline among African American men. This means that the widely quoted unemployment rate understates the real problem of the labor market (Bushway 2011). But the result was the same: less crime.

Something else is going on and it probably has little to do with jobs, the labor market, or how consumers feel. One obvious thing is that there are a lot more people in prison. Experts differ on how big this effect is on the crime rate. But I think those, such as William Spelman (2000) and Steven Levitt (1996), who believe it explains about one-quarter or more of the decline, have got it about right. I say this knowing that many thoughtful people think we have too many people in prison for too long. For some offenders, such as low-level drug dealers and ex-inmates returned to prison for violating the terms of their parole, this may be true. But most prisoners are being kept off the streets so they can only attack each other, not your wife or sister.

The crime reduction effect of imprisonment helps us explain why the burglary, car theft, and robbery rates are lower in this country than they are in Denmark, England, and New Zealand. This difference does not result from our willingness to send a convicted offender to prison; that is about the same in all of these countries. The big difference lies in how long we keep them there. You spend more time in prison in the United States than you do for the same offense in England or the Netherlands (Lynch and Pridemore 2011). But though prison was important in explaining the crime drop in this country, it cannot be the sole explanation. Canada has had the same crime drop as America, yet Canada did not sharply increase its use of prison (Zimring 2007).

Policing has become more disciplined and is driven today more by the desire to reduce crime rates than to simply maximize arrests. There are several techniques that have been carefully evaluated and others that might be tested if anyone got around to it. One is "hot spots" policing. The great majority of crimes tend to occur in the same places. Put active police resources in those spots rather than telling officers to drive around waiting for a 911 call and crime can be reduced.

Criminologists Lawrence Sherman and David Weisburd (1995), after analyzing data from more than 7,000 police arrivals in Minneapolis, showed that if the officer had been there for 15 minutes and then left, the number of crimes went down during the next 15 minutes. Crime went down—not because the officer did anything but simply because he or she had been there.

This idea helped make the COMPSTAT program of the New York Police Department so effective. If the cops focus on hot spots and active offenders instead of driving around on random patrol and if police chiefs back that up by holding precinct captains responsible for this task, crime rates will go down.

Some cities now use a computer-based system to map traffic accidents and crime reports. The two measures tended to coincide: where there were more accidents there was more crime. In Shawnee, Kansas, the police spent a lot more time in 4 percent of the city's land area than they did in the city as a whole; in that territory, one-third of all crime took place. Because of the police presence, the number of burglaries fell by 60 percent even though in the city as a whole it only dropped by 8 percent (Kerrigan 2011).

In 1974, the EPA required oil companies to stop putting lead in gasoline. The program cut gasoline lead by 99 percent. Medical tests showed that the amount of lead in Americans fell by four-fifths between 1975 and 1991. Studies have shown that this reduction in lead has apparently caused a sharp reduction in violent crime (Reyes 2007). The same argument has been made for other nations (Nevin 2007).

Another environmental change that probably has helped reduce the crime rate is the drop in heavy cocaine use in many states. Measuring cocaine use is not an easy matter. It has to be inferred from interviews or from hospital admission rates. Between 1992 and 2009, the number of drug treatment admissions for cocaine or crack use has fallen by nearly two-thirds. In 1987, 4.3 percent of students in the twelfth grade said they had tried cocaine in the last 30 days, but by 2002 that had fallen to 1.4 percent (Monitoring the Future 2002).

What we really need to know is not how many people tried coke but how many are heavy users. Many casual users are probably less likely than dedicated ones to commit serious crimes; for them, it is a "party drug." But other new users may be more likely to commit crimes if they are not wealthy or have easy access to the drug; instead, they must steal to get money and find distributors who do not know if they can be trusted. Theft and violence may increase among these users. Heavy users are much more likely to break other laws because they need the money to buy the drug and are unable to hold a legitimate job. If these numbers are down, it will help explain the drop in crime.

A study by scholars at the Rand Corporation found that the total consumption of cocaine dropped by 61 percent between 1988 and 2000 (Kilmer et al. 2010). Such data are uncertain since it is hard to estimate consumption, but this estimated decline is large enough to suggest that the drop was real. This decline in demand may help explain why coke has become cheaper despite intense law enforcement efforts aimed at its distribution. Illegal markets, like legal ones, cut prices when demand falls. The drop in coke use may contribute to the decline in crime rates.

All of these noneconomic explanations, to the extent they are true, come together in accounting for the drop in the African American crime rate. Knowing the crime rate of any ethnic or racial group is no easy matter since most crimes do not result in an arrest or conviction and those that do produce a conviction may be an unrepresentative fraction of all criminal acts. But we know the racial characteristics among those arrested for a crime and of those seen by their victims and reported to the Census Bureau when they are interviewed as part of the National Crime Victimization Survey.

What we learn is this: there has been a sharp decrease in the number of blacks arrested. Barry Latzer (2011) has shown that between 1980 and 2005 black arrests for homicide and other violent crimes fell by about half. In the five New York City precincts whose population was at least 80 percent black, the murder rate fell by 78 percent between 1990 and 2000.

Much the same story occurred in Chicago. Over half of the drop in the city's homicide rate was attributed to the decline in the seven districts where the population was at least 90 percent black. Criminologist Wesley Skogan (2006) confirmed this: in 1991–1992 the 52 police beats that were heavily poor and 98 percent black had the highest robbery rates in the city. But in 2001–2002 only four of these beats had the city's highest robbery rates. In black neighborhoods between 1991 and 2003, burglary fell by 52 percent, robbery by 62 percent, and homicide by 33 percent.

A skeptic might suggest that all these gains can be explained by saying that the police gave up on this matter. They stopped recording crimes in black areas and arresting crimes committed by African Americans. But if that is their belief, the skeptics will have a hard time explaining why opinion surveys in Chicago show that among blacks fear of crime was cut in half during this period.

In this crime drop, Chicago improved at about the same rate as the other nine cities with more than one million residents. These were broad changes, not ones that can be easily linked to one city's particular strategy. And some people gained more than others. In its Supplementary Homicide Reports, the FBI has shown that the biggest decline among African American homicides has occurred among family members. In 1976, 1,529 blacks killed an intimate partner; in 2005 only 475 did so, a decline of more than two-thirds. And this decline occurred despite the growth in the size of the African American population (Fox and Zawitz 2011).

The Bureau of Justice Statistics (2007) has shown that, using the Uniform Crime Reports and the National Crime Victimization Survey, black robbery victims fell from 13 per thousand in 1993 to only four per thousand in 2001 and nonfatal but violent attacks on blacks dropped from about 70 per thousand people in 1993 to about 25 per thousand in 2001. This sharp decline in how often blacks are victimized suggests rather strongly that the drop is not the result of the police arresting fewer people.

African Americans still constitute part of America's crime problem, but they have changed. The changes include the growth of a black middle class, the migration of many blacks back to the South, and the large fraction of young black males sent to prison. All of these changes probably contributed to this remarkable reduction in criminality.

But there is one more factor that many people overlook. Drug use has changed. Persons born in New York City between 1948 and 1969 were heavily involved in using crack cocaine, while those born after 1969 had little to do with crack or heroin and instead confined themselves to marijuana (Johnson et al. 2000).

The reason was simple: crack and heroin use sent people they knew to prisons, hospitals, and the morgue. They had these unhappy fates because of drug-induced diseases, being arrested for stealing or selling, or getting shot by a rival user or dealer. There were some risks from using marijuana, but they were vastly less serious. The shift in drug use, if the New York City experience is borne out in other places, helps explain the drop in inner-city crime rates after the early 1990s.

There is one remaining possibility, and I think an important one: our culture has changed. This will strike many of you as so vague a claim as to be meaningless. But we have relied on it in the past to explain less crime (as in the Great Depression) and more crime (as in the 1960s). In the first period people took self-control seriously, in the latter they took self-expression seriously. How do you measure those qualities? We don't know how to study culture in a way that produces hard numbers and tested theories. Scholars can't do it very well. It is a task for novelists, biographers, and clinicians.

I wish I could suggest ways of creating a useful macrocriminology, but I cannot. I doubt anyone can. We have no good advance measures of how people react to drugs, what effects gangs may have on crime, the speed with which local police adopt new methods, or how culture changes. Even without those measures, we can say a lot about these issues, but we cannot prove much. The best we can do is to explain what has happened in the past.

References

Becker, Gary. 1968. "Crime and Punishment: An Empirical Approach." *Journal of Political Economy* 76: 169–217.

Bureau of Justice Statistics. 2007. *Criminal Victimization*. Washington, DC: US Department of Justice, Office of Justice Programs.

Bushway, Shawn D. 2011. "Labor Markets and Crime." In *Crime and Public Policy*, edited by James Q. Wilson and Joan Petersilia, 183–209. New York: Oxford University Press.

Elder, Glen H. 1974. *Children of the Great Depression*. Chicago: University of Chicago Press.

Fox, James A., and Marianne W. Zawitz. 2011. "Homicide Trends in the United States." Bureau of Justice Statistics. http://bjs.ojp.usdoj.gov/content/pub/pdf/htius.pdf

Johnson, Bruce D., Andrew Golub, and Eloise Dunlap. 2000. "The Rise and Decline of Hard Drugs, Drug Markets, and Violence in Inner-City New York." In *The Crime Drop in America*, edited by Alfred Blumstein and Joel Wallman, 164–206. New York: Cambridge University Press.

Kerrigan, Heather. 2011. "Data-Driven Policing." *Governing*, May, 54–55.

Kilmer, Beau, Jonathan P. Caulkins, Brittany M. Bond, and Peter H. Reuter. 2010. *Reducing Drug Trafficking Revenues and Violence in Mexico: Would Legalizing Marijuana in California Help?* Santa Monica, CA: RAND.

Latzer, Barry. 2011. "The Great Black Hope: How Race Drove the Crime Drop." Unpublished manuscript. John Jay College of Criminal Justice.

Levitt, Steven D. 1996. "The Effect of Prison Population Size on Crime Rates: Evidence from Prison Overcrowding Litigation." *Quarterly Journal of Economics* 111: 319–352.

Lynch, James P., and William A. Pridemore. 2011. "Crime in International Perspective." In *Crime and Public Policy*, edited by James Q. Wilson and Joan Petersilia, 5–52. New York: Oxford University Press.

Monitoring the Future. 2002. Available at www.monitoringthefuture.org/data/02data.html.

Nevin, Rick. 2007. "Understanding International Crime Trends: The Legacy of Preschool Lead Exposure." *Environmental Research* 104: 315–336.

Reyes, Jessica Wolpaw. 2007. "Environmental Policy as Social Policy? The Impact of Childhood Lead Exposure on Crime." Working Paper 13097. Cambridge, MA: National Bureau of Economic Research.

Sherman, Lawrence W., and David Weisburd. 1995. "General Deterrent Effects of Police Patrol in Crime Hot Spots." *Justice Quarterly* 12: 635–648.

Simpson, Sally S., and David Weisburd. 2009. "Introduction." In *The Criminology of White-Collar Crime*, edited by Sally S. Simpson and David Weisburd, 3–14. New York: Springer.

Skogan, Wesley G. 2006. *Police and Community in Chicago*. New York: Oxford University Press.

Spelman, William. 2000. "The Limited Importance of Prison Expansion." In *The Crime Drop in America*, edited by Alfred Blumstein and Joel Wallman, 97–129. New York: Cambridge University Press.

Zimring, Franklin E. 2007. *The Great American Crime Decline*. New York: Oxford University Press.

30

Staking out the Next Generation of Studies of the Criminology of Place

COLLECTING PROSPECTIVE LONGITUDINAL DATA AT CRIME HOT SPOTS

David Weisburd, Brian Lawton, and Justin Ready

Generally, the academic literature on crime takes one of two perspectives, either emphasizing the role of the individual (see, e.g., Becker 1953; Taniguchi, Rengert, and McCord 2009) or examining crime from an ecological perspective at a macro level of geography (see, e.g., Bursik and Grasmick 1993). These latter studies have generally focused on fairly large units of aggregation such as the community, neighborhood, or census-defined levels such as tracts and block groups. Recently, however, there has been a growing interest in the distribution of antisocial behaviors at much lower levels of geography (Weisburd, Groff, and Yang in press). These studies have focused on geographic units such as street segments, or small groups of street segments that evidence similar types of disorder or crime problems.

As we describe below, an emphasis on micro geographic units has led to notable findings. First, street segments show considerable heterogeneity in environmental, sociodemographic, and antisocial behaviors even within relatively low levels of aggregation, such as census block groups (Groff, Weisburd, and Yang 2010). Second, prior research has demonstrated the utility of identifying places with very strong crime concentrations, that is, "hot spots" (Weisburd and Maze-rolle 2000). Third, these hot spots of antisocial behavior are relatively stable over time (Weisburd et al. 2004), suggesting important potential for interventions to have long-term influences on crime. Finally, these places have identifiable attributes that make them highly predictable and which provide opportunities for better understanding and more effectively ameliorating crime.

In this chapter, we review recent contributions of micro place studies of crime, and then draw insights from the seminal work of David Farrington in studies of individual criminality to suggest a next generation of study of the "criminology of place." David Farrington has been criminology's most effective advocate of prospective longitudinal studies (Farrington 1979; Farrington 2006). More than three decades ago in a seminal volume titled *Understanding and Controlling Crime*

(1986), written with Lloyd Ohlin and James Q. Wilson, Farrington was able to literally reform the criminological enterprise. Responding to a generation of scholars that had argued that criminology could provide little knowledge of utility for doing something about crime problems, Farrington, Ohlin, and Wilson argued that prospective longitudinal studies would provide insights into the core features of human development that impacted upon crime. Farrington has built upon this advocacy over more than three decades, not only producing a wealth of knowledge, but spawning a series of prospective longitudinal studies (including his own Cambridge Study in Delinquent Development; see Farrington and Hawkins 1991) that have transformed the ways in which criminologists understand the development of crime. Farrington has noted in building the case for prospective longitudinal study: "In criminology, the main advantage of such surveys is that they provide information about the development of offending over time, including data on ages of onset and desistance, frequency and seriousness of offending, duration of criminal careers, continuity or discontinuity of offending, and specialization and escalation" (Farrington 1979, 290). Below we argue that David Farrington's call more than 30 years ago for prospective longitudinal studies of individual offending is as critical for advancing the criminology of place today as it was for the advancement of our understanding of individual criminality in the 1980s.

The Importance of Micro Place Units in Understanding Crime

While the individual and "macro" units of place such as the community have long been a focus of research and theory regarding social problems, only recently have scholars begun to explore crime and other antisocial behavior at very small "micro" units of geography. The roots of such approaches can be found in the efforts of scholars to identify the relationship between specific aspects of urban design (Jeffrey 1971) or urban architecture (Newman 1972) and antisocial behavior, but broadened to take into account a much larger set of characteristics of physical space and criminal opportunity (e.g., Brantingham and Brantingham 1975). These studies drew important distinctions between the specific location of antisocial behavior and the larger geographical area (such as neighborhood, community, police beat, or city) that surrounds it.

The main theoretical impetus to the micro place approach to antisocial behavior is found in a group of theoretical perspectives that emerged in the late 1970s. In a seminal article on routine activities and crime, for example, Cohen and Felson (1979) suggested that a fuller understanding of crime must include a recognition that the availability of suitable crime targets and the presence or absence of capable guardians influence crime events. Routine activities focused attention on the specific ecological contexts in which suitable targets, motivated offenders, and the absence of capable guardians occurred. Researchers at the British Home Office in a series of studies examining the effects of "situational crime prevention" also challenged the traditional focus on offenders and communities (Clarke 1983). In contrast to offender-based approaches to crime prevention, which usually focus on the dispositions of criminals, situational crime prevention begins with the opportunity structure (and immediate physical context) of the crime situation (Felson and Clarke 1998). Paul and Patricia Brantingham also emphasized the role of place characteristics in shaping the type and frequency of human interaction in their work on environmental criminology (Brantingham and Brantingham 1991).

One implication of these emerging perspectives was that places at a micro geographic level should be an important focus of scholarly inquiry. While concern with the relationship between social problems and place is not new and indeed goes back to the founding generations of modern criminology, the micro approach to places suggested by recent theories has just begun to be examined. Places in this micro context are specific locations within the larger social environments of communities and neighborhoods (Eck and Weisburd 1995).

Recent studies point to the potential theoretical and practical benefits of focusing research on crime places. A number of studies, for example, suggest that there is a very significant clustering of crime at places, irrespective of the specific unit of analysis that is defined (Brantingham and Brantingham 1999). The extent of the concentration of crime at place is dramatic. In one of the pioneering studies in this area, Lawrence Sherman and colleagues (1989) found that only 3.5 percent of the addresses in Minneapolis produced 50 percent of all calls to the police. Fifteen years later in a retrospective longitudinal study in Seattle, Washington, Weisburd et al. (2004) reported that between 4 and 5 percent of street segments in the city accounted for 50 percent of crime incidents for each year over 14 years.

The findings of remarkable concentrations of crime suggest a "tight coupling" of antisocial behaviors and place. Research indicating that these concentrations remain stable over time reinforces this idea. Spelman (1995) for example found evidence of a high degree of stability of crime events at hot-spot schools, housing projects, subway stations, and parks over a three-year period. Taylor (1999) also reported evidence of a high degree of stability of antisocial behavior at places over time when he examined crime and fear of crime at 90 street blocks in Baltimore, Maryland. Using group-based trajectory models, Weisburd et al. (2004) found strong stability in chronic hot spots over a 14-year period in Seattle.

Because such social problems have often been seen to be the result of community-level processes (e.g., see Sampson, Raudenbush, and Earls 1997), scholars have also examined whether the focus on hot spots is in fact adding new information beyond a community level of analysis. Recent research shows that there is considerable variability of patterns of antisocial behavior street by street in a city, and that this variability indicates that social forces are not simply pushing down on places, but rather that forces at a very micro geographic level are exerting pressures upward in developing what we normally think of as the crime problem (see Groff, Weisburd, and Yang 2010). This means that there are antisocial behavior hot spots in what are generally considered "good areas" of a city, and even in most areas defined as problematic, most streets are generally free of such problems.

A recent retrospective longitudinal study by Weisburd and colleagues (in press) shows that it is not just antisocial behaviors that are concentrated and relatively stable at hot spots; so are the situational and social characteristics of places at a micro level of analysis. That study provides strong evidence of the importance of routine activities, and crime opportunities more generally, to the generation of antisocial behavior. For example, the number of possible "targets" that live, work, or visit a street (e.g., as represented by population density, number of employees, and high-risk juveniles) strongly impacts crime levels. But Weisburd and colleagues also find that social and structural factors that are more often associated with community-based theories of crime (e.g., as reflected by indices of poverty and collective efficacy) are also important in understanding trends in antisocial behavior at micro places.

Key Questions for Future Study

In short, the existing literature suggests that micro geographic units of analysis are important in understanding and studying antisocial behavior. But prior studies have been restricted by the retrospective nature of data collection. One key problem is simply that appropriate data are difficult to identify retrospectively. While there are a large number of archival data sources on micro geographies now available, many characteristics of places cannot be identified retrospectively. In turn, there are few data sources available on the people who live in hot-spot areas, or their attitudes and experiences. The census, which could provide important information, does not allow release of data at micro geographic levels such as street segments. Moreover, existing studies have not been able to examine the ways in which crime hot spots influence the trajectories of crime, drug use, and other antisocial behaviors of people who live in these areas because social surveys are not focused on these geographic units and generally are not collected with enough cases to examine micro place processes.

Prospective longitudinal studies in the criminology of place would answer key questions that have so far eluded study. How does living in a crime hot spot affect individuals, and do different types of hot spots affect individuals in different ways? For example, do people who live in drug hot spots as compared with predatory crime hot spots and places without persistent crime or drug problems experience fear, physical and mental health problems, and safety risks in the same way? What are the long-term implications for these place-specific effects on individual lifestyles, criminal behavior, and health and social outcomes of residents living in those places? What structural factors are correlated with places being crime hot spots, and do different types of hot spots have different factors that are correlated with crime? And just as important, what risk and protective factors, if any, predict developmental trends related to areas becoming associated with crime? For example, are streets with insufficient levels of collective efficacy and residential stability and high levels of public disorder at greater risk of becoming predatory crime or drug crime hot spots? Are streets that are typified by facilities that attract potential victims (e.g., public libraries, schools, or malls) or that have transportation nodes that facilitate movement of victims and potential offenders more likely to become crime hot spots?

Possible Study Design

What would a prospective longitudinal study of the criminology of place look like? What would be the key unit of analysis for such a study? What data sources and methods would be critical? Below we focus on these issues in order to provide a possible model for how prospective longitudinal studies of places would be carried out.

The unit of analysis for examining micro places is a critical choice. In the past, micro place studies have focused on addresses, street blocks or street segments, and small clusters of these units. The problem, of course, is that there is no ideal level of geography, and no given unit of analysis that can be assumed at the outset. While there is no clear rule regarding the appropriate unit for studying antisocial behavior at places, there is a growing consensus among scholars in this area that this unit should be very small. We would suggest that this approach be followed in prospective longitudinal studies in the criminology of place. The street segment (sometimes referred to as a street block or block face) defined as both sides of the street between two intersections seems to us the most reasonable choice for unit of analysis.

The sampling design for a prospective study of places would have to define sites with serious enough crime problems that effects could be observed. It would also have to collect a large enough sample of residents at each place to allow the study to have sufficient statistical power. We suggest that a minimum of 10 interviews be collected at each geographic unit studied, and that the number of geographic units be at least 150 per group identified. At the very least there should be a "control group" for comparison to the hot-spot street segments identified. Following Farrington (1979), we think it is important to also recognize that crime hot spots may be of different types, and that it is critically important to recognize that variability. For example, a study might focus on predatory crime hot spots and on drug crime hot spots, including a "cool spot" comparison group—a design we have used in a proposed prospective longitudinal study in Baltimore City, Maryland (Weisburd et al. 2011). We would suggest a buffer of at least one street segment around each site selected in the study to prevent possible contamination due to the research processes, and to allow for isolating patterns at specific places.

Data collection for a prospective study would involve multiple data sources. The first would be an annual, or biennial, survey of residents conducted over an extended period of time. The second would be systematic social and physical observations also to be conducted over time, in conjunction with the survey. The third component would include archival data, information routinely collected by local government. Finally, we would recommend qualitative fieldwork to allow researchers to "look inside the black box" of what is happening at the places studied.

We think that the strongest method for collecting survey data would be as face-to-face interviews with interviewers walking door to door to the households in the sample. A sampling frame could be taken from a census of households on each street segment that would be conducted at the outset of the study. The survey instrument should contain a broad range of measures related to the topics of health, safety, drug use, and crime. In addition, respondents should also be asked to report on their use of public space, social interactions with neighbors, the role of neighbors in providing guardianship over children and property, and efforts on the part of the respondent to become involved in collective actions to ameliorate problems in their community.

While household interviews would constitute a major data collection component for a prospective study, we also suggest that information be collected concerning the physical layout and architectural attributes of the street segments in order to better understand the relationship between the physical environment and behavioral patterns in hot spots. It would also be of great use to have "systematic social observations" of places that are included in the study (Sampson and Raudenbush 1999; Sherman and Weisburd 1995). What is the extent and type of street-level activity? Who are the types of people who hang out on the street? How does street-level activity change over time?

Qualitative data are sometimes neglected in longitudinal research, but we think that it is critical to also observe the nature of street relationships in the hot and cool spots. Data collection might include ecological mapping, direct observation of street segments (including the businesses, individuals, and groups within them) and in-depth, semistructured interviews.

A final study component would be archival data. Many city and state agencies collect geographically specific data on topics such as housing, population characteristics, transit locations, places of interest (i.e., schools, airports, etc.), as well as special topics such as educational and truancy data, and crime data.

Conclusions

David Farrington has played a critical role in advancing criminological knowledge about individual offending through his advocacy of prospective longitudinal study. In this chapter, we have argued that it is time to add Farrington's insights to the study of the criminology of place. One of the more compelling contributions of a longitudinal study would be the prospective nature of examining crime hot spots over time. Specifically, such data would allow for an analysis of individual- and street segment-level predictors of areas being classified as hot spots. Such research would also be able to examine developmental trajectories of crime at place and explore the etiology of these patterns. The proposed design would also fill important theoretical gaps in the literature on the influences of place on individuals, by sampling enough individuals at a micro geographic level to allow for a careful examination of risk factors of places that increase criminality, and protective factors that discourage criminal behavior. At a policy level this work would provide guidance on how place characteristics of street segments can be altered to discourage development of antisocial behavior, and how individual risk and protective factors can be encouraged to reduce the negative influences of antisocial hot-spot places.

References

Becker, Howard. 1953. "Becoming a Marijuana User." *American Journal of Sociology* 59: 235–242.

Brantingham, Patricia L., and Paul J. Brantingham. 1975. "Residential Burglary and Urban Form." *Urban Studies* 12: 104–125.

Brantingham, Patricia L., and Paul J. Brantingham. 1999. "A Theoretical Model of Crime Hot Spot Generation." *Studies on Crime & Crime Prevention* 8: 7–26.

Brantingham, Paul J., and Patricia L. Brantingham. 1991. *Environmental Criminology*. Prospect Heights, IL: Waveland Press.

Bursik, Robert J., Jr., and Harold G. Grasmick. 1993. *Neighborhoods and Crime: The Dimensions of Effective Community Control.* New York: Lexington Books.

Clarke, Ronald V. 1983. "Situational Crime Prevention: Its Theoretical Basis and Practical Scope." In *Crime and Justice: A Review of Research*, vol. 14, edited by Michael Tonry and Norval Morris, 225–256. Chicago: University of Chicago Press.

Cohen, Lawrence E., and Marcus Felson. 1979. "Social Change and Crime Rate Trends: A Routine Activity Approach." *American Sociological Review* 44: 588–608.

Eck, John E., and David Weisburd. 1995. "Crime Places in Crime Theory." In *Crime and Place: Crime Prevention Studies*, vol. 4, edited by John E. Eck and David Weisburd, 1–34. Monsey, NY: Willow Tree Press.

Farrington, David P. 1979. "Longitudinal Research on Crime and Delinquency." In *Crime and Justice: An Annual Review of Research*, vol. 1, edited by Norval Morris and Michael Tonry, 289–348. Chicago: University of Chicago Press.

Farrington, David P. 2006. "Building Developmental and Life-Course Theories of Offending." In *Advances in Criminological Theory*, vol. 15: *Taking Stock: The Status of Criminological Theory*, edited by Francis T. Cullen, John Paul Wright, and Kristie R. Blevins, 355–366. New Brunswick, NJ: Transaction.

Farrington, David P., and J. David Hawkins. 1991. "Predicting Participation: Early Onset and Later Persistence in Officially Recorded Offending." *Criminal Behaviour and Mental Health* 1: 1–33.

Farrington, David P., Lloyd Ohlin, and James Q. Wilson. 1986. *Understanding and Controlling Crime.* New York: Springer.

Felson, Marcus, and Ronald V. Clarke. 1998. "Opportunity Makes the Thief: Practical Theory for Crime Prevention." Police Research Series Paper 98. London: Policing and Reducing Crime Unit; Research, Development and Statistics Directorate, Home Office.

Groff, Elizabeth R., David Weisburd, and Sue-Ming Yang. 2010. "Is It Important to Examine Crime Trends at a Local 'Micro' Level: A Longitudinal Analysis of Street to Street Variability in Crime Trajectories." *Journal of Quantitative Criminology* 26: 7–32.

Jeffrey, Clarence R. 1971. *Crime Prevention through Environmental Design.* Beverly Hills, CA: Sage.

Newman, Oscar. 1972. *Defensible Space.* New York: Macmillan.

Sampson, Robert J., and Stephen W. Raudenbush. 1999. "Systematic Social Observation of Public Spaces: A New Look at Disorder in Urban Neighborhoods." *American Journal of Sociology* 105: 603–651.

Sampson, Robert J., Stephen W. Raudenbush, and Felton Earls. 1997. "Neighborhoods and Violent Crime: A Multilevel Study of Collective Efficacy." *Science* 277: 918–924.

Sherman, Lawrence, and David Weisburd. 1995. "General Deterrent Effects of Police Patrol in Crime 'Hot Spots': A Randomized Study." *Justice Quarterly* 12: 625–648.

Spelman, William. 1995. "Criminal Careers of Public Places." In *Crime and Place: Crime Prevention Studies,* edited by John E. Eck and David Weisburd, 115–144. Monsey, NY: Willow Tree Press.

Taniguchi, Travis, George Rengert, and Eric McCord. 2009. "Where Size Matters: Agglomeration Economies of Illegal Drug Markets in Philadelphia." *Justice Quarterly* 26: 670–694.

Taylor, Ralph B. 1999. *Crime, Grime, Fear, and Decline: A Longitudinal Look.* Research in Brief. Washington, DC: National Institute of Justice, US Department of Justice.

Weisburd, David, Shawn Bushway, Cynthia Lum, and Sue-Ming Yang. 2004. "Trajectories of Crime at Places: A Longitudinal Study of Street Segments in the City of Seattle." *Criminology* 42: 283–322.

Weisburd, David, Elizabeth Groff, and Sue-Ming Yang. In press. *The Criminology of Place: Street Segments and Our Understanding of the Crime Problem.* New York: Oxford University Press.

Weisburd, David, Brian Lawton, Justin Ready, Katherine Sikkema, and Danielle Rudes. 2011. "Community Behavior and Anti-social Behavior at Drug Hot Spots." Proposal to NIDA/NIH.

Weisburd, David, Cynthia Lum, and Sue-Ming Yang. 2004. *The Criminal Careers of Places: A Longitudinal Study.* Washington, DC: US Department of Justice, National Institute of Justice.

Weisburd, David, and Lorraine G. Mazerolle. 2000. "Crime and Disorder in Drug Hot Spots: Implications for Theory and Practice in Policing." *Police Quarterly* 3: 331–349.

31

The Futures of Experimental Criminology

Lawrence W. Sherman

In 1983, David Farrington published his landmark review "Randomized Experiments on Crime and Justice." In that same year, the *New York Times* (Boffey 1983) published the preliminary results of the Minneapolis Domestic Violence Arrest Experiment (Sherman and Berk 1984), the first randomized controlled field trial of police discretion to arrest, which was reported widely and influentially (perhaps to a fault) around the world. Of the two events, Farrington's review was far more influential on my own life course as a scholar. Until then, I had defined myself primarily as a police scholar. After reading the broad sweep of Farrington's essay, I became an experimental criminologist.

Today, that identity is claimed by more scholars than ever before. Since 2005, the *Journal of Experimental Criminology* has served as a forum for publications in this new field. Since 1998, with David Farrington as cofounder and second president, the Academy of Experimental Criminology has honored people who have led experiments on crime and justice. Since 2009, the Division of Experimental Criminology of the American Society of Criminology has attracted a wide range of members from around the world. And in 2005, Farrington and Welsh (2005) reported the publication of another 83 randomized experiments between 1982 and 2004, since the original 35 Farrington (1983) had identified in the period 1957 to 1981—from a mean of 1.5 per year in 1957–1981 to a mean of 3.8 per year in 1982–2004.

While the growth in experimental criminology is far from geometric, it is presently at a crossroads. This chapter describes that crossroads in terms of two models of experimental criminology. It then describes the several possible futures experimental criminology could take as it enters the crossroads.

Two Models of Experimental Criminology: Center and Periphery

FROM CENTER TO PERIPHERY

For most of its history, experimental criminology has been driven from various centers of influence in research funding. In the United States, experiments began with funding from private foundations, which was channeled through university-based scholars who were linked to foundations through social networks. Empey and Lubeck (1971), for example, were funded by the Ford Foundation to randomly assign juvenile delinquents to institutional or community treatment. The principal investigators, working at the University of Southern California, then served as brokers between the funding organization in New York City and the juvenile justice system in Los Angeles. Similarly, the California Youth Agency based in Sacramento funded and conducted many experiments across California, many of which had international influence.

By the late 1960s, both the US Department of Justice and the UK Home Office had become centers for initiating research, including (at least intermittently) randomized field experiments (Farrington 2003). The creation of the Police Foundation by the Ford Foundation placed experimentalist Herbert Sturz, the founding director of the Vera Institute of Justice, onto its board. With the support of several other key board members, the Police Foundation in Washington then reached across the nation to find local police agencies willing to conduct experiments.

In 1979, the National Institute of Justice explicitly requested proposals for randomized field experiments for its Crime Control Theory Program, which was created based on a recommendation from the National Research Council of the National Academy of Sciences. In the model of that program, a research scholar was to approach an operating agency to ask permission to conduct an experiment, and then request funding. Based on that model, as director of research for the Police Foundation, I asked the police chief of Minneapolis, Anthony V. Bouza, as well as his mayor and city council, if they would allow police to randomly assign arrest. With a unanimous vote of support from the Minneapolis City Council, the National Institute of Justice approved the research funding. I then persuaded over 30 Minneapolis police officers to volunteer for the experiment, and to comply with its protocol to a greater or lesser degree. At all times it was a center-driven project supported by a police chief committed to research in general, but not one driven by the Minneapolis Police Department's own officers' vocational concerns.

This story could be told with different names and places by all of the experimental criminologists of that generation: Peter Greenwood, David Weisburd, Joan Petersilia, and many others. Why would criminal justice professionals want to formulate their own experiments? There was no demand from those workers on the periphery of national policy for the information that could make their work more effective. Rather, they were simply being helpful to people from the center, in a spirit of cooperation rather than thirst for knowledge. Criminology was something for academics and policymakers, not for workers in the trenches.

FROM PERIPHERY TO CENTER

In 1995, the Cambridge University Institute of Criminology made a historic decision that may eventually transform the direction of energy in experimental criminology from periphery to the center. The decision was to accept the invitation of the Bramshill Police College to teach six weeks of the long course preparing senior police officers to become chief constables. For the first time, police chiefs were required to study criminology at a graduate level in a leading research university in order to be deemed qualified for their jobs in policing. This mandate lasted most of 10 years. While it is no longer mandatory, the Cambridge program has expanded to teach senior police from countries around the world. From London to Sydney, from Sacramento to New Delhi, and from Hong Kong to Stockholm, hundreds of police chiefs a year are being taught applied criminology and police management at Cambridge University—by faculty including David Farrington.

It is a very small step from teaching criminology to teaching *experimental* criminology. Building on the foundations laid by Professor Sir Anthony Bottoms and his colleagues, the Cambridge Police Executive Programme at Cambridge was given a strong boost by the Jerry Lee Foundation in Philadelphia. In 2007, Jerry Lee committed 10 years of funding to the new Jerry Lee Centre for Experimental Criminology at Cambridge University. With a governing committee including experimental criminologists Friedrich Lösel, Manuel Eisner, and David Farrington, the new center appointed a postdoctoral fellow trained by David Weisburd at Hebrew University, Barak Ariel, who immediately started teaching the police chiefs in the graduate program.

By 2009, the combination of the Jerry Lee Centre and the Police Executive Programme had begun to reverse the tide from center to periphery. Police leaders who had been drilled in the methods and findings of randomized experiments in policing started coming back to Cambridge for help in designing their own experiments. From Manchester to Birmingham, from Staffordshire to the London Underground, police leaders responsible for making communities safer asked for Cambridge to help them design experiments.

In the early years of this development, the police were able to go to the National Policing Improvement Agency (NPIA) for modest support for surveys or other research costs. But in 2010, the election of a new Government in Britain led to the announcement of plans to close the NPIA. In addition, police in England and Wales were told to cut their budgets by 20 percent over three years. Nothing could have seemed less propitious for developing experimental criminology. Yet nothing else could have been so misleading.

By mid-2011, the Cambridge Institute of Criminology was in partnership with four police agencies committing substantial personnel and cash costs to conducting experiments that were designed at the initiative of the police agencies. The experiments were designed to be as lean and low-cost as the times required, and as the support of the Jerry Lee Foundation allowed. But their protocols provide an example of one possible future of experimental criminology, what Weisburd and Neyroud (2011) call "police-led science" (rather than science-led policing).

A second future of experimental criminology can build on this approach. In what might be called periphery-to-periphery collaborations, crime and justice policies can be tested simultaneously in multiple sites. The remainder of this chapter considers those two possibilities, as well as the prospects for the survival of center-to-periphery criminology.

Profession-Driven Science

Several examples at Cambridge illustrate what may already be happening around the world in other settings where police and criminologists are in ongoing dialogue. When British Transport Police (BTP) attended the Third International Cambridge-NPIA Conference on Evidence-Based Policing, they were very impressed with findings from various experiments on policing hot spots. They then approached Barak Ariel at Cambridge to ask him to design a hot-spots patrol experiment for them. When he analyzed the data on the very low volume of crime in the London Underground, Ariel found over 100 high-crime "platforms" (out of thousands) within the subway stations. He then worked closely with the BTP to identify options for research questions that could be answered with different levels of statistical power. The entire premise of the negotiation was that the BTP would supply the operational personnel for conducting the experiment, the field supervision, and the data collected of the conduct and outcomes of the experiment. The Cambridge role, supported with a small subvention from BTP to Cambridge, would be to design and analyze the experiment on completion.

When Assistant Chief Constable Gordon Scobbie of the West-Midlands Police in England brought a planning team to Cambridge in early 2010, the team had spent several months discussing how they might improve a critical policy in a way that followed principles of "evidence-based policing" (Sherman 1998). They had been stuck over issues of how a new policy on antisocial behavior might be designed. After a meeting at Cambridge, they accepted the idea of random assignment of a new specialist team approach versus the existing neighborhood team approach. With a small grant from the NPIA, they sent three sergeants and some 15 constables back to Cambridge for five days of planning and designing both the new police practices and the experimental design for evaluating those practices. From the outset, Cambridge insisted that the practices themselves be owned and chosen by the constables and sergeants in the new specialist units. While they also requested some training in restorative justice, more of their work qualified as creative problem-solving in managing neighborhood disputes.

When Hampshire Police asked Cambridge about testing the effect of prosecution on domestic common assaults, Cambridge suggested a research design that required extensive and wide-ranging consultation. After almost a year, the chief constable of Hampshire and his team conducted that consultation, ultimately receiving approval from Cabinet-level officials. At that point, he came back to Cambridge to help design and carry out the experiment, randomly assigning conditional cautions versus prosecutions in cases of minor domestic violence. In an earlier government with a highly centralized view of policymaking, such permission would have been inconceivable. But as England moves toward an announced policy of locally elected police and crime commissioners, the idea of local autonomy opens the door to more periphery-to-center initiatives. (And how did the Hampshire Police become linked to Cambridge? This came about through its senior officers attending the graduate courses at the Cambridge Police Executive Programme.) This was not a Cambridge idea. This was a Hampshire Police idea.

The "Cambridge Randomizer"

One Cambridge idea that has facilitated police developing their own experiments is Barak Ariel's invention, the Cambridge Randomizer (Ariel et al. 2011). This device is simply a standardized web tool, available by password-protected access at the Cambridge Institute of Criminology website (for the Jerry Lee Centre of Experimental Criminology). This tool can be customized very quickly for any kind of experimental design, with various units of analyses and sequences of random assignment. It allows operational personnel from field settings to enter identifying details on eligible cases and to check on their eligibility, prior to random assignment. Once the details are entered and the computer confirms the eligibility criteria answers are correct, the web tool then generates a randomly assigned treatment for that case. The operating staff receives the information instantly and can immediately apply the treatment as assigned. At the same time, the case can be audited based on the website data to check whether the assigned treatment turned out to be what was delivered, according to field records of the operating agencies.

Anyone on the planet who wants to register a protocol on the Cambridge registry of randomized trials in policing or corrections (see www.crim.cam.ac.uk) can ask Cambridge to set up a customized Cambridge Randomizer for their experiment. This tool, we hope, will further encourage periphery-to-center experiments by reducing the costs of randomized trials. When one considers that this web tool may replace as many as three full-time staff entering the information, it is a major cost-cutter. Whether it will provide as effective a mechanism of quality control as full-time staff is the key question to be monitored.

The Society for Evidence-Based Policing

Another idea that came out of the Cambridge Police Executive Programme is a professional society for promoting evidence-based policing, founded in November 2010. Originally cast as the *British* Society of Evidence-Based Policing, professionals and academics from around the world asked that the national identity be dropped in favor of a society without borders. Led by two Cambridge alumni, Superintendent Alex Murray of the West-Midlands Police, and Assistant Chief Constable Neil Wain of Greater Manchester Police, the board of the new Society agreed to the requests for the name change, with the same mission statement of aims: (1) increased use of best available research evidence to solve policing problems; (2) the production of new research evidence by police practitioners and researchers; and (3) communication of research evidence to police practitioners and the public.

Multinational Science

Once the Society becomes a truly global network of police seeking knowledge, the potential for even better science will increase. The use of "prospective meta-analysis" though simultaneous conduct of the same experiment in separate locations is already developing within the same nations. Several experiments in the UK are heading in that direction. Other experiments that have been developed in Australia have also been replicated in the United States and UK. By planning for replication from the outset of testing any new strategy, professionals can increase not only the internal validity of their tests, but also the generalizability (external validity) of the results they find in conducting experiments.

Prospects for Center-Driven Experiments

In the economic tsunami that hit the Western world in 2008, the prospects for multi-million-dollar randomized field experiments dimmed considerably. While the hopes for such big science are not yet crushed entirely, it is unlikely to reappear in the UK in the near future. While the Home Office put £5 million into experiments in restorative justice in the first decade of the twenty-first century, the second decade seems unlikely to witness center-driven experiments on that scale.

Paradoxically, the demise of center-driven funding may lead to more experiments rather than less. As Farrington (2003) reports, center-driven funding for experiments can depend highly on the preferences of a few key officials. Yet as the foregoing account suggests, a rising demand for experiments within crime and justice policy professions can become an irresistible tide. By using graduate education to diffuse understanding of the value of experimental criminology, academics can foster far more experiments than they could ever organize and conduct on their own. Police call this kind of leverage a "force multiplier," in which each academic consulting with professionals can yield much more research evidence than under the traditional model of experimental criminology.

Both the traditional and the new models of field experiments may well be in our future. One way or the other, the demand for experimental criminology seems likely to grow with the general demand for knowledge about public safety. Whether the profession-driven science can be held to high standards of research quality and integrity is the challenge of the new world that is emerging. But with strong emphasis on peer review and collaboration between highly trained academics and practitioners, the challenges ahead should not be insuperable. And however the field develops, it will always owe a lot to the man who first mapped it out and invited us to explore it: David Farrington.

References

Ariel, Barak, Jordi Vila, and Lawrence W. Sherman. 2011. "Random Assignment without Tears: How I Learned to Stop Worrying and Love the Cambridge Randomizer." Unpublished Ms. thesis. Cambridge, UK: Jerry Lee Centre for Experimental Criminology, Institute of Criminology, Cambridge University.

Boffey, Philip M. 1983. "Domestic Violence: Study Favors Arrest." *New York Times*, April 5. Available at http://www.nytimes.com/1983/04/05/science/domestic-violence-study-favors-arrest.html.

Empey, Lamar, and Steven G. Lubeck. 1971. *The Silverlake Experiment*. Chicago: Aldine.

Farrington, David P. 1983. "Randomized Experiments on Crime and Justice." In *Crime and Justice: An Annual Review of Research*, vol. 4, edited by Michael Tonry and Norval Morris, 257–308. Chicago: University of Chicago Press.

Farrington, David P. 2003. "British Randomized Experiments on Crime and Justice." *Annals of the American Academy of Political and Social Science* 589: 150–167.

Farrington, David P., and Brandon C. Welsh. 2005. "Randomized Experiments in Criminology: What Have We Learned in the Last Two Decades?" *Journal of Experimental Criminology* 1: 9–38.

Sherman, Lawrence W. 1998. *Evidence-Based Policing*. Washington, DC: Police Foundation.

Sherman, Lawrence W., and Richard A. Berk. 1984. "The Specific Deterrent Effects of Arrest for Domestic Assault." *American Sociological Review* 49: 261–272.

Weisburd, David, and Peter Neyroud. 2011. "Police Science: Toward a New Paradigm." Paper presented at the Harvard Kennedy School / National Institute of Justice Executive Session on Policing and Public Safety.

32

Stopping Crime Requires Successful Implementation of What Works

Irvin Waller

Even with large reductions in rates of victimization in the United States and other countries, there are too many victims of homicide and drunk drivers, too many victims of forcible rape, too many victims of robbery and much more. We know about the losses and emotional pain from each individual case. We also know that that pain, if it can be measured in financial terms, still accumulates to $450 billion in the United States (Waller 2010) and $83 billion in Canada (Zhang 2011).

Criminology stars such as David Farrington and his collaborators have provided us with proof that these rates of victimization and the harm done to victims has been reduced in experiments in the past (Loeber and Farrington 2011; Farrington and Welsh 2007; Sherman et al. 2006). But the harm to victims will not be further reduced until we help governments to reinvest in the processes that get effective prevention implemented in every community. It is time for criminology to get better at implementing its knowledge successfully in the mainstream.

The current fiscal crisis in both the UK and the United States provides a special opportunity to get a shift from unaffordable and ineffective policing and prisons to cost-effective prevention. This chapter identifies for criminologists some of the key steps for shifting government policy to success and some examples of implementation (WHO 2004; Waller 2008; Institute for Prevention of Crime 2009). I demonstrated how a reinvestment of 10 percent of what we are spending on reactive policies now could achieve a reduction of 50 percent in rates of victimization (Waller 2008).

The Limits and Costs of Massive Expenditures on the Traditional System

In the last four decades, the biggest criminological experiment of all time took place when the United States went from levels of 200 persons incarcerated per 100,000 in the 1970s to 750 in 2011 and so became the number one jailer in the world, with one in four of all persons incarcerated in the world (Waller 2008). To achieve this, it expanded expenditures on policing to surpass $100 billion, on prisons to more than $70 billion, and on lawyers and criminal courts to more than $50 billion (Waller 2008). These expansions were not the result of random policy reform at the state or local level, but the result of federal dollars used to get states to invest in what the evidence available shows would not have worked in a cost-effective manner (Waller 2008).

This spike in spending occurred despite criminology rather than because of it. In those same four decades, the teaching of criminology multiplied in US universities. Criminological researchers interpreted statistics, critiqued the trends, and published in their journals but failed to reach the policymakers and stem the tide. Even the well-written summaries of the evaluations of what works for Congress (Sherman et al. 2006) did not make a chink in the traditional criminal justice expenditures.

The traditional justice system focuses on individual responsibility and cases, not social science research. It largely reacts to crime and is framed in legal dogma going back to Beccaria. It also fails victims in many different ways, as they are not protected, recognized, or included in the process (Waller 2008; 2010). The publicity machine of Giuliani fooled some criminologists, but those who looked at the evaluations saw how limited any impact could have been.

Despite the expenditures, the rates of most property and violent crime in the United States are little different from countries such as Canada or England and Wales, which have made much more moderate use of more police and prisons. Further, the US murder rate is still 5 per 100,000, which is 200 percent higher than Canada and the UK. Worse still, the stratospherically high rates of incarceration for African Americans still leave disproportionate numbers of African Americans as victims of violence.

The Effectiveness and Dividends of Proven Prevention

David Farrington's leadership has provided us with a rich bank of empirical data on the risk factors correlated with the onset and persistence of delinquency (e.g., Farrington 2005). His contributions have provided clear conclusions, particularly about which negative life experiences in child development predispose young children to persistent offending. They have shown the extent to which these risk factors are concentrated geographically within cities. Five percent of families account for 50 percent or more of the offending.

But they have gone further to provide strong evidence to prove that specific projects that tackle these risk factors can reduce victimizations (e.g., Farrington and Welsh 2007; Loeber and Farrington 2011). There are now many well-known examples of projects that have prevented street violence, suppressed property crime, and avoided child abuse (Waller 2008; Sherman et al. 2006). In 2011, the US

Justice Department announced a new website (http://crimesolutions.gov) to help taxpayers judge the effectiveness of state and local anticrime programs. The programs are divided into eight categories, of which interestingly crime and crime prevention had the most evaluations, as these are exactly the areas where the United States has lagged the civilized world.

A 5 or 10 percent reinvestment from criminal justice into these cost-effective programs would provide huge benefits to potential victims of crime (Waller 2008). Every dollar spent on prevention saves at least seven dollars associated with incarcerating the individual in question (Waller 2008; Institute for Prevention of Crime 2009).

Governance and Other Key Concepts of Implementation

Proof that programs work is not sufficient to get mainstream investments in the programs. Every applied criminologist knows that what happens after a program has been evaluated as a success in reducing the number of crime victims is that the program shuts down.

WHO PROPOSALS FOR IMPLEMENTATION

In 2004, the World Health Organization produced its first report on how to get this knowledge implemented. It points to six critical steps, including increasing the capacity for collecting data on violence; researching violence—its causes, consequences, and prevention; promoting the primary prevention of violence; promoting gender and social equality and equity to prevent violence; strengthening care and support services for victims; and bringing it all together—developing a national plan of action.

But these programs have to be directed by good governance strategies that are sustained, comprehensive, and results oriented. These need a responsibility center at the highest level with sustained investment in training, standards, and capacity development as well as 3-year action plans with a 10-year vision. These must be multipronged (enforcement, design, social, and so on) and a portfolio of short- and long-term investments (Waller 2008). They need to be multiagency problem solving: diagnosis, plan, implementation, and evaluation; collaborative effort that brings together key agencies such as schools and social services; and engagement with the public.

The Winnipeg auto theft suppression strategy is a spectacular Canadian success story using the same proven ingredients of diagnosing a problem, involving key sectors and then implementing a solution with adequate funding. It invested $20 million to reduce car theft and so saved many lives and more than $80 million so far.

Cities such as Boston in the 1990s did some of the analysis and so reduced the number of gang-related homicides between young men by 50 percent or more within only two years of finishing the diagnosing phase and implementing its city-wide strategy. It used strategic approaches that combined existing police resources, programs to help young men complete school and get jobs, and the mobilization of mothers to pressure their sons to abandon violent associates. Unfortunately, it neglected to establish a permanent responsibility center and so is facing the same problems again today.

Communities That Care (Catalano et al. 2011) has strong evidence for success. It has spread to a number of different countries and is widely used in Pennsylvania and some other states. But in terms of widespread application, it is another example where the lack of a permanent leadership center leaves the communities without sustained collaboration.

The process of establishing a permanent leadership center to diagnose problems and implement solutions is what a growing number of municipalities have done in the UK in the safe community partnerships and also in Canadian cities, such as Edmonton, Montreal, Ottawa, and Waterloo Region, but without the reinvestment that the data would justify in the proven programs.

Establishing the governance processes at all orders of government requires immediate investment and capacity development—a city of 100,000 will require two trained crime reduction planners—a national government of 10 million will require an initial group of 30–40 exclusive of statistical instruments and analysis (Institute for Prevention of Crime 2009).

Once the responsibility center is in place, it can multiply the use of proven strategies. In the City of Ottawa, the "4th R," which was tested in a large-scale randomized controlled trial in Canada (Crooke et al. 2008), has been promoted by the city's crime prevention responsibility center known as Crime Prevention Ottawa to stop violence against women.

Convincing Governments to Reinvest in Prevention

ENGAGING THE PUBLIC

One of the most important steps for helping legislators to make the reinvestments is to get the knowledge out to voters, taxpayers, and (potential) victims of crime. This was the reason for the success of Proposition 36 in California. It was the purpose of a book written for this audience (Waller 2008). Its success in English has led to translations in Chinese, French, German, and Spanish. This combines the science with examples of successful programs that show that national and local government could reduce the number of crime victims by 50 percent or more, by shifting from overreliance on policing and corrections to smart use of police and smart investments in prevention. It shows how the shift to prevention is in the interest of (potential) victims and taxpayers.

Social media provide another opportunity to influence government policy. Clearly they have influenced elections in the United States and Canada. They get the messages about the potential for prevention to reduce violence to a wide public and so persuade governments to reinvest.

The US Department of Justice is funding a data bank on cost-benefit knowledge for criminal justice at the renowned Vera Institute for Justice in New York City. This group, like the Washington State Institute for Public Policy and many leading think-tanks, is using Twitter to share key reports with the general public.

The Spanish version of the book has momentum of its own with legislation based on the book recommended by a congressional commission of the Mexican parliament and two states with a similar process leading to comprehensive policies.

IMPORTANCE OF COMMISSIONS

Another important way for this material to be put into the mainstream of government action is through commissions. In the United States in the 1960s, presidential commissions started major reforms. Recently, in other countries commissions have influenced large-scale implementation of what works. In England, for instance, the Audit Commission undertook a review of the situation in England to report on what should happen. Just two years later, the British government introduced the Crime and Disorder Act that created the Youth Justice Board, which implemented the Youth Inclusion Programs in 72 different estates (Waller 2008).

A commission analyzes what we are currently doing, identifies the gaps with international knowledge, and then recommends the necessary actions. Among those using this book are Senator Webb, who is proposing special legislation in the US Congress, and the Cameron government in the UK (Chambers et al. 2009).

The Province of Alberta established a task force in 2007 using in part Waller (2008) and so became the leading jurisdiction in North America on implementing the best approaches for reducing crime. It is investing $40 per capita per year in new dollars into a strategy that balances enforcement, treatment, and prevention— the three-pronged strategy. It is run by SafeCom, which is a modern-day responsibility center that co-locates senior officials from five ministries and is mandated to follow a sustained strategy to significantly reduce crime and prevent victimization over a 10-year period.

The City of Ottawa established a task force in 2004 that resulted in a permanent citywide crime prevention strategy. The University of Ottawa developed proposals for a national strategy, contracted with experts across the world to inform Canadian crime prevention, and launched a network of major Canadian cities to implement collaborative and evidence-based governance strategies. This institute and the network developed action briefs for municipal stakeholders (2009) as a significant tool for cities to plan better and invest smartly, which are encouraging more cities to shift their policies in Canada and across the world. The mayor of Edmonton established a task force in 2009 that resulted in a citywide community safety strategy.

The vice president of Argentina recently held a meeting to look at application of the book in Argentina. The Soros Foundation took an interest in establishing a violence prevention fund inspired by the conclusions from the various chapters in the book. Ecuador and other Latin American countries are looking at strategies similar to Alberta. But until these initiatives lead to commissions as in Mexico or Canada, it is unlikely to see concrete reinvestment.

World Bank

In 2010, the World Bank began to look at the book together with expertise from leading American crime prevention experts to solve violence in Latin America (Waller 2008; Sherman et al. 2006). My conclusions from that meeting reemphasize the following:

- Key to success is a sustained, comprehensive, and results-oriented approach led at the highest level of government—not just enforcement and courts.
- Potential for successful return on investment in effective prevention is significant (in reduced numbers of victims and climate of safety)—continued growth in expenditures on reaction depletes economic and human development.

It is also important to provide a checklist of the programs with promise of short- and/or long-term reductions in violence, including the following:

- Programs addressing parenting, such as those provided by public health nurses, and addressing youth problems through mentoring and inclusion projects.
- Reducing the availability and harmful use of alcohol, guns, and knives.
- Neighborhood programs that create or reinforce collective efficacy.
- Public health strategies to tackle criminal youth gangs such as Chicago's Operation Ceasefire (also original Boston project).
- Empowerment of women, including all-female police stations.
- Restorative justice and victim assistance.

The World Bank's development report in 2011 concludes that governments must reduce violence in order to increase domestic product. If the Bank goes the next step, then it will set conditions on governments to ensure investments in effective prevention.

Conclusion

The rights of citizens not to be victims of crime require national and local governments to get to know the results of scientific analyses of the causes of crime and the results of programs tackling those causes. Waller (2008) makes this part easy. As part of the effort to frame investments in crime reduction in terms of reducing harm to victims, there is now a sequel focusing on crime victims (Waller 2010), where a combination of Twitter and other social media are being used to reach the general public.

Governments must establish commissions to develop recommendations for permanent leadership centers to make the shift from traditional strategies that are costly to taxpayers and ineffective in preventing victimization. Governments concerned about doing it right and protecting taxpayers are making this shift. Governments like those in the UK and United States are being forced to do it by fiscal crises.

Several proposals are of top priority:

1. Shift crime policies to preemptive strategies orchestrated by a small secretariat to diagnose problems and mobilize key sectors such as schools, housing, and policing in all orders of government.
2. Invest adequately in effective (what works) programs, such as youth inclusion, mentoring, repeat victimization, Boston-Chicago gang strategies, compulsory curricula—4th R—to reduce sexual assault, programs to stop child abuse, and Winnipeg strategies to stop car theft.
3. Continue to tackle alcohol, guns, and drug abuse among younger adults (Waller 2010).

References

Catalano, Richard F., Kevin P. Haggerty, J. David Hawkins, and Jenna Elgin. 2011. "Prevention of Substance Use Disorders: Role of Risk and Protective Factors." In *Clinical Manual of Adolescent Substance Abuse Treatment*, edited by Yifrah Kaminer and Ken C. Winters, 25–63. Washington, DC: American Psychiatric Publishing.

Crooke, Claire, D., David A.Wolfe, Ray Hughes, Peter G. Jaffe, and Debbie Chiodo. 2008. *Development, Evaluation and National Implementation of a School Based Program to Reduce Violence and Related Risk Behaviours: Lessons from the 4th R*. IPC Review, vol. 2. Ottawa: Institute for the Prevention of Crime.

Farrington, David P. 2005. "Childhood Origins of Antisocial Behaviour." *Clinical Psychology and Psychotherapy* 12: 177–190.

Farrington, David P., and Brandon C. Welsh. 2007. *Saving Children from a Life of Crime: Early Risk Factors and Effective Interventions*. New York: Oxford University Press.

Institute for the Prevention of Crime. 2009. *Making Cities Safer: Action Briefs for Municipal Stakeholders*. Ottawa: University of Ottawa.

Chambers, Max, Ben Ullmann, Irvin Waller, and Gavin Lockhart. 2009. *Less Crime, Lower Costs: Implementing Effective Early Crime Reduction Programmes in England and Wales*. London: Policy Exchange.

Loeber, Rolf, and David P. Farrington. 2011. *Young Homicide Offenders and Victims: Risk Factors, Prediction, and Prevention from Childhood*. New York: Springer.

Sherman, Lawrence W., David P. Farrington, Brandon C. Welsh, and Doris L. MacKenzie, eds. 2006. *Evidence-Based Crime Prevention*. Rev. ed. New York: Routledge.

Waller, Irvin. 2008. *Less Law, More Order: The Truth about Reducing Crime.* Westport, CT: Praeger.

Waller, Irvin. 2010. *Rights for Victims of Crime: Rebalancing Justice.* New York: Rowman and Littlefield.

World Bank. 2011. *World Bank Development Report: Conflict, Security, and Development.* Washington, DC: World Bank.

World Health Organization. 2004. *Preventing Violence: A Guide to Implementing the Recommendations of the World Report on Violence and Health.* Geneva: WHO.

Zhang, Ting. 2011. *Costs of Crime in Canada, 2008.* Ottawa: Department of Justice Canada.

33

The Future of Sentencing and Its Control

Michael Tonry

Sentencing should matter. The stakes are high. It is the ultimate conflict between the interests of the individual and the state, in which citizens are denounced for wrongdoing and lose their properties, liberties, and lives. In our time it matters more than usual. Beginning in the 1980s, something went fundamentally wrong. Many policymakers lost sight of a moral and semantic truth: "criminal justice" is about crime and it is about justice. Most legal systems seek to prevent crime and to punish offenders justly. Most American and English policymakers and practitioners long understood that. After 1984 in the United States and 1993 in England and Wales (hereafter England), many acted as if they had forgotten.

We don't know why the American and English criminal justice systems became so large and so severe—common explanations include rising crime rates, political cynicism, public attitudes, existentialist angst, and the history of American race relations (Garland 2001; Simon 2007; Tonry 2011a)—but we know how it happened. New laws mandated prison sentences of historically unprecedented lengths, and practitioners applied them. Judges sent more people to prison. Parole boards became more risk-averse; many fewer prisoners were released. Those released were held longer and were more likely to have their parole revoked and be sent back. Police became more aggressive, engaged in racial profiling on a large scale, and targeted places and circumstances that disproportionately ensnared young minority men and women.

David Farrington and I organized projects that aimed to advance understanding of the effectiveness of various approaches to crime prevention and of crime and punishment trends in developed countries.[1] In the first we assumed, and believed the then available evidence showed, that criminal justice system approaches to crime prevention are largely ineffective and focused instead on situational, developmental, and community approaches (Tonry and Farrington 1995). There was substantial evidence of the effectiveness of situational and developmental prevention and weaker, mixed evidence concerning community prevention. In the second we attempted to standardize official and victimization data on crime and operationalize data on sentencing and sanctions for seven developed countries in part to look for cross-national evidence of the effects of punishment policies on crime rates (Tonry and Farrington 2004). None was found.

The state of knowledge today stands pretty much where it did when those projects were published. Evidence concerning the effectiveness of situational and developmental prevention continues to accumulate. Evidence concerning community approaches when they are not at heart primarily situational remains ambiguous. Near consensus now exists that the deterrent effects of harsher sanctions are small to nonexistent (e.g., Durlauf and Nagin 2011). New evidence suggests that prisons are criminogenic, increasing rather than decreasing the likelihood a released prisoner will reoffend (Nagin, Cullen, and Jonson 2009). Some people believe new policing techniques significantly affect crime rates (e.g., Durlauf and Nagin 2011; Sherman 2011). Others disagree (e.g., Lappi-Seppälä 2008; Tonry 2011b).

With that background in mind, this chapter identifies how American and English sentencing and punishment policies need to and will change by 2025. I make two heroic assumptions, contrary to recent experience in both countries. The first is that policymakers will pay attention to systematic evidence. If so, they will invest money and imagination in situational and developmental approaches and decrease emphasis on sentencing and sanctions. The second is that policymakers will remember that convicted offenders should be justly punished.

In the minds of practitioners, theorists, and ordinary people, offenders should be punished as much as they deserve, not more. The severity of the punishment, almost everyone agrees as a matter of private belief, should be proportionate to the seriousness of the crime. Between 1984 and 1996 in the United States and between 1993 and 2010 in England and Wales, many policymakers and some prosecutors and judges acted as if they believed otherwise. The classic American examples are California's 1994 "three-strikes" law and a 1986 federal law that punished crack offenses, usually involving young black men, as severely as powder cocaine offenses 100 times larger, usually involving white sellers. The classic English examples are the Labour Government's mantra about "rebalancing the system in favor of the victim" and the enactment in the Criminal Justice Act of 2003 of provisions permitting indeterminate, potentially lifetime sentences for "dangerous offenders" convicted of designated offenses, some not self-evidently threatening to human life and safety (e.g., sexual congress with a sheep).

The people who enacted these laws cannot possibly have thought much about their effects on the people they would send to prison. Losing large chunks of life would damage anyone. The most typical offenders, young minority and working-class people and drug-dependent people of all types, are more damaged by imprisonment than are more prosperous, less troubled people. They have less financial, family, and other resources to fall back on. While in prison, ties with wives, husbands, and children atrophy. Families break up, parents die, and skills become obsolete. Chances of living decent, contributing lives are reduced. The well-known negative aftereffects operate—stigma, depression, difficulty finding work, family problems.

Imprisonment has always damaged people, but for people who deserved their punishments that was seen as a regrettable but necessary evil. John Howard, the first high-profile prison reformer, 200 years ago called prisons "schools for crime." The most recent sophisticated research shows what informed people have always suspected—imprisonment makes people worse, more likely to commit crimes than before they were sent away.

Judges have responsibility for sentencing convicted offenders, and have immense power over offenders' lives. They want to be wise and to be just. They want, and should be allowed, to fashion punishments that take account of offender's crimes, and their effects on victims, and the circumstances of offenders' lives. It is in everyone's interest that crimes be appropriately punished and that offenders be helped to build conventional, law-abiding, satisfying lives. To do that, judges need the authority they had before sentencing was radically transformed, but subject to restraints earlier judges did not face. The problems that discredited sentencing in earlier times—unjustifiable disparities, risks of biased and capricious decisions, lack of procedural fairness and official accountability—were real problems. The problems that afflict contemporary sentencing—undue harshness, rigidity, arbitrariness—are real problems. They can all be solved. The remainder of this chapter describes what needs to be undone and done.

Disassembly

In the United States, all three-strikes, mandatory minimum sentence, life-without-possibility-of-parole (LWOP), and "dangerous offender" laws should be repealed. Laws in England permitting indeterminate sentences, mandating minimum sentences, and limiting parole release eligibility likewise should be repealed. There is no credible evidence that they make either country a safer place. Mountains of evidence show that they are applied inconsistently and disproportionately to minority offenders. Even for the comparatively small number of unacceptably dangerous people, those laws are not needed. The most dangerous can be civilly committed if they are "dangerous to themselves or others." Offenders who fall short of that test but fairly can be described as unacceptably violence-prone can be sentenced to long prison sentences on a case-by-case basis. And if following release they continue to seem unacceptably violent, civil commitment is available.

It is natural to wonder—people in other countries do wonder—why manifestly unjust and astonishingly severe three-strikes, LWOP, and mandatory minimum sentence laws proliferated in the United States and why England's Labour Government adopted repressive rhetoric and laws and worked systematically to reduce defendant's procedural protections. No one has a really good explanation. Some academic theories focus on crime as an emotionally powerful proxy issue for political conflicts between liberals and conservatives, as a politically potent symbol of our insecure "late modern world," or as a field on which the latest chapter of

America's complicated history of race relations plays out. However recent crime control politics and public attitudes are explained or understood, laws of unprecedented severity were enacted. Drug laws routinely mandated sentences measured in decades for offenses mostly committed by teenagers and people in their early twenties. LWOP laws applied to crimes committed by minors, including in some cases crimes other than homicide. That is why the US Supreme Court in *Graham v. Florida* (2010),[2] stepped in to declare LWOPs unconstitutional for nonhomicide offenses committed by minors. That decision affected several hundred people. Several thousand more continue to serve LWOPs for crimes committed as juveniles (Nellis and King 2009).

The juvenile LWOP story illustrates the proposition that policymakers during the 1980s and 1990s stopped thinking about the effects of the laws they passed on the people they would affect. Legal systems in all Western countries for at least a century have recognized that juvenile offenders are different from adults and treated them differently. They are intellectually and emotionally immature, are in a risk-taking phase of life, and have their whole lives ahead of them. That's why juvenile justice systems exist and why maximum sentences in juvenile courts are much lower than in adult courts. In many places, for similar reasons, including Germany and the Scandinavian countries, courts are required or allowed to impose mitigated punishments on young adults aged 18 to 20. Legislators who made 12- to 17-year-olds eligible for LWOPs forgot that those young people are not adults, but are especially fallible, immature human beings.

What is true of LWOPs for juveniles is true of LWOPs generally, three-strikes laws, minimum sentence, and "dangerous offender" laws mandating prison terms measured in decades for adults. If the interests of kids did not count, beyond uncertainty, the interests of adult offenders did not either.

Construction

In principle it would be simple to build sentencing systems that allow judges to come close to treating like cases alike and different cases differently.[3] In practice, vested interests, inertia, and resistance to change make transformation of legal processes inordinately difficult. The path forward, however, is clear. New sentencing systems could be made incomparably fairer, more consistent, and more just than any existing American or English system.

PRESUMPTIVE SENTENCING GUIDELINES

First, systems of presumptive sentencing guidelines would be established; following them would not be mandatory, but when judges impose some other sentence they would have to explain why; the adequacy of their reasons could be appealed to a higher court. Substantial evidence from Minnesota, Oregon,

Washington, and Kansas shows that presumptive guidelines can bring the rule of law to sentencing. They can make decisions more consistent, fair, predictable, and transparent, reduce racial and other unwarranted disparities, and make judges more accountable.

The record with other kinds of sentencing guidelines is less extensive and less convincing. North Carolina's mandatory guidelines for prison sentences improved consistency among those sent to prison but drove plea bargaining underground to avoid prison sentences for sympathetic offenders and created stark disparities between offenders dealt with under and above ground. The mandatory federal sentencing guidelines are universally recognized to have been a disaster—mechanical, rigid, overly severe, and widely circumvented. The record with voluntary guidelines is ambiguous. Research findings from the 1980s and 1990s consistently showed that they neither reduced sentencing disparities nor enhanced consistency or predictability.

SENTENCE REVIEW

Second, realistic systems would be established for review of the adequacy of judges' decisions to depart from guidelines. There are a number of ways to do it. Jurisdictions could, as in Kansas, Minnesota, Oregon, and Washington, establish presumptive guidelines backed up by appellate review. Those systems have worked reasonably well. Alternatively, parole boards could be revitalized or reestablished and directed to establish parole release guidelines that aim to avoid unwarranted disparities in prison sentences. The most comprehensive and cost-effective approach would call for identical guidelines for sentencing and release decisions. The parole agency would review every case in which a judge imposed a sentence longer than guidelines prescribed. This would cost much less than appellate review and be more systematic, comprehensive, and consistent.

PROPORTIONATE MAXIMUM SENTENCES

Third, meaningful upper limits of sentence severity would be established for each type of crime; this could be done in a number of ways. First, criminal codes can be revised to define offenses more precisely and designate proportionate maximums for each. This is what most European criminal codes do. Second, a considerably less ambitious job, new laws superseding existing provisions on maximum sentences could be enacted that set new proportionate maximums for all offenses. A substantial research literature shows that there is wide agreement among most people in most countries about the relative seriousness of crimes. Once crimes are ranked according to seriousness, it is a simple mechanical task to attach proportionate maximum punishments to each. A third option, partly adopted in the *Model Penal Code* and more fully developed in a 1978 report of the British Advisory

Committee on the Penal System, is to provide in legislation a normal maximum sentence for each type of crime. Judges could exceptionally impose longer sentences but would have to explain why. The adequacy of those explanations could then be reviewed by an appellate court.

SECOND-LOOK MECHANISMS

Fourth, mechanisms would be established to allow a second look at the need for continued confinement of offenders serving sentences beyond a designated period. No human being should be denied the possibility of hope for a better life. LWOPs do that, and so do three-strikes and mandatory minimum sentences measured in decades. So do sentences of those lengths imposed under sentencing guidelines or as departures from them.

Second-look mechanisms could take a number of forms. A parole board could do it. Following the Canadian model, a specially constituted jury could do it. For many years in Minnesota, the commissioner of corrections could do it. The original sentencing judge, if he or she remained available, could do it. In Germany, a panel of appellate judges decides when and whether long-term prisoners should be released. Exactly how it is done is less important than that there be meaningful review of whether valid reasons continue to exist to hold the prisoner.

The reasons second-look mechanisms are needed are straightforward. Most American states do not have meaningful systems of appellate sentence review. When unconscionably long sentences are imposed, appellate judges can remedy them only by disingenuously overturning a conviction for, usually, overly technical reasons. Forced to choose between doing justice and literally applying the law, some judges go one way and some the other. That is unjust.

A second reason is that many American sentencing laws and guidelines mandate or presume sentences measured in decades or lifetimes and English indeterminate sentences have no fixed limit. A third reason is that times change and people change. For most crimes, public passions abate. Offenders whom, in the emotional aftermath of a notorious or much publicized crime, judges and citizens want to exile forever, in time come to seem less threatening.

The first and second of the preceding proposals address major weaknesses of indeterminate sentencing: unwarranted disparities and risks of bias, and lack of procedural fairness, transparency, and judicial accountability. The third and fourth address major weaknesses of contemporary sentencing systems: arbitrariness, inconsistency, rigidity, and excessive severity. Examples of all four components operate successfully in various places. A sentencing system incorporating all four would provide reasons for expecting sentences to be reasonably just, fair, consistent, predictable, and transparent, for judges to be held accountable, for seemingly inconsistent or idiosyncratic sentences to be subjected to searching review, and for unjustly severe or extraordinarily long sentences to be reexamined and held to a minimum.

Notes

1. We also organized a third large project, which gave rise to the Chicago Program on Human Development and Crime, but that was on an entirely separate subject (Tonry, Ohlin, and Farrington 1991).

2. *Graham v. Florida*, 560 U.S. (2010).

3. Sources on which the following discussion is based can be found in Tonry (1996) and Tonry (2012), each of which surveys empirical and policy work on sentencing through its date.

References

Advisory Committee on the Penal System, Great Britain. 1978. *Sentences of Imprisonment.* London: Home Office.

Durlauf, Steven N., and Daniel S. Nagin. 2011. "Imprisonment and Crime: Can Both Be Reduced?" *Criminology and Public Policy* 10: 13–54.

Garland, David. 2001. *The Culture of Control.* New York: Oxford University Press.

Lappi-Seppälä, Tapio. 2008. "Trust, Welfare, and Political Culture: Explaining Differences in National Penal Culture." In *Crime and Justice: A Review of Research*, vol. 37, edited by Michael Tonry, 313–387. Chicago: University of Chicago Press.

Nagin, Daniel S., Francis T. Cullen, and Cheryl Jonson. 2009. "Imprisonment and Re-offending." In *Crime and Justice: A Review of Research*, vol. 38, edited by Michael Tonry, 115–200. Chicago: University of Chicago Press.

Nellis, Ashley, and Ryan S. King. 2009. *No Exit: The Expanding Use of Life Sentences in America.* Washington, DC: Sentencing Project.

Sherman, Lawrence W. 2011. "Al Capone, the Sword of Damocles, and the Police— Corrections Budget Ratio." *Criminology and Public Policy* 10: 195–206.

Simon, Jonathan. 2007. *Governing Through Crime.* New York: Oxford University Press.

Tonry, Michael. 1996. *Sentencing Matters.* New York: Oxford University Press.

Tonry, Michael. 2011a. *Punishing Race: A Continuing American Dilemma.* New York: Oxford University Press.

Tonry, Michael. 2011b. "Less Imprisonment Is No Doubt a Good Thing; More Policing Probably is Not." *Criminology and Public Policy* 10: 137–152.

Tonry, Michael. In press. *Sentencing Fragments.* New York: Oxford University Press.

Tonry, Michael, and David P. Farrington, eds. 1995. *Building a Safer Society.* Chicago: University of Chicago Press.

Tonry, Michael, and David P. Farrington, eds. 2004. *Crime and Punishment in Western Countries, 1980–1999.* Chicago: University of Chicago Press.

Tonry, Michael, Lloyd E. Ohlin, and David P. Farrington. 1991. *Human Development and Criminal Behavior.* New York: Springer.

{ INDEX }